BOMBAY BEFORE *B*OLLYWOOD

Film City, original hand-coloured photograph. © Olivier Richon.
Reproduced by permission of Olivier Richon.

BOMBAY BEFORE *B*OLLYWOOD

Film City Fantasies

ROSIE THOMAS

Orient BlackSwan

BOMBAY BEFORE BOLLYWOOD

ORIENT BLACKSWAN PRIVATE LIMITED

Registered Office
3-6-752 Himayatnagar, Hyderabad 500 029 (A.P.), INDIA
E-mail: centraloffice@orientblackswan.com

Other Offices
Bangalore, Bhopal, Bhubaneshwar, Chennai,
Ernakulam, Guwahati, Hyderabad, Jaipur, Kolkata,
Lucknow, Mumbai, New Delhi, Noida, Patna

ISBN 978 81 250 5362 0

Typeset in
Adobe Jenson Pro 11/13
by Eleven Arts, Delhi

Printed in India at
Glorious Printers, Delhi

Published by
Orient Blackswan Private Limited
1/24 Asaf Ali Road
New Delhi 110 002
E-mail: delhi@orientblackswan.com

For sale only in India, Pakistan, Nepal, Bhutan, Bangladesh, Sri Lanka
and the Maldives

Contents

$\mathcal{T}$ables and Figures

Publisher's Acknowledgements

A version of Chapter Three in the volume, 'Distant Voices, Magic Knives: *Lal-e-Yaman* and the Transition to Sound in Bombay Cinema', first published in Rachel Dwyer and Jerry Pinto (eds), *Beyond the Boundaries of Bollywood: The Many Forms of Hindi Cinema*, New Delhi: Oxford University Press, 2011, pp. 53–76. Reprinted with permission of Oxford University Press and © Rosie Thomas.

A version of Chapter Four in this volume 'Not Quite (Pearl) White: Fearless Nadia, Queen of the Stunts' was originally published in Raminder Kaur and Ajay Sinha (eds), *Bollyworld: Indian Cinema through a Transnational Lens*, New Delhi: Sage, 2005, pp. 35–69. Reprinted with permission of Sage Publications and © Rosie Thomas.

A version of Chapter Five in this volume was originally published as 'Zimbo and Son Meet the Girl with a Gun', in David Blamey and Robert d'Souza (eds) *Living Pictures: Perspectives on the Film Poster in India*, London: Open Editions Press, 2005, pp. 27–44. Reprinted with permission of Open Editions Press and © Rosie Thomas.

A version of Chapter Six was originally published online as 'Still Magic: An Aladdin's Cave of 1950s B Movie Fantasy' on the website of Tasveer Ghar, edited by Sumathi Ramaswamy, Christiane Brosius, Yousuf Saeed. http://tasveerghar.net/cmsdesk/essay/103/. Reprinted with permission of Tasveer Ghar.

Chapter Eight was originally published as 'Indian Cinema: Pleasures and Popularity' in *Screen*, vol. 26, nos 3–4, pp. 116–32, May–August

1985. Reprinted with permission of Oxford University Press journals and © Rosie Thomas.

Chapter Nine was originally published as 'Sanctity and Scandal: The Mythologization of Mother India' in *Quarterly Review of Film and Video*, vol. 11, no. 3, pp. 11–30, 1989. Reprinted with permission of Taylor and Francis and © Rosie Thomas.

We would like to thank—

Olivier Richon for the cover photograph: 'On the set of Razia Sultan', original hand-coloured photograph © Olivier Richon; and frontispiece, 'Film City', original hand-coloured photograph © Olivier Richon.

Roy Wadia and Wadia Movietone for the following: **Figure 1.1**: *Hatimtai* (1956) lobby card (also courtesy the Priya Paul Collection); **Figure 1.2**: Basant's *Alibaba* (1954) postcard; **Figure I.1**: Booklet cover for *Hunterwali* (1935); **Figure 2.2**: Still of *Lal-e-Yaman* (1933); **Figure 3.1**: Still of *Lal-e-Yaman* (1933); **Figure 3.2**: Booklet cover of *Noor-e-Yaman* (1935); **Figure 4.1**: Booklet cover of *Lootaru Lalna* (1938); **Figure 4.2**: The one and only Fearless Nadia; **Figure 4.3**: Poster of *Hunterwali ki Beti* (1943); **Figure 4.4**: Still of *Hunterwali* (1935); **Figure 4.5**: A still from *Diamond Queen* (1940); **Figure 5.1**: Poster of *Zimbo Finds a Son* (1966) (also image courtesy Open Editions Collection); **Figure 5.2**: Poster of *Khilari* (1968) (also image courtesy Open Editions Collection); **Figure 6.3**: *Aladdin and the Wonderful Lamp* (1952) lobby card for the movie theatres (also image courtesy of Tasveer Ghar); **Figure 6.5**: *Aladdin and the Wonderful Lamp* (1952) lobby card for the movie theatres (image courtesy of Tasveer Ghar); **Figure 6.7**: *Aladdin and the Wonderful Lamp* (1952) lobby card for the movie theatres (image courtesy of Tasveer Ghar); and **Figure 6.8**: *Zimbo* (1958) hand-coloured collage used as lobby card for the movie theatres (image courtesy of Tasveer Ghar). **Figures I.1, 2.2, 3.1, 3.2, 4.1, 4.2, 4.4 and 4.5 © Wadia Movietone/Roy Wadia. Figures 1.1, 1.2, 4.3, 5.1, 5.2, 6.3, 6.5, 6.7 and 6.8 © Basant Pictures**.

Virchand Dharamsey for **Figure** 2.1: *Gul-e-Bakavali* (1932).

Tasveer Ghar for **Figure 6.1**: *Alif Laila* (1953) lobby card for the movie theatres; **Figure 6.2**: Textile label for Ralli Brothers; **Figure 6.4**: *Jahan Ara* (1964) lobby card for the movie theatres; **Figure 6.6**: Poster of Anglo-Burmese star, Helen, as cabaret dancer 'Chin Chin Chu', from the film *Howrah Bridge* (1958); and **Figure 6.9**: *Aladdin and the Wonderful Lamp* (1952) reverse of lobby card for the movie theatres.

Neha Kamat at Kamat Foto Flash for **Figure II.1**: A still from *Kartavya* (1979). **Image © Kamat Foto Flash**.

Ketan M. Desai for **Figure 8.1:** *Naseeb* (1981); **Figure 8.2**: *Naseeb*: sword fight; and **Figure 8.3**: *Naseeb* party scene. **All images © MKD Films**.

Mehboob Productions Private Ltd, Mumbai, India for **Figure 9.1**: Poster for *Mother India* (1957) and **Figure 9.2**: Still from *Mother India*. **Images © Shaukat Khan**.

Behroze Gandhy for **Figure 9.3**: Poster on Bombay streets in 1985. **Image © Behroze Gandhy**.

Mahesh Bhatt for **Figure 10.1**: A still from *Sadak* (1991). **Image © Vishesh Films Private Limited**.

Sujoy Ghose for **Figure 10.2**: A still from *Aladin* (2009). **Image © Eros International & Bound Script**.

Dharma Productions for **Figure 10.3**: A still from *Agneepath* (2012).

$\mathcal{A}$cknowledgements

As this book draws on more than three decades of my research and writing, the many intellectual and other debts I have accrued are impossible to acknowledge in full. Numerous people have helped me at different stages of my project and I have been overwhelmed by the generosity and kindness shown me by so many friends, colleagues and complete strangers.

For intellectual support and stimulation, collegiality and friendship at different points over the years, I am grateful to, amongst many others, Richard Allen, David Bate, Daniela Berghahn, Ira Bhaskar, Kaushik Bhaumik, Adina Bradeanu, Carol Breckenridge, Christie Brown, Stella Bruzzi, Ed Buscombe, Gayatri Chatterjee, Ranita Chatterjee, Tom Corby, Corey Creekmur, Aurogeeta Das, Radha Dayal, Virchand Dharamsey, Rajinder Dudrah, Rachel Dwyer, Sabeena Gadihoke, Behroze Gandhy, Shohini Ghosh, Christine Gledhill, Moti Gokulsing, Lalitha Gopalan, Nitin Govil, Kathryn Hansen, Daisy Hasan, Jim Hillier, Adam Hodgkins, Steve Hughes, May Adadol Ingawanij, Dina Iordanova, Nasreen Munni Kabir, Raminder Kaur, Philip Kennedy, Karen Knorr, Lawrence Liang, Philip Lutgendorf, Neepa Majumdar, Michael Maziere, Ranjani Mazumdar, Vijay Mishra, Debashree Mukherjee, Pushpamala N., Ashis Nandy, Joshua Oppenheimer, Uriel Orlow, Christopher Pinney, Jerry Pinto, Ashish Rajadhyaksha, Olivier Richon, Chris Rodley, Yousuf Saeed, Jean Seaton, Salma Siddique, Margherita Sprio, Ravi Sundaram, Mitra Tabrizian, Joram ten Brink, Patricia Uberoi, Ravi Vasudevan, Valentina Vitali, Marina Warner, Clare Wilkinson-Weber, Christopher Williams and John Wyver, along with legions of interesting and encouraging scholars and students with whom I have discussed my work at conferences, invited lectures and workshops around the world.

I thank the Social Science Research Council (SSRC), the British Academy (BA) and the Arts and Humanities Research Council (AHRC) for grants at key phases of my project, without which none of this work would have been possible. I thank colleagues at the University of Westminster for stalwart institutional support over the years, especially Fauzia Ahmad, Peter Goodwin, Myszka Guzkowska, Annette Hill, Philip Lee, Geoff Petts, Vincent Porter, and too many others to name individually.

Numerous people in India have offered generous help and shown extraordinary faith in me and my project. From my earliest periods of fieldwork I remember with deep fondness and gratitude a host of friends, acquaintances and industry professionals, some of whom are no longer with us, others of whom I have sadly lost touch with. These include Lolly Agarwal, Parag Amladi, Kamal Amrohi, Dev Anand, Johnny Bakshi, Shyam Benegal, Satish Bhatnagar, Mahesh Bhatt, Manmohan Desai, B. Dharap, Nargis and Sunil Dutt, the Gandhy family, Dileep Halbe, Raj Kapoor, Raj Khosla, Shekhar Kapur, Smita Patil, Devika Rani, Rahul Rawail, Uday Row Kavi, Joy Roy, Mohan Segal, Uma Segal, B.R. Sharan, Nilima Sharma, K.K. Shukla, Suraj Sunim, Homi Wadia, Mary Wadia and Jamshed Wadia.

From more recent times, underpinning my work on the history of stunt and fantasy films, I have been lucky enough to enjoy the friendship and unstinting generosity of the Wadia family: Nargis, Roy and the late Riyad and Vinci. I have also had the privilege of the support, assistance and friendship of Anuja Ghosalkar, Arun Khopkar, Geetha Mehra, Leo Mirani, Vinod Mirani, Sanjit Narwekar, Sumit Roy and Dorothy Wenner, amongst very many others. I have an enduring debt to the staff at the National Film Archive of India (NFAI), especially Mrs Joshi in the library, Aarti Kharkanis and Laxmi Iyer in the documentation department, various NFAI directors over the years, most recently K.S. Sasidharan, and above all, the legendary archivist P.K. Nair, who has been an inspiration and bedrock to our whole field as it has grown.

Perhaps my longest-standing debt is to one family: Niru and Abhijeet Rao and the late Uday Row Kavi. Uday was a pillar of support during my original fieldwork: through his patient explanations I first understood how the film industry really worked, and through his immense network of industry contacts I was able to meet whomever I wanted. Niru and Abhijeet have become like my own family and I cannot thank them enough for their kind hospitality over the years. My friendship with Behroze Gandhy has been similarly long-standing and precious to me: she was the first person in London with whom I could really discuss Hindi cinema and, as fellow travellers, we worked together on educational and television projects around Indian cinema for decades, long before 'Bollywood' became fashionable.

In putting this book together I owe a big thank you to the staff of Orient BlackSwan—Rinita Banerjee, Mimi Choudhury and Vidya Rao—all of whom have been a delight to work with and unerringly efficient, as well as to their anonymous peer reviewer whose incisive feedback helped me to understand my own project.

My final heartfelt thanks and love go to Tom and Steve Brookes, who have put up with this project in their home lives for far too many decades. This book—now it is finally done—is for Steve.

one

Bombay before Bollywood

Film City Fantasies

When I first arrived in autumn 1979 at the modest bungalow in the leafy outskirts of Pune that housed the National Film Archive of India (NFAI), eager to see their paperwork collections, I was directed to one dusty cupboard in the corner of the small library. Inside, higgledy-piggledy, was a random collection of posters and film stills from the 'new' or 'art' cinema, alongside some stills from Hindi and Marathi classics of the 1950s and earlier. Once I had explained—to the consternation and bemusement of the library staff—that I was interested in the contemporary popular or mainstream Hindi cinema, a script of Vijay Anand's 1965 film *Guide* was reluctantly retrieved for me. As it had been nominated for an Academy Award, I was assured that it was a 'good' mainstream film—a film of a better kind. I spent a few weeks dutifully working my way through this script and usefully improving my Hindi. But little more was on offer, although it is now clear that their vaults must have held much other uncatalogued material, albeit little of the then recent popular.

I soon gave up and made my way down to Bombay where I started to build my own collection of fan postcards and calendars of stars, film song-books and dialogue cassettes from the ubiquitous pavement vendors and small street stalls. I found a film-crazy college student as my unofficial tutor, visited the cinema with her twice or thrice a week, watched Doordarshan's Sunday night movie and its film song show *Chitrahaar* with determined regularity and gradually, pincer-movement, made my way into the industry, watching first-hand how films were made. After a confusing twenty months in which I met almost all the Bombay cinema 'greats' alive in that era, I returned to London to attempt to make sense of it all, with no more than a handful of other scholarly works or databases to refer to. It was a daunting task. When I had first suggested this doctoral project to my social anthropology department, I was firmly discouraged on the grounds that 'cinema isn't culture'. When I presented a paper on Manmohan Desai's films at a Pesaro conference in 1985, I was slow-clapped by the entire contingent of *Cahiers du Cinema* critics aligned along the front row. Today the situation for any researcher of Indian cinema has changed beyond all recognition, both at the National Film Archive in Pune and elsewhere. Part of the journey of this book is also the journey of this transformation.

THE CHALLENGE

Now that Indian cinema is at least a hundred years old—and possibly a decade older than that—it is time to take stock. Indian cinema studies has, largely over the past decade, become an established academic discipline with a fast-growing community of scholars based around the world. Much has been achieved since Barnouw and Krishnaswamy's groundbreaking *Indian Film* of 1963, which had been my bible in the early 1980s.[1] We have two scholarly encyclopaedias, a burgeoning body of academic and journalistic books and articles, at least three peer-reviewed journals in the field, digitised archives at NFAI, any number of films and film clips online—many with subtitles—and a mushrooming of databases, including collections of visual ephemera and songs, as well as a pioneering online encyclopaedia wiki project.[2] It has never been easier to find material.

But, with this plenitude comes a danger: as academic and journalistic projects accumulate, certain versions of Indian cinema history are becoming fossilised and assumptions and assertions about the form are being uncritically recycled, as I will discuss. While there is an abundance of online and other information, the resources for critical evaluation of this material are more limited. Moreover, the archives of early Indian cinema, both films and documents, are notoriously scanty in comparison with film industries elsewhere in the world, a point to which I will return.

The current book is both an intervention and itself an archival repository of sorts. By way of intervention, I will be arguing that, now that the discipline has reached critical mass and is ready for take-off, it is urgent that we encourage more stories to be told about Indian cinema and that we reassess some of the myths and hazy generalisations that have grown up around its history. This includes building—and stressing—a more nuanced picture of India's earliest films and film-makers that, among other things, represents the true balance between mythologicals, stunts, fantasies and other genres within that early history, as well as the dominance of American and European films in that era.[3] This process should also include a reassessment of the significance of the B- and C-circuits throughout Indian cinema history and recognition of the dangers of carving this history into monolithic eras.[4] While some scholarly works—notably Ashish Rajadhyaksha and Paul Willemen's *Encyclopaedia of Indian Cinema*, together with groundbreaking studies of the silent era by Kaushik Bhaumik and Virchand Dharamsey (on Bombay) and Stephen Hughes (on Madras)—have long been clear about this, their findings do not always get through to the accounts that flourish in the mainstream.[5] Although the more journalistic histories are rarely completely *wrong*, their emphases can be decidedly misleading. But now that scholarship is growing and Indian cinema history can afford to become more complex and less pat, it is time for orthodoxies to be challenged.

Alongside this polemical thrust, the impetus for the current book stems from the recognition that I have myself accumulated a body of writing and research material over the past thirty years and it is time to reassess my own collection and to see what patterns emerge. The chapters that follow track a broadly chronological path, from the silent era to 1994, with a brief coda bringing us up to 2013. However, this is in no conventional sense a history of Bombay cinema. Instead, the book draws eclectically on diverse cinematic tropes and film artefacts across two key eras, pre-independence and the early 1980s. From these 'clues and myths', for the most part serendipitously found and intuitively followed, a map emerges that opens up alternative historical narratives and debates to shed new light on the films, their industry and their circulation.[6] Thus, for example, two chapters in part one take ephemeral visual artefacts as their starting point (lobby cards, film stills, posters), while the chapters of part two are substantially based around ethnographic fieldwork. Although the book builds on discrete essays researched and written at different points in time and within varying conceptual frameworks, its overarching themes and arguments emerged as the chapters spoke to each other across three decades of Indian cinema scholarship.

BOMBAY BEFORE BOLLYWOOD

My title is a knowingly controversial one. At its simplest, *Bombay Before Bollywood* signals no more than that the book's content focuses on mainstream Hindi cinema in the years before 1995—before the Shiv Sena renamed Bombay as Mumbai and before the moniker 'Bollywood' gained international currency as changes began to take root within India's film industry in the wake of economic liberalisation. But the title also points up conundrums around two equally—if differently—contentious and slippery terms. The use or refusal of both has become significant in the modern world: while both 'Mumbai' and 'Bollywood' had been in use for many years before the mid-1990s, both terms are today crucially marked by who speaks them and from where.

For many Marathi and Gujarati speakers of Mumbai/Bombay, their home city has always been 'Mumbai' in their vernacular languages. Moreover, for many people outside India, both diasporic Asian and non-Asian, as well as for others within India, there is a compelling case for refusing the term Bombay, given its colonialist history and connotations. The city's official name has been Mumbai since November 1995. On the other hand, many of the city's inhabitants of all backgrounds, brought up within a proudly cosmopolitan metropolis, have always called their home Bombay and continue to assert their right to do so or to slip between Mumbai and Bombay, often within the same sentence.[7] The term, for them, signals a celebration of the secular, multi-faith city with which they identify. In this book I have chosen to use the term Bombay to refer to the city and its film industry as I knew—and lived with—them before 1995 and the term Mumbai to refer to the city after that point.

The term 'Bollywood' is more subtly—and less politically—complicated. A well-rehearsed debate on what, exactly, Bollywood means, how it evolved and how it should—or should not—be used is still unresolved. As with all good histories there are contested myths of origin, with several people claiming to have invented the term.[8] In fact, as Madhava Prasad points out, the term 'Tollywood' had existed since the 1930s to refer to films made in Tollygunge, Calcutta.[9] The follow-on coinage of the term 'Bollywood' is likely to have arisen in a number of places independently. This matter is of little importance. For what it is worth, while I do remember the term's occasional usage within Bombay film circles in the early 1980s, it had little wider currency at the time and was a flippant, slightly derogatory term that expressed the ambivalence of educated English-speaking middle-class Indians towards their own popular cinema.

The debate about the term 'Bollywood' today revolves around three issues: what it means, who uses it, and where. Crucially, the term is not unanimously used within the Mumbai industry, although it is becoming increasingly common among the younger generation. But many film-makers are openly hostile to the term—although they will happily tolerate it in the context of the global success of their own films. 'Bollywood' is of course widely used outside India, by both diasporic South Asians and non-Asians, and Rajinder Dudrah has argued for its special importance within this context.[10] While Dudrah uses the term carefully and consistently, many others do not.[11] To be fair, its meaning is extraordinarily elastic: most usually it refers to films made in Mumbai/Bombay within the populist conventions of spectacle and action, song and dance, music and stars. At times 'Bollywood' refers to those conventions themselves. Sometimes the term is used only of films made in Mumbai since the mid-1990s with a targeted appeal to the non-resident Indian (NRI) market; at other times, in popular parlance, Bollywood refers to all Indian films of all eras, or even to all films made by people of Indian origin anywhere in the world. The term may also refer, more broadly, to the contemporary Mumbai film industry, while more nuanced arguments building on a key intervention by Ashish Rajadhyaksha use it to refer to the agglomeration of cultural and entertainment industries that revolve around Hindi/Mumbai/Bombay/Indian cinema, in which the films themselves play a comparatively minor role.[12] Whether the term refers to a set of conventions, a body of films or an industry, 'Bollywood' is a brand that sells everything from face cream to barbers' stalls; from fashion to food; from dance classes to academic books. Crucially, as Ravi Vasudevan notes, it is a brand that sells India to the world.[13] But, as Prasad and others point out, the effect of the term 'Bollywood' is to promote, on the world stage, the notion of an unchanging essence of Indian cinema.[14] This is not a sound basis for a serious study of India's multiple cinemas.

The battle to control the term's use—both by film industry folk and by India-based academics—appears to have been lost. 'Bollywood' is here to stay, even though, as Prasad argues, 'in the end it must be admitted that there is no hope of giving it a definite meaning' and its growing usage is perhaps best read as 'a cultural symptom'.[15] I have chosen, perhaps hopelessly, to follow the practice of most Indian academics and some in the film industry itself and limit my use of the term to the mainstream output—in the broadest sense—of the Mumbai-based, commercial Hindi cinema industry since 1995. The 'before' of my title, therefore, gestures towards the 'once upon a time' of an equally hopeless celebration of a mythologised past.[16]

What the debate over nomenclature signalled by my title also points to is a broader question that has haunted me throughout my decades of study of this cinema. It is the perennial quandary of any work of cultural translation: from where am I speaking and to whom? With every audience I address, I must modify my exposition. As I pointed out in the 1980s, it was one thing for educated Indians to dismiss or celebrate their own cinema but quite a different matter for 'foreigners' to do the same. I was imbued, at that time, with liberal ideals—to understand Indian films and film-making in their own terms (or in their film-makers' own terms) and to escape the dismissive and patronising gaze of Western cultural imperialism. But today, to whom am I speaking and on what terms? I hope that by my title I signal, however obliquely, something of the complexity of this conundrum. Moreover, given that an ongoing theme of this book concerns the paradoxes of cultural flows and cultural translation, the two contested terms of my title highlight the slippery nature of this terrain.

My subtitle, *Film City Fantasies*, is more straightforward, although this, again, condenses a number of associations and ideas. The first half of the book, which builds on my research over recent years, explores the more popular genres of pre-independence cinema, including a body of films known within the industry as *Arabian Nights* fantasy films, together with their sister genres on the B- and C-circuits, notably stunt and action films. The book is a plea for these more fantastical and popular films, the genres that refused 'realism' outright and were—for much of the pre-1970s era—largely aimed at subaltern[17] or lower-class audiences, to be reinstated and given proper attention within Indian cinema history and for their importance to the subsequent development of film form within India to be recognised.[18]

On the other hand, the second half of the book draws primarily on my period of ethnographic fieldwork in the early 1980s within the film industry of Bombay, film city par excellence. In that phase of my project, I was as much concerned with the beliefs and fantasies that film-makers had about their film-making as with the operations of the industry on the ground. I became particularly interested in the beliefs film-makers developed about their audiences. I was also, of course, interested in the fantastical tales that were the films themselves. All of these concerns find expression in the chapters in part two.

Finally, the term fantasies is also a synonym for popular misconceptions, in which case the subtitle refers back to the other overarching project of this book, which is to challenge and complicate a number of myths about Indian cinema and its history, as already described. In all these senses, this book addresses the 'fantasies' of Bombay cinema.

TOWARDS SOME ALTERNATIVE HISTORIES

One of the most widely circulating stories about Indian cinema is that its first film—and many of its silent films—were Hindu mythologicals. The celebration of Dhundiraj Govind Phalke's first Indian feature film, released in 1913, tells a triumphal tale of Indian nationalism bending modern technology to an essentially Indian form, with an episode from the Hindu epics, King Harishchandra, providing a conveniently pure Indian subject matter. Since at least the mid-1930s Phalke has been feted internationally as the first Indian film-maker and, as his films represent a significant proportion of the twenty or so silent films to have survived, Phalke has been championed in each successive era as the 'founding father of Indian cinema'.[19]

The story is not quite so simple. However remarkable Phalke's achievements undoubtedly were, it is well documented that in the early twentieth century a number of people in different parts of India were experimenting with the new technology of film. These include Dadasaheb Torne, whose *Shree Pundalik* was released in 1912, as well as others in Calcutta and Bombay.[20] Even as late as 1917, Phalke's unique contribution was not widely known: as Ranita Chatterjee points out, the Bombay-based *Times of India* film critic was still blissfully unaware of any Indian film-making in the Bombay area and excitedly informed his readers that he had news of a 'Mr Madon' (*sic*) who had just made an Indian film, *Harishchandra*, 'played by Indians', which had met with great success at the Elphinstone tent in Calcutta.[21]

In fact, quite another man may have claims to being Indian cinema's unsung pioneer. Hiralal Sen, a Calcutta-based photographer and founder of the Royal Bioscope Company, was making films around the turn of the century and, as others have pointed out, by 1913 had two dozen or so productions under his belt. As I describe in chapter two, he had allegedly already made a number of dance shorts by 1903, when, according to anecdotal reports, he made *Ali Baba and the Forty Thieves,* a two-hour version of an evergreen hit of the Calcutta stage. The play was based on K.P. Vidyavinode's version of this classic fantasy tale and referred to as an '*Arabian Nights* opera'. We know nothing more about Hiralal Sen's film apart from rumour and anecdote: his life's work went up in flames in 1917 and there are no records of any screenings, although considerable talk of the film circulated in old Calcutta.

The question of 'firsts' and 'founding fathers' is not, in itself, of any great significance and I am not proposing a simplistic, revisionist history. But let us speculate. What if Hiralal Sen's feature film did exist? What if *Ali Baba* and not *Raja Harishchandra* was Indian cinema's foundational text? What if India's first celluloid hero was not a noble royal from the Hindu epics but a feckless young woodcutter from a quasi-Arabian/European orientalist tale? The implications are intriguing. Rather than beginning with a forty-minute Hindu myth,

Indian cinema history would kick off with a two-hour, confusingly culturally-hybrid tale from the *Arabian Nights*, set within an Islamic fantasy world and keying into global orientalist obsessions at the high point of cosmopolitan modernity. Crucially, such a history would stress Indian cinema's interconnectedness with world cinema and culture, not its exotic difference—a point to which I will return throughout this book.

If we continue our speculation and we tell Indian cinema history through the fantasy film, different emphases and different films and film-makers hove into view. Let us, for now, briefly assume that the *Arabian Nights* fantasy, *Ali Baba*, was India's first feature film. If we follow this trail, other landmark films then become more visible. The first all-India super hit, a storm across the country in 1924, was *Gul-e-Bakavali* (The Bakavali Flower, Kanjibhai Rathod), a fantasy film that was made and released a year before Douglas Fairbanks's Hollywood film *Thief of Bagdad* (Raoul Walsh, 1924) arrived to captivate India's audiences.[22] Two years later India's first woman film-maker Fatma Begum, a star of *Gul-e-Bakavali*, wrote and directed her first film, the fantasy *Bulbul-e-Paristan* (Nightingale in Fairyland, 1926), starring her daughters Zubeida and Shazadi. The following year, three of the top ten box-office favourites cited in the 1927 evidence to the Indian Cinematograph Committee (ICC) were fantasy films, including an *Aladdin Ane Jadui Fanas* (Aladdin and the Wonderful Lamp, B.P. Mishra, 1927) that kick-started the success of Ardeshir Irani's Imperial Studios. Imperial quickly followed this with an equally successful *Alibaba Chalis Chor* (Alibaba and Forty Thieves, B.P. Mishra, 1927) that was a milestone in Sulochana's career as a super-star. Four years later, Irani's studio made history by producing India's first talkie, *Alam Ara* (Beauty of the World, Ardeshir Irani, 1931), also an *Arabian Nights* fantasy film.

While mythologicals and devotionals did indeed dominate Bombay production in the years between 1913 and 1921, by the early 1920s these were fading out of view. From the mid-1920s onwards, production was dominated by stunt and action, costume and fantasy films, alongside, of course, a growing trend for 'socials'.[23] However, the latter were appreciated primarily by film-makers and audiences with pretensions to respectability.[24] As I describe in chapter two, in the later silent era between 1925 and 1934, fantasy and costume genres represented around 40 per cent of production, alongside a significant percentage of stunt films per se. Precise quantification is difficult as, from what we can judge in the absence of the films themselves, there was considerable overlap between genres: for example, stunts, 'thrills' and special effects were aspects of both mythologicals and fantasies. There was, however, a clear perception of a mass or 'C-grade' class of audience for all such films.[25]

With the coming of sound, *Arabian Nights* fantasies that drew on Urdu-Parsi theatre productions and their personnel flooded the early talkies, given the opportunities they offered for extravagant spectacle, music and dance. In chapter three, I examine one of these, *Lal-e-Yaman*, in some detail. While the social films came into their own on the respectable A-grade circuits from the mid-1930s onwards, stunt and action films continued to dominate what I refer to as the subaltern circuits, and therefore the box office, as chapter four describes.[26] Even when the 1930s stunt era was dying, fantasy films could still make money. In 1940, Mehboob Khan's *Ali Baba*, shot in Hindi and Punjabi, was the super hit that allowed him to leave Sagar Studios and set up on his own.[27] It was also a film about which Mehboob felt particularly sentimental: his first break in the film industry had been a cameo role as one of the forty thieves in Imperial Studio's 1927 hit, the Sulochana-starrer *Alibaba*, although he used to grumble that he spent most of his on-screen time inside a jar.

If the significance of fantasy and action films during the pre-independence era has been underplayed to date, the received histories of the post-independence era are even more partial. These have tended to privilege the socials as the monolithic form of the 1950s and 1960s, along with occasional references to mythologicals and historicals.[28] In this they have taken their cue from the official film industry discourse of the day. Thus, according to an anonymous author writing an overview of 'Indian films' for a 1956 publication *India Talkie: Silver Jubilee* to celebrate the twenty-fifth anniversary of the Indian sound film:

After Independence and the new censorship policy of the Government of Bombay, which did not look favourably on magic and fighting scenes, production of 'stunts' of the type popular in the silent days and the early days of the Talkie, virtually ceased. Social, mythological and historical stories continued to be the main subjects for picturisation.[29]

This is misleading. For 1956, the year that this article was published—and also the year when, for example, *Mother India* was shooting on the studio floors—the editors of the industry trade paper, *Trade Guide,* named three box-office super hits.[30] Two of these were indeed socials—B.R. Chopra's *Ek Hi Rasta* (Just One Road) and Raj Khosla's *CID,* a crime thriller starring Dev Anand.[31] The third was Basant Pictures' *Hatimtai,* directed by Homi Wadia, an unadulterated *Arabian Nights* fantasy film based on a favourite Indian story of the Parsi stage, handed down through the oral traditions of *qissa-dastan.*[32] The film of *Hatimtai,* 'the most generous man of the Arab world' according to its song-book publicity, was set in a spectacular never-

Figure 1.1   *Hatimtai* (1956) lobby card

Source: © Basant Pictures. From the Priya Paul collection. Courtesy Roy Wadia and Wadia Movietone.

never land of fairies, monsters and giants. It boasted stunts and action, glorious music and special effects magic, including an ornate underwater palace and a tree from which the heads of beautiful water nymphs hung like fruit (Figure 1.1). It was Homi Wadia's first full-colour film and his own personal favourite among all his movies.

Nor was the success of *Hatimtai* a flash in the pan: just two years earlier, Homi Wadia's *Alibaba and the Forty Thieves* was firmly in 1954's top four super hits (Figure 1.2). The film was shot in black and white but its novelties included choice scenes in so-called *bhoji* colour, for which prints were painstakingly hand-coloured by specially trained Gujarati craftsmen. *Alibaba* is premised on memorable songs and buffoonish comedy, together with stunts and action, with Alibaba, played by Mahipal, as a Douglas Fairbanks–style fighting hero. Although its special effects fantasy was less marked than *Hatimtai*, it was directly based on an *Arabian Nights* tale: it was hardly a social.

Even more significantly, two years before that, Homi Wadia's *Aladdin and the Wonderful Lamp* (1952), starring a young, beautiful Meena Kumari, together with a flying *jinni* / genie and exquisite special

Figure 1.2   Basant's *Alibaba* (1954) postcard

Source: © Basant Pictures. Courtesy Roy Wadia and Wadia Movietone.

Bombay before Bollywood

effects magical happenings, was also among India's top ten box-office successes of the year. As in the silent era, there was overlap between the fantasy and mythological films: studios such as Basant Pictures made both, drawing on the same pool of actors, stuntmen and special effects technicians. *Aladdin's pahalwan* (wrestler) jinni, flying through the skies, bearing the magic carpet that transports Aladdin and his princess to safety (see Figure 6.3 in chapter six), had visual echoes of familiar mythological scenes of Hanuman flying to Lanka.[33] Moreover, Mahipal, who here played Aladdin, was nicknamed 'Ram' by his co-workers at Basant, as he strutted around the sets, because he so often played that role. Indeed, there are grounds for arguing that, especially in the 1950s, it was the fantasy films that drove the market for the mythologicals, at least among certain audiences. Vijay Mishra, a schoolboy in Fiji in the 1950s, still remembers the Basant fantasy films almost frame by frame and tells me that these were the films most eagerly anticipated within his community: mythologicals, when they came, were a poor substitute.[34]

It is true that stunt films 'of the type popular in the silent days' dwindled away in the 1950s—before taking off again with a vengeance in the early 1960s. It is also true that some populist elements of 'magic and fighting' were incorporated within some (but not all) socials. But the B- and C-circuits, which had been part of the exhibition landscape since the silent era, did not disappear. On the contrary, Basant and other studios knew only too well the commercial viability of the subaltern audience. The stunt queen of the 1930s, Fearless Nadia, continued to be a box-office success throughout the 1940s and 1950s on these circuits. Once social films had replaced stunt thrillers among the more 'respectable' audiences, who increasingly dominated the film industry's aspirations, Homi Wadia started to produce cheap genre versions of Nadia's earlier hits, beginning with *Hunterwali ki Beti* (Daughter of the Woman with the Whip, Nanabhai Bhatt, 1943), as I describe in chapter four. Indeed, in 1956 Nadia starred in an *Arabian Nights'* spoof, *Baghdad ka Jadu* (Magic of Baghdad, John Cawas). Moreover, Homi Wadia's action films—drawing on other globally popular stories such as Tarzan and James Bond—continued to make money right through the 1960s, as described in chapter five.

A more complete account of the 1950s would show that for most of that decade the makers of C-circuit stunt and mythological films turned to other forms within which to incorporate the attractions of 'magic and fighting'. The costume and fantasy genres provided these forms. Moreover, these genres were especially popular with children, including middle-class children, many of whom still fondly remember the fantasy films of their youth. In 1955 and 1956, costume and fantasy films made up around 30 per cent of all productions, only dropping to less than 20 per cent in the late 1950s, when stunt films took off again.[35] Rather astutely and somewhat tongue-in-cheek, the more cynical of the Bombay industry started to refer to such films as 'semi-socials' in order to keep the more snobbish of their critics at bay.[36]

Crucially, Indian cinema in the 1950s and 1960s was not homogeneous. Accounts that privilege the socials within a so-called 'classic era' of Bombay cinema tell only half the story. It is true that, in a spirit of Nehruvian optimism, many 1950s socials engaged with the project of Indian nationalist modernity, whether through the essentialist values of Mother India's chastity and the 'timeless' Indian village or through the exciting new cityscapes of Bombay in the Navketan films. But the fantasy films of Bombay's subaltern circuits were equally, if differently, engaging with that modernity: they related to more global forms of cosmopolitan modernity in which an exotic Orient, full of magical delights, provided the Other to the nation's self-image of rationalist modernity and socialist utopia. The fantasy films of the 1950s can be seen as the flip side of *Mother India* and *CID*. Moreover, we should remember that the *Arabian Nights* themselves were essentially *city* stories and until recently dismissed as trash by Arabist literary intellectuals. As Robert Irwin puts it, they were 'the collective dreaming of commercial folk in the great cities of the medieval Arab world' whose stories 'pander to the tradesman's fascination with commodities'.[37] As such the *Nights* were far from irrelevant to the new India. Furthermore, while always 'Indianising' their material, these fantasy films invariably made direct visual references to Hollywood versions of such tales, as later chapters will describe.[38] On the other hand, the stunt films of the late 1950s onwards also openly bought into the transnational popular culture—as they had in the 1920s and 1930s—drawing on global icons such as Tarzan,

James Bond and King Kong. Indian stars such as Dara Singh, Fearless Nadia and John Cawas brought 'Indianised' versions of this global culture to lower-class audiences, and these stars thereby became counter-heroes and counter-heroines to the mainstream heroes of Bombay's socials, as discussed in chapter five.

Turning to the 1970s and 1980s, the focus of the second half of this book, our project of looking at Indian cinema history afresh through the lens of the fantasy film uncovers a rather different picture. In this period, now often referred to as the *masala* era,[39] on account of the 'spicy' form of the attractions of the dominant mainstream blockbusters, fantasy films per se were fewer, even on the lower-class circuits. Nevertheless, there were some straight *Arabian Nights* productions, including a big-budget, Indo-Soviet co-production of *Alibaba aur 40 Chor* (Latif Faiziyev and Umesh Mehra, 1980) starring Hema Malini, Zeenat Aman and Dharmendra, and, even as late as 1990, a *Hatimtai* from Babubhai Mistry that starred Jeetendra.[40] However, B- and C-circuit stunt films persisted throughout the 1970s and 1980s and even mythologicals and devotionals had a half-life in this era: in April 1980, I visited the sets of the last film to shoot at Basant studios and watched Homi Wadia direct the mythological *Mahabali Hanuman* (1981).[41] But by then change was well under way in the film industry. On the other hand, the fantasy and mythological genres found a new life on television in the 1980s and early 1990s. Ramanand Sagar followed his phenomenally successful 1980s television serial of the *Ramayana* with the equally popular *Alif Laila*, two series of stories from the *Arabian Nights*, broadcast on Doordarshan and SAB TV between 1993 and 1996.

The importance of a history of Bombay cinema told 'from below'—through the frame of the magic and fighting films—is that it brings to our attention the crucial role played by these lower-brow forms in the rise of the big-budget masala film in the 1970s. The spectacle, action and special effects magic of the B-movies[42] were all greedily incorporated within the conventions of the mega-masala films that ruled the box office of that decade—a cinema of attractions that predated Hollywood's own turn to big-budget, visceral spectacle in the 1980s. A different sensibility about verisimilitude emerged through this: social 'realism' was no longer of much relevance to the masala blockbuster. Rather, the suspension of disbelief of the B-grade fantasy, stunt and mythological films moved into the mainstream. *Naseeb* (Manmohan Desai, 1981), for example, not only references popular Hollywood and Hong Kong action films but also plays out across three different registers of verisimilitude, as described in chapter eight.

Most significantly, some of the biggest names in the Bombay industry of the 1970s and early 1980s—directors, producers and stars—learnt their trade directly from the older B-studios. Manmohan Desai, the masala king of the 1970s, used to refer to 'trick wizard' Babubhai Mistry, the special effects genius of Basant studios, as his guru: Desai was apprenticed to Mistry in 1957 and told me he learnt all he knew about populist, spectacle-based film-making from this legendary figure.[43] Moreover, Manmohan Desai's own father was Kikubhai Desai, a fantasy and stunt film-maker, who founded Paramount Studio and was a close friend of J.B.H. Wadia. Even Mahesh Bhatt's father was one of Basant's top directors, Nanabhai (aka Batuk) Bhatt, who directed more than a hundred fantasy, stunt and mythological films over the course of his lifetime. One of Bhatt's earliest memories is of visiting his father directing *Sinbad the Sailor* (Nanabhai Bhatt, 1952) on the studio sets of a grand ship and of 'an enchanting land which mesmerised me'.[44] The masala films were, almost literally, born in the B-studios.

If we reduce the so-called 'classical' era of the 1950s and 1960s to a monolithic form of social film, as some accounts of Indian cinema have implied, these other threads and influences become less visible. It makes no sense to talk about the 'Bollywoodisation' of the masala era (whatever that means) as Sangita Gopal does, without recognising that this spirit of cosmopolitan, visceral, lowbrow, popular culture was kept alive within the B-circuit throughout the 1950s and 1960s.[45] The B-films implicitly challenged the dominant paradigm of the Indian nation: if, as has been said of Hollywood, B-films are the space within which the 'return of the repressed' of the A-film erupts, the Bombay B-films of the 1950s and 1960s were arguably the place where the idealised Nehruvian 'nation' became messy and porous and could not be neatly severed from global popular culture. As I suggest in the first part of this book, the Wadia brothers' films—from the 1930s to the 1960s—embodied a somewhat different vision of nationalism and a modernising India from that of the mainstream elite. This brought together transnational popular culture with traditional Indian subaltern performance forms in an inclusive, hybrid, ludic space. A crucial aspect of the Wadias' cosmopolitan worldview was that their thrillers and fantasies engaged audiences at a visceral level, through thrilling action, spectacle and songs, which linked in to the culturally hybrid traditions of lower-class entertainment, including circus and variety entertainment, magic shows, cabaret and wrestling, as well as to Hollywood's so-called 'lower genres'.[46] The *Arabian Nights* and fantasy tropes figured within many of these traditions, as we shall see in subsequent chapters.

To recap, the beauty of an account of Indian cinema that begins with *Ali Baba* rather than *Raja Harishchandra* is that, for a change, cultural syncretism is placed at its heart: as we will see, the *Arabian Nights* are a transcultural body of stories that have developed over the centuries through an accretion of cultural borrowings. They are as Indian, Persian or European as they are Arabian. Indian films have always been simultaneously 'Indian' and in touch with the global. An undue emphasis on the mythological in some earlier scholarship has encouraged essentialist celebration of Indian cinema's exotic difference and an ultimately distracting focus on features such as the 'darshanic gaze'.[47] Meanwhile, such emphases have sidelined the contribution of the much-maligned stunt and fantasy films to the development of mainstream Bombay cinema's conventions, including the introduction of global cinema codes of both form and subject matter, as Ashish Rajadhyaksha and others have pointed out.[48] It is time to redress the balance.

LOOKING BACK: THE LONGER VIEW

There are a number of lessons here, not least the perils of generalisation. In practice, there are both similarities and differences between Bombay cinema and other forms of world cinema, between one period and another, and across a body of films within any one period. Film-makers themselves work within an economy of both repetition and difference. For example, it is in many ways true that one form—the social—dominated from the early 1950s to the 1990s, a period between two more cosmopolitan eras of global flows. Uncovering the ground rules of this was the focus of much of my own work in the 1980s. Madhava Prasad took this further and outlined the ascendance over this period of the dominant super-genre of the 'feudal family romance'.[49] But, as argued above and *pace* Prasad, we must not over-generalise. To take one example, Sangita Gopal asserts of the very long period between independence and the early 1990s: 'The films themselves were ... cut-and-paste—dialogue, songs, dance numbers and fight sequences were manufactured piecemeal and then assembled to create the final product.'[50] This was undoubtedly true of a number of film-makers at different points within that period. However, now that a more nuanced picture of production is emerging through new ethnographic and historical research by younger scholars, such generalisations become problematic. For my own fieldwork of the 1980s, I visited the productions of mainstream directors/producers as contrasting as Kamal Amrohi, Manmohan Desai, Subhash Ghai, Raj Kapoor, Raj Khosla, Hrishikesh Mukherjee, the Ramsay brothers, Mohan Segal and Homi Wadia. I saw as many differences as similarities in how individual film-makers worked. Production norms differed not only between production companies but also at different points over those four decades. In the 1950s and 1960s, 'cut-and-paste' was not the norm with the established film-makers and it never was with the Raj Kapoors, Guru Dutts and Mehboob Khans of the film industry. Moreover, there was always, even in the silent era, a complex network of circuits targeting different audiences with appetites for different kinds of cinema.[51]

If the anthropologist is one who 'stays long enough', as Trinh T. Minh-ha's memorably ironic voice-over put it in her essay film, *Re-assemblage* (1979), I still have to wonder whether I qualify, even after more than thirty years of research on Bombay cinema—albeit not continuously. Indeed I have amassed my own archive: a series of notebooks, interviews, tapes and trunks of ephemera that I can—and should—plunder and put into the public domain before they turn to dust.[52] While the Indian cinema archive is notorious for its gaps and irrevocable acts of destruction and neglect, it is nevertheless growing exponentially today, as the very concept of what an archive might be and contain is transformed and as the digital opens new doors.[53] Different forms of collections are emerging across a plethora of sites, both within public institutions and among private collectors: material ignored by the NFAI in Pune in the 1970s now has commercial as well as academic value.

There is still a wealth of resources out there to be tapped. Some, like the websites of the film song fanatics of Kanpur, are already in the public domain; others—from *Movie Mahal's* priceless collection of film industry interviews of the 1980s to Osians' enviable collection of cinematic artefacts and ephemera, or to the million-plus negatives of classic Bombay film stills held by Kamat Foto Flash—await a viable commercial vehicle before being put into the public domain.[54] As a consequence of all this, the nature of academic labour itself has to be re-evaluated: where is value to be located in the collection, analysis and contextualisation of archival materials? What is to be rewarded and how? Who can own what? Whether or not such questions can be resolved, this 'living archive' must be tracked down vigorously before it is too late, for, as Stephen Hughes points out, 'film history dwells alongside us as a part of the living present; it is an ongoing, unfinished and open-ended project.'[55]

An additional advantage of being around 'long enough' is the privilege of the longer perspective. One can better see the continuities across the years, not just the changes. While a perennial theme within the film industry has been that major changes are afoot—and even that crisis is imminent—in the longer term these changes seem less significant than the continuities. For example, when I briefly returned to the film industry in the context of a television documentary I was making in 1994, after a gap of almost a decade, I was astonished to watch the top hits of the day—*Khalnayak* (The Villain, Subhash Ghai, 1993) and *Sadak* (The Street, Mahesh Bhatt, 1991). As I discuss in the final chapter of this book, they were both in some ways quite different from the films of the 1970s and 1980s but in others very much the same.

Currently (in 2013), it is true that almost every aspect of film production has been transformed—as has India—and the Mumbai film industry is now full of sophisticated, elite, young people, many internationally educated, whose range of cinematic references spans world cinema in a way that was almost unheard of thirty years ago.[56] Nevertheless, *Agneepath* (Path of Fire, Karan Malhotra, 2012), which I discuss in the coda to this book, not only reflects world cinema but is also a remake of a 1990 Bombay film which itself draws on motifs and an underlying structure and grammar that looks back to *Mother India* and, arguably, earlier. The challenge is on to analyse cultural flows in a complex new world. But it was ever more or less thus. *Plus ça change, plus c'est la même chose.*[57]

NOTES

1. Erik Barnouw and S. Krishnaswamy, *Indian Film*, second edition, New York: Oxford University Press, 1980 [1963].

2. See Ashish Rajadhyaksha and Paul Willemen (eds), *Encyclopaedia of Indian Cinema*, new revised edition, London: British Film Institute and Oxford University Press, 1999, and Encyclopaedia Britannica, *Encyclopaedia of Hindi Cinema*, New Delhi: Encyclopaedia Britannica (India) Pvt. Ltd, 2003. Journals include Sage's *BioScope: South Asian Screen Studies*; Routledge's *South Asian Popular Culture*; and Intellect's *Studies in South Asian Film and Media*. For the online wiki project set up by Lawrence Liang and Ashish Rajadhyaksha and hosted by pad.ma, see: www.cinemaofindia.org.

3. Genres in the Indian context (as elsewhere) are notoriously difficult to define. Broadly, mythologicals are films about the Hindu gods drawn from the epics and puranas; devotionals are stories of their devotees, including the medieval saint-poets; fantasies are set in magical worlds and mostly draw on Persian-Arabian storytelling traditions; stunt films are action films set in a contemporary world. For a brief gloss of these and other terms see Rosie Thomas, 'India: Mythologies and Modern India', in *World Cinema since 1945*, ed. William Luhr, New York: Ungar, 1987, pp. 304–5. As I will later discuss, there is considerable overlap between these genres.

4. According to industry parlance from the 1930s onwards, the 'A-circuit' comprised prestigious metropolitan cinemas; the 'B-circuit' referred to middle-ranking and 'second-run' cinemas in cities and larger towns; the 'C-circuit' comprised cinemas in rural districts, smaller towns and the poorest urban areas, where the lower-class and unlettered audiences lived, and included travelling cinemas.

5. A growing body of academic research is excavating this. However, these interventions have made little impact to date in the non-specialist public domain. See, for example, Kaushik Bhaumik, 'The Emergence of the Bombay Film Industry, 1913–36', unpublished DPhil thesis, University of Oxford, 2001; and 'Cinematograph to Cinema: Bombay 1896–1928', *BioScope*, vol. 2, no. 1, 2011, pp. 41–67; Suresh Chabria and Paolo Cherchi Usai (eds), *Light of Asia: Indian Silent Cinema, 1912–1935*, New Delhi: Wiley Eastern, 1994; Virchand Dharamsey's work ('Filmography', pp. 69–235) in Chabria (above) and elsewhere, including 'The Advent of Sound in Indian Cinema: Theatre, Orientalism, Action, Magic', *Journal of the Moving Image*,

vol. 9, 2010; Rachel Dwyer, *Filming the Gods: Religion and Indian Cinema*, London: Routledge, 2006; Stephen Putnam Hughes, 'Is There Anyone Out There? Exhibition and the Formation of Silent Film Audiences in South India', unpublished PhD thesis, University of Chicago, 1996; and 'When Film Came to Madras', *BioScope*, vol. 1, no. 2, 2010, pp. 147–68; Rosie Thomas '*Miss Frontier Mail*: The Film That Mistook Its Star for a Train', in *Sarai Reader 07: Frontiers*, eds Monica Narula, Shuddhabrata Sengupta, Jeebesh Bagshi and Ravi Sundaram, Delhi: Centre for Study of Developing Societies, 2007, pp. 294–308; and Valentina Vitali, *Hindi Action Cinema*, New Delhi: Oxford University Press, 2008.

6. This methodology acknowledges the inspiration of Carlo Ginzburg, *Clues, Myths and the Historical Method*, trans. from the Italian by John and Anne C. Tedeschi, Baltimore: Johns Hopkins University Press, 1989 [1986].

7. Moreover, there are official anomalies, such as the continued use of the term Bombay High Court.

8. *Cine Blitz* journalist Bevinda Collaco and producer Amit Khanna, among others.

9. For an excellent, succinct overview of the debate and nuances of the phenomenon see M. Madhava Prasad's 'Surviving Bollywood' in *Global Bollywood*, eds Anandam P. Kavoori and Aswin Punathambekar, New York: New York University Press, 2008, pp. 41–51.

10. Rajinder Dudrah, *Bollywood Travels: Culture, Diaspora and Border Crossings in Popular Hindi Cinema*, London: Routledge, 2012, pp. 4–7.

11. For example, Sangita Gopal, *Conjugations*, Chicago: Chicago University Press, 2011. Although this is an otherwise useful and insightful American academic book on what it calls 'the New Bollywood', Gopal flounders in her attempts to define its terms, admitting that 'when I do use [Bollywood] at all, I mean it to signify Hindi film in general', while referring to a mysterious process of 'Bollywoodisation' that she argues was in process from the 1970s.

12. Ashish Rajadhyaksha, 'The "Bollywoodization" of the Indian Cinema: Cultural Nationalism in a Global Arena', in *Global Bollywood*, eds Anandam P. Kavoori and Aswin Punathambekar, New York: New York University Press, pp. 17–40.

13. Ravi Vasudevan, *The Melodramatic Public: Film Form and Spectatorship in Indian Cinema*, New Delhi: Permanent Black, 2010, p. 339.

14. Prasad, 'Surviving Bollywood', p. 49.

15. Ibid., p. 44.

16. N.B. the 'new Bollywood' trend of nostalgic celebration of the 1970s and early 1980s, for example, *Once Upon a Time in Mumbaai* (Milan Luthria, 2010).

17. I use the term subaltern to refer to the disempowered, mostly unlettered, urban and rural poor, broadly in line with the use of the term within the academic discourse of subaltern studies. This word would not be used among film industry workers, for whom terms such as the 'masses', 'C-grade' or 'C-class' were most commonly used.

18. Valentina Vitali's research on action cinema is important in this context. Vitali, *Hindi Action Cinema*.

19. This is not to deny that Dadasaheb Phalke was the first Indian feature film-maker with a conscious project to build a national film industry, as Ashish Rajadhyaksha argued cogently in 'The Phalke Era: Conflict of Traditional Form and Modern Technology', in *Interrogating Modernity: Culture and Colonialism in India*, eds Tejaswini Niranjana, P. Sudhir and Vivek Dhareshwar, Calcutta: Seagull Books, 1993, pp. 47–82.

20. Rajadhyaksha and Willemen, *Encyclopaedia of Indian Cinema*.

21. Ranita Chatterjee, 'Journeys In and Beyond the City: Cinema in Calcutta 1897–1939', unpublished PhD thesis, University of Westminster, 2011. The reference will be to *Satyawadi Raja Harishchandra*, produced by Elphinstone Bioscope Company and released in March 1917 in Calcutta.

22. *Gul-e-Bakavali* was released in India in March 1924, two months before *Thief of Bagdad* was released in the United States of America (USA) and a year before its Indian release.

23. In Bombay film industry parlance, the social has been broadly understood as any film in a contemporary setting not otherwise classified.

24. Kaushik Bhaumik describes how the desire for 'respectability' underpinned the Bombay silent film industry's move towards the social film. See Bhaumik, 'The Emergence of the Bombay Film Industry'; see also Kaushik Bhaumik, 'Sulochana: Clothes, Stardom and Gender in Early Indian Cinema', in *Fashioning Film Stars: Dress, Culture, Identity*, ed. Rachel Moseley, London: British Film Institute, 2005, pp. 87–97.

25. J.B.H. Wadia uses this term in his memoirs. For more on elite perceptions of the Indian mass audience, see also Manishita Dass, 'The Crowd Outside the Lettered City: Imagining the Mass Audience in 1920s India', *Cinema Journal*, vol. 48, no. 4, 2009, pp. 77–98.

26. My use of the term 'subaltern circuits' refers primarily to the distribution circuits where 'C-grade' audiences lived, that is, underclass and unlettered audiences.

27. Bunny Reuben, *Mehboob: India's De Mille*, New Delhi: Indus, 1999, p. 63.

28. To take three examples from across the decades: Barnouw and Krishnaswamy, *Indian Film*; M. Madhava Prasad, *Ideology of the Hindi Film: A Historical Construction*, New Delhi: Oxford University Press, 1998; Gopal, *Conjugations*. My own early work was also somewhat guilty of this.

29. Anonymous in *Indian Talkie, 1931–56, Silver Jubilee Souvenir*, Bombay: Film Federation of India, 1956, p. 81.

30. I base these rankings on discussions and correspondence with Uday Row Kavi, Associate Editor of *Trade Guide*, in the early 1980s. His lists replicate those published by his employer, B.K. Adarsh, *Film Industry of India, 1913–1963*, Bombay: Trade Guide, 1963, p. 59, which were drawn on by Vinayak Purohit, *Some Aspects of Sociology of Indian Films and Profile of the Hindi Hit Movie, 1951–1989*, Bombay: Indian Institute of Social Research, 1990. However, Row Kavi's lists also include the trade distinctions between A+ (super hit), A (hit), and B (successful) films. He also adds four more 1952 'hits' to Purohit's two, one of which is Homi Wadia's *Aladdin and the Wonderful Lamp*.

31. *CID* is a social in the film industry's own usage of the term, that is, a film set in the contemporary era.

32. Indo-Persian story tradition. See chapter two for more on qissa-dastan.

33. This also drew directly on the representation of the genie in Alexander Korda's *Thief of Bagdad* (Michael Powell, Ludwig Berger, Tim Whelan, 1940), as discussed in chapter six.

34. Personal communication, February 2013.

35. Around 50 per cent were socials, 30 per cent costume and fantasy and less than 10 per cent mythologicals in the mid-1950s. These estimates are my own calculations, based on genre classifications in filmographies by Firoze Rangoonwalla, *Indian Filmography*, Bombay: J. Udeshi, 1970; and Rajendra Ojha, *75 Glorious Years of Indian Cinema*, Bombay: Screen World Publication, 1988.

36. I first heard this term in an interview with H.S. Rawail in January 1981.

37. Robert Irwin, 'Introduction', in *The Arabian Nights: Tales of 1001 Nights*, trans. from the Arabic by Malcolm C. Lyons, with Ursula Lyons, London: Penguin, 2008, vol. 1, p. xv.

38. See chapter six. Moreover, as chapter two argues, India's 1930s fantasy films made much less direct reference to Hollywood than their 1950s counterparts.

39. Masala: (lit.) spices. For more on the conventions of the masala films see chapter eight. Depending on how one defines the term (which is almost as slippery as 'Bollywood'), not all films were 'masala' films in that era: it was a tendency. In fact, in one account written in 1990, the masala era was considered to have run from 1964. See Purohit, *Some Aspects of Sociology of Indian Films*.

40. For more on the 1980 film, see Masha Salazkina, 'Soviet-Indian Co-productions: Alibaba as Political Allegory', *Cinema Journal*, vol. 49, no. 4, Summer 2010, pp. 71–89.

41. Although Babubhai Mistry was credited as the film's director, on the day I visited he had gone to Madras and Homi had taken over for the day.

42. My use here of the term 'B-movie' or 'B-film' covers films that would be referred to within the industry as either 'B-grade' or 'C-grade' (sometimes interchangeably), that is, films made cheaply, without expensive stars, that would play on both the B- and C-circuits.

43. Interview with author, May 1981. He was, however, particularly adamant that although he saw Mistry as his guru he would never touch his feet.

44. Interview with author, March 2006.

45. While Gopal does acknowledge the B-circuit of 1947–70 in passing (via a footnote reference to Valentina Vitali's work), she underplays its significance and elsewhere implies that the B-circuit only emerged in the 1980s. Gopal, *Conjugations*, pp. 9, 93).

46. Miriam Hansen uses the term 'lower genres' in the context of her argument about vernacular modernism, positing a 'sensory-reflective horizon for the contradictory experience of modernity', which is of some relevance here. See Miriam Bratu Hansen, 'The Mass Production of the Senses: Classical Cinema as Vernacular

Modernism', in *Reinventing Film Studies*, eds Christine Gledhill and Linda Williams, London: Arnold Publishers, 2000, pp. 332–50.

47. Ashish Rajadhyaksha and Geeta Kapur first described the workings of 'frontal address' and 'iconicity' in early Indian cinema. See Rajadhyaksha, 'The Phalke Era', and Geeta Kapur, 'Revelation and Doubt: *Sant Tukaram* and *Devi*', in *Interrogating Modernity: Culture and Colonialism in India*, eds Tejaswini Niranjana, P. Sudhir and Vivek Dhareshwar, Calcutta: Seagull Books, 1993, pp. 19–46. Their ideas have been taken up and developed widely elsewhere, including most rigorously by Ravi Vasudevan in 'The Politics of Cultural Address in a "Transitional" Cinema: A Case Study of Indian Popular Cinema', in *Rethinking Film Theory*, eds Christine Gledhill and Linda Williams, London: Arnold, 2000, pp. 130–64. Iftikhar Dadi counters this by suggesting that what he calls 'the *dastan* (story) mode' might better reflect the spectatorial practices of Muslim audiences. See Iftikhar Dadi, 'Registering Crisis: Ethnicity in Pakistani Cinema of the 1960s and 1970s', in *Beyond Crisis: Re-evaluating Pakistan*, ed. Naveeda Khan, New Delhi: Routledge, 2010, pp. 145–76.

48. Only since the 1990s has re-evaluation of the stunt film begun to acknowledge its importance in the development of storytelling, editing and mise-en-scène in Indian cinema. Film-maker Shyam Benegal pointed this out in an interview in Riyad Wadia's documentary *Fearless: The Hunterwali Story*, 1993. Ashish Rajadhyaksha later makes a similar point in 'India's Silent Cinema: A "Viewer's View"', in Chabria and Usai, *Light of Asia*, p. 15 and pp. 33–4.

49. Prasad, *Ideology of the Hindi Film*.

50. Gopal, *Conjugations*, p. 5.

51. As Ranita Chatterjee, drawing on documentation in the Aurora studio archive, has usefully begun to sketch out in her PhD thesis, 'Journeys In and Beyond the City'.

52. Dust (and archival work) being the sine qua non of modern academic historical method as Carolyn Steedman wittily argues in *Dust*, Manchester: Manchester University Press, 2001.

53. In turn, Ranjani Mazumdar writes of Bombay cinema itself as 'an archive of the city'. See her *Bombay Cinema: An Archive of the City*, Minneapolis: University of Minnesota Press, 2007.

54. Nasreen Munni Kabir's interviews with key figures of the Bombay film industry were filmed for her series *Movie Mahal*, a popular programme which edited together film song clips and interviews with film-makers and ran on United Kingdom's Channel Four television throughout the 1990s; Osians is a private limited company that buys and sells all kinds of artwork including film memorabilia and also runs a film festival; Kamat Foto Flash is the longest-running photographic stills company in the Bombay film industry, a family concern that started in 1945.

55. Stephen P. Hughes, 'The Production of the Past: Early Tamil Film History as a Living Archive', *BioScope*, vol. 4, no. 1, 2013, pp. 71–80.

56. Tejaswini Ganti, *Producing Bollywood: Inside the Contemporary Hindi Film Industry*, Durham: Duke University Press, 2012, pp. 144–51.

57. The more things change, the more they remain the same.

Bombay before Bollywood

part one

Introduction

Part one of this book—chapters two to six—takes an alternative look at Bombay cinema history from its inception until the late 1960s. In this account, the focus is not on the socials and mythologicals, which have been well covered elsewhere and are the basis for most Indian cinema scholarship over the years, but on Bombay's extremely popular action and fantasy films, in particular the films that drew on global popular culture and repackaged this primarily, but not exclusively, for India's subaltern audiences.

Key figures in this history—and in my research—are the brothers Jamshed and Homi Wadia, film-makers whose extraordinarily successful working lives spanned the silent and sound eras. Homi was still producing and directing films in 1980 when I visited him on set at Basant's studios; Jamshed was writing his memoirs when I interviewed him at around the same time. Both have left an invaluable legacy for film historians. Moreover, Jamshed had the foresight to deposit a number of prints of their films at the Pune National Film Archive, as well as leaving a collection of visual ephemera, studio documents and his own writings for safekeeping with his own family.[1] While this is not a book about the Wadias per se—their fascinating history is the focus of a separate monograph—their work provides a common thread to my discussions in part one. A brief introduction is therefore appropriate at this point.

Jamshed and Homi Wadia were born into a respectable Bombay Parsi family, master shipbuilders to the East India Company.[2] Like many young men growing up in the early decades of the twentieth century, the brothers were avid movie fans, eagerly consuming the Hollywood westerns, comedies, stunt films and serials that ran to packed houses across the subcontinent. In 1926, aged twenty-five, Jamshed (widely known and referred to henceforth as JBH) scandalised his family by throwing away a promising career in law and banking to become a freelance writer and director for the silent movies. Homi, ten years his junior, soon joined him, working first as his assistant at the Devare Film Laboratory at Kohinoor Studios, then as his 'trusted lieutenant' and partner in Wadia Brothers' Productions, perfecting his camera and editing skills and soon directing his first silent film, *Diler Daku/Thunderbolt* (Homi Wadia, 1931). Between them, the Wadia brothers showed remarkable populist flair, and a run of successful silent films, all written by JBH, proved that big money could be made in the movies.[3] These five silent stunt thrillers—all successful 'in their class ... which was of course C-grade'[4]—had drawn unapologetically on Hollywood's 'lower' genres, notably the stunt serials of stars such as Douglas Fairbanks, Helen Holmes and Pearl White. Through 'Indianisation' of these, the Wadias' films had constructed a terrain upon which a Westernised Indian modernity, in touch with global popular culture, could be forged—an argument I develop across the later chapters of this section.

The release of *Alam Ara* (Beauty of the World, Ardeshir Irani, 1931), India's first sound film, caused some panic among other Bombay producers but JBH and Homi quickly linked up with Parsi entrepreneurs and industrialists—M.B. Bilimoria, and Nadirshaw and Burjorji Tata—who offered to set them up with their own studios, as well as to start a distribution office for both Indian and foreign films. Wadia Movietone was launched in 1933.

The studio's first sound film, *Lal-e-Yaman* (Jewel of Yemen,[5] J.B.H. Wadia, 1933) was a melodramatic *Arabian Nights* fantasy, a musical which drew its storyline and visual style from Parsi theatre: JBH had shrewdly invested in the talent of Joseph David, the acclaimed theatre director who had written *Alam Ara*. The film was a major hit and, on the proceeds of this and other early successes, Wadia Movietone was soon able to build impressive studios in the grounds of the Wadias' ancestral home, Lovji Castle, in the well-heeled Parel area of Bombay. The runaway success of *Hunterwali* (Woman with the Whip, Homi Wadia, 1935) and their new stunt star Fearless Nadia, followed by a series of hit 'thrillers' with Nadia—and, a little later, John Cawas—

Figure I.1 Booklet cover for *Hunterwali* (1935)

Source: © Roy Wadia/Wadia Movietone.

ensured that by 1938 theirs was the most profitable studio of its day. As Jamshed wrote in his memoirs: 'The figures showed that the earnings of Wadia Movietone films ... were unquestionably more than those of other companies.... Wadia films were decidedly more popular in rural cinemas and second-run cinema houses in cities like Bombay and Poona.'[6]

This well-oiled business enterprise, run along factory lines, had, by the late 1930s, around 600 people on its payroll, ranging from carpenters and cleaners to its top stars. Homi, reminiscing, described the discipline as 'like a school': when the ten o'clock bell rang, stars clocked in along with everyone else and a register was called to check for absences. Those not needed on set would rehearse or go home or, in the case of the stunt artistes, work out in the studio gym. Studio production specialised in comedy, stunt and action films and, in the early years, orientalist fantasies.

In the early 1940s, as socials became the genre of choice in 'respectable' circles when stunt and fantasy films appeared to fall out of fashion, the brothers set up Basant Pictures, ostensibly to increase their raw stock allocation in the context of wartime rationing. However, as tensions between the brothers developed, the company was split in 1943 and the two went their separate ways. Homi found renewed success at Basant by making populist stunt films aimed at the lower-class audiences, while Jamshed struggled on at Wadia Movietone producing mostly socials and documentaries. As we saw in the first chapter, Homi's Basant Pictures became the most successful B studio of the 1940s and 1950s, making cheap mythologicals, stunt and fantasy films that starred their own company of actors, including Fearless Nadia and John Cawas. The brothers came together again in 1948 with the success of the mythological *Shri Ram Bhakta Hanuman*, written by Jamshed and produced and directed by Homi Wadia, after which the announcement, 'A Wadia Brothers Film', prefaced many of the most successful films produced by Homi at Basant.

While the Wadia Movietone legacy is better documented than that of most Bombay studios, largely due to the vision—or egotism—of JBH, and while more than a dozen or so films have survived, albeit largely from Basant, any researcher is still clutching at clues. Thus each of the five chapters in this section begins with—and develops around—a different focus: dance and setting; sound and song; costume and performance; posters; lobby cards and stills. From these traces we uncover a complex, partial and less than orthodox picture of Bombay's B-movies over five decades.

Chapter two is an overview of the 'oriental genre' in early Indian cinema. It focuses on how the tales of the *Arabian Nights* circulated—and were adapted—in the early twentieth century and explores how orientalism played out within India. Tracing curious cultural borrowings across the interconnected paths of twentieth-century Indian and Western orientalist theatre, film, dance and variety entertainment, the chapter suggests that the *Arabian Nights* became, somewhat paradoxically, a signifier of cosmopolitan modernity in 1920s and 1930s India. Kohinoor's silent fantasy *Gul-e-Bakavali* (Kanjibhai Rathod, 1924), Wadia Movietone's *Lal-e-Yaman* (1933) and *Noor-e-Yaman* (1935), and, from Calcutta, Madhu Bose's *Alibaba* (1937) illustrate how films drew eclectically on both transcultural orientalist trends and on local traditions. I suggest that the so-called Islamicate was India's preferred orientalist mode.

Bombay before Bollywood

Chapter three offers a close reading of the fantasy film *Lal-e-Yaman* (J.B.H. Wadia, 1933), one of the earliest and most successful Indian sound films to have survived. The chapter argues that the film is structured around an opposition between the visual and the aural in which the power of the voice prevails over the illusory qualities of the visual, with Wadia innovatively using the acousmatic (disembodied) voice to represent truth and God. Comparing *Lal-e-Yaman* with Wadia's penultimate silent film *Vantolio* (Whirlwind, Homi Wadia, 1933), two modes of subaltern cosmopolitan modernity are contrasted, both increasingly disparaged in public discourse as the 1930s progressed.

A study of Fearless Nadia, Bombay's top box-office female star of the 1930s and 1940s, and her producers at Wadia Movietone is the focus of chapter four. It examines the apparent paradox of a white European woman being celebrated as a feisty nationalist heroine. The chapter links Nadia's appeal to the *virangana* (warrior woman) motif that circulated widely in early twentieth-century Indian popular culture. Using *Diamond Queen* (Homi Wadia, 1940) as an example, it argues that Nadia's persona is usefully understood as a form of mimicry in reverse, to be viewed in the context of the transnational flows of cinema distribution of the era.

Chapter five was inspired by two 1960s film posters aimed at 'C-grade' audiences: *Zimbo and Son* (John Cawas, 1966) and *Khilari* (The Player, Homi Wadia, 1968), Indian versions of Tarzan and James Bond respectively. Through analysis of these posters in relation to an earlier film, *Toofani Tarzan* (Homi Wadia, 1937), the chapter shows how globally popular subject matter was 'Indianised'. It argues that Tarzan and James Bond had particular resonances for subaltern Indian audiences for whom notions of masculinity were under negotiation in the nationalist era. By the 1960s, a game of mimicry and pastiche was being played with—and through—these references, with Basant recycling its own history to exploit two of its key brands, Fearless Nadia and John Cawas.

Chapter six emerged from—and is structured as a response to—the online archive Tasveer Ghar's collection of Indian popular visual culture ephemera. It focuses on stills from 1950s B-movie fantasy and action films. Spinning off from the half-dozen lobby cards displayed there from Homi Wadia's 1952 fantasy film *Aladdin and the Wonderful*

Lamp, it places these in the context of stills from other 1950s B-movies and alongside imagery as diverse as nineteenth-century textile labels, European travellers' postcards, matchbox covers, wrestling posters and calendar art. Rather different in form from the other chapters in this book, it was designed originally as a web-based visual essay. But as it draws together the themes of the other chapters of part one, it seemed appropriate to include it here.

NOTES

1. Riyad Wadia, Jamshed's grandson, did much to excavate and publicise this archive, which consists of both Wadia Movietone and some Basant Pictures material. While most of Basant's records were unfortunately destroyed when Homi sold the studio grounds to developers in the mid-2000s, he had also kept DVDs and VCDs of a number of his favourite films in his home. Since Riyad's untimely death in 2003, first his father Vinci, then his brother Roy, have continued as custodians. I am extremely grateful to all three, together with Nargis Wadia, for their unwavering and generous support of my research project over the years.

2. Information on the early days of the Wadias draws on J.B.H. Wadia's own published and unpublished writings, my own 1986 interviews with Homi and Mary Wadia, Riyad Wadia's 1993 documentary *Fearless: The Hunterwali Story*, Riyad Wadia's unpublished 1994 research dossier, together with other papers he kindly provided.

3. Although sound had arrived in India in 1931, there were still a couple of years within which silent films could make a profit on the B- or C-grade circuits—which were not yet geared for the new medium. *Diler Daku/Thunderbolt* (1931), *Sinh Garjana/Lion Man* (1931), *Toofan Mail* (1932), *Vantolio/Whirlwind* (1933) and *Dilruba Daku/Amazon* (1933) were all cheaply made stunt and action films which 'clicked in their class' and established the brothers' credibility in the industry.

4. J.B.H. Wadia, 'Those Were the Days', unpublished memoirs, 1980.

5. *Lal* can be translated as 'son' or as 'ruby' (or similar terms connoting preciousness). Whilst J.B.H. Wadia chose 'Darling of Yemen' as the film's English title, this does not read well to a contemporary ear (and was almost never used at the time). The translation 'Jewel of Yemen' better matches the range of the Urdu word.

6. J.B.H. Wadia, 'Those Were the Days'.

two

𝒯hieves of the Orient

The *Arabian Nights* in Early Indian Cinema*

In 1917, a fire broke out in a Calcutta warehouse, destroying a priceless haul of film history riches. Inside was the life's work of Hiralal Sen, India's unsung film pioneer. It is claimed the treasures included footage of a dance from *Flower of Persia*, an 1898 'Arabian Nights opera' of the Calcutta stage, as well as a one-hour compilation of dance scenes from another big theatre hit, K.P. Vidyavinode's *Ali Baba*, that had been screened alongside the play from Classic Theatres in 1901. But, even more astonishing if true, the warehouse is said to have contained a 'full length' film version of the same *Ali Baba* stage play, which included close-ups, pans and tilts and was edited to a length of over two hours and screened at the theatre in 1903 or 1904.[1]

While lists of cinema 'firsts' are always contentious and ultimately irrelevant, revelations that hint at stolen glories are irresistibly intriguing. If the tales of Hiralal Sen's film-making are correct, it would mean not only that India's own first feature film was an *Arabian Nights* tale with a loosely Islamicate[2] setting, but that India produced both the world's first *Arabian Nights* film footage and its first full-length *Arabian Nights* film. These claims are controversial: Edison's catalogue included a European *Ali Baba* made in 1902, but this was a short, as was the French *Aladdin and the Wonderful Lamp* 'in 45 tableaux', which played in Madras in 1902.[3] Moreover, the Indian film industry has long celebrated as its founding moment a 1913 film version of a story from Hindu mythology, Dadasaheb Phalke's *Raja Harishchandra*. Hiralal Sen's *Ali Baba and the Forty Thieves* has, for the past hundred years, been mostly either quietly ignored or dismissed as 'just' a film record of a Bengali stage hit and, without any hard evidence to go on, sceptical historians have been free to dispute its length and significance.

Whatever the truth about Sen's films, there is no doubt that stories from the *Arabian Nights* were present at the birth of cinema in India, just as they were in America, France and Germany. Moreover, Indian film-makers' enthusiasm for the *Nights* owed little to film pioneers elsewhere in the world. At least one Indian film in the oriental fantasy genre was a box-office hit well before Douglas Fairbanks's *Thief of Bagdad* (Raoul Walsh, 1924) took India by storm from mid-1925.[4] In these early years, Indian film-makers were borrowing less from Hollywood than from their own local traditions of 'oriental' tales, albeit refracted through an Urdu-Parsi theatre as steeped in European theatre and literature as in the Indian vernacular forms that circulated orally and through the popular printing presses. Tales and tropes from the *Arabian Nights* fed Indian cinema's fantasy and costume genres throughout the late 1920s and early 1930s and remained a mainstay of the subaltern cinema audience circuits until the 1960s and beyond.

This chapter explores what Ira Bhaskar and Richard Allen refer to as the 'oriental genre' in early Indian cinema.[5] Given the centrality of the *Arabian Nights* to these predominantly fantasy films, I focus on how that body of stories and motifs—with its complex transcultural history—circulated within India and was drawn on by Indian film-makers in the pre-independence years.[6] I argue that while films referencing the *Arabian Nights* had much in common with others with a Muslim ethos (such as Muslim socials, historicals and courtesan films)—offering a strong cultural appeal to Muslim and subaltern audiences as well as scope for spectacle, poetry, romance, stunts and anti-communalist politics—their appeal was broader and their construction of an 'Islamicate' world somewhat looser than those other genres. Key to India's oriental fantasy film was its setting within an imaginary world outside India. Although sometimes coded as quasi-Arabian and/or ancient Iranian, this was in fact a hybrid never-never land, as we shall see. This fantastical Orient—its magical qualities invariably conjured up through inventive special effects—also drew heavily, both directly and indirectly, on the fashionable orientalism that infused Euro-American art, literature, cinema and performing arts of the eighteenth to early twentieth centuries, in the construction of which the *Arabian Nights* had played a major role.[7] This transnational orientalism penetrated both high- and low-culture performance forms of 1920s and 1930s India, rendering them spaces of multiple and curious appropriations—a veritable hall of mirrors. Cross-fertilisation with the ubiquitous traces of Mughal or Rajput courtly culture and a Hinduising nationalism complicated things further. Through all these processes, India constructed its own imaginary, quasi-Islamicate Orient. Although marked by both similarities to and differences from the European Orient, this was equally a site of essentialist 'othering' and cultural thievery.

I argue that within India the *Arabian Nights* fantasy film operated on two levels, perceived not only as local and 'traditional' but also, apparently paradoxically, as international and 'modern'. Focusing on *Lal-e-Yaman* (Jewel of Yemen, J.B.H. Wadia, 1933), Bombay cinema's earliest surviving *Arabian Nights* fantasy film and one of the most successful of its day, and drawing comparisons with *Gul-e-Bakavali* (The Bakavali Flower, Kanjibhai Rathod, 1924), this chapter begins to tease out this conundrum. The first part examines the processes of adaption and circulation of the *Nights* in early Indian cinema; the second part explores India's Islamicate Orient in the context of Euro-American orientalism; the conclusion discusses the appeal of Indian cinema's fantasy genre and its complex series of appropriations.

THE *ARABIAN NIGHTS* IN INDIA: CIRCULATION AND ADAPTATION

In the Bombay film industry context, an *Arabian Nights* film was not just a film that reworked recognisable tales such as 'Ali Baba' and 'Aladdin'.[8] Echoing the Hollywood producers of *Thief of Bagdad*, the term 'Arabian Nights fantasy film' was used by Indian filmmakers to describe film hybrids created from a number of different *Nights*' stories and motifs. These included fantasy films based on Persian qissa-dastan literature and legend, notably the so-called *pari*/fairy films.[9] Although not strictly *Arabian Nights* tales, many of their storylines and motifs overlap with the *Nights* as pari stories evolved from similar original sources.[10] Thus, in India, the term's colloquial usage referred to all films with an *Arabian Nights* ethos, which meant, broadly, films of magical and wondrous happenings set in a quasi-Persian/Arabic, and usually loosely Islamicate culture. Older cinema workers I have met referred to such films as *jadoo* (magic) films, and a 1930s source suggests they were also known as 'Mahomedan [sic] pictures'.[11] As we will see, what they all drew on, alongside their common indigenous roots, was a transnational, imaginary Orient. Indeed, the Indian film industry trade press of the early 1930s advertised distributors' lists of imported 'Oriental' and 'Semi-Oriental' films.[12] Moreover, the hybridity of such fantasy films was in keeping with the spirit of the *Nights'* own evolution through oral traditions over many centuries. As Robert Irwin explains: 'Plot motifs within the *Nights* combine and recombine…. The stories are full of echoes and half echoes of one another, like recurrent dreams in which the landscape is thoroughly familiar, though what is to come is utterly unpredictable.'[13]

The *Arabian Nights*, also known as *The Thousand and One Nights* (and in Arabic as *Alf Layla wa-Layla*, or in Urdu as *Alif Laila*), is best described as a labyrinth or 'sea of stories' which originated—and evolved—within ancient Indian, Persian and Arabic low-culture oral traditions. There is no definitive canon—certainly not 1,001 tales—and the *Nights* exist in many differing versions and translations.[14] Key continuities are the formal device of tales that spring from within other tales and the frame story of Scheherazade, the clever queen who keeps postponing her own execution by telling her sexually jealous husband such engaging bedtime stories that, when she stops abruptly as each day breaks, he extends her life for a further day at a time. Finally, after 1,001 nights of fantastical stories—and the birth of three sons—he magnanimously agrees to spare her. Little is known about the *Nights'* early history, although India is, without doubt, an important source and, as Emmanuel Cosquin has shown, the origin of the frame tale.[15] By the fourteenth to sixteenth centuries, several Arabic manuscripts were circulating across the bazaars of Damascus, Cairo and Baghdad. On the basis of what survived of these, Antoine Galland published the first European translation, *Les Mille et Une Nuits* (1704–17). This sparked a veritable craze in European arts and the literary culture of its day, influencing writers and artists from

Voltaire to Coleridge and even the Brothers Grimm. Numerous retranslations followed Galland—including some from French back into Arabic and several hoaxes. Somewhat curiously, the *Nights* found its way back to India in the form of two nineteenth-century Arabic manuscripts published in Calcutta (known as *Calcutta 1* and *Calcutta 2*), originally as textbooks for British officers to learn Arabic. New European versions of the *Nights* introduced different stories, with some, like Richard Burton and Joseph Mardrus, shamelessly accentuating the erotic and exotic content for the delectation of European literary salons, while others, like Edward Lane, prudishly censored the erotica.[16]

Some core tales remain throughout all versions of the *Nights*, while others, notably 'Ali Baba', 'Aladdin' and 'Sinbad'—those best known in the modern world—cannot be traced to any Arabic source that pre-dates Galland's translation. These are now referred to as the 'orphan stories' and believed to be largely Galland's own improvisation around the outline of tales he heard from a Syrian monk, Hanna Diab. But this does not mean they are not 'really' part of the *Arabian Nights* canon. As Ulrich Marzolph argues, despite its undisputed oriental origins, the *Arabian Nights* has now to be seen as a transcultural creative work 'shaped into its presently visible form by European demand and influence'.[17]

While little is known about the *Nights*' early history and development within India, there is no doubt that the stories were circulating widely here in Victorian times—alongside the qissa-dastan from which they were mostly indistinguishable in the popular imagination. This was in part a continuation of local and vernacular performance traditions, notably theatre and oral storytelling cultures, but it was also inspired by the popularity of the *Nights*' various European translations around the world. Although the publication of the two Arabic manuscripts in Calcutta in 1814–18 and 1839–42 did not immediately filter through to Indian readers, with the rise of vernacular commercial presses from the mid-nineteenth century Indian language translations began to proliferate. Thus, for example, while an (abridged) Urdu translation of the *Nights* was published in Lahore in 1844, it was largely after 1867, with the more ornate Urdu prose and poetry versions (considered more 'authentic') from Naval Kishore's Lucknow press, that the *Nights* 'became popular reading for all'.[18] Meanwhile, in late-nineteenth-century Calcutta, the cheap, popular *bat-tala* presses hawked *Arabian Nights* stories in Bengali.[19]

It is impossible to unravel precisely how much of the *Nights'* presence in Victorian India evolved from the earliest Indian tales, how much derived directly from Persian legend and the bazaars of the Arab world, what came through local printing presses and their *munshis*,[20] and what arrived back in India through the detour of eighteenth-century European high culture or, indeed, nineteenth-century low culture. Suffice it to say that Indian film-makers and their audiences in the 1920s and 1930s would have encountered the *Nights* through a number of overlapping routes, foremost amongst these being urban theatre.

Nineteenth-century Urdu-Parsi theatre did much to popularise the *Nights* across India's cities. *Arabian Nights* plays were staples of the commercial theatre repertoire from at least the 1870s: *Ali Baba*, *Aladdin* and *Hatimtai* all figure in the records, presumably reflecting not only popular reading tastes but also the *Nights'* prevalence in eighteenth- and nineteenth-century British theatre and pantomime. But the Indian playwrights were reworking these stories on their own terms. Empress Victoria Theatrical Company, for example, was touring an Urdu *Ali Baba aur Chalis Chor* across north India in the 1870s, playing it in Chinese costumes and Chinese-style sets as part of its repertory over a five-month stay in Lahore in 1878.[21] Meanwhile, on India's east coast, as we have seen, Vidyavinode's Bengali adaptation of the 'Ali Baba' story, advertised as a 'magnificent Comic Opera' and a 'genuine Fountain of Mirth and Merriment', dominated the turn-of-the-century Calcutta theatre.[22]

In Indian theatre, as in cinema, straightforward adaptations of well-known *Arabian Nights* tales existed alongside more hybrid fantasies. The Urdu-Parsi theatre was a notoriously eclectic form: elements of the *Arabian Nights* coexisted with Shakespeare, Victorian literature and a range of Persian, Indian and Arabic literatures and legends, from the eleventh-century Persian *shahnama* to the tales-within-tales of Sufi *masnavi* or the pari/fairy romances of the qissa-dastan oral repertoire such as *Gul Sanobar* and *Gul-e-Bakavali*, not to mention the ever popular tales from Hindu mythology. Thus a vernacular tradition

of integrating the *Arabian Nights* within other local and foreign forms
was well established by the time the cinema arrived in India and was
an obvious port of call for film writers and directors.

The first *Arabian Nights* films were effectively filmed stage plays,
like Hiralal Sen's *Ali Baba*. Dance shorts were common: J.F. Madan
& Sons' Elphinstone Bioscope Company was showing 'the tableaux
dance of *Kamr-al-Zaman-Badoora*' on 'bioscope worked by electricity'
at the Corinthian Theatre, Calcutta, alongside a Parsi theatre
version of *Hamlet,* in 1905.[23] This same Madan family, whose vast
cinema distribution and exhibition empire of the 1920s evolved out
of its Urdu-Parsi theatre business ventures, produced India's first
(recognised) *Arabian Nights* fantasy film, *Princess Budur (The Story of
Qamar-e-Zaman,* J.J. Madan), in 1922.[24] The Madans went on to make
a string of such films throughout the silent era, notably *Hoor-e-Arab,*
1928, *Aladdin,* 1931, and (the talkie) *Ali Baba,* 1932, all starring their
top actress, the 'Anglo-Indian' Patience Cooper.

A sudden surge in fantasy film production in India from 1925
onwards undoubtedly, in part, reflected the extraordinary box-office
success of the pari/fairy fantasy film *Gul-e-Bakavali,* Bombay's first
all-India super hit.[25] Based on a Persian legend about the fairy princess,
Bakavali, the handsome prince, Taj-al-Mulk, and his quest for Gul-
e-Bakavali, the magic flower that will cure his father's blindness, the
qissa had circulated orally in poetry and prose for centuries. Fort
William College published the first Urdu translation in 1803 (in press
alongside an Urdu *Alif Laila*) as part of its language curriculum.[26] By
the mid- to late nineteenth century, *Gul-e-Bakavali* (Figure 2.1), like
the *Nights*, was a staple of the vernacular commercial presses.

Gul-e-Bakavali became an Urdu-Parsi theatre favourite,
capitalising on the scope it offered for staging spectacular magical
transformations, and it is no surprise that early film-makers also
saw its potential. A shooting script of Kohinoor's 1924 film has
recently come to light, courtesy of Virchand Dharamsey, revealing
conclusively that tropes we associate with *Arabian Nights* films were
already well established in cinema before *Thief of Bagdad* arrived in
India: the hero receives 'magical gifts' from a *fakir*[27] to assist in his
fights against evil beings; he finds his entrancing fairy princess asleep
on a couch and exchanges a magic ring with her; with a 'trick shot'

Figure 2.1   *Gul-e-Bakavali* (1932)

Source: Courtesy Virchand Dharamsey.

she emerges 'slowly slowly' from a giant flower painted on a curtain; an elixir poured on another ring opens the door to her secret garden; horses gallop 'at the speed of wind' and several characters fly through the clouds, including fairies who scatter flowers on the earth below.[28] Such fantastical material, with strong echoes of the *Nights'* magical worlds, would have offered many opportunities for the 'trick shots' that had been such a favourite of the earlier mythological films of the 1910s and early 1920s. A cameraman working for Krishna Film Company described the ingenious, if low-tech, special effects he used in another contemporary fantasy, *Jalkumari/Hoor-al-Bahar*[29] (H. Mehta, 1925), in which he filmed fairies in flight dodging oncoming clouds by suspending the 'celestial creatures' on wires against a black curtain, filming them waving their arms, and then double exposing this footage with a live panning shot of the sky.[30]

By 1927, when the ICC was taking its evidence, three fantasy films, including *Gul-e-Bakavali* and *Aladdin and the Wonderful Lamp* (B.P. Mishra, 1927), turn up repeatedly on witnesses' lists of the top eight or nine Indian box-office successes.[31] Films from the *Arabian Nights* were cited approvingly as 'films of general appeal' that could bridge provincial—and even religious—differences of taste.[32] The proprietors of Imperial Film Company reported that *Aladdin* was their most popular film ever—'wherever it is sent it is popular'—and some exhibitors confirmed that Indian films such as *Aladdin* could be more profitable than Western films.[33] However, the final ICC report categorically concluded, 'The most popular film ever shown in India was the *Thief of Baghdad* [*sic*] with Douglas Fairbanks in an Oriental setting.'[34] Billed in its opening titles as 'An Arabian Nights Fantasy', the *Thief of Bagdad*, which hit Calcutta in March 1925, was a hybrid spun—with considerable latitude—from the tales of 'Aladdin', 'The Magic Horse' and 'Prince Achmed'. Witness after witness testified to the success of this Hollywood extravaganza, which would have made its distributors/exhibitors, Madan Theatres, far more money than all their own *Arabian Nights* films put together. Resonating with indigenous fantasy traditions, this was, almost certainly, the most important catalyst for the surge of *Arabian Nights* fantasy films in the late 1920s and early 1930s.

We can no longer properly assess the scale of the *Nights'* influence on Indian silent cinema. Only two dozen of India's 1,300 or so silent films have survived, none of them fantasy films.[35] Apart from the ICC evidence—and now the *Gul-e-Bakavali* script—our only resources are film titles, newspaper advertisements, censorship records, a few film stills and earlier historians' genre classifications. Somewhat confusingly, while some historians distinguish between 'fantasy' and 'costume' films, others subsume under 'costume film' everything from Ruritanian swashbuckling adventures, Rajput, Mughal and Sultanate courtly dramas to the more overtly Islamicate fantasy films that interest us here.[36] We can, nevertheless, draw a few tentative conclusions. Between 1925 and 1934 (when silent film production ceased) more than 40 per cent of all productions can be classified as 'costume film' in its widest sense. Less than

20 per cent of these costume films can be confidently said to be 'fantasy', 'pari' or 'jadoo' films.[37] In other words, direct *Arabian Nights'* (including qissa-dastan) influence accounted for a steady trickle of films throughout the silent cinema of the late 1920s and early 1930s—half-a-dozen to a dozen films each year. However, a number of so-called costume films would have been hybrids that incorporated *Nights* and qissa motifs, and many others would have been influenced by Fairbanks's swashbuckling persona and thus, less directly, the *Arabian Nights*.[38]

Such statistics say nothing about the scale, popularity and influence of individual films or how the landscape appeared to people at the time. One or two 'straight' *Nights* tales were made each year between 1927 and 1931—in the Indian context the favourites were the universally popular 'orphan stories' *Aladdin* and *Ali Baba*, together with *Hatimtai*, *Qamar-al-Zaman* (aka *Princess Budur*) and, to a lesser extent, *Sinbad*. As these films were produced by wealthy, high-profile companies such as Madan and Imperial—predominantly but not exclusively companies run by Parsis—they would have had disproportionate impact and status. Thus, for example, Krishna Film Company's *Hatimtai* (Prafulla Ghosh, 1929), which drew on a crossover tale more familiar from qissa-dastan than the *Nights* (the seven adventures of Hatim, the exemplarily generous traveller, and the fairy Gulnar), made waves as a big-budget, spectacular, four-part serial with extravagant sets. Other films appear to have been more opportunistically hybrid: Madan's *Hoor-e-Arab* was, according to Firoze Rangoonwalla, another reworking of *Aladdin*, while Ranjit Studio's *Siren of Bagdad* (*Bagdad ka Bulbul*, Nanubhai Vakil, 1931) traded shamelessly not only on the *Thief of Bagdad* brand but also on the audience's prurient interest in erotic display, according to hints in a not untypical *Bombay Chronicle* advertisement of the day. Beside a silhouette of a naked dancing girl, the text gently titillates its readers.

> Do you know the fascination of Arabian atmosphere! Bagdad, where moonbeams light the blue sky, where pure love is the religion, where nature dances in a nude form. If you want to be thrilled by such a romance then you must see: SIREN OF BAGDAD.[39]

In 1931, 55 per cent of the silent films released were costume films, many in the Rajput idiom, but a significant number of others were in the quasi-Islamicate hybrid idiom that brought *Nights*-qissa 'marvels' and 'enchantments' together with stunt action. These were all part of what Kaushik Bhaumik describes as the 'adventure romance' genre that dominated the era.[40]

With the arrival of sound in 1931 and an influx of talented writers, directors and actors from Parsi theatre, the trend for fantasy and costume films accelerated. India's first talkie, Imperial's *Alam Ara* (Beauty of the World, Ardeshir Irani, 1931), written by the Urdu-Parsi theatre writer/director Joseph David, boasted seven songs, extravagant spectacle, a loosely Persianate setting, and a story of romance between a gypsy girl and a prince, and of harem rivalry between two queens after a Sufi fakir predicts that the younger will produce the king's heir. Its success, and that of other similar films, including Wadia Movietone's first sound venture *Lal-e-Yaman*, produced a rash of *Arabian Nights* hybrids up until the mid-1930s. The trend petered out by the end of the decade, as the 'realist' social melodramas became increasingly fashionable, although a trickle of cheaply made fantasy films fed the subaltern audiences throughout the 1940s. With the success of Basant's *Aladdin and the Wonderful Lamp* (Homi Wadia, 1952), a new vogue for fantasy films on the B- and C-grade cinema circuits began in the 1950s, with films such as K. Amarnath's *Alif Laila* (A Thousand Nights, 1953) and a string of cult classics from the Wadia brothers. These include *Gul Sanobar* (Aspi, 1953), *Alibaba and the Forty Thieves* (Homi Wadia, 1954), *Hatimtai* (Homi Wadia, 1956) and *Baghdad ka Jadu* (Magic of Baghdad, John Cawas, 1956), a comedy spoof starring Fearless Nadia, after which the studio returned to producing mostly stunt and mythological films. By the mid-1950s, fantasy and costume films together accounted for almost a third of all productions, with a constant stream of fantasy films from other B- and C-circuit directors such as Nanubhai Vakil and Dhirubhai Desai throughout that period.[41] *Arabian Nights* fantasy films only died away as a genre in the 1970s, although occasional revivals have continued even to 2009.[42] Moreover, Ramanand Sagar's 260-episode *Alif Laila* was one of Indian television's most popular series of the mid-1990s.[43]

LAL-E-YAMAN (1933) AND *NOOR-E-YAMAN* (1935)

J.B.H. Wadia always referred to *Lal-e-Yaman* and its sequel, *Noor-e-Yaman* (Light of Yemen, J.B.H. Wadia, 1935), as 'Arabian Nights fantasies', although he explained in his memoirs that he chose *Lal-e-Yaman*'s story precisely because of its generic mix: 'At last my choice fell upon an Arabian Nights story.... I was impressed with its dramatic potential. Behind the veneer of fantasy, it had all the elements of a social film—rich in human values.'[44]

Lal-e-Yaman is of interest today as the earliest Indian *Arabian Nights* film to have survived and one of the biggest cinema hits of its day. But unlike other films of the era that were straight adaptations of theatre productions of favourite *Nights* stories such as 'Ali Baba' and 'Aladdin', *Lal-e-Yaman* was an *Arabian Nights*-qissa hybrid. Based on no individual known tale, the story was dreamed up for the film by the Urdu-Parsi theatre impresario Joseph David (*Alam Ara*'s writer), in collaboration with J.B.H. Wadia, whose family had long enjoyed David's Islamicate plays, such as *Hoor-e-Arab*,[45] *Khaki Putla, Noor-e-Watan* and *Baagh-e-Iran,* performed by the Parsi Imperial Theatre Company at Bombay's Coronation Theatre in the 1910s.

Wadia's memoirs give a vivid insight into the process of constructing this *Arabian Nights* hybrid—as well as the intellectual and cultural backgrounds of the people involved. While Wadia was an upper-class Parsi, with an LLB and postgraduate degrees in English literature and Avesta Pehlavi, David was a self-taught man of Indian Jewish (Bene Israeli) origin, who had left school young and began working in his local theatre in rural Maharashtra as a child, first as a stage prompt and later as actor, writer and director.[46] However, by the time David was in his sixties, when Wadia met him, his modest flat at Dongri, Central Bombay, housed a vast library that ranged across European and Indian literature, arts and drama. He not only read voraciously in English but also wrote and read in Urdu, Hindi, Marathi, Gujarati and Hebrew. Wadia was thrilled to be able to discuss world theatre with this erudite and cultured man, whom he admiringly referred to as 'Dada'.[47]

[His flat] contained more books and manuscripts in his favourite languages than household furniture. His study of the World drama was remarkable and his memory phenomenal. It was a real pleasure for me to discuss with Joseph David not only Shakespeare, Marlowe and B Johnson but even lesser Elizabethan dramatists like Beaumont and Fletcher, Massingham and Greene, the eighteenth-century English dramatists and early moderns like Ibsen and Shaw.

Not only was David steeped in a European literature replete with *Arabian Nights* references, but he was also *au fait* with Asian and Middle Eastern literary traditions. Moreover, he was himself a prolific storyteller, constantly creating new plots out of this rich sea of stories from around the world.

> Joseph David, respected Dada to us all, had only to pull out the papers from his fabulous collection of stories and plays written out in Gujarati script in his own hand for future use.... They consist of story kernels and an endless stream of quotations in Hindi and Urdu (couplets, quatrains, etc.).

In a process of creative dialogue and bricolage amongst these 'story kernels', the two men narrowed down the options for Wadia's first talkie. When the team finally got to work, Dada was involved in every aspect, from writing the script, dialogues and music to casting and rehearsing the actors.

Lal-e-Yaman is set in a mythical time past, advertised in the *Bombay Chronicle* as 'a golden chapter from the legendary history of humanity, when angels stalked the earth and men believed in miracles'.[48] The film tells of a Yemeni royal family torn apart by a woman's jealousy and human greed; the family eventually finds truth and happiness through a fakir's[49] wisdom and supernatural powers. The opening scene shows the wedding celebrations of the King of Yemen and his new second wife. A female dancer and musicians are entertaining the assembled court when the mournful singing of a fakir passing by outside catches the king's attention. The blind fakir is invited in but proceeds to warn the king that his new wife's poisonous nature will ruin him. When the queen protests her innocence, the fakir is whipped for his insolence. The rest of the film unfolds ten years later. The ruthless queen tries to kill the king's first son, Parviz, so that Nadir, her own son, can become king. However, the fakir helps Parviz escape from the palace dungeon, giving him a magic knife that can make him invisible. After melodramatic twists and turns and adventures in an enchanted land ruled by a wicked jinni, Parviz rescues the Egyptian princess Parizad, killing the jinni by means of a magic rose. The prince returns home to find his father in exile in the fakir's forest retreat. The king is now a widower, ranting and confused, his only consolation the beautiful singing of his younger son, Prince Nadir. With the fakir's help—and the magic knife—Parviz reclaims the family's kingdom and marries Parizad. But just as Parviz is about to be crowned king, the fakir intervenes and announces God's will: Nadir must be king, while Parviz and Parizad must go to her land, Misr (Egypt), to spread the word of Islam and sing the praises of Allah there. They depart, blessed by the old king, while the new king, Nadir, sings against the background of a flag embroidered with the Islamic crescent moon and star. [50]

Although the film does not derive from an existing *Arabian Nights* or qissa tale, we recognise these tales both thematically and structurally. Like many *Nights* stories *Lal-e-Yaman* moves between three realms: the jinni's magic land, the Yemeni royal court, and an (implicit) celestial realm that controls human destinies. Moreover, the film alludes directly to existing *Nights* tales: for example, Princess Parizad is guarded by a capricious parrot, echoing not only the *Nights* story of the jealous merchant who leaves a talking parrot to keep watch over his beautiful but deceitful wife but also a qissa along similar lines. [51] Familiar generic motifs abound: the prince on his quest is lured into the jinni's land by a semi-naked nymph frolicking in a lake; he becomes entranced by the sight of a bejewelled princess asleep on a gilded couch who can only be woken by rubbing two sticks together; and he must use his magic dagger's cloak of invisibility to vanquish the monstrously ugly being who has kept her captive. In fact, the fakir's magic powers centre primarily on visibility and invisibility: crude optical effects create his miracles—weeping trees, illusory beings, snakes and prison chains that turn into garlands. This visual magic draws on conventions of Parsi theatre and of the costume, fantasy and action genres of India's later silent cinema, as seen in *Gul-e-Bakavali*, but also, somewhat eclectically, the film cites both Shakespeare and Hollywood: the king is a King Lear figure, while the jinni's bodyguard is an ape-like monster that swings through the jungle just like Johnny Weissmuller's Tarzan. *Lal-e-Yaman* is an improvisation around *Arabian Nights* themes and storylines, combining these with contemporary popular culture references, much in the spirit of the *Arabian Nights'* own evolution.

Wadia Movietone worked closely with Joseph David on five Islamicate films between 1933 and 1935, including two 'historicals', *Bagh-e-Misr* (Tiger of Egypt, J.B.H. Wadia, 1934), set in ancient Egypt, and *Josh-e-Watan/Desh Deepak* (Light of the Homeland J.B.H. Wadia, 1935), set in ancient Iran, as well as *Kala Gulab/Black Rose* (J.B.H. Wadia, 1934), based on an Urdu stage play set in a Muslim milieu.[52] But the studio's two *Arabian Nights'* fantasies were by far the most successful at the box office.[53] *Noor-e-Yaman* appears to have pushed the fantasy elements much further than *Lal-e-Yaman*. Its convoluted plot again stars the wise fakir and the prince (now king) with the golden voice but adds bevies of bathing nymphs, a flying carpet, messenger parrots and doves, a skull and a ring for distance seeing, a magic pebble to make its owners invisible, mystic incense that makes a man fall in love, a magic spell that transforms a wicked man's lower body into a tree trunk, which can only be undone by sprinkling jinni's blood onto him, and much besides.[54] Judging by images in *Noor-e-Yaman's* song booklet, the film was also considerably more spectacular than its predecessor, with chorus lines of fairies and nymphs, dungeons of skeletons and ornate Islamicate court settings. Most intriguingly, the seductress Princess Parizad, who spent much of the film imprisoned and tortured for refusing to forsake Islam, was played by an exotic, blue-eyed blonde in her first proper screen role: the former cabaret dancer then known as Miss Nadia.[55] This was the Islamicate never-never land at its most excessive, drawing deliriously from a cosmopolitan repertoire of orientalist signifiers.

What can these films tell us about India's home-grown Orient— this imaginary (magical) space that is 'other than' India? We must return to the question of where the fantasy genre sits within the spectrum of India's so-called Islamicate cinematic forms and examine the relationship between orientalism and the Islamicate.

ORIENTALISM AND THE ISLAMICATE

The question of orientalism within Indian performing arts has been surprisingly little explored, although Gregory Booth's groundbreaking essay on musical orientalism in Hindi cinema usefully sets out its complexities.[56] His discussion includes the conventionalised use of the oboe and the 'gapped scale' for 'Arab spice'—a conscious borrowing from Hollywood—as well as Hindi cinema's more idiosyncratic tendency to exoticise background (non-diegetic) rather than diegetic music and songs. However, Booth's central focus on post-independence cinema oversimplifies matters. While he correctly notes that 'orientalist baggage' was imported into Hindi cinema through the traditions of Euro-American film and theatre on which it drew so closely—and, as he puts it, 'Orientals can indeed be Orientalist'—it is misleading to contend that this was primarily a post-independence development. As we have just seen, an orientalist sensibility was rife in early Indian cinema, especially in *Arabian Nights* fantasy films, and this included a tendency to 'other' its Muslims. But as the term 'orientalism' nowadays subsumes a variety of differing practices and forms, it would be useful to unravel its complex histories within both Euro-American and Indian contexts.

It has been well documented that throughout the eighteenth and nineteenth centuries, European arts and literature were fascinated by representations of an Orient that was largely a projection of Western political fears and erotic fantasies—as Edward Said and many others have described.[57] Antoine Galland's French translation of the *Arabian Nights* in 1704–17 undoubtedly helped to fuel this obsession. This European popular Orient was a confused imaginary space in which the harem and the despot primarily defined the Arab world, while South Asia became the domain of magic, mysticism and sensual dancing girls, the latter pruriently fantasised as 'a symbol for oriental opulence ... and uncurbed sensuousness'.[58] Aspects of this orientalist imagination were embraced, with some enthusiasm, within India itself, finding expression, as discussed earlier, in nineteenth-century Urdu-Parsi theatre as well as in other fields, including painting and architecture. From an Indian perspective, although chinoiserie did make its mark here, the gaze was in fact mostly directed *westward* towards an 'Orient' broadly associated with Persia, the Arab world, and Central Asia and marked loosely, but not exclusively, by an Islamicate ethos. Although India's Orient was not identical with that of the Europeans, it was similarly hazy.

In the context of early Indian cinema, however, it was the second wave of European orientalist fantasy in the early decades of the twentieth century that was most significant. This arrived from several directions simultaneously—France, England, America—with the *Arabian Nights* recurring yet again as a catalyst. In France, the new orientalism had been importantly inspired by the publication of Joseph Mardrus's translation of the *Nights* between 1899 and 1904. This was a decidedly loose and flamboyantly eroticised adaptation that epitomised *fin-de-siècle* decadence. Nevertheless, it was wildly popular and directly inspired Serge Diaghilev's *Schéhérazade*, the 'oriental ballet' with which the Ballets Russes conquered Paris in 1910, before making waves around the world. Starring Vaslav Nijinsky as the Golden Slave, whose 'frenzied voluptuousness' both scandalised and titillated its audiences, *Schéhérazade* was even more of a travesty of the *Arabian Nights* than Mardrus's work. Shamelessly dispensing with the clever woman storyteller—Scheherazade herself—the ballet was confected around one scene of the introductory frame story, which revelled in the despot, slave, harem and orgy motifs that so excited the European imagination. But, as Peter Wollen describes, with its sensationalist spectacle and Leon Bakst's jewel-coloured sets and costumes, this twenty-minute extravaganza set the agenda for an explosion of orientalist modernism across the European decorative arts. Paul Poiret's influential 'oriental look' fashions helped to popularise this sensibility: by the time the Exhibition of Decorative Arts opened in Paris in 1925, French department stores were awash with art deco orientalist clothing accessories, and turbans and harem pants had become de rigueur for the fashionable of both sexes.[59] The new orientalism, now a consumer movement, had extraordinary global reach—with art deco coming to connote modernity around the world, including India.[60]

Cinema in Europe and America was deeply influenced by the Ballets Russes' modernist orientalism (and Poiret's fashions), especially after the dance company's 1916 American tour, on which it performed its full oriental cycle. Matthew Bernstein, building on Wollen and Gaylyn Studlar, suggests, 'Serge Diaghilev's Ballets Russes with its staging of *Cleopatra*, *Thamar* and *Schéhérazade* ... contributed decisively to the mise-en-scène of Orientalist cinema.'[61] In Hollywood, admirers of 'the Diaghilev ballet' included Douglas Fairbanks and the creative team of *Thief of Bagdad*.[62] But *Schéhérazade*'s influence on this film touched far more than its mise-en-scène. As Studlar argues, '*Thief of Bagdad* ... is driven by dance aesthetics at every level in spite of not containing one conventional dance scene'—a telling observation in the context of the film's popularity across India.[63]

Considerable as Diaghilev's influence was on twentieth-century orientalism, it should not be overstated. Orientalist performance was already well established in European and American popular entertainment. Joan Erdman reminds us that 'the 1909 season of Diaghilev's Russian dancers, with their elaborate costumes, exquisite sets, and extraordinary themes, brought to ballet what had already been viewed on the stages of music hall and in the Folies Bergère: the exotic Orient.'[64] Salome's Dance of the Seven Veils—veils removed with wild abandon in the course of the dance, as immortalised by Maud Allen—was a vaudeville craze in Paris, London, Vienna, New York and elsewhere in America at the turn of the century, as were Loie Fuller and her diaphanous 'Hindu skirt' and Mata Hari as Shiva's temptress, all familiar to early Indian filmgoers.[65] There were strange cross-currents and multiple appropriations. As Wollen points out, while in earlier years fashionable St Petersburg had eagerly imported Parisian orientalism, after Diaghilev's arrival in 1909 Paris started to import a Russian orientalism marked by Central Asian cultural forms—arguably one of the Ballets Russes' key contributions to the international orientalist imaginary and one that resonated with India's experience of Central Asian cultures.[66]

However, other currents influenced Indian film, dance and arts more directly and bizarrely. In turn-of-the-century USA, an 'aesthetic dance' movement was evolving out of vaudeville. This new breed of dancers, amongst them Isadora Duncan and Ruth St Denis, was even more committed to orientalist masquerade than their music hall predecessors. Ruth St Denis, who became particularly influential both in Hollywood and within India's new dance movement of the

1930s, began her solo career touring with her 'Radha', 'Cobra' and 'Incense' dances in the 1900s, in which little distinction was made between Hindu, Jain, Buddhist and Islamic influences. [67] According to Adrienne McLean, St Denis's 'Indian dances' and exotic props and costumes were mostly inspired by imaginative encounters with found imagery, just as her 'Egyptian dance' was allegedly based on an advertisement she had seen for Turkish cigarettes. Like all her peers, she had never seen any Indian dance. In 1915, she and her husband, Ted Shawn, set up a dance school in Hollywood, which trained many future leading choreographers, dancers and Hollywood stars, including Martha Graham, Louise Brooks and Jack Cole. By this point Ruth and Ted, calling themselves 'Denishawn' and openly influenced by the Ballets Russes, advertised as the school's speciality its 'Oriental Suite' routines—in which fuzzy notions of ancient Egypt, Persia, Siam, Greece and India were pilfered interchangeably. Denishawn's stage-show tours repeated this popular—and much imitated—formula with relentless enthusiasm. One disillusioned former Denishawn protégé, the dancer and choreographer Doris Humphrey, later grumbled: 'I just got tired of being Siamese, Burmese, Japanese, all the other "eses". I came from Oak Park Illinois and I wanted to find out as a dancer who I was.' [68]

England's answers to *Schéhérazade*—the stage shows *Kismet* (1911) and *Chu Chin Chow* (1916)—were just as hazy about their Orient, which was similarly derived from popular theatre and music hall traditions. Once again, the *Arabian Nights* has much to answer for and 'Ali Baba' turns up again here. Oscar Ashe's musical comedy *Chu Chin Chow*, a version of the 'Ali Baba' story, broke all London theatre box-office records between 1916 and 1921, toured North America in the 1920s, and was made into a successful film by Gainsborough Studios in 1934, spreading its racist stereotypes and quasi-oriental styles around the globe, including India. [69] An illustration in the *Tatler* to mark the first anniversary of the show's 'reconstruction of the days of Haroun al Raschid [sic]' depicts six 'new dresses for *Chu Chin Chow*, very suitable to the sultry climate of old Bagdad'. The caption continues,

Mr Oscar Ashe is one of the greatest manufacturers of Eastern atmosphere that the stage has ever seen, and fanciful as some of his colour schemes may perhaps sometimes appear they are not very far wide of things that can be seen to-day [*sic*] in almost any of the big native cities of Ajmere and Rajputana.[70]

The influence of Euro-American popular culture—and its higher-culture variants via Diaghilev and Poiret—is clear: China, India and 'old Bagdad' were interchangeable; the 'Islamic' was barely marked; and ultimately no one cared too much about authenticity. This was a fashionable, fantastical Orient that existed only in its consumers' imaginations. It no longer referenced any putatively real geographical space 'over there'. As David Bate puts it, orientalism had become 'a type of cultural practice internalized, paradoxically, as modern forms for pleasure, eroticism and leisure'.[71]

Within urban India, the new orientalism was enthusiastically received, especially in film and performance circles. The pervasive orientalist motifs and masquerade that had become a mainstay of Euro-American theatrical dance and vaudeville were exported directly onto India's own variety entertainment circuit, where they fused with new forms of *nautch* in the public domain. Bombay, Madras and Calcutta were major stopover destinations on the tours that followed the steamship routes between England and Australia. European artistes on the Indian circuits rubbed shoulders with entertainers of Anglo-Indian, Eastern European, Central Asian, and South and Southeast Asian backgrounds, all touting the 'oriental dance' that so conveniently legitimised the display of eroticised female bodies. By the 1920s and early 1930s, the form had trickled down to the lowest levels and its lure was inescapable. Again and again the Indian newspapers of the day advertised exotic 'oriental dance': Turkish, Russian, Armenian, Japanese, Burmese—where these dancers were originally from is anyone's guess. A number of these women soon found careers in India's emerging film industry, including the Madans' Patience Cooper, a former variety show dancer with impresario Maurice Bandmann's company, as well as the Wadias' Mary Evans aka Fearless Nadia, an Anglo-Greek soldier's daughter of Australian origin. Advertisements for Miss Nadia, making her cabaret debut at the Regal Cinema in Lahore in 1934, describe her 'Gypsy' and 'Persian' dances, while a series of images from her photo album of the same year shows the range of her exotic stage costumes, which include the bare midriff, harem pants and veil of an *Arabian Nights* temptress whose distant roots stretch visibly back to the imaginings of Bakst and Poiret.[72]

However, Indian film-makers were also enthralled by other imported—and confused—orientalist forms, notably in the dance field. Alongside vaudeville, the Indian entertainment circuits hosted the higher-culture variants of 'oriental dance' that boasted allegiances with—and even direct links to—the prestigious Ballet Russes and the new Euro-American modernist dance arts. Both Anna Pavlova and Denishawn came to India on their world tours in the 1920s, not only to perform for enraptured Indian audiences but also to see the 'real' Indian dance for themselves at last. Both were sadly disappointed. Pavlova had been performing as a *devadasi* temple dancer in *La Bayadere* since 1909, her routines based on an India imagined on the basis of books, paintings and vague notions of Central Asian culture remembered from her Russian youth. The Madans, her Parsi hosts in both Bombay and Calcutta in 1922, obliged her with displays of local nautch dancers but she was not impressed. 'But where is your dance?' she is rumoured to have exclaimed.[73] When Denishawn visited India in 1925, their entourage was similarly feted by high society, including a glittering soiree at the Nizam of Hyderabad's 'palace' on Malabar Hill in Bombay. But they were even more disparaging about the dancers they were shown. Comparing the dances they found in India with a vaudeville act, 'The Dancing Girl of Delhi', by their own American protégé Vanda Hoff, Ted Shawn later claimed, 'In loveliness, charm and real ability, what infinite worlds above the real dancing girls of Delhi was our Vanda.'[74]

Pavlova's disappointment fired a determination to change things: on returning to London she developed and choreographed her own *Oriental Impressions* suite—a series of dances that included *Krishna and Radha* and *A Hindu Wedding*, for which she enlisted the help of Uday Shankar, a wealthy young Bengali art student she met on London's fashionable Hampstead social scene. The results, once again, had more to do with European dance and fantasy than with any authentic Indian traditions. However, this did not deter the ecstatic Indian elites who thronged to see her around the world, including in Calcutta and Bombay in 1928–29. Thereafter, Uday Shankar and Rukmini Devi, Pavlova's two young, cosmopolitan, upper-class, Indian associates, were tasked by her with reviving and (re)inventing Indian classical dance. Throughout the 1930s, while Rukmini energetically championed the emergent Bharat Natyam, Uday Shankar introduced the modernist movement into Indian dance.[75] Thus, out of a fusion of European 'oriental dance', Euro-American modernist free expression, and dutifully researched Indian vernacular and folk forms, the new Indian 'classical' dance was born. It was ineffably 'modern' and unquestionably nationalistic.

We have strayed into curious territory—a universe of shifting sands. As Joan Erdman points out, 'In India ... oriental dance meant dance from Europe.'[76] Ultimately, of course, oriental dance (everywhere) meant modernity. India's creative practitioners and audiences borrowed an already incoherent Euro-American fantasy Orient, took from it what they wanted—just as Europe had pilfered for its own Orient—and used this to reinvent their own modern forms (and India's own modern self). It was an orgy of cultural theft but, in the spirit of the 'Ali Baba' story, stealing from robbers was questioned no more than living comfortably on the proceeds of stolen property. Broadly speaking, by the 1930s the purportedly Hindu Orient was appropriated and reworked within India's nationalist high culture, while the quasi-Islamic elements of this Orient were relegated to lower cultural forms, where, cross-fertilised with local vestiges of Mughal and Persian cultural forms, they fed into a more cosmopolitan Indian modernity. So how did this doubly phantasmagoric Orient play out in early Indian cinema?

Many Indian film-makers and their audiences—both highbrow and lowbrow—enthusiastically embraced the fashionable international orientalism, as can be seen both by films celebrating the new 'classical' dance forms (for example Madhu Bose's films *Alibaba* [1937] and *Court Dancer* [1942], starring his dancer wife Sadhana Bose) and by the popularity of the lower-brow oriental fantasy genre.[77] In so doing these film-makers took their place at the table of global modernity. As this Orient was an imaginary space— without precise geographical or historical referent—it could be more or less unproblematically accepted: the Orient of India's early-twentieth-century performing arts was a space of magic and wondrous happenings, of spirituality and sensuality. Clichés often projected onto India by the West could in turn be deflected onto a predominantly Islamicate never-never land. This was an imaginary Middle Eastern, Central and Western Asian world, comprising a fuzzy mix of Afghan, Persian, 'Arab' and even, loosely, Eastern European subaltern 'others', which recycled international orientalist tropes. As we have seen, not only was 'oriental dance' understood to mean European dance (and hence nothing to do with India), but also a blonde European cabaret dancer was considered sufficiently exotic to play the Egyptian princess Parizad who proselytises for Islam in *Noor-e-Yaman*. Insofar as we can generalise from the few surviving films, it appears that, unlike Euro-American orientalism, which merged quasi-Hindu and Islamic elements without distinction, India's popular Orient from the 1930s onwards was effectively that which was outside or 'other' than—a putatively Hindu—India.

Lal-e-Yaman provides a useful example of this process, situated within Indo-Persian storytelling forms but referencing on its own terms the Orient of international subaltern popular culture and Hollywood 'lower genres'.[78] The film's opening scene, shot on a set of the King of Yemen's palace as he celebrates his second wedding, begins with a mid-shot of the back of a young woman, clad in diaphanous 'harem pants' and a skimpy *choli*, dancing seductively—with bare midriff—to a slow, rhythmic musical accompaniment of violin, sarangi and tabla (Figure 2.2). The scene pulls out to reveal the full court *durbar*, including the king, his new queen and his older son, arranged in a semi-circle across a palatial set, extravagantly painted with ornate, quasi-Islamicate motifs. Wadia in later years admitted that he drew inspiration for all his Islamicate sets primarily from 'profusely illustrated books on art, architecture, costumes and furniture designs', including 'beautifully bound German volumes' that he and his art director, formerly a Parsi theatre set designer, owned. 'How many times must Homi and I have gone through them for modelling sets in our umpteen films?'[79] Moreover, *Lal-e-Yaman*'s court dancer was neither Arab nor Indian but a European cabaret dancer, Miss Lola, married to the German Agfa representative in

Figure 2.2 Still of *Lal-e-Yaman* court dancer (1933)

Source: © Roy Wadia/Wadia Movietone.

Bombay and paid by the hour to perform the mimic oriental dance of the Indian variety circuit.

On the other hand, Wadia and David paid great attention to composing music based on classical Indian ragas. J.B.H. Wadia was a passionate devotee of Indian music and his decision to promote the classical singing abilities of the young Firoz Dastur, the prince with the golden voice, was a bold one.

> Suddenly a thought came to me that if I was to assign the pivotal role of the boy prince to Firoz why should I not make him sing in the classical music vein? I took Dada into my confidence and he too fell in line with my idea which was rather crazy from a box-office angle.[80]

Dastur's role was increased to include six classical songs and these soon became a craze throughout the city.

However, *Lal-e-Yaman's* most marked difference from the Euro-American Orient lies in its depiction—and celebration—of a recognisable Islamic religion and philosophy. In this it differs from the earlier film *Gul-e-Bakavali*, which had, in Dharamsey's words, 'secularised' its source story.[81] *Gul-e-Bakavali*, as published by Naval Kishore in 1882, was set in an unambiguously Islamic context, with direct references to God and the Prophet Muhammed.[82] The 1924 film blithely changed the king's name from Zeen-ul-Mulk to Raja Jalad Sang/Singh (albeit with a son called Taj-ul-Mulk) and introduced *yakshas*, Indra, sati, views of Bombay and Rajputana skirts alongside paris, fakirs and burqas. While box-office and nationalist pressures undoubtedly drove this syncretism, which was already a feature of the Parsi stage, it also reflected the ubiquitous, transnational, hybrid Orient, traces of which pepper the *Gul-e-Bakavali* film script.

With *Lal-e-Yaman*, on the other hand, Sufi mystical philosophy sits at the heart of the film: truth is reached by hearing the voice of God and avoiding distraction by the illusory spectacle of the material world, as I detail in chapter three. The film's ending celebrates Islam visually (the Caliphate flag), aurally (a song praising God and enjoining Parviz to devote his life to spreading the word of Allah), and as narrative resolution (Nadir becomes king through divine will). Its sequel, *Noor-e-Yaman*, similarly stars the wise fakir and even introduces a second heroine who refuses to renounce Islam. For Wadia this undoubtedly involved a political dimension: he was a committed nationalist, with what he later referred to as a 'passion' for Hindu–Muslim unity and anti-communalist politics. As I argue in the next chapter, Wadia's use of the Islamicate idiom may also be seen as a counter to the already incipient hegemony of a Hinduising *bhakti* movement, as reflected in some films of rival studios such as Prabhat.[83] But while Wadia was undoubtedly unusual in his political aspirations for his films, the Indian *Arabian Nights* fantasy films' greater respect for—and knowledge of—Islam (than their Euro-American counterparts), especially after 1933, reflected their very real engagement with India's Muslim communities.

Perhaps more surprisingly, given the influence that the Douglas Fairbanks persona had on Wadia's earlier stunt films, *Lal-e-Yaman* makes limited reference to *Thief of Bagdad*. On the surface there are generic echoes—for example the sword fights, invisible swashbucklers, and the hero's discovery of his beautiful princess asleep on a couch—but *Lal-e-Yaman*'s visual and aural references are closer to Urdu theatre and qissa traditions than to Hollywood, building on motifs already present in *Gul-e-Bakavali*. *Lal-e-Yaman* is not, as Studlar observed (earlier) of *Thief of Bagdad*, 'driven by dance aesthetics at every level': neither the costume nor the balletic movements and androgynous eroticism of Fairbanks's thief are emulated, nor is the scale of the sets and the all-encompassing dream-like quality of the *Thief of Bagdad* world.[84] *Lal-e-Yaman* moves, like most *Arabian Nights* and qissa stories and unlike *Thief of Bagdad*, between different domains of reality. Moreover, whereas *Thief of Bagdad* is a quasi-morality tale about theft, the dignity of labour and the irresistible lure of unearned wealth, *Lal-e-Yaman* is about the power of spirituality, music and divine destiny.

The early sound era appears to mark a turning point in screen depictions of India's Orient. Certainly, by the 1950s the fantasy films were consistently set within a recognisably Muslim milieu but were, at the same time (and apparently paradoxically), more closely derivative of British and Hollywood orientalist films than in the 1930s, as comparison between the Wadias' 1930s and 1950s *Arabian Nights* films shows.[85] *Lal-e-Yaman* illustrates that 1930s transitional moment and also highlights the complexity—and futility—of essentialist attempts to disentangle influences: the 'Islamicate' and the orientalist are not easily distinguished. But, I argue, the *Arabian Nights* film as a genre puts the notion of the Islamicate under particular strain. As we have seen, India's fantasy films drew, like the Muslim socials, historicals and courtesan films, on an imagined Mughal past and Indo-Persian culture as expressed in theatre, visual arts and performing arts. However, unlike those other genres, fantasy films simultaneously referenced fashionable international orientalism. Consequently, their 'Islamicate' world was a double—even treble—mirage, reflecting a transnational Orient that had evolved through a complex series of borrowings and projections. Moreover, the *Arabian Nights* themselves had, by the twentieth century, become a curiously hybrid transnational form, albeit within India popularly—and uniquely—conflated with Indo-Persian stories little known in Europe. But precisely these factors ensured the genre's wide appeal. Just as 'oriental dance' was understood within India to be European dance, so, I suggest, by the early 1930s 'oriental film'—the 'Arabian Nights fantasy film'—was importantly understood to be film that engaged with international cosmopolitan modernity.

THE APPEAL

Finally, we must ask why the Arabian Nights were so key to India's fantasy genre. What work did the Arabian Nights do or allow to be done? On the one hand, the Nights provided recognisable motifs from a familiar body of stories that had cultural resonance within the Indian subcontinent and beyond. As we saw, these offered unparalleled licence for spectacular excess and surprising twists and turns in the storylines: the films could boast splendid sets and gorgeous costumes, memorable song and dance, as well as Urduised poetic and theatrical dialogue. Moreover the Nights tales are full of magical transformations and masquerade, with all the potential for drama and special effects that these open up. These films—like the Nights stories that inspired them—offer the extravagant pleasures of utopian worlds.

On the other hand, as I will argue in the next chapter, there may well have been a deliberate bid to reach out to the Muslim audience: as the ICC evidence cited earlier suggests, there was a need to find films that appealed across the board. It should be stressed that, despite the disparaging tag 'Mahomedan pictures', fantasy films were popular not just with Muslims.

I suggest that the Arabian Nights fantasy film worked well with Indian audiences because of its inherent ambiguity. It was modern and Western on the one hand—carrying the prestige and branding of the genre's Hollywood successes and a fashionable Europeanism— but it also carried an apparent cultural authenticity as a refusal of all things Western. While the films' settings were outside—and 'other than'—contemporary India, motifs from the stories reverberated with audiences' broader cultural knowledge and histories. The Arabian Nights were, above all, a shared set of fantasies of the culture, a set of exciting reference points, celebrating the non-rationality that was the integral flip side of cosmopolitan modernity around the world. But such films played on a knife-edge between glorifying India's Islamic heritage and dismissing its Muslims as exotic and 'other'. This was a complex hybrid space, used to different effects by different producers at different periods.

In contrast to Wadia Movietone's contemporary films in other genres, its stunt and fantasy films opened up spaces for a nationalist modernity that differed from both the Hinduised and the Westernised forms found within, for example, the mythologicals and socials.[86] *Lal-e-Yaman* effortlessly combines motifs from Indo-Persian story traditions with the modernity of Hollywood, as the fleeting appearance of Tarzan within the land of the jinni suggests. But this eclecticism is brought to the service of an alternative nationalist sensibility, which in Wadia's case included a call for 'Hindu–Muslim unity' or, more specifically, for a cosmopolitan modernity that recognised the heterogeneity of India and its porous borders within a transnational world. Of course this opened Wadia up to criticism. *Varieties Weekly*, for example, smugly asserted that films such as *Lal-e-Yaman* were for 'the Muslim class' and while 'welcome entertainment', they 'should not become the order of the day'.[87] While oriental fantasy films were undeniably mostly lowbrow, even the best would be routinely disparaged as 'Muslim' films by a Hindu supremacist tendency that wished to exorcise—or exoticise—Islamic influences. Wadia suffered for this throughout his career.

Revealingly, while films of magical and wondrous happenings within an Islamicate world were known—and invariably dismissed—as 'fantasies', those of wondrous happenings within a Hindu cosmology were celebrated as 'mythologicals'. It may be no accident that claims that Hiralal Sen's *Ali Baba and the Forty Thieves* was India's first film have been largely forgotten in favour of a conveniently Hindu mythological, *Raja Harishchandra*. 'Ali Baba' is a story about thieving that has been a perennial hit, but perhaps the tragic irony of Hiralal Sen's film is to have had its glory, as probably the world's first *Arabian Nights* film, stolen from it by histories written, on the one hand, by a complacent West that has remained for the most part blithely ignorant of Indian cinema history and, on the other, by an Indian nationalism that has preferred to champion a Hindu mythological as Indian cinema's moment of origin.

NOTES

*Originally written for—and will be eventually published in—Philip Kennedy and Marina Warner (eds), *Scheherazade's Children: Global Encounters with the Arabian Nights*, New York: New York University Press, 2013.

1. This account draws on several (somewhat contradictory) secondary sources, primarily: Sajal Chattopadhyay, *Aar Rekho Na Andhare*, Calcutta: Jogomaya Prakashani, 1998; B. Jha, 'Profiles of Pioneers', *Cinema Vision India*, vol. 1, no. 1, 1980, pp. 54–5; Prabhat Mukherjee, 'Hiralal Sen', in *70 Years of Indian Cinema, 1913–1983*, ed. T.M. Ramachandran, Bombay: CINEMA India-International, 1985, pp. 49–53; Firoze Rangoonwalla, *Indian Cinema: Past and Present*, New Delhi: Clarion Books, 1983, pp. 12–14. I thank Ranita Chatterjee for finding and translating Bengali sources for me throughout this essay.

2. Although the term 'Islamicate' is controversial, it has gained currency amongst Indian film scholars since Mukul Kesavan first used it in connection with Hindi cinema in 'Urdu, Awadh and the Tawaif: The Islamicate Roots of Hindi Cinema', in *Forging Identities: Gender, Communities, and the State in India*, ed. Zoya Hasan, Boulder, Colorado: Westview Press, 1994, pp. 244–57. He draws on Marshall G.S. Hodgson, who coined 'Islamicate' to refer not directly to the Islamic religion per se, 'but to the social and cultural complex historically associated with Islam and the Muslims, both among Muslims themselves and even when found among non-Muslims'. Marshall G.S. Hodgson, *The Venture of Islam: Conscience and History in a World Civilisation*, 3 vols, Chicago: University of Chicago Press, 1974, pp. 1–57. See also Dwyer, *Filming the Gods*, pp. 97–131. My own use of the term in this essay refers to stereotyped conventions that construct an exotic fantasy of an historical cultural complex associated with Islam. This bears no necessary relationship to 'real' Islamic cultures—nor can one disentangle essentially 'Muslim', 'Hindu' or any other elements within this.

3. Advertised in the *Madras Mail*, 24 January 1902. I thank Stephen Hughes for this reference.

4. *Gul-e-Bakavali* (The Bakavali Flower, Kanjibhai Rathod, 1924) released in Bombay in March 1924. *Thief of Bagdad* opened in Calcutta in March 1925 and in Bombay in May 1925 (and in the USA in May 1924).

5. Ira Bhaskar and Richard Allen, *Islamicate Cultures of Bombay Cinema*, New Delhi: Tulika, 2009, p. xiii.

6. The scope of this essay is limited to northern India, including Bombay and Calcutta. While evidence exists of the *Nights'* popularity in southern India—and *Nights* films certainly played there—more research is needed.

7. For consistency, I use upper case 'O' for the proper noun, Orient, to refer to a fantastical imaginary space, and the lower case 'o' for all its derivatives, including adjectives and nouns that describe a critical position, as in 'orientalist' and 'orientalism'.

8. I use inverted commas to refer to the generic tale ('Ali Baba', 'Aladdin') and italics for the titles of specific versions of these tales.

9. Qissa-dastan (two Persian/Urdu words for 'story') refers to a traditional Persian—and subsequently Urdu/Hindi—narrative genre that evolved out of

medieval Persian-Arabic folk forms, usually involving adventurous quests, romantic love and magic 'enchantments' across human and fairy/spirit worlds. Famous qissa-dastan include *Hatimtai, Char Darvesh, Gul-e-Bakavali, Gul Sanobar* and *Amir Hamza*. First published from 1803 at Calcutta's Fort William College, qissa-dastan storytelling survived as an oral tradition in north India until the late 1920s. See Frances Pritchett, *Marvellous Encounters: Folk Romances in Urdu and Hindi*, Delhi: Manohar, 1985, pp. 1–19; and Francesca Orsini, *Print and Pleasure: Popular Literature and Entertaining Fictions in Colonial North India*, New Delhi: Permanent Black, 2009, pp. 106–16.

10. For example, the full-length story *Hatimtai* was both a well-known qissa-dastan and also a cycle of Arabic folktales, to which just one episode in the *Nights* alludes.

11. Jatindra Nath Mitra, 'A Review of Indian Pictures', *Filmland*, Puja issue, 1934, [reprinted] in *Indian Cinema: Contemporary Perceptions from the Thirties*, ed. Samik Bandyopadhyay, Jamshedpur: Celluloid Chapter, 1993, p. 31.

12. See a series of advertisements for Variety Film Services (distributors/exhibitors) in the trade journal *Cinema* in 1931–32.

13. Irwin, 'Introduction', *The Arabian Nights*, pp. ix–x.

14. Malcolm Lyons's Penguin Classic version of the *Nights* is, for all practical purposes, the most complete. Lyons translates the eighteenth-century Arabic text/manuscript known as *Calcutta 2*, which collated a number of earlier versions and divided the stories into 1,001 chapters, or nights. *Calcutta 2* was also the basis of Richard Burton's famous but flawed translation. The 2008 Penguin edition also includes Ursula Lyons's translation of Galland's three 'orphan tales'. Robert Irwin's introductions to each volume are an invaluable guide to the latest thinking in *Nights* scholarship. Malcolm C. Lyons, with Ursula Lyons, trans., *The Arabian Nights: Tales of 1001 Nights*, 3 vols, London: Penguin, 2008.

15. Emmanuel Cosquin demonstrated similarities between three elements of the *Arabian Nights* frame story and numerous ancient Indian tales including the Buddhist Tripitaka, the Sanskrit *Sukasaptati*, the Buddhist Jatakas and the eleventh-century Sanskrit *Kathasaritsagara*. See Emmanuel Cosquin, 'Le Prologue-cadre des Mille et Une Nuits', *Revue Biblique*, vol. 6, no. 7, 1909, pp. 7–49. Moreover, the talking animals of the *Tales of Bidpai* (a Pehlavi translation of the *Panchatantra*) also suggest Indian precursors. However, as the *Arabian Nights Encyclopedia* points out, 'There is no evidence to suggest a direct relationship between the mentioned texts and the *Arabian Nights*. All that one can say with certainty is that the compiler of the frame story of the *Arabian Nights* relied on various components from Sanskrit texts to compose a new story.' See Ulrich Marzolph, Richard van Leeuwen, Hassan Wassouf (eds), *Arabian Nights Encyclopedia*, Santa Barbara, CA: ABC-CLIO, 2004, vol. 1, p. 372.

16. For an excellent account of the complexity of the *Nights* phenomenon see Robert Irwin's *The Arabian Nights: A Companion*, London: Allen Lane, 1994.

17. Ulrich Marzolph (ed.), *Arabian Nights Reader*, Detroit: Wayne State University Press, 2006, p. vii.

18. See Ulrike Stark, *An Empire of Books: The Naval Kishore Press and the Diffusion of the Printed Word in Colonial India*, Ranikhet: Permanent Black, 2007, pp. 308–10.

Regarding Urdu translations see Shaista Akhtar Banu Suhrawardy, *A Critical Survey of the Development of the Urdu Novel and Short Story*, London: Longmans, Green, 1945, p. 26.

19. Nikhil Sarkar, 'Printing and the Spirit of Calcutta', in *Calcutta Living City*, vol. 1, ed. Sukanta Chaudhuri, Calcutta: Oxford University Press, 1995 [1990], pp. 133–4.

20. Munshi: scribe, secretary, clerk. Although often credited as the stories' authors, they did not invent the stories, only the mode of telling them: they were primarily editors/translators/transcribers. See Sisir Kumar Das, *Sahibs and Munshis: An Account of the College of Fort William*, Calcutta: Orion Publications, 1978. Interestingly, Wadia writes of a munshi involved in script-writing for *Lal-e-Yaman*.

21. It is not clear whether this was the play written originally by Vinayak Prasad Talib for the Victoria Company and published in 1900 or a different adaptation by star actor Kavasji Khatau, who played Ali Baba in 1878, with the female impersonator Naslu Sarkari as Marjana (or if these are the same). See Somnath Gupt, *The Parsi Theatre: Its Origins and Development*, trans. from the Hindi and edited by Kathryn Hansen, New Delhi: Seagull Books, 2005 [1981], pp. 70–1 and 126.

22. See Sushil Kumar Mukherjee, *The Story of the Calcutta Theatres: 1753–1980*, Calcutta: K.P. Bagchi, 1982, pp. 99, 594 and 797.

23. Ranabir Ray Choudhury, *Early Calcutta Advertisements, 1875–1925*, Bombay: Nichiketa Publications, 1992, p. 108.

24. The stories about Prince Qamar-al-Zaman run across nights 170 to 249 (Lyons, *The Arabian Nights*, vol. 1, pp. 693–807), only parts of which concern his lover and wife, Princess Budur.

25. Rajadhyaksha and Willemen, *Encyclopaedia of Indian Cinema*.

26. Nihal Chand's Urdu *Gul-e-Bakavali* was published in 1803/4 according to Pritchett, *Marvellous Encounters*, p. 21 (1803); p. 197 (1804). Pritchett's subsequent (1991) catalogue of Fort William publications (http://www.columbia.edu/itc/mealac/pritchett/00urdu/baghobahar/BBFORTWM.pdf) mentions an Urdu *Alif Laila* as 'preparing for press' in 1803—a decade before its famous Arabic translation, *Calcutta 1*.

27. Fakir: Sufi holy man.

28. Indian film scholarship is indebted to Virchand Dharamsey for sharing this extraordinary manuscript. See Dharamsey, 'The Script of *Gul-e-Bakavali* (Kohinoor, 1924)'.

29. Unlike many other films of the silent era, no English title was given to *Jalkumari/Hoor-al-Bahar* as far as we know. Literally these titles mean fairy/beautiful young woman of the ocean/water, with slightly different connotations in Urdu and Hindi.

30. He added, 'Most of the films in those years … were either mythologicals or fantasies that abounded in trick scenes.' See Ram Mohan, 'The Closely Guarded Secrets of the Special Effects Men', *Cinema Vision India*, vol. 1, no. 1, 1980, pp. 89–90.

31. The third was *Magician of Bengal* (*Gaud Bangal*, aka *Kamroo Deshni Kamini*, K.P. Bhave, 1925).

32. Indian Cinematograph Committee, *Report of the Indian Cinematograph Committee, 1927–28*, Calcutta: Government of India Central Publication Branch, 1928, p. 40. (Hereafter *ICCR*.)

33. Indian Cinematograph Committee, *Indian Cinematograph Committee 1927–28, Evidence*, vol. 1, Calcutta: Government of India Central Publication Branch, 1928, pp. 24, 172 and 288. (Hereafter *ICCE*.)

34. *ICCR*, p. 21. Witness testimonies include, for example, *ICCE*, vol. 1, pp. 70, 442, 457, 505 and 594.

35. Chabria and Usai, *Light of Asia*.

36. We have insufficient evidence to assess how distinguishable these actually were.

37. Out of 1,051 silent films between 1925 and 1934, 425 were classified by Virchand Dharamsey (in Chabria and Usai, *Light of Asia*, pp. 69–211) as 'costume' films. As Dharamsey here eschews the 'fantasy' category, I cross-reference his more reliable filmography with Rangoonwalla, *Indian Filmography*, and Ojha, *75 Glorious Years*, despite some inconsistencies between the three. More recently, Dharamsey appears to argue for 'costume' films to be distinguished from 'oriental' films on the basis that the latter were set in Arabia or Rome and the former had Rajput, Mughal or Sultanate settings. However, this not only confuses industry classifications with post-hoc critical classification, but is also unworkable in a context where settings are hybrid or fantastical. Dharamsey, 'The Advent of Sound in Indian Cinema'. As with all attributions of genre, definitive classifications are neither possible nor useful: approximations are all we need in the present context.

38. As we will see, although *Lal-e-Yaman* was classified as a costume film by Rangoonwalla, *Indian Filmography*, and Ojha, *75 Glorious Years*, it was explicitly seen as an *Arabian Nights* fantasy film by its makers.

39. *Bombay Chronicle*, 14 February 1931.

40. Kaushik Bhaumik, 'Querying the "Traditional" Roots of Silent Cinema in Asia', *Journal of the Moving Image*, no. 7, 2008, http://www.jmionline.org/jmi7.htm (accessed 6 January 2011).

41. In 1950 there were no fantasy films and just three 'costume' films released; by 1955, out of 125 releases there were eight fantasy and thirty-two costume films (Rangoonwalla, *Indian Filmography*). Basant itself made *Aladdin* (1952), *Alibaba* (1954), *Gul Sanobar* (1955), *Hatimtai* (1956), as well as *Baghdad ka Jadu* (1956).

42. For example, *Aladin* (Sujoy Ghosh, 2009) with Amitabh Bachchan and Sanjay Dutt playing, respectively, good and bad genies/jinns.

43. *Alif Laila*, directed by Ramanand Sagar, was broadcast on Doordarshan and SAB TV between 1993 and 1996.

44. J. B. H. Wadia, 'JBH in Talkieland', *Cinema Vision India*, vol. 1, no. 2, 1980, p. 82.

45. Literally *Hoor-e-Arab* would be 'Arab Beauty' or 'Arab Fairy'—but no other film scholars translate this, apart from Rangoonwala who calls it 'Aladdin'.

46. Material on Joseph David and all quotes are from J.B.H. Wadia's essay, 'Joseph David—Tribute to a Forgotten Pioneer' from unpublished memoirs, 1980, in Wadia Movietone archives, Bombay. Accessed with kind permission of Vinci Wadia.

47. Dada: respected elder male, literally, grandfather or older brother.

48. *Bombay Chronicle*, 24 September 1933.

49. The terms *pir mard*, *darvesh* and fakir (all terms for a Sufi holy man) are used interchangeably within the film.

50. For more analysis and a more detailed plot outline of *Lal-e-Yaman*'s complex narrative, see chapter three.

51. In the *Nights* the wife ingeniously fools the parrot with sounds of thunder, lightning and rain—so when the merchant returns, knowing there was no storm, he kills what he thinks is an untrustworthy parrot, only to repent when he realises it is his wayward wife who is untrustworthy. The qissa-dastan *Tota Kahani* (Parrot's Tale), narrated by the parrot, also involves a parrot guarding a potentially unfaithful wife, as does the Sanskrit *Sukasaptati*. See chapter three for more details.

52. Wadia Movietone also made a mythological *Vaman Avtar* (Vaman is the name of a mythological character who was an incarnation of Vishnu) in 1934.

53. According to figures, in a 1941 document in the Wadia Movietone archive, *Lal-e-Yaman* was Wadia Movietone's tenth most profitable film, making a respectable Rs 152,000 in its first eight years. Although *Noor-e-Yaman* did not do quite so well (121K compared with 152K), it earned more than *Lal-e-Yaman* in every territory apart from Bombay and Delhi, and especially overseas. For a detailed breakdown of *Lal-e-Yaman* box-office figures, see chapter three, note 38.

54. Storyline and visuals are deduced from the song booklet—all that survives of this film.

55. Just one year later, as Fearless Nadia aka *Hunterwali*, she transformed Wadia Movietone's fortunes and changed its production priorities from Islamicate melodrama to stunt films. See chapter four.

56. Gregory D. Booth, 'Musicking the Other: Orientalism in the Hindi Cinema' in *Music and Orientalism in the British Empire 1780s–1940s: Portrayal of the East*, eds Martin Clayton and Bennett Zon, Aldershot: Ashgate, 2007, pp. 315–38.

57. The key text is Edward W. Said, *Orientalism*, London: Routledge and Kegan Paul, 1978. See also Linda Nochlin 'The Imaginary Orient', *Art in America*, no. 71, 1983, pp. 118–31 and 187–91, amongst very many others.

58. Otto Rothfeld, *Women of India*, London: Simpkin, Marshall, Hamilton, Kent & Co. Ltd, 1920, p. 154.

59. Peter Wollen, *Raiding the Icebox: Reflections on Twentieth-Century Culture*, London: Verso, 1993, pp. 1–34.

60. The term art deco was used only from the 1960s. For more on art deco in India see Rachel Dwyer and Divia Patel, *Cinema India: The Visual Culture of Hindi Film*, London: Reaktion Books, 2002, pp. 124–35.

61. Matthew Bernstein, 'Introduction', in *Visions of the East: Orientalism in Film*, eds Matthew Bernstein and Gaylyn Studlar, London: I.B. Tauris, 1997, p. 4.

62. As Douglas Fairbanks's son recounts, in an interview released on the VHS of *Thief of Bagdad* (Thames Television for Channel Four, 1985).

63. Gaylyn Studlar, 'Douglas Fairbanks: Thief of the Ballets Russes', in *Bodies of the Text: Dance as Theory, Literature as Dance*, eds Ellen W. Goellner and Jacqueline Shea Murphy, New Brunswick, NJ: Rutgers University Press, 1995, p. 109.

64. Joan L. Erdman, 'Dance Discourses: Rethinking the History of the "Oriental Dance"', in *Moving Words: Rewriting Dance*, ed. Gay Morris, London: Routledge, 1996, p. 289.

65. Gaylyn Studlar, 'Out-Salomeing Salome: Dance, the New Woman, and Fan Magazine Orientalism', in Bernstein and Studlar, *Visions of the East*, pp. 106–7.

66. Wollen, *Raiding the Icebox*, p. 10.

67. Material on Ruth St Denis/Denishawn draws on a number of sources, notably Elizabeth Kendall, *Where She Danced*, New York: Kopf, 1979; Ted Shawn, *Gods Who Dance*, New York: Dutton, 1929; Adrienne L. McLean, 'The Thousand Ways There Are to Move' and Gaylyn Studlar, 'Out-Salomeing Salome', both in Bernstein and Studlar, *Visions of the East*, pp. 99–158.

68. Quoted in McLean, 'The Thousand Ways There Are to Move', p. 155.

69. William A. Everett, '*Chu Chin Chow* and Orientalist Musical Theatre in Britain during the First World War', in *Music and Orientalism in the British Empire, 1780s–1940s*, eds Martin Clayton and Bennett Zon, Aldershot: Ashgate, 2007, pp. 277–96. The influence of the 1934 Gainsborough Studios' film is visible in Homi Wadia's 1954 *Alibaba*.

70. *The Tatler*, 12 September 1917.

71. David Bate, *Photography and Surrealism: Sexuality, Colonialism and Social Dissent*, London: I.B. Tauris, 2004, p. 127.

72. Photo album filmed by author during an interview with Mary Wadia in January 1986.

73. Pushpa Sunder, *Patrons and Philistines: Arts and the State in British India, 1773–1947*, New Delhi: Oxford University Press, 1995, p. 249.

74. Shawn, *Gods Who Dance*, p. 99.

75. I thank Ann David for a useful discussion of ideas in this section.

76. Erdman, 'Dance Discourses', p. 289.

77. Madhu Bose's 1937 Bengali *Alibaba*, based on the same Calcutta stage play as Hiralal Sen's 1903/4 film, was widely celebrated and seen as more 'respectable' than the Wadias' Islamicate films, despite being more obviously derivative of Hollywood (and Western theatre) and less directly related to indigenous traditions.

78. My use of the terms 'low' and 'lower' genre follows Miriam Hansen and others to denote the 'sensational, attractionist genres' of early cinema or, following Yuri Tsivian, the 'adventure serials, detective thrillers and slap-stick comedies' so beloved of the Soviet modernists. See Hansen, 'The Mass Production of the Senses'.

79. J.B.H. Wadia, 'How *Bagh-e-Misr* Came to Be Produced', from unpublished memoirs, 1980, in Wadia Movietone archives, Bombay. Accessed with kind permission of Vinci Wadia.

80. J.B.H. Wadia, 'The Story Behind the Making of *Lal-e-Yaman*', from unpublished memoirs, 1980, in Wadia Movietone archives, Bombay. Accessed with kind permission of Vinci Wadia.

81. Dharamsey, 'The Script of *Gul-e-Bakavali* (Kohinoor, 1924).

82. *Gool-i Bukawulee*, trans. from the Urdu by Thomas Philip Manuel, Lucknow: Naval Kishore Press, 1882.

83. See chapter three.

84. As Wadia's first talkie, *Lal-e-Yaman* was a much more cheaply and crudely made film, as Wadia himself admits.

85. Homi Wadia's *Aladdin* (1952) and *Alibaba* (1954) both copy visual and plot motifs from British and Hollywood versions of the stories—albeit integrated within distinctively 'Indianised' tellings of the tales. See chapter six.

86. See chapters 4 and 5 in this book.

87. *Varieties Weekly*, 23 February 1934, pp. 9–10, quoted in Bhaumik, 'The Emergence of the Bombay Film Industry'.

three

$\mathcal{D}$istant Voices, Magic Knives
Lal-e-Yaman and the Transition to Sound in Bombay Cinema

When Prince Parviz arrives with his magic knife in the land of the jinni, the *Arabian Nights* world at the heart of the film *Lal-e-Yaman* (Jewel of Yemen, J.B.H. Wadia, 1933), he is greeted by a capricious parrot. Seen only in silhouette, the bird balances on an elegant perch high above the action whilst his captive, the beautiful Princess Parizad, sleeps below on a gilded couch. Behind them the painted backdrop of a verdant, orientalist landscape hints at the hedonistic excesses of this exotic world. In the voice of an automaton, the parrot repeatedly squawks his warning, 'You have seen the world with your eyes, now see this *tamasha* [charade/playacting].'[1] It is indeed a tamasha that sweeps Parviz up, as he negotiates the forces of greed, lust and desire within this supernatural realm and its shadow world of court intrigue. But more presciently, the parrot's mantra—aimed equally at the spectators in the cinema as at the actors within the diegesis—neatly condenses the themes of the film, which centre on the illusory nature of the visual and the power of the voice.

Lal-e-Yaman is of interest for a number of reasons. Not only is the film, made by Wadia Movietone in 1933, the earliest example that survives of Indian cinema's so-called *Arabian Nights* fantasy films,[2] but it was also one of the major successes of its day.[3] As Wadia Movietone's inaugural venture and producer/director J.B.H. Wadia's first talkie, it offers a fascinating glimpse of the diverse elements at play in Indian sound cinema's earliest days, before the conventions that ultimately became 'Bollywood' had settled down.

I will undertake a detailed examination of this one film to explore how J.B.H. Wadia experimented with and exploited the new potential of sound, using it in innovative ways to represent the powers of truth and God. I begin by outlining details of the film's production and reception to suggest the pioneering and amateur nature of this unexpectedly successful venture. I move on to examine the film itself and how it works, taking the opening scene to show how the power of the voice—and its divinity—is established. I argue that this is reinforced by the film's underlying structure, which revolves around two divine voices that are opposed on every level to the fallibility of the visual—a world of special effect miracles. In the final section I compare *Lal-e-Yaman* with what we know of Wadia's silent stunt films to suggest that not only is *Lal-e-Yaman* a comment on this transition itself, but that a different kind of modernity is privileged in each. Moreover, in the political context of the Indian nationalist movement, where there were attempts to purge both classical music and—as the 1930s went on—also film of Islamic influences in order to build a Hinduised nationalist modernity, *Lal-e-Yaman*'s visceral appeal, Sufi ethos and hybrid modernity hint at directions that were stifled as mainstream Indian cinema—and eventually Bollywood—developed over subsequent decades.

BACKGROUND

India's first talkie, *Alam Ara* (Light of the World, Ardeshir Irani, 1931), had, just two years before *Lal-e-Yaman*, pioneered the popularity of *Arabian Nights* themes—including qissa-dastan—in the early sound era, wowing Indian audiences with its seven songs and extravagant spectacle. Written by the retired theatre director and writer Joseph David, Imperial Studios' *Alam Ara* had drawn directly on the populist conventions of the Urdu-Parsi theatre, the eclectic urban form that combined gaudy spectacle with influences from European melodrama, Hindu cosmology and Indo-Muslim and Persian romantic tales. *Alam Ara* immediately established the paradigm for Bombay cinema's distinctive form, integrating song and dance within melodrama. As described in the last chapter, such costume and fantasy melodramas in Islamicate settings quickly became popular in the early 1930s, outperforming the so-called social, devotional and mythological films, mostly set in a Hindu milieu, which have, in recent years, been more extensively studied.[4]

In the silent era, J.B.H. Wadia had built up a strong track record by producing profitable low-budget 'stunt thrillers' for the 'C-grade' circuit. By 1933 it was clear that, if he was going to survive, he had to learn how to make sound films. Smartly, his new company, Wadia Movietone, approached theatre 'impresario' Joseph David, who had written *Alam Ara* for Ardeshir Irani. JBH had been a fan of David's since his schooldays, when he regularly attended shows of David's Parsi Imperial Theatrical Company at the Coronation Theatre. Having fallen on hard times financially, David, who was an accomplished writer, director and musician, was more than ready to share his vast theatrical experience—and large bank of handwritten story plotlines—with JBH.[5]

Between 1933 and 1935, JBH worked with Joseph David on six talkies before the success of Fearless Nadia's *Hunterwali* (Woman with the Whip, Homi Wadia, 1935) refocused Wadia Movietone's energies on the more lucrative stunt thrillers.[6] Wadia himself remembered those six films, all of which he directed, as 'melodramatic stories culled out of the voluminous stock of handwritten books of the veteran Joseph David, the beloved "Dada" of Wadia Movietone ... backed up with good music and production values'.[7]

JBH explains how, when he came to sound cinema, he 'had developed the itch to do something different, something more ambitious ... [and] decided to make talkies of dramatic and musical value', adding, '"Dramatic" is a euphemism. "Melodramatic" is a more appropriate description.'[8] Already concerned about the low regard in which his stunt thrillers were held in polite society, he saw his move to the talkies as a chance to redeem his cultural reputation with a foray into the more respectable socials.

As described in the previous chapter, the film is set in a magical past and follows the fortunes of a doomed Yemeni royal family, whose follies and human greed lead to tragic consequences, which are only overcome with the help of a wise Sufi fakir and his mystical powers. One of the film's central storylines is of a handsome prince's quest in a magical land ruled by an evil jinni, where the hero rescues a beautiful princess held captive by an ugly monster and a talking parrot before reclaiming his own family's kingdom through his brave fighting skills and some magic. The other central narrative thread is woven around the beautiful singing voice of the younger prince, which consoles the family in their darkest hours and opens up a channel to the divine on earth.

PRODUCTION

Wadia's memoirs give a colourful account of the excitement and amateurism of *Lal-e-Yaman*'s production.[9] JBH and his production team rented cheap office space in Parel, by then a working-class area of Bombay, bringing a tabla and his harmonium from home, along with a couple of desks, some hard chairs and old crockery. The team of seven adventurers spent long hours together absorbed in the pre-production of *Lal-e-Yaman*.

> There Joseph David, Essa, Master Mohmed, Munshi 'Ashiq', our tabalchi,[10] Homi and myself would meet every day—Sunday and holidays not excepted. Dada and I would attend to the routine of our book work and music. All of us would share our frugal luncheon together on a mattress; and the ubiquitous cups of tea freshly prepared every time in the office would go round four or five times a day.

Dada's role went beyond writing script and dialogues and helping to cast and eventually coach the actors. He was also centrally involved, with JBH, in devising the music and songs strictly in accordance with raga theory.

Clueless about how talkies were actually made, Wadia tells of his hopeless attempts to infiltrate the sets of other producers, including unsuccessfully trying to bribe the doorman at Imperial Studios to let him onto the sets of *Alam Ara*, in a bid to learn the tricks of the trade of the new sound technology. When finally, in May 1933, he had raised enough cash from his partner, M.B. Bilimoria, to hire the night shift at Ajanta studios, he was reduced to learning on the job, relying not only on earnest study of Hollywood studio magazines but also on obliging studio hands. Isher Singh, Ajanta's sound engineer, had to spell out precisely what to do, whistling Wadia his cues to instruct clapper boys and actors: 'But I was like a boatman who had gone to sea for the first time.... I fumbled and blundered and began giving wrong instructions at inopportune moments.' The sound engineer begged him to simplify his overly complicated shooting script but he refused. 'Paradoxically, my strength lay in my weakness as an inexperienced director. Isher Singh gave me up as a lost cause and I carried on "to my heart's content".' They shot their first scene from one in the morning until six a.m., when the sounds of parrots, crows and singing milkmen started to intrude onto the soundtrack. By then, he says, word was out around the studios 'that the film was bound to end in a hopeless mess'.

The opening scene that they shot that night is the one described in the previous chapter. It is set in the Yemeni royal court where a dancing girl and musicians are entertaining the king's wedding party. Of particular interest to the current chapter is the culmination of this scene, in which a blind fakir interrupts the proceedings to tell the king that his new second wife will bring trouble, although his warning goes unheeded. Structurally, the fakir's warning is the disruption that sets the narrative in motion. The body of the film begins a decade later, with the new queen plotting to kill Prince Parviz, the king's son by his first wife, so that Prince Nadir, her own son, can inherit the throne. While Parviz must escape to a supernatural never-never land to fulfil his hero's destiny, Nadir remains to comfort his increasingly disaster-prone family.

The film's action intercuts between these two arenas. Parviz, aided by the fakir and armed only with a magic knife that can make him invisible, undergoes a string of adventures in the land of the wicked jinni, Big Foot. He falls in love with and rescues Princess Parizad, the Egyptian beauty held captive by the jinni's monstrous ape-man servant and the parrot. Meanwhile, back in Yemen, the queen is blinded and dies; the mad king retreats, alone, to exile in the forest; and a wicked minister takes over the kingdom. Resolution is finally effected—evil is vanquished and order is restored to the kingdom—when Parviz, with the help of the wise fakir, kills the minister by virtue of his acrobatic strength and the magic knife. He marries Parizad and, at the command of the fakir (and

Figure 3.1 Still of *Lal-e-Yaman* (1933) showing the Fakir, Prince Nadir and the King of Yemen

Source: © Roy Wadia/Wadia Movietone.

God), agrees to devote his life to spreading the word of Allah. His younger step-brother, the innocent Prince Nadir, whose heavenly singing voice has conferred on him the divine right to rule Yemen, is crowned king. For readers who would like more details of this very convoluted and melodramatic plot, I include a fuller account in the endnote.[11]

Wadia was the first to admit that the film was flawed, writing: 'Let me make it plain that *Lal-e-Yaman* was far from being a perfect film. In fact as a pioneering effort on my part it simply could not be.' It was made on a 'shoe-string budget' and had 'low production values', which are especially evident today. The team had also taken a number of box-office risks. Joseph David had brought Master Mohamed, an experienced Urdu stage actor with a strong singing voice and musical talent, to play the fakir. He had also encouraged Wadia to cast Jal Khambatta, a renowned Shakespearean actor, as the mad king, a role overtly modelled on King Lear. But all other roles went to amateurs or minor actors from the Wadias' silent stunt films. Crucially, the younger prince was played by Firoz Dastur, an unknown thirteen-year-old Parsi boy that Wadia and David met through their friend 'Bawaji', Seth Ruttonshaw Dorabji Wellington, who owned the Super Cinema and used to hang out late nights in Dastur's father's billiard salon opposite the cinema on Grant Road. Dastur senior was himself a classical music aficionado, who was already organising singing lessons for his talented young son. When J.B.H. Wadia and Joseph David met the boy, Firoz, they knew they had their prince. He was immediately enrolled for Urdu lessons with their munshi. As rehearsals went on they became increasingly impressed with his potential and, carried away by his beautiful voice, modified their script and increased his role from two to six classical songs, despite what they saw as the box-office risks involved.

SUCCESS

Their gamble paid off. *Lal-e-Yaman* became the most successful talkie of its day. Bawaji had refurbished Super Cinema to launch the film for the Dussera festival on 28 September 1933, where it ran for fourteen house-full weeks before moving on to second-run theatres and other circuits. This was a record at that time: neither of the talkie hits to date—Imperial's *Alam Ara* and J.J. Madan's *Shirin Farhad* (1931)—had lasted more than eleven weeks each, and the concept of the Silver Jubilee was scarcely known. In fact, the only reason *Lal-e-Yaman* was pulled from the Super was because Bawaji had already promised the cinema to another producer for an Id special release. Wadia writes charmingly of his success:

> When the film became the talk of the town I was human enough to feel elated. For some time I walked about unfolding my peacock feathers if not also dance [sic] like our Country's symbolic bird. Had I not become 'somebody'?[12]

Lal-e-Yaman recouped its Rs 60,000 cost within six months and was still in distribution in the early 1950s.[13] On the profits from this and their next film, *Bagh-e-Misr* (Tiger of Egypt, J.B.H. Wadia, 1934), the Wadias were able to build their studios at Lovji castle. Eighteen months later, they felt confident enough of the film's appeal to make a sequel, *Noor-e-Yaman* (Light of Yemen, J.B.H. Wadia, 1935) with the same two singing stars—Master Mohamed again playing the fakir and Firoz Dastur the new king of Yemen.[14] This time Dastur, the child star, had top billing.

So why was this apparently flawed film so successful? Undoubtedly, one key to *Lal-e-Yaman*'s impact was its music and, specifically, Firoz Dastur's charm and charismatic presence as the teenage prince. Dastur's voice became something of a sensation, with adverts of the day hyping him as the 'Golden Voiced Wonder-Boy of Radio Fame'.[15] Originally selling the film on its 'Golden Melodies, Melodramatic Splendour, Dramatic Punch, Galaxy of Stars',[16] the advertising campaign took some interesting directions. The opening week's news item—undoubtedly either written directly by the Wadia Movietone press office or based very closely on its press release—stressed the 'respectability' of the venture:

> The director Mr Wadia holds the university degree of M.A., L.L.B. His ideal seems to be to strive at a harmonious blending of the dramatic qualities in the Cinema art with a genial spirit of entertainment to please the audiences and educate the masses.

It also made much of Jal Khambatta being admired by Sir Rabindranath Tagore, as well as of Bawaji's conversion of the Super Cinema to sound, having 'bought in at a great cost the latest RCA machine, universally recognised as one of the finest machines for recording'.[17] But as the weeks went by, the adverts and 'reviews' changed tack and attempts to highlight its respectability were dropped in favour of a stress on the film's popular appeal, especially that of the songs. By the seventh week: 'Its melodious music and sweetest songs have become so popular that they are heard being sung and repeated at many street-corners in the city.'[18] Now the adverts were stressing the visceral appeal of the film as the key to its success. The *Bombay Chronicle* trumpeted: 'Melodious music and sweetest songs that will return to your lips over and over again. Romance and mystery with soul-stirring scenes, vigorous dialogue and gripping plot that would make you jump in your seats.'[19]

While the film's ability to engage its audiences in powerful, corporeal ways was proven by its box-office takings, its strengths were less well recognised by the middle-class critics and intellectuals. Thus, as we saw in chapter two, a review in *Varieties Weekly* (in fact a mouthpiece of the Calcutta-based New Theatres) damned it with faint praise in comparison with the accolades heaped on the films of New Theatres and Prabhat Film Company, asserting that films such as *Lal-e-Yaman* were for 'the Muslim class' and whilst 'welcome entertainment', they 'should not become the order of the day'.[20] Such disparagements—to which Wadia's oeuvre was subjected throughout his career—fail to acknowledge the fact that, despite its obvious naïveté and Wadia's description of his own bumbling amateurism, *Lal-e-Yaman* is conceptually and cinematically quite sophisticated, especially in its experimentation with the dramatic potential of sound technology. Most remarkable is the fact that Wadia understood immediately—on his first night's sound shoot— what was unique about sound film.

THE DISEMBODIED VOICE

As Michel Chion has pointed out, the significant breakthrough of sound cinema was not the fact of words: silent cinema had always had words through its intertitles. Nor was music a novelty: there were always onsite musicians. What was new and uniquely powerful was the possibility sound opened up of a *disembodied* voice, an *unseen* presence, disrupting the narrative.

> The sound film also has an offscreen field that can be populated by acousmatic voices, founding voices, determining voices—voices that command, invade, and vampirise the image; voices that often have the omnipotence to guide the action, call it up, make it happen, and sometimes lose it on the borderline between land and sea.[21]

The disembodied voice, Chion's *acousmatic* voice, hovers: it exists both within and outside the diegetic space and, as Chion argues, it has a special 'magic and power', an inherent quality of the divine, which may relate to our earliest memories.[22] Moreover, revealing its origins invariably disempowers this voice, a trope that Chion describes across the history of cinema, from Lang to Hitchcock and Kubrick.

The five-minute scene that JBH shot on his first night on a sound stage begins with the seductive—if somewhat artless—gyrations of a dancing girl in full 'oriental' dress, on the set of a royal court in an ornate Islamicate palace, as described in the last chapter. King, queen and courtiers watch the display. The following sequence is particularly interesting in the context of Wadia's use of sound. After a minute or two, the king gestures for the music and dance to stop, as an off-screen male voice rises from the background, mournfully singing a series of verses in praise of Allah. 'Whose soulful voice is this? Bring him here', commands the king. The courtiers lead in a blind fakir, who introduces himself as a passing *khuda ka bandaa* (servant/man of God). In mid-shot, he warns the king, 'Although you have eyes, you are blind.' His new queen is a treacherous woman, whose evil nature will ruin him. When the queen beguilingly—and with the exaggerated gestures of the stage or silent movies—protests her innocence, the king demands that the fakir be taken away and whipped. The music and dance resume, this time punctuated by the off-screen sounds of the whip and the fakir's cries of pain, whilst silhouette images of the fakir being lashed are intercut with the sensuous dancer before the court.

Lal-e-Yaman's introduction of the fakir is like a case-book example of Chion's acousmêtre, his voice emerging out of an unknown void outside the action, but commanding a central presence within the diegetic space. The fakir's disembodied singing is the film's first voice and the trigger that sets the whole narrative in motion. It prompts the very first dialogue of the Wadias' first talkie, 'Whose soulful voice is this? Bring him here.' It is both the voice of truth (and God) and the voice of doom as the fakir warns the king about his new wife. In this crucial opening scene, the (male) *voice* literally interrupts and stops the *spectacle* of the (female) court dancer, but as soon as the fakir has been revealed, the narrative must punish him. As an apparent 'trouble in the text', the logic of the narrative means that he must be tortured (whipped) before the story can move on and the 'real trouble'—the wicked queen (and women more broadly)—can be exposed as villainous and killed off. When the music and dance resume, the spectacle of the dancer is dominated by the sounds of the whip and the fakir's cries of pain, interrupted only occasionally by cutaways to two-dimensional silhouette images of the fakir, filmed like a shadow play behind a screen that has no coherent location within the diegetic space. Although the source of the sound has been revealed (we have seen the fakir) and now has a shadowy visual presence (the silhouette shadows), the voice is once again ambiguously located. In Chion's terminology, the voice has moved from *acousmatic* to *semi-acousmatic*, but still retains its power to dominate the spectacle.

In this context it is relevant to note how insistent Wadia had been on filming this latter sequence according to a complicated scenario he had naïvely devised before stepping into the studio.

> It was the usual practice in those days to shoot a song or dance at a stretch. But carried away by my theoretical study of sequences of Hollywood films I had divided my script in four parts. It demanded the simultaneous sound recording of dance shots along with whip lashes on the back of [the holy man].[23]

The cries of pain and whipping noises were recorded—with considerable difficulty—at the same time as the dance was filmed despite the protests of Isher Singh, the studio's sound recordist. Whilst this was in part a result of Wadia's limited knowledge and reliance on Hollywood models inappropriate to available Indian technology, it also suggests that he instinctively understood that, for its full power to work, the fakir's disembodied voice and cries of whip-lashing had to be both inside and outside the action. While it might be argued that this was nothing more than an adaptation of the 'off-stage' space in theatre, Chion reminds us of a crucial difference: the acousmatic voice in early cinema emanated from the same speaker in the cinema hall as the on-screen sounds and was therefore identically located for the audience.

Wadia had spent a great deal of time studying Hollywood and European cinema and was an admirer of, amongst others, Fritz Lang, from whom he undoubtedly gained—consciously or unconsciously—something of his understanding of the power of the acousmêtre. Somewhat unusually for Wadia, in his memoirs on *Lal-e-Yaman* he also acknowledged some contemporary Indian influences, including Imperial's *Alam Ara*, New Theatres' *Puran Bhagat* (Debaki Bose, 1933) and Prabhat Films' *Maya Machhindra* (Illusion, V. Shantaram, 1932). While we have no footage of the first two, the latter has survived, which makes for interesting comparison. The Prabhat film is undoubtedly visually more assured and sophisticated than *Lal-e-Yaman*, to some extent a function of the better sound technology they used, which allowed for greater camera movement than Wadia found at Ajanta. Wadia was well aware of the limitations this imposed on him.

> It was the dictat of Isher Singh who wanted every artiste to render his or her dialogue and song always facing the microphone and more or less in a static position. Moreover the mike had to be placed as near to the artiste as possible and often barely out of field of ... the camera frame. This was necessary to ensure audible sound and an even tone. It was not just a whim on the part of Isher Singh who was certainly a most competent recordist of the time. Microphones then were rather primitive when compared to those that came in the market later on. And Playback was an unknown quantity. As a director who was used to taking 'trucking' shots [*sic*] in Silent films I had naturally felt handicapped. I had naïvely preconceived many movement shots in my script. They had to be abandoned in favor of simpler ones devised on set.[24]

However, despite their technical advantages, the Prabhat film-makers had not yet exploited the dramatic potential of the disembodied voice to any significant degree. In this context, Wadia's understanding of the visceral power and magic of the acousmatic voice is impressive and his use of this to construct the voice of the divine appears, on the evidence we have, to be more sophisticated than his contemporaries. However, it is the film's underlying structure that is most surprising: *Lal-e-Yaman* presents the power of the voice in comparison with the illusory qualities of the visual through building the film around a fundamental opposition between the aural and the visual.

SOUND AND VISION

Two 'divine' voices dominate and structure *Lal-e-Yaman*: the spiritual wisdom of the fakir and the 'God-given gift' of the young prince's beautiful singing voice. The devotional songs of both Prince Nadir and the fakir praise God and call on man to wake up to the traps, delusions and temporary nature of the material world. Interestingly, these are the only two uncomplicatedly 'good' characters of the film. While the fakir's voice sets the narrative in motion and orchestrates the unfolding of events, the beautiful singing of the teenage prince Nadir is the compelling centre of the film and its resolution. Like the fakir, this prince's singing voice is first introduced acousmatically: we hear him singing God's praises over the image of the king in rapt attention. As the film goes on, the Prince Nadir character becomes

Figure 3.2   Booklet cover of *Noor-e-Yaman* (1935)

Source: © Roy Wadia/Wadia Movietone.

defined primarily *by* his divine voice: its innocence, purity and truth alone entitle him to inherit the kingdom. Firoz Dastur became the film's central attraction, with the charismatic star presence and charm of a boy with a melodious voice on the edge of manhood. He provides the film with a still, pure centre that anchors the chaos and neuroses of the older characters and the theatrical excess of their acting styles. Significantly, both divine voices are male and these stars were subsequently chosen to market the sequel *Noor-e-Yaman* (Figure 3.2).

In contrast to these voices, *Lal-e-Yaman* represents the visual as inherently unreliable. Continuous play on the theme of blindness and blinding runs throughout the film. In the first scene the blind fakir accuses the king of being metaphorically blind because he cannot see the queen's evil nature. Later, when the king recognises his mistake and the queen's villainous plot has been unmasked, he orders her to be literally blinded, her eyes gouged out with an iron rod. Laughing hysterically when he sees her stumbling towards him, he exclaims, 'Now we are both blind. With eyes I have been blind, without them now so are you.' As she staggers around unable to see, she plunges from a high cliff to her death. Throughout the film, dialogue and song lyrics repeat phrases such as 'your eyes are empty vessels' or 'my eyes are playing tricks on me'.

The fakir's supernatural powers centre primarily on visibility and invisibility. Parviz's long-suffering first wife receives magical powers of long-distance vision from the fakir, through which she is able to spy on her husband's flirtations with Parizad and, disguised as a young man by the fakir, bring Parviz back home. The miracles that the fakir performs are created by the film's crude but effective optical effects: prison chains and snakes dissolve into garlands of flowers, trees weep, illusory beings spring out of nowhere and a holy flag descends from the heavens with a message from God. Crucially, the fakir's gift to Prince Parviz—and the source of his power—is a magic knife that grants him the boon of invisibility. Visual illusions such as these were staples of the silent era, particularly of the fantasy and fairy or *pari* genres in which the potential of cinema's optical effects was particularly enthusiastically exploited, as described in chapter two. In this, early Indian cinema was echoing not just the experiments of European silent cinema but also the Urdu-Parsi theatre's predilection for harnessing the latest technological tools to construct extravagant visual illusion as one of its attractions.

In *Lal-e-Yaman*, while the dramatic events in the kingdom of Yemen are dominated by the power of the voice, most of the action in the jinni's land draws on the visual register of the most popular genres of India's later silent cinema: the costume, fantasy and action genres of the late 1920s and early 1930s. Within the jinni's world spectacle and illusion rule: a scantily clad, beautiful nymph bathing in the open air tempts Parviz into the supernatural land; he falls in love when his gaze falls upon a sleeping (unseeing) princess who can only be woken by magic sticks; and his ability to move between invisibility and visibility through the fakir's knife gives him superhuman powers over her monstrous captors. *Arabian Nights* tales of visual magic within an Islamicate never-never land came into silent cinema largely through their influence on the Urdu-Parsi theatre, as discussed in the last chapter. On the other hand, the jinni's world also boasts echoes of the American silent films that were phenomenally popular throughout India at that time, including Hollywood's own famous adaptation of *Arabian Nights* exotica, *Thief of Bagdad* (Raoul Walsh, 1924). Hollywood had also provided Wadia with inspiration for his action films, not least the Tarzan series, and visual echoes of Johnny Weissmuller are unmistakable in the ape-like creature that guards Parizad.[25] However, music and song appear to have been much more important selling points for *Lal-e-Yaman* than its visual attractions: apart from one small photograph of the Tarzan-like figure in the film's song booklet and some images of the beautiful Padma, none of the contemporary publicity and newspaper coverage mentioned *Lal-e-Yaman*'s visual illusions and spectacular attractions.

Two elements within the jinni's land provide a bridge between this and the world of the royal court of Yemen, hinting at its status as a shadow world of reversals. One is a dance that Princess Parizad is forced to perform for the jinni, Big Foot. In a grotesque reprise of the film's opening scene, Parizad must dance before her captor, while Parviz watches impotently from the sidelines. But where in the opening scene it is the voice (of the fakir) that interrupts and overpowers the spectacle of the female dancer, here the arrival of the Tarzan-like ape-man stops the dancing, provoking a fight sequence that culminates in a form of visual magic through which the villainous captor is killed, as Parviz wins Parizad's freedom by plucking a magic rose that controls the jinni's heart.

The other bridge between the two worlds is the talking parrot that greets all comers with the playful mantra, 'You have seen the world with your eyes, now see this tamasha.' The parrot's voice is the only word of warning within this world premised on the illusory nature of spectacle. But its source is mysterious. As Claudia Gorbman has pointed out in relation to Hollywood's first talkie, *The Jazz Singer* (Alfred Coslan, 1927), 'for the first time in a feature story film, the voice ... contributes toward the constitution of a diegetic space'.[26] So what contribution does our parrot make? In this case the parrot's voice is, just like the fakir's, both inside and ambiguously outside the diegetic space of *Lal-e-Yaman*. Interestingly, in a direct echo of the whipped fakir, the parrot is always shown in silhouette as shadow-play.[27] Like the fakir, his is a distanced voice that comments on the action. Although his perch *is* located within the frame and hovers over the action, the parrot has clear acousmatic qualities: we never see clearly the parrot's face or beak (the voice's precise source), and with its machine-like tone[28] his voice is at root a riddle. We can never know whether this is wisdom or mimicry and, being a consummate mimic, whether there can be such a thing as an *authentic* parrot voice. This innovative device, only possible with sound cinema, further unsettles the stability of the jinni's world of visual illusion. It can also be argued that the parrot unsettles the reality effect on which sound cinema itself is based—pointing up the ultimate impossibility of the unity of voice and body.[29] As in his use of the disembodied fakir's voice to underscore divine power, Wadia's use of a semi-acousmatic parrot to comment on the action and underline the core themes of the film demonstrates an impressively inventive understanding of the potential of the new era of sound technology to create cinematic magic.[30]

To summarise my argument so far, *Lal-e-Yaman* is structured, at its core, around an opposition between the visual and the aural, in which the power of the voice prevails over the illusory qualities of the visual. The fantasy land of the jinni—where spectacle and visual illusion rule—is narratively contained by the world of divine voices.

Technologies of visual effects—staples of the silent era—lose out to the magic of sound recording. And whilst the older prince, with his magic knife and athletic, active body, wins the kingdom through physical action and visual illusion, it is the younger prince, with the divine voice, who is crowned king in deference to God's will.

MODERNITIES

Curiously, the film can be read as an allegory of the arrival of the talkies themselves: it narrates the struggle to accept the incursions of voice and song into the cinema of pure vision. Made at the point when J.B.H. Wadia finally—and we know somewhat reluctantly—accepted the demise of silent cinema (the primarily visual) and the inevitability of the talkies (voice and song), he chose for his first talkie a story in which the voice (of doom and of truth) has to be punished before redeeming itself and being accepted as the pinnacle and motor of the new world order.

Wadia had been a late convert to sound film.

> I indulged in wishful thinking that both the Silent Film and the Talkies would prosper side by side. I found welcome support in the pronouncements ex-cathedra of no less a world celebrity than Charlie Chaplin berating the advent of the Talkies as a retrograde step in good film making. But facts are stubborn creatures, and the fact of facts was staring us in the face. In the wake of the newly-arisen threat, the returns from Silent Films were going down, down like the prices of shares caught in the vortex of mandi in the Share Bazaar.[31]

Only one short trailer has survived of the brothers' silent work, that of their penultimate silent film, *Vantolio* (Whirlwind, Homi Wadia, 1933). The frenzied four-minute montage includes images of a rapacious villain (Sayani), a sari-clad but modern heroine in peril (Padma) and courageous heroes (notably Boman Shroff) who ride the gamut of modern technological marvels: trains, cars, ships and sailboats. We see a fight atop a moving train as a white horse gallops alongside, a perilous climb up a ship's masthead, 'death-inviting' jumps, and much swinging from ropes, including the heroine's plucky retort to the villain's unwelcome advances with her kicking, ankle-boot-clad feet. Edited as a trailer, it is hard to deduce much about the pace and editing style of the film itself, and we know little about the story beyond the stock motifs that recur in the Wadias' later sound films. But adverts in the Gujarati film journal *Mouj Majah* give some sense of its targeted appeal: 'Coming with more speed than *Toofan Mail*' and 'more astonishing than *Sinhgarjana*',[32] *Vantolio* also boasted 'death-defying stunts on cars, trains and steamers moving at lightning speed'.[33]

Comparison between *Vantolio*, released in April 1933, and *Lal-e-Yaman*, released just six months later, is instructive. Apart from the obvious gulf between the settings—from futuristic Westernised modernity to a fantasy Islamicate past—there are important structural distinctions. Where *Vantolio* celebrates the power of the body and its visuality, its appeal lying in the spectacle of what the all-powerful modern body can do, *Lal-e-Yaman* celebrates the power of the (traditional) word, spoken or sung, and the marvels of sound recording. Whilst *Vantolio*'s heroes are acrobats and bodybuilders with superhuman physical powers, who defy the laws of nature through their control of modern technologies of speed as well as through cinema's own technologies of visual illusion, *Lal-e-Yaman*'s two central heroes, the young Prince Nadir and the Sufi holy man, are singers with divine voices.

Lal-e-Yaman is overtly about Sufi mystical wisdom: the material world is an illusory spectacle and the path to truth lies in listening to the voice of God, just as the parrot's voice warned. Parrots were familiar motifs in Urdu romantic literature, as well as in Sanskrit literature, with the *Sukasaptati* (Seventy Tales of the Parrot) claimed, alongside other early medieval stories, as an ancestor of the *Arabian Nights*.[34] The *Arabian Nights* tales themselves include a parrot story that *Lal-e-Yaman* clearly references, both in detail and in theme: a jealous merchant leaves a parrot to keep watch over his beautiful wife.[35] An equally resonant reference in this context is to an earlier story from a key text of Sufi mysticism, Rumi's thirteenth-century masnavi. Here the parrot is taught to speak by being placed in front of a mirror, behind which his trainer hides and speaks. When the parrot looks into the mirror he believes he is hearing the voice of another parrot and so listens attentively and learns to talk to it. Here we have the classic acousmêtre scenario: an unseen voice speaks from behind a mirror or screen, thereby both signalling its existing power and accruing further potency. Chion reminds us that the term 'acousmatic' itself derives from the name of a Pythagorean sect whose followers had to listen to their master's voice from behind a curtain, so that the sight of the speaker would not distract them from the master's message.[36] The interdiction against looking, which transforms the master/God into an acousmatic presence, permeates a number of religions, including, importantly, Islam.[37]

The Islamicate world of the film was undoubtedly designed to a considerable extent to appeal to India's large Muslim audiences of the day—although, as we saw in chapter two, not exclusively so: the aim was to reach a large crossover audience. But we do know from box-office figures in the Wadia Movietone archive that *Lal-e-Yaman* was particularly popular in Bombay and the north Indian territories, where a significant proportion of the cinema audience was Muslim: the film made 45 per cent of its profits in the Bombay territory, 25 per cent in the Delhi territory and 9 per cent in Lahore.[38] *Lal-e-Yaman* also had substantial overseas sales in the 1930s, accounting for around 5 per cent of its returns, and it is more than likely that this and other Wadia films played in Baghdad and across parts of the Arab world.[39] But the issue is undoubtedly more complex than this and, given the scale of *Lal-e-Yaman*'s success, the film's appeal cannot have been limited to Muslims, nor should scholars today essentialise these audiences.

The ending of *Lal-e-Yaman* is particularly interesting in this context. In an echo of the opening scene, the court has assembled for the marriage between Prince Parviz and Princess Parizad, which is to be followed by the prince's coronation. The king blesses the union and is about to hand his crown to his eldest son when the fakir intervenes with a message from God, received through a flag that drops from the clouds. God has pronounced that Parviz's younger step-brother, Prince Nadir, must be king, whilst Parviz and Parizad must go to her homeland, Misr (Egypt), to spread the word of Islam and sing God's praises there. Nadir is duly crowned instead and Parviz and Parizad depart, blessed by the old king, while the new king Nadir sings them off.

Jaawo sadhaaro fat-ha paawo, tumpe saaya rabka
Mishra mein jaake danka bajawo, name ahadse deen jagawo
Har ghar ko islam banawo, naam ko tum chamkawo—tumpe saaya rabka
Rakhkhe amaanmein tumko woh daav fat-ha, wa dewe khalique akbar
Hai ye dua 'Aashq' ki aksar majahab pe mit jaawo, tumpe saaya rab ka.[40]

The song's words command them to take Islam to every home and immerse themselves in the religion/*mazahab*. Meanwhile, unfurling behind the new king is a flag adorned with the Caliphate[41] crescent moon and star.

On the face of it, and especially from today's perspective, this seems a surprising resolution, given that J.B.H. Wadia was a committed humanist, secularist and rationalist. Quite how the scene was read in the context of nationalist politics in 1933 is unclear, although it would necessarily have meant different things to different audiences. In fact, the film's closing song, while clearly appealing to the large Muslim audiences, may also have been seen more broadly as a nationalist allegory, a celebration of the importance of the homeland, a theme which other songs within the Wadias' films present more explicitly.[42] We saw earlier from the press of the day that *Lal-e-Yaman*'s songs had a life of their own, with a visceral quality 'that will return to your lips over and over again', which indicates that the film's songs would have been particularly significant in the circulation of its nationalist political messages.

However, there is another important dimension to this. In the early decades of the twentieth century there was a craze for bhakti nationalism. Hindu devotional songs or bhajans were popularised as a vehicle for the nationalist cause, as part of a relentless movement to 'Sanskritise' Indian culture—and particularly its music. As Janaki Bakhle argues, an Indian classical music was being invented that was to be purged, wherever possible, of Islamic influences.[43] Inevitably, this made its mark on the film industry, notably with the film-makers at the Prabhat Film Company in Pune, whose first sound films—devotionals and mythologicals like *Ayodhyecha Raja* (King of Ayodhya, V. Shantaram, 1932) and *Maya Machhindra*—drew directly on the craze for bhakti nationalism, presumably inspired by V.D. Paluskar's popularising of the bhajan as a nationalist form.[44]

In this context, the so-called *Arabian Nights* films—of Wadia at least—opened up spaces for a different kind of nationalist modernity from either the Hinduised versions of early Prabhat Films, or Westernised versions in films such as *Vantolio*. As Kaushik Bhaumik has noted, this alternative modernity was fed by the nineteenth-century Urdu romantic literary movement, masnavi poetry, Urdu-Parsi theatre (with its Indo-Muslim fairy romances) and the flowering of Urdu modernism in the north Indian bazaar cultures of the 1920s and 1930s, and arguably across much of the Persian and Arabian world.[45] Themes and motifs of these forms, including the *Arabian Nights* and qissa-dastan, provided a shared cultural reference point.

In contrast to the Hinduising tendencies of some of their contemporaries, the Wadias' films brought together a range of alternative models for Indian modernity, from Indo-Persian story forms to popular Hollywood, as I will elaborate in the following chapters. In its hybrid Islamicate form and its stress on the visceral, *Lal-e-Yaman* was soon out of step with the direction in which 'respectable' Bombay cinema was moving. However, within it we can already see the seeds of a stream of later, post-independence B-movies that were emphatically 'beyond the boundaries' of the socials of mainstream Indian cinema that developed over the next decades.

In conclusion, Wadia keyed straight into the unique new powers sound cinema offered and harnessed these to the vision of a nationalist modernity, exploiting, like other film-makers, the visceral power of song, with its long after-life outside the cinema. But unlike other early sound films before 1933—mythologicals and devotionals in a Hindu ethos—Wadia also immediately exploited, in quite sophisticated ways, the magic of the off-screen voice, using it to construct divinity within a world with a Sufi ethos, in which sound wins out over the purely visual, divine voices over acrobatic bodies, and distant voices over magic knives.

NOTES

1. *In ankhon se duniya dekhi / Ye bhii tamasha ab tu dekh.*
2. See chapter two for discussion of the term '*Arabian Nights* fantasy film'.

3. The copy that survives, running at around two hours, is a slightly shortened version re-edited by JBH in the late 1950s from the one worn-out print he managed to recover.

4. Much of the scholarship on this period has focused on the films of Bombay Talkies and Prabhat Studios.

5. Material on Joseph David is from J.B.H. Wadia's unpublished essay, 'Joseph David—Tribute to a Forgotten Pioneer'. According to this, Joseph David was born in 1872 at Rev Danda (a village south of Alibagh). In the late 1930s, he returned to Rev Danda and died in 1940 at 'a ripe old age'. So 'forgotten' a pioneer was he that Somnath Gupt's classic text on Urdu-Parsi theatre incorrectly asserts that David 'did not live a long life' and 'died at the age of thirty'. Ironically in this context, the author continues: 'The Parsi stage has never forgotten the services of Joseph David nor can it ever forget him.' Gupt, *The Parsi Theatre*, p. 100.

6. Order of release: *Lal-e-Yaman* (September 1933), *Bagh-e-Misr* (1934), *Vaman Avtar* (August 1934), *Kala Gulab/Black Rose* (1934), *Noor-e-Yaman* (April 1935), *Josh-e-Watan/Desh Deepak* (October 1935). David worked on all of the above and is also credited for music (alongside Master Mohamed) on the first three. He also wrote dialogues for *Hunterwali*. *Kala Gulab* was based on *Khaki Putla*, a successful stage play David had directed, which Wadia tells us was an adaptation of a Marie Corelli novel, *Sorrows of Satan*.

7. The quotations from Wadia's unpublished memoirs are drawn primarily from the essays, 'The Story Behind the Making of *Lal-e-Yaman*', 'Joseph David—Tribute to a Forgotten Pioneer', 'The Wadia Movietone Partnership' and the first chapter of 'Those Were the Days, Part Two'. All these were accessed with the kind permission of Riyad, Vinci and other members of the Wadia family. Page numbers are unreliable as there is much repetition and the memoirs currently exist in several versions. Some of this material was also published by J.B.H. Wadia as 'JBH in Talkieland', in *Cinema Vision India*.

8. J.B.H. Wadia, 'Those Were the Days, Part Two'.

9. This material all comes from Wadia's own colourful account in 'The Story behind the Making of Lal-e-Yaman', some of it repeated in print in Wadia, 'JBH in Talkieland', pp. 82–3.

10. Essa was assistant director. Tabalchi: tabla player; Munshi aashiq: poet/lyricist/scribe.

11. In the interests of readability, the details of this convoluted plot from this point on have been simplified within the main body of the essay. For those who wish to pursue this further, a more detailed synopsis follows here. Inevitably, the emphases in such retellings reflect my own interests; for example, a fascinating analysis could be made of the representation of gender within the film, which I do not attempt to point up here.

Prince Parviz arrives in the land of the jinni where he falls in love with the beautiful Princess Parizad who is being held captive by the monstrous Big Foot and his ape-man retainer, helped by a talking parrot. Through a combination of physical strength, cunning and supernatural powers, Parviz kills Big Foot and frees Parizad. Their subsequent embrace is 'seen' many miles away by Prince Parviz's wife, who has come, in an ascetic's garb, to ask the fakir's help. Meanwhile, back at the palace, the distraught king, whose only solace is his younger son's beautiful singing, orders his wife to be punished by blinding. Her only support is her daughter, who is soon abducted by the prime minister's soldiers. Alone and unable to see, the queen falls off a cliff to her death. As his whole family, apart from Prince Nadir, has now left him, the king abandons his kingdom to his prime minister and retreats into the forest. Here he goes mad and, with his son Prince Nadir, is taken in by the fakir, who sings wise songs and attempts to restore order.

Transforming Prince Parviz's wife into a man, the fakir sends 'her' as a messenger to bring back her husband. Told of his father's dementia and the loss of his kingdom, Prince Parviz immediately leaves with the messenger for Yemen, despite his lover Princess Parizad's pleas to stay with her. Egged on by the malicious parrot, Princess Parizad uses a magic ring to unleash water devils to try and stop Parviz's journey. As Parviz approaches the kingdom and the king's dementia deepens, the prime minister reveals himself as a murderous villain who is attempting to marry the absent king's daughter by force. In a showdown of the forces of good against evil, aided by the fakir's knife which makes him invisible, Prince Parviz destroys the prime minister's men, whilst his wife (still disguised as a man) rescues the king's daughter (her own sister-in-law). However, Parviz's loyal wife gets caught in the struggle between Parviz and the wicked prime minister and, after revealing her true identity, dies saving her husband.

Some time later ('when the dark clouds of tragedy had rolled by'), the king, happy once more, his beloved son Nadir singing at his side, gratefully recognises the fakir's help. He blesses the marriage between his elder son, Parviz, and Parizad and is about to crown him king when a flagpole descends with a message from the heavens. The fakir intervenes and announces God's will: Nadir must be king, while Parviz and Parizad must go to her land, Misr (Egypt), to spread the word of Islam and sing the praises of Allah there. They depart, blessed by the old king, while the new king Nadir sings against the background of a flag embroidered with the Caliphate crescent moon and star.

12. See J.B.H. Wadia, 'Those Were the Days, Part Two', chapter one.

13. Distributor M.B. Bilimoria (MBB) struck the last print around 1953. Considered by Wadia to have been 'made on a shoestring', Lal-e-Yaman's production costs of Rs 60,000 included 25 prints and 50 trailers, together with all publicity and advertisements. Originally, JBH proposed that he would advance Rs 20,000 of his own savings, if MBB matched this with an investment of Rs 20,000. MBB made a counterproposal that they should go into business together, along with the brothers Nadirshaw and Burjorji Tata, wealthy landowners with an import–export business from MBB's hometown Bilimoria in Baroda—a partnership of five Parsi men (see Wadia, 'The Story behind the Making of Lal-e-Yaman' and 'The Wadia Movietone Partnership'). Valentina Vitali has suggested that the deal struck between JBH and MBB was strongly weighted in MBB's favour, thereby paving the way for India's unique exhibition/distribution system comprising vertical deals with a multitude of small operators. See Vitali, Hindi Action Cinema, pp. 97–9.

14. It was in *Noor-e-Yaman* that Fearless Nadia made her debut as a second heroine, seductress Princess Parizad, as Padma had been 'spirited away' to join Baburao Patel's Gandharva Cinetone. Wadia was still experimenting with his stable of actors and Master Mohammed was not allowed to play the romantic lead after a disastrous experiment in *Bagh-e-Misr*: 'Doll-like Padma was my heroine and as the stars were very favorable to Master Mohmed (the Pir Mard of *Lal-E-Yaman*) the hero's role was assigned to him. His one big asset was his stentorian voice. Otherwise he was not carved out to play the romantic lead. He was heavy built with a protruding paunch, which had to be strapped tightly during "takes".' Unfortunately audiences 'could not stomach him as a romantic lead against the eye-filling beauty of Padma'. See J.B.H. Wadia, 'How *Bagh-e-Misr* Came to Be Produced'.

15. *Bombay Chronicle*, 24 September 1933. Wadia subsequently called Dastur 'Sangeet Ratna'; see 'JBH in Talkieland', p. 83. Dastur later left films for a career in classical music, becoming a foremost exponent of Kirana Gharana and, from 1969, professor of Hindustani classical music at the University of Bombay.

16. *Bombay Chronicle*, 24 September 1933.

17. *Bombay Chronicle*, 30 September 1933.

18. *Bombay Chronicle*, 11 November 1933.

19. *Bombay Chronicle*, 10 November 1933.

20. *Varieties Weekly*, 23 February 1934, quoted in Bhaumik, 'The Emergence of the Bombay Film Industry, 1913–36', p. 174. Bhaumik also compares the acting style of *Lal-e-Yaman* with New Theatres' *Chandidas* (Nitin Bose, 1934) and argues that, although *Lal-e-Yaman* was disparaged and *Chandidas* praised as the 'acme of screen realism', there is little objective difference between the two (ibid., p. 160).

21. Michel Chion, *The Voice in Cinema*, trans. from the French by Claudia Gorbman, New York: Columbia University Press, 1999 [1982], p. 27.

22. 'Why all these powers in a voice? Maybe because this voice without a place that belongs to the acousmêtre takes us back to an archaic original stage: of the first months of life or even before birth, during which the voice was everything and it was everywhere' (ibid., p. 27).

23. Wadia, 'The Story Behind the Making of *Lal-e-Yaman*'.

24. Ibid.

25. For more on Tarzan in India see chapter five.

26. Claudia Gorbman, *Unheard Melodies: Narrative Film Music*, London: British Film Institute and Bloomington: Indiana University Press, 1987, p. 46.

27. The only time he is not in silhouette is at a moment of tension where he risks losing control, when Parviz and Parizad proclaim their desire to be together for ever more.

28. An 'acousmachine' in Chion's terminology (Chion, *Voice in Cinema*, pp. 42–5).

29. In this it arguably also foreshadows the ubiquitous acceptance of 'playback' in Indian cinema from the mid-1940s onwards. For a stimulating discussion of playback singing in Indian cinema see Neepa Majumdar, *Wanted Cultured Ladies Only! Female Stardom and Cinema in India 1930s–1950s*, Urbana: University of Illinois Press, 2009, pp. 173–202.

30. This parrot had a key narrative role in the sequel, *Noor-e-Yaman*, initiating the narrative action. According to the song booklet, the film opens with the parrot bringing to the evil jinni's brother the message that Parizad and Parviz had killed Big Foot and escaped.

31. J.B.H. Wadia, 'The Story Behind the Making of *Lal-e-Yaman*'. Wadia's memoirs are peppered with such (somewhat laboured) word play.

32. *Sinhgarjana*: lion's roar. This is also the title of a 1932 Wadia stunt film.

33. *Mouj Majah*, March 1933.

34. In the *Sukasaptati*, written some time before the twelfth century, the talking parrot provides the frame story, telling such beguiling tales that his mistress stays in the house and is prevented from committing adultery. See Irwin, *The Arabian Nights*, pp. 67–8.

35. Husain Haddawy, trans., *The Arabian Nights* (based on the text edited by Muhsin Mahdi), New York: Norton, 1995/2008, pp. 50–1 in Lyons, *The Arabian Nights*, pp. 549–50.

36. Chion, *Voice in Cinema*, p. 19.

37. A more contemporary nationalist connotation of the parrot should also be noted: Christopher Pinney points out that, in 1920s and 1930s India, the caged parrot was a visual metaphor for a colonised nation. Postcard images of caged and uncaged parrots (many by Chitrashala Press) were sent out by nationalists as coded anti-colonial messages that would escape the notice of the British censors. Christopher Pinney, *'Photos of the Gods': The Printed Image and Political Struggle in India*, London: Reaktion Books, 2004, p. 56.

38. By 1941, *Lal-e-Yaman*'s total profits across the seven distribution territories were Rs 152,793: that is, Bombay: Rs 68,131 (c. 45 per cent); Lahore: Rs 14,072 (c. 9 per cent); Delhi: Rs 34,396 (c. 25 per cent); Central Provinces: Rs 4,223 (c. 3 per cent); Calcutta: Rs 13,899 (c. 9 per cent); Madrid: Rs 9,000 (c. 6 per cent); and Overseas: Rs 7,654 (c. 5 per cent) (figures from documents in the Wadia Movietone archive).

39. According to Bilimoria, writing in 1957, overseas sales only really got off the ground after 1935. However, by the late 1930s, two Bombay distributors had offices in Baghdad, distributing throughout the Middle East, and 'popular action pictures of India were as much popular in the city of Baghdad as in any first-run house of Bombay'. As Bilimoria distributed Wadias' action films alongside *Lal-e-Yaman*, we might assume that the significant 'foreign' sales for *Lal-e-Yaman* reflect its popularity in the Middle East. See M.B. Bilimoria, 'Foreign Market for Indian Films', in *Indian Talkie: Silver Jubilee Souvenir 1931–56*, Bombay: Film Federation of India, 1956, p. 53.

40. Go, be victorious, God's blessings are with you;
Beat the drum in Misr (Egypt) and show them the religion;
Bring Islam to every home, spread the word, God's blessings are with you;
If you stay in peace, the great Creator will make you victorious;
This is the boon of *aashq* (poet or passion/love), immerse yourself in the religion (mazahab), God's blessings are with you.

41. Appropriately, Nadir is a ruler by divine will, in the Caliph tradition.

42. Wadia discusses this in his memoirs on *Josh-e-Watan* and his later film *Jai Bharat* (Homi Wadia, 1936). One might also argue that Sufi mysticism is the benign or 'secular' face of the Islamic movement, with the potential to effect a resolution not only between Hindu and Muslim (the Hindu bhakti movement draws on Sufism), but also between Indian tradition and Western modernity, especially given the celebration within Sufi poetry of erotic desire, consumption of alcohol and freedom from social constraint.

43. See Janaki Bakhle, *Two Men and Music: Nationalism in the Making of an Indian Classical Tradition*, New York: Oxford University Press, 2005.

44. This is not to argue that Prabhat in the 1930s was in any obvious way a 'Hindu studio' or made films for 'Hindu audiences'. Not only was one of its five founders the Muslim producer/director S. Fatehlal, who produced several of Prabhat's devotionals set in a Hindu universe, but Indian audiences and their cultural knowledges could not be neatly segregated along community lines. See Ravi Vasudevan, 'Genre and the Imagination of Identity, 1935–1945', in *From Ali Baba to Jodhaa Akbar: Islamicate Cultures of Bombay Cinema*, eds Ira Bhaskar and Richard Allen, New Delhi: Tulika Press, 2014 (forthcoming).

45. Bhaumik, 'The Emergence of the Bombay Film Industry'.

four

*N*ot Quite (Pearl) White

Fearless Nadia, Queen of the Stunts

It was June 1935 on a dark, monsoon-lashed Bombay night and J.B.H. Wadia was taking one of the biggest gambles of his film production career. His new venture, *Hunterwali* (Woman with the Whip, Homi Wadia, 1935), was premiering at the Super Cinema in downtown Grant Road. The film had been an unprecedented six months in the making and cost more than Rs 80,000 but no distributor had come forward to buy it. Rumours in the industry suggested it was a turkey: the film starred a large blonde-haired muscle-woman with fearsome fighting skills who thrashed Indian men into the ground—on the face of it an unlikely proposition for Indian audiences at the height of the nationalist movement. JBH and his partners had been reduced to pooling their own resources to secure a release. Extravagant pre-publicity had reeled in the crowds for the opening night. It was now down to their new star, Fearless Nadia, aka Mary Evans, in her role as a masked avenging angel, to deliver the goods. Billed as the 'Indian Pearl White' and playing a swashbuckling princess in disguise, she roamed the countryside on horseback sporting hot pants, big bosom and bare white thighs and, when she wasn't swinging from chandeliers, kicking or whipping men, she was righting wrongs with her bare fists and an imperious scowl. By the time Nadia hitched up her sari and cracked her whip in the third reel, declaring: '*Aaj se main Hunterwali hoon*'[1] the audience was cheering. Within days the Wadias knew they were sitting on a goldmine: the film ran to packed houses for more than twenty-five weeks and became the

Figure 4.1 Booklet cover of *Lootaru Lalna* (1938)

Source: © Roy Wadia/Wadia Movietone.

major money-spinner of the year. Fearless Nadia became a sensation across the country and unofficial merchandising followed: Fearless Nadia whips, belts, matchboxes and playing cards appeared and her famous yell '*hey-y-y*' became a catchphrase. Nadia went on to secure a reputation as one of the biggest female stars of the Indian screen of the 1930s and early 1940s.

In the same year, just outside Bombay in rural Malad, an urbane Brahmin beauty, Devika Rani, and her charismatic husband, producer Himansu Rai, were launching a visionary new studio enterprise, Bombay Talkies. Already the toast of London high society for her debut as a glamorous oriental princess in Rai's Anglo-Indian co-production, *Karma* (Fate, J.L. Freer-Hunt, 1933), Devika quickly established her own and Bombay Talkies' reputation at home with the phenomenal box-office and critical success of *Achhut Kanya*

(Untouchable Girl, Franz Osten, 1936). This premiere was a grand affair at Bombay's Roxy Cinema, boasting a glittering cosmopolitan audience which, legend has it, included Jawaharlal Nehru. Devika's role as a doe-eyed tragic heroine, an untouchable village belle trapped in a doomed romance, was seen as a social comment on caste iniquities, establishing her as a major icon of Indian cinema and the other top female star of the era.

The two women could scarcely have been more different: where Nadia was big, buxom, blonde and blue eyed, a white-skinned former circus artiste who had been the darling of the soldiers in the North-West Frontier, Devika was a conventional Indian beauty. Petite, almost childlike, with long dark hair and large velvety brown eyes, she was upper-class and upper-caste, London-educated at South Hampstead High School and the Royal Academy of Dramatic Arts, and widely known to be a grand-niece of Tagore. While Nadia and her director (later to be her husband), Homi Wadia, moved in the world of Bombay clubs and horse racing, and openly admired and adapted the popular comic-book fare of Hollywood action serials and comedies, Devika and her husband and director, Himansu Rai, moved amongst the European cosmopolitan elite, learning their craft at Berlin's UFA studios and drawing their inspiration—and many of their technicians—from German cinema. Where Devika was the aristocrat who made her screen reputation through playing an outcaste, Nadia was the outcaste who played princess. The two star personae—neither of them the most likely of nationalist icons and both of them speaking poor Hindi—are in interesting ways inversions of each other. In examining the late colonial period, we might see the two as complementary exotic fictions, speaking to the project of defining Indianness while simultaneously exploding the idea of Indian cinema as isolated from the rest of the world.

Nadia, in her heyday, was the queen of the box office. It was, however, Devika who became 'the first lady' of Indian cinema, celebrated by the critics and feted throughout Europe. Until recently, Devika dominated the histories of Indian cinema of this period as the embodiment of good, serious and patriotic cinema, her films seminal in establishing the genre of Indian film melodrama.[2] Nadia, despite her extraordinary popularity with the mass audience, both in India and throughout the diasporic distribution networks of Southeast Asia, the Middle East, the Caribbean and Africa, was virtually unknown in Europe or America and had been largely erased from official Indian cinema histories until recent years, although since her death in 1996, interest in Nadia has been growing.[3]

Focusing on the intriguing figure of Fearless Nadia, this chapter explores the construction of one form of modern Indian femininity in the late colonial period, examining Nadia within the film production context of 1930s Bombay and, in passing, drawing comparisons with her complementary-opposite persona, Devika. I ask why Nadia was chosen by the Wadias and why she was so popular with her contemporary audiences. In particular, I examine how the Wadia brothers dealt with her whiteness/Otherness and negotiated the points of tension in her image, especially in the context of the nationalist movement. I also ask to what extent she simply 'copied' Hollywood stunt stars such as Pearl White and how these role models were 'Indianised'. Finally, I consider why Nadia became so peripheral to later histories of Indian cinema and why the Wadias' films were given so little status, particularly in relation to studios such as Bombay Talkies.

The chapter begins by setting up the context of Nadia's arrival at Wadia Movietone. It moves on to examine the Nadia persona in greater depth, arguing that the films produce her as a modern Indian woman through a complex process which refers to Hollywood (not quite Pearl White), cosmopolitan Indian modernity and the warrior women of India's virangana tradition. The argument is illustrated through the examination of her classic *Diamond Queen* (Homi Wadia, 1940). Finally, the Wadias' oeuvre is considered in the context of debates on mimicry and nationalism and it is suggested that, given their eclectic vision of Indian modernity, J.B.H. Wadia's lifelong quest for respectability was inherently doomed within the framework of mainstream nationalist discourse. However, the hybridity and playful impersonations of the Wadia brothers' films were major factors in their contemporary success and are what today reverberates—for better or for worse—with global popular culture.

EARLY YEARS OF BOMBAY CINEMA

It is well documented that the arena of Indian cinema in the early decades of the century boasted very real exchanges between Bombay and the cinemas of both Hollywood and Europe.[4] Indian audiences had been exposed to Hollywood from the earliest years: the young Wadia brothers were among the many enthusiastic fans of the stunt and action films, and serials of stars such as Pearl White, Ruth Roland, Charlie Chaplin, Eddie Polo and Douglas Fairbanks ran to full houses throughout the 1910s and 1920s, when four out of five films screened were foreign. Hollywood stars—including Fairbanks—visited Bombay and producers such as Ardeshir Irani forged their own links with Hollywood personnel.[5]

Alongside the Hollywood influences, a parallel stream was fed by European cinema. Dadasaheb Phalke's vision of producing the first Indian feature film was famously inspired by a viewing of *The Life of Christ* and a desire to promote Indian religion and culture. Rajadhyaksha has documented how, in doing this, Phalke established the template for a nationalist aesthetic.[6] Phalke himself made three trips to Europe and, between 1922 and 1924, Himansu Rai trained with Pabst and Pommer at Germany's most prestigious studio, UFA. Rai later brought his bride-to-be, Devika Rani, to Berlin to begin her own art direction apprenticeship, working first as Marlene Dietrich's make-up assistant and later attending acting master-classes under Pabst. In 1933, after a successful run of Indo-European co-productions, Rai decided they should return to India. They brought with them a cohort of German technicians, including Franz Osten and Joseph Wirsching, to work at Bombay Talkies and train local talent. Inspired by the ideals of the nationalist movement to bring international glory to India's heritage and build a world-class film industry, Rai told Devika: 'Let us learn from these people, but let us put the knowledge to work in our country.'[7]

Despite these influences it is true to say that throughout the years Indian cinema has shown a remarkable resistance to Hollywood cultural imperialism. Since it could build its own distribution networks capable of sustaining the industry—within India and throughout much of Asia, the Middle East and Africa—its conventions could develop without conforming to expectations of wider international audiences. While most film-makers have openly borrowed some elements from Hollywood and elsewhere, successful films always 'Indianised' such borrowings through integration within what evolved as Indian conventions. The Wadias' films starring Fearless Nadia exemplify this process.

WADIA MOVIETONE AND NADIA

When Nadia arrived in Bombay in 1934, the Wadia Movietone studio was buzzing. Foreign dignitaries were welcome guests and JBH openly acknowledged the influence of Hollywood film-makers such as Douglas Fairbanks. But the studio also prided itself on its home-grown talent: local musicians, theatre writers and self-taught film technicians. The ambience fitted well with Nadia's own culturally heterogeneous background.

Nadia was born Mary Evans in Perth in 1908[8] to a Greek mother and British father, arriving in India in 1911 with her father's army unit. Following his death on the French battlefields in 1915, Mary's mother, a one-time belly dancer, decided to settle in Bombay where her daughter became a weekly boarder at Claire Road convent school. In 1922, they joined an uncle, an army veterinarian in Peshawar, and Mary spent an idyllic adolescence learning dancing, horse riding and other outdoor skills from her army friends. She was also an enthusiastic movie fan, enviously enjoying the exploits of Pearl White in *Perils of Pauline* (Louis J. Gasnier, 1914) and Ruth Roland's *Adventures of Ruth* (George Marshall, 1919). Back in Bombay in 1926 with a baby son, Bobby, politely referred to as her 'brother', she needed work. Finding shop life at the Army and Navy Stores too dull and law office work stultifying, she decided to take up her hobby, dancing, professionally. She toured the country first with Madame Astrova's Russian ballet troupe, making her name as an acrobat, singer and dancer. After a brief stint with Isako's circus she became a vaudeville singer and dancer touring army and civilian clubs and cinemas, where she might sing playback to silent stars or perform risqué songs in Hindustani. After flirting with a number of names, including the highly inappropriate Carmen Miranda—'Quite ridiculous, I didn't look at all Spanish'—she became Nadia, a name suggested by an Armenian fortune-teller who promised it would bring her fame and fortune. Mary was pleased because 'Nadia ... was accepted as being both Indian and foreign enough'.[9] In 1934, her screen potential was spotted by the manager of Regal Theatres, Lahore, Mr Kanga, who offered to introduce her to his old friend, J.B.H. Wadia. Nadia recalls her first visit.

> I was very nervous when Kanga told me he had organised a meeting with these Wadia brothers. While I had never heard of them myself or seen any of their films, my friends on hearing about my audition said that they were a reputable firm. I remember catching the tram. ... Parel was a very posh area and the studio was located right next to the Governor's Palace of that time ... [and] was surrounded by miles of green paddy fields.... I recall wearing this lovely blue sun dress that I had treated myself to and this white fedora with a sunflower arrangement. When I got off the tram Mr Kanga was waiting for me in his bright red Chrysler and we drove in through the large wrought iron gates [of] the studio.... I had expected to see tin sheds as I had previously seen when I had gone to see some shooting at the Imperial Studio in the silent days but here was this massive mansion of stone, very imposing and all.[10]

The meeting was a success. The brothers were clearly captivated by her sense of fun, charming lack of deference and plucky 'can-do' attitude, as well as her obvious stage talents: singing, dancing, gymnastics and a wonderful curvaceous body that she displayed with little inhibition. She was hired at Rs 150 per month on condition that she passed a screen test.

JBH clearly had qualms about introducing a buxom, blue-eyed, blonde as an Indian heroine. Nadia herself noted that he seemed surprised when she arrived: 'I don't think he expected me to be quite so large or fair.' The screen test seven days later was apparently disastrous, her Hindi diction laughable. She was told she would have to work hard with a voice coach on her Hindi, to change her name and to wear a wig or dye her hair: 'Otherwise people will think you are a *buddhi*.'[11] She claims she did try an auburn tint but it went lighter than before so she decided to let it be. But she flatly refused a black wig with long plaits: 'Look here Mr Wadia, I am a white woman and I'll look foolish with long black hair.' She also refused to change her name to the Hinduised Nanda Devi: 'That's not part of my contract. Nadia rhymes with Wadia and besides ... I'm no *devi*.'[12]

At the time she arrived, Wadia Movietone was still flush with *Lal-e-Yaman*'s success and was attempting to capitalise on this with further *Arabian Nights* and Islamicate melodramas. JBH decided to try Nadia out with a tiny role in his orientalist historical, *Desh Deepak/Josh-e-Watan* (Light of the Homeland, J.B.H. Wadia, 1935), a costume melodrama being shot at the studios in collaboration with Joseph David. Although she had only three minutes of screen time, Nadia's sequence—as a skimpily clad slave girl and nationalist supporter—hit the cinemas in full colour. Wadia had organised hand-colouring on twenty-five prints, emphasising her golden curls, bright blue eyes and ample flesh spilling out of a tight *choli* and diaphanous golden sarong. As a slave market auctioneer details Nadia's considerable physical charms, the camera obliges us with cutaway close-ups on her teeth, her mouth, her eyes. JBH had already decided on the two features that, together, would sell Nadia to Indian audiences: a voluptuous white body and populist nationalism. Audiences went wild and fan mail started pouring in, especially from the North-Western Provinces where she already had a reputation as a stage performer.

With her additional success as Princess Parizad in the *Arabian Nights* fantasy sequel to *Lal-e-Yaman*, titled *Noor-e-Yaman* (Light of Yemen, J.B.H. Wadia, 1935), playing a small role in which she had to speak, sing, dance and cry,[13] J.B.H. Wadia felt confident enough to let Nadia take the lead in the remake of his final silent film success, *Dilruba Daku/The Amazon* (A.H. Essa, 1933), which had introduced a swashbuckling female lead for the studio's 'beautiful and doll-like' Bengali star, Padma, resplendent in mask and sword. Openly inspired by both *Mark of Zorro* (Fred Niblo, 1920) and *The Perils of Pauline*, the new script was *Hunterwali*. Twenty-four-year-old Homi Wadia was chosen to direct this, only his second 'talkie' film. Shooting began as soon as a gap appeared in the studio schedules and, carried away by enthusiastic reports from the floor and impressive rushes, JBH extended the production period from six weeks to six months as songs and a romantic subplot (starring another actress) were added. However, when the film was finished his business partner, Bilimoria, got cold feet about Nadia, considering her feisty persona too risky in the Indian context: 'An Indian woman doing all that fighting—the public may not like it. We must sell the picture.' Fortunately for the Wadias there were no serious takers and they were forced to release the picture themselves, thereby retaining for Wadia Movietone one of the biggest box-office hits of the decade.

NATIONALIST POLITICS

Over the next few years, a run of stunt and action films—with and without Nadia—enriched the studios, which produced around six films a year. Nationalism and the freedom movement were a constant subtext of the 1930s Wadia Movietone films, including *Hunterwali*. Like many in the film industry, the Wadias were early Congress supporters and these beliefs underpinned their films. Although strict British censorship forbade overt references to the freedom movement, film-makers of the 1930s and 1940s would slip casual references to Congress songs and symbols into the soundtrack or screen. A princess rescuing an oppressed kingdom from a wicked foreign tyrant would have obvious resonances in 1930s India.[14] Nadia saw her role—on screen and off—as supporting the nationalist movement and stated explicitly, 'In all the pictures there was a propaganda message, something to fight for, for example for people to educate themselves or to become a strong nation.'[15]

Socially responsible themes were becoming de rigueur at this time for producers who wanted critical status. The 1936 box-office and critical success of Devika Rani's *Achhut Kanya* had upped the stakes and, while Wadia Movietone's reputation for 'cheap' films for the 'masses' was unassailable, Bombay Talkies—and other studios making socials, such as Prabhat—were considered more respectable. JBH responded to *Achhut Kanya* with a jokey twist on the caste theme in *Hurricane Hansa* (R.N. Vaidya, 1937) in which Nadia plays a harijan[16] girl who transforms her name from 'harijan Hansa' to 'Hurricane Hansa', dons her trademark mask and takes revenge on a villain who had destroyed her family.

Inspired by the ideas of the radical Bengali Marxist and humanist M.N. Roy, JBH left the Congress Party and in 1940 became a founder member of Roy's Radical Democratic Party.[17] As his political commitment grew, JBH became increasingly frustrated with his own film-making. While he wanted to follow his peers and make socials, his business partners had no intention of killing the golden goose—theirs was the most profitable studio of the day. Reluctantly they allowed JBH one non-stunt film a year. His formal experiment *Naujawan* (Youth, Aspi, 1937), billed as the first Indian sound film without songs, had been a flop. He now focused on infusing his stunt films with social issues: Nadia starred in *Lootaru Lalna* (Dacoit Damsel, Homi Wadia, 1938), taking on the explosive issue of Hindu–Muslim unity, and in *Punjab Mail* (Homi Wadia, 1939) (Figure 4.2), attacking

The one and only Fearless NADIA.

Figure 4.2   The one and only Fearless Nadia
(*Punjab Mail*, 1939)

Source: © Roy Wadia/Wadia Movietone.

the class system and championing women's rights.[18] The influence of M.N. Roy's humanist ideas became increasingly visible, culminating in *Diamond Queen* (Homi Wadia, 1940), which dealt with women's emancipation and presented the tough and capable Nadia for the first time without her whip and mask. This film hit the jackpot of combining box-office glory with the critical acclaim JBH so desired, prompting even the usually acerbic *Film India* to praise 'a thought-provoking film that enlightens as it entertains'.[19]

With *Diamond Queen's* success—and the fact that wartime film stock rationing limited studios to two films per producer—Homi was promoted from director to producer. JBH became actively involved in the war effort, chairing the Film Advisory Board and making pro-war documentaries.[20] Wadia Movietone became increasingly schizophrenic as the two brothers followed their own paths. Homi, flush with the success of the latest Nadia films, pursued ever more extravagant production values. For *Bombaiwali* (Woman from Bombay, Homi Wadia, 1941) and *Jungle Princess* (Homi Wadia, 1942) he constructed fine sets and brought in a host of new special effect technicians—clever local boys such as Babubhai Mistry—building a forty-foot jungle model for an ambitious storm in the jungle and introducing high-speed car chases. However, JBH's authorial hand on script and screenplay simultaneously reduced the number of stunts and increased the 'plausibility' and social themes of these stories. The industry believed the stunt film was dead and the comparatively small profits made by these two films appeared to confirm the view. Primarily to augment their raw stock allocation, the brothers set up Basant Pictures in 1942, initially geared to producing more socials. Notionally Homi's company, JBH was in fact a silent partner.[21]

However, JBH's central obsession was his radical project, *Raj Natarki* aka *Court Dancer* (Madhu Bose, 1941), a prestige production on which he was relying for the intellectual and critical credibility that still eluded him. Starring celebrated classical dancer Sadhana Bose and top thespian Prithviraj Kapoor, JBH boasted this was the first Indian film shot simultaneously in English, Bengali and Hindi. His final coup was to secure it, as a 100 per cent English-language film, a US and European distribution deal through Columbia in Hollywood. The film undoubtedly helped to redeem his reputation with the Bombay intelligentsia but, although it recouped its costs across three language versions, a crisis was brewing at Wadia Movietone. While JBH wanted to pursue the now fashionable social melodramas, Homi and Bilimoria wanted to go aggressively for box-office hits. In Autumn 1942, the company was split. With the box-office failure just months later of Basant's first film, *Mauj* (Wave, Batuk/Nanabhai Bhatt and Babubhai Mistry, 1943), a social drama in which the Wadias experimented with Nadia playing a vampish femme fatale, JBH suggested cancelling the stunt stars' contracts. At this point the brothers fell out, their differences apparently irresolvable.

Homi, ever loyal to Nadia, who was by now also his long-term lover and unofficial partner, decided to concentrate on making the most

Figure 4.3   Poster of *Hunterwali ki Beti* (1943)

Source: © Basant Pictures. Courtesy Roy Wadia and Wadia Movietone.

of his assets: the stunt star contracts. He decided to follow a hunch that what a sizeable section of the audience really wanted was the old whip-cracking Nadia. He suspected that if produced cheaply enough the films could make money. Produced on a shoestring, *Hunterwali ki Beti* (Daughter of Woman with the Whip, Batuk/Nanabhai Bhatt, 1943) (Figure 4.3) was an immediate success and Homi had found his formula. Cheap, quickly-made action, stunt, jungle and fantasy films followed and Basant went from strength to strength with such films as *Flying Prince* (Homi Wadia, 1946), *Tigress* (K. Talpade, 1948), *11 o'clock* (Homi Wadia, 1948), *Baghdad ka Jadoo* (The Magic of Baghdad, John Cawas, 1956) and *Circus Queen* (Nosir Engineer, 1956). Meanwhile, JBH's fortunes at Wadia Movietone dwindled and by 1946 he had to sell his studio buildings to his old rival, V. Shantaram. The brothers had by now teamed up again and, following the 1948 success of *Shri Ram Bhakta Hanuman* (Homi Wadia), they discovered a lucrative market niche in quality mythologicals—and from the 1950s onwards *Arabian Nights* fantasy films—which sustained Basant for many years. Meanwhile, Homi continued to knock out cheap action films for Nadia until she retired in 1959.[22]

TWO VISIONS

The split between the Wadia brothers is invariably characterised as the clash of two visions. Homi was the shy, conservative, technical genius and astute business brain who left school at sixteen, unashamedly loved lowbrow entertainment and despised intellectual pretensions. J.B.H. Wadia, MA, LLB, was the self-assured, cultured, radical humanist, a teacher and writer who craved critical acclaim and international recognition. The situation was, in fact, more complex as JBH was himself torn between the high ideals of his political and intellectual passions and his own love of Hollywood entertainment and brilliant understanding of the popular Indian imagination.

This perceived conflict between 'respectability' and 'popularity'— or profit—echoed that between professionals and the business community, the two emergent and competing forces of urban India, and permeated contemporary thinking. On release the press had applauded Wadia Movietone's distinctly melodramatic *Lal-e-Yaman* for being a 'serious drama' rather than a 'cheap' stunt film.[23] Rajadhyaksha has described how Bombay film melodrama became 'the privileged form of representation' for the nationalist consciousness.[24] In the Indian context, melodramatic 'socials' became equated with 'realism' and were harnessed to the nationalist project with a mission to project images not of what is, but of what India *should* be. As Chakravarty puts it: 'Realism is the masquerading moral conscience of the Indian intelligentsia in their assumed (though not uncontested) role of national leadership during the fifties.'[25] Film history was rewritten to celebrate the golden age of 'realist' 1930s socials. Bombay Talkies eclipsed Wadia Movietone.

At stake were two different visions of the nationalist project— and two different relationships to modernity and the West. 'India is most truly national when it is international', Nehru famously wrote, but the tug between national self-definition and global modernity could be articulated in different ways. JBH straddled the two. Like the European-educated Congress intellectuals of the 1930s, he saw the nation-building project as comprising humanist social reform at home and proud display of modern India's classical heritage abroad. Modernity meant a national self-definition that drew on the roots of a 'pure' tradition, setting these within 'modern' European social values: a humanistic and scientific worldview. This worthy vision valued 'realist' melodramas on social issues and orientalised classical dance films for European audiences.

However, JBH also understood market forces and saw that popular passions would be the seed of new modernities that could not be neatly controlled from the centre. He valued aspects of the West that the intellectuals dismissed as Hollywood 'trash', as well as popular Indian entertainment forms. It appears that he brilliantly understood hybridity and recognised that national identities would be forged through playful negotiation, rather than simply imposed from above. This vision of modern India drew comfortably on global popular culture but looked to its home markets, rather than the international stage, for its validation.

While wholeheartedly celebrating the remarkable achievements of Indian film-makers, JBH unashamedly paid homage to Hollywood pioneers of technical skills and storytelling conventions naming, amongst others, Charlie Chaplin, Douglas Fairbanks, Harold Lloyd and D.W. Griffiths.[26] He also openly acknowledged the influences of character and storyline: as we have seen, Nadia was billed as the 'Indian Pearl White', her co-star John Cawas as the 'Indian Eddie Polo'.[27] Moreover, JBH spoke uninhibitedly about adapting such films as *Mark of Zorro* and the Tarzan series for Indian audiences. This might be seen as an example of the mimicry we associate with sites of anti-colonial struggle, but it was also sharp marketing: these were huge brand names and the Wadias understood their value. At the same time, they knew how to 'Indianise'—in subject matter and in form. Their films were, at their core, sites of negotiation of a new Indian modernity: alongside Hollywood they drew on Urdu-Parsi theatre (via Joseph David), Indian myth and legend and contemporary political debate.

While both visions acknowledged the transnational, the first was largely premised on an essentialised Indian cultural tradition, while the second better recognised the hybridity and fluidity within the porous borders of this modern 'India'. The former tended towards melodrama as a film form, the latter action, comedy and masquerade. As Vijay Mishra has noted, stunt films are 'the only form [in Indian cinema history] that arguably escapes from [melodramatic] staging'.[28] The Wadias' films embodied an ongoing tension between these two forms and the two visions of the transnational arena. Fearless Nadia was constructed within the framework of this dual vision.

THE NADIA PERSONA

Nadia was undoubtedly the Wadias' most brilliant discovery and creation. If they were looking for an Indian heroine, she was not an obvious choice, and at first sight perhaps the strangest aspect of the Nadia phenomenon was that, despite her indisputable whiteness, she was so easily accepted as an Indian heroine in films that were read by many audiences as anti-British allegories.

From the start her ethnicity was an issue for the Wadias and Indianising her was a conscious project: hair colour, name, Hindi diction were all areas they sought to control. Interestingly, while JBH's original concern had been that Nadia might appear too European for Indian audiences, on *Hunterwali*'s release Bilimoria was worried that audiences might reject her for behaviour inappropriate to an *Indian* woman.[29] A number of strategies were used to fix her identity as Indian. Taking no chances, *Hunterwali*'s promotional booklet introduced her as a 'brave Indian girl who sacrificed royal luxuries to the cause of her people and her country'. As the films went on she was increasingly referred to as 'Bombaiwali' (the woman from Bombay), connoting cosmopolitan sophistication and modernity, thereby justifying her apparent transgressions of traditional Indian female dress codes and mores, while retaining her as an all-Indian heroine. A certain fluidity did accompany her physical appearance in posters and on screen: although she was adamant about refusing a wig, in posters her hair was sometimes hand-coloured light brown and, in black and white films, shadows could render her colouring ambiguous. The mask itself helped weaken the visual impact of her ethnic identity. In fact, in the context of the nationalist movement, Nadia's heroism and support of the underdog was almost enough in itself to place her on the Indian side. Girish Karnad recalls:

The single most memorable sound of my childhood is the clarion call of Hey-y-y as Fearless Nadia, regal upon her horse, her hand raised defiantly in the air, rode down upon the bad guys. To us school kids of the mid-forties Fearless Nadia meant courage, strength, idealism.[30]

However, her Western looks were undeniably part of her exotic appeal and, in choosing her, the Wadias were involved in a careful calculation. Billing her as India's Pearl White, they could attract to their films all the glamour of the Pearl White brand and the exoticism of the 'white *mem*' while simultaneously constructing an all-Indian Nadia. Played cleverly, they could have it both ways, conflating two traditions: the Hollywood stunt queen (and by implication the whole Hollywood stunt genre—her persona referred as much to Fairbanks as to White) and the legendary Indian warrior woman. Through these a cosmopolitan modern femininity could be forged.

The Wadias did not invent the masked fighting woman. This was a well-established convention of the silent cinema and Wadia's *Dilruba Daku/The Amazon*, *Hunterwali*'s immediate predecessor, was part of a contemporary vogue for warrior women, known as viranganas.[31] Kathryn Hansen, in her study of Nautanki theatre, describes how historical and legendary figures from various eras and different parts of India (from Razia Sultana to Lakshmibai, Queen of Jhansi) fed the imagery and stories of a significant body of work within popular theatre and early cinema, as well as folk songs, comic books and calendar art.[32] The virangana prototype describes a good queen, who takes over the throne when a male kinsman dies, leads her people into battle dressed as a man, displays astonishing military skills and dies defending her kingdom against invaders. The key image—a turbaned woman on horseback brandishing a sword above her head—has been enthusiastically exploited by female politicians over the years, notably Indira Gandhi.

British government censorship of overt references to the nationalist movement fuelled the popularity of virangana stories in all forms of popular entertainment between 1910 and 1940, as figures such as the Queen of Jhansi had become a focus for nationalist activism.[33] Thus, fictionalised biographies of historical and legendary female warriors as well as fictional warrior queens, princesses and female outlaws became popular staples of early cinema.[34]

Hansen suggests that the distinction between different conceptions of *sat* (truth) generally considered appropriate to men and women is key to understanding what she refers to as 'this startling counterparadigm of Indian womanhood'.[35] The virangana, usually dressed as a male, is seen to operate within the widest sphere of morality, the upholding of justice and truth (*sat*), in a way which is more usually associated with men, rather than *stridharma*, the traditional female sphere of sat, which proposes passive suffering, sexual fidelity and chastity for the sati (woman who embodies sat). As the virangana's status derives from her own noble deeds rather than her relationship to a man, she is allowed an independence denied other women. Four aspects of this counterparadigm are relevant to Nadia.

The first concerns the body. Hansen writes: 'The virangana ideal commends physical training and active deployment of the body in combat.'[36] Nadia's proud display of a muscular and athletic body, her fighting skills and championing of exercise and gym sessions are pure virangana. Like her American counterparts, Pearl White and Douglas

Figure 4.4   Still of *Hunterwali* (1935)

Source: © Roy Wadia/Wadia Movietone.

Fairbanks, she was always admired for doing all her own stunts,[37] and was, from the first, identified with her body and its power, in a way that heroines such as Devika Rani (who frequently suffered and died) were not. Secondly, the virangana shows moral strength. 'The virangana arrives not simply when force is required but when moral order needs to be restored.'[38] Nadia always occupies the position of moral strength within her films—she rights wrongs and restores order and justice, being introduced from her first *Hunterwali* appearance as a 'protector of the poor and punisher of evildoers'. Thirdly, the virangana has unprecedented sexual freedom. 'Because her virtue is not reducible to the sexual transactions of the female body, physical relations cannot impugn her truth.'[39] In the virangana tradition sexuality is irrelevant—women can have lovers without being defined by their sexual transgressions. While her sexuality was not explicitly marked within the films' diegeses, Nadia's on-screen sexual and erotic appeal was enormous—she could carry off an (almost) nude bathing scene in *Hunterwali* and still be seen by fans as 'voluptuous but prim' (Figure 4.4).

Finally, the virangana cross-dresses. 'The virangana ... in these dramas claims male positions for the female body; she rides on horseback, wears male dress, wields weapons ordinarily carried by men.'[40] Nadia regularly wore masculinised clothing, especially in confrontations with the villains. This ranged from riding breeches and hacking jackets to sailor suits or Fairbanks-style cloaks and swords. However, Nadia invariably played a split persona, with either a double life (*Hunterwali*) or the complex Bombaiwali construction (*Diamond Queen*), so she also regularly wore a sari—the ultimate signifier of Indian femininity.[41]

Even the Wadias underestimated the extent to which the virangana ideal underpinned and legitimised Nadia's persona, discovering to their cost how limited a range of roles she could play. While she could champion the cause of the oppressed on almost any issue—from caste to class, from anti-communalism to women's issues—she was never allowed to show weakness. 'Nadia cannot cry', one distributor exclaimed, insisting an emotional scene in *Mauj* be cut from the final film. Moreover, while she could wear clothes that revealed more female flesh than any other Indian actress of her day and her image was undeniably erotically charged, her appearance as a 'vamp', smoking, drinking and flirting as part of a double role in *Muqabla* (Competition, Batuk/Nanabhai Bhatt and Babubhai Mistry, 1942), was not a box-office success. She had to be emphatically coded as the 'good girl', albeit only within the conventions of virangana morality. A telling anecdote describes how, in later years, a churlish Homi responded to his brother's request that he direct a mythological for him with the retort, 'only if Nadia plays Sita'—a calculatedly provocative suggestion as the Ramayana heroine, Sita, is the embodiment of stridharma, becoming a sati by walking into fire to prove her chastity.

In an earlier essay examining the contradictions within the star persona of Nadia, I had proposed two answers to the question of her popularity as an icon within a nationalist context despite her whiteness.[42] First, as a white woman her status was liminal—the threat of her physical prowess could be contained and her sexuality could be vicariously enjoyed. Her whiteness, simultaneously recognised and disavowed, undoubtedly underpinned the ambivalent frisson of her erotic appeal, the classic colonial miscegenation fantasy. Second, her identity was fixed within the films' diegeses through identifying her not with whiteness but with the cosmopolitanism and modernity of the Bombaiwali. What the Wadias spotted was the potential to build Nadia as a virangana for a modern world. The Wadia films are importantly a reverie of potency within modernity and Nadia was, throughout the films, associated with a gamut of signifiers of Western technology: cars, planes and, importantly, trains.

Partha Chatterjee has described how developments within the nationalist movement of nineteenth-century Bengal created the figure of a 'new Indian woman'. Identified with spiritual qualities symbolised by the 'home', she could preserve the purity of an essentialised Indian culture while allowing Indian men to operate in the Westernised 'world' of rationality and technological progress.[43] Although this formulation empowered middle-class women to benefit from education and equality in the workplace as well as to champion social reform, the power of (at least mainstream versions of) the new nationalist woman lay ultimately in embracing a more limited and essentialised femininity, and was consequently comparatively constrained. This was a different model from the virangana counterparadigm that implied recognition of gender ambivalence and multiple models of femininity. The distinction is relevant to the comparison between Nadia and stars of the melodramatic social films, notably Devika Rani.

While Devika Rani's modernity constructed her as both a cipher for humanist values and fount of purity within an orientalised 'tradition', Nadia's was firmly situated within the (male, Western) world of technological progress, where she was unambiguously in control, whether driving a car or riding the roof of a hurtling train. Fearless Nadia was frequently shown running triumphantly along the tops of trains, fist-fighting her male tormentors, parading burly men high above her shoulders before chucking them to their deaths on the tracks below. While Devika's attempts to challenge traditional orthodoxies in *Achhut Kanya* left her crushed under the wheels of an oncoming train, the tragically wronged woman, a victim of social ills, Nadia championed the oppressed and effected change in the world from the giddy heights of the train roof, empowered rather than crushed by technology.

The significance of both stars as key icons of the era emerges through Qurratulain Hyder's autobiographical essay, *Memories of an Indian Childhood*. Devika Rani is remembered for her family background, *Achhut Kanya* being one of the few films Hyder's parents allowed her to watch on the grounds that 'India had at last entered the era of cultural revolution because Gurudev's [Tagore's] own niece had become a cinema actress'.[44] Meanwhile 'Miss Nadia of *Hunterwali* fame' was a cultural reference point against which children compared the skills of a local circus Well (*sic*) of Death motorbike queen. In what appears as a dichotomy between substance and performance, Devika's significance stemmed from her social status as an upper-middle-class Brahmin—*who she was*—and Nadia's from her body and its skills—*what she could do*.

DIAMOND QUEEN

Diamond Queen, often celebrated as the Wadias' best film, and probably the most seamless fusion of the brothers' two visions, offers fascinating insights into the balancing act that was the Nadia persona. It was the seventh in the Diamond Thriller series that began with Homi's first sound film, *Veer Bharat* (Indian Warrior, Homi Wadia, 1934). *Hunterwali* had been the second and audiences were by now fond of its cast of side characters: the faithful horse, Punjab ka Beta (Son of the Punjab), a baby Austin car christened Rolls Royce ki Beti (Daughter of Rolls Royce) and Moti, the plucky dog.

In *Diamond Queen* Nadia plays Madhurika, a modern cosmopolitan girl who returns to her small town, Diamond Town, after five years of education in Bombay. She finds the people terrorised by villain Kedarnath and his gang, who have taken over the kingdom during the ten years that the good prince has been abroad. Their corrupt and decadent regime sabotages local literacy campaigns, steals taxes from the poor and threatens the chastity of local women. Madhurika links up with Diler, a bandit with a heart of gold and his own reasons for seeking revenge, to expose Kedarnath's corruption and restore order. With the help of her friends including Miss Radha, the pretty school teacher, Radha's father Sevakram, a respected elder of the community, and Prince Ranjiit Singh who has disguised himself as a Westernised bumbling fool in order to find out the truth about Kedarnath's rule, Madhurika defeats the villains and allows the good prince to return and rule benignly. In the process she espouses the causes of women's independence, education and physical exercise programmes.

Madhurika is undoubtedly the film's central pivot. Although Diler's life story bookends the film—his boyhood and his marriage—Madhurika is the Diamond Queen of the film's title and focus of the villain's wrath. 'I fear bandit Diler less than the free and fearless Madhurika—her poisonous thinking will spread through Diamond Town unless we get rid of her,'[45] Kedarnath snarls from his palatial den. Madhurika motivates the action and *she* ultimately kills Kedarnath.

Madhurika is visually constructed within virangana codes. We first meet her through a sequence of eroticised body parts emphasising her physical strength: a close-up of a white fist, swiftly followed by a muscular arm which lands a sharp punch in the face of the lascivious brute who is threatening to abduct Miss Radha. The camera moves to Madhurika's feet as she crushes a male hand attempting to grab a fallen knife, then pans slowly up her body—wide black trousers, taut across her large hips, tight white blouse and big bosom, natty neck-scarf and brooch—eventually revealing a regal blonde dominatrix, high cheekbones, aquiline Greek nose, tight blonde curls. When she has disposed of the villains—kicked, thrown and spectacularly detrousered—she greets her father's and friends' astonishment at the way she's changed in Bombay with a smile and the casual throwaway, 'I've been training in a women's gym.'[46]

Madhurika unequivocally upholds the moral order. She punishes villainy and protects and rescues the vulnerable good: virtuous young women who epitomise Indian traditional arts and culture (Miss Radha), tortured animals (her horse, Punjab ka Beta), benevolent wise old men (Sevakram) and the community itself that has been cheated for years by their corrupt rulers. While Diler enthusiastically supports Madhurika, seeing her as a potential partner in his own lone campaign to rid Diamond Town of its corrupt rulers, as well as a future lover and wife, she primly rejects his criminal methods. Demurely draped in a white embroidered sari and sporting a halo of backlit blonde curls,[47] she entreats him to give himself up to the law. 'A criminal cannot arrest a criminal,' she gently cajoles. Only when he has paid his dues in jail will she consider marrying him. Throughout the final assault on the villains Madhurika is at the helm: she organises her gang, draws up the plans, is at the driving wheel

Figure 4.5 Nadia with co-star John Cawas. A still from
Diamond Queen (1940).

Source: © Roy Wadia/Wadia Movietone.

throughout the car chase and finally wrestles Kedarnath to his death
on top of a hurtling tonga, with Diler looking on admiringly.

Comparison with Nadia's Hollywood counterparts, notably the
Pearl White character in the *Perils of Pauline* serials, is relevant here.
Although Nadia was always accompanied by a male hero, usually
John Cawas, for romantic interest (Figure 4.5), we see here that
Nadia was primarily a fighter and rather more than Pearl White's
plucky daredevil stunt woman. Nadia was always the primary agent
of the villains' demise and as likely to rescue her hero as be rescued.
Invariably, a second heroine, in this case Miss Radha, provided the
focus for romance, emotion and song and dance in Nadia's films.

Two narrative threads run through *Diamond Queen*, both set up in
an intriguing opening scene in which mother, father and boy child,
Diler, are having dinner in their simple hut in a rural paradise. The
utopian family romance is shattered when the father's treacherous
business partner, Kedarnath, bursts in and, wanting their gold-mining
spoils for himself, shoots both parents. In the ensuing scuffle between
boy Diler and villain Kedarnath the hut catches fire, but Diler escapes,
having promised his dying father that he will take revenge. The rest
of the film unfolds sixteen years later.

An opening reel which sets up the action—and the polarities of good and evil—in the hero's childhood is usual within Indian cinema conventions. Here we find a schematic equilibrium and disruption: happy family life in harmony with nature is disrupted by the villain's greed and insensitivity to family and friendship loyalties. But in *Diamond Queen*, unusually, a second discordant note also surfaces. As boy Diler excitedly chatters about the freedom he has to roam and play in the jungle, the mother, most uncharacteristically for the genre, complains: 'You may enjoy it but it's hard work for me.' We discover they are about to leave the jungle paradise because she will no longer tolerate her unequal workload, raising the spectre of women challenging their traditional subservient roles.[48]

These two narrative threads need resolution: treachery and greed must be punished by destroying the villains, and a viable model of contemporary Indian womanhood must be held together. While in most films the boy hero grows up to effect narrative resolution, here the eruption of women's issues changes things: neither Diler nor any of the other men in this film can fully restore order. Only Madhurika has the physical and moral power to resolve both threads.

Madhurika sets out her terms in her first scene. When the disgruntled boor she has just pulped complains of the insult to his virility: '*main mard hoon, mard*',[49] Madhurika retorts with what, within the 1940s context, appears astonishing: 'Hey mister, don't think today's women are so weak they'll submit to the brutality of men.... if India is to be free, women must be given their freedom.... if you try and stop them you'll face the consequences.'

Thread one, the fight between good and evil, is told through action scenes which push the narrative forward, where Madhurika, in her most masculinised outfits, challenges the tyranny of the villains. These include scenes of greatest tension: fights, car chases and choreographed swashbuckling, building excitement through skilful editing and intercutting storylines. Madhurika wears eroticised, Westernised clothes: trousers and blouse in two key scenes, riding breeches and hacking jacket in a third, while for the only other major showdown with the villains she wears the knee-length black dress in which she kills Kedarnath. In these revealing costumes she performs all her most physically demanding feats, while simultaneously commanding the moral authority of the film. Douglas Fairbanks meets the virangana queen.

Thread two, which challenges outdated traditions, notably women's subservient roles, unfolds predominantly through spectacular excess—songs, love scenes, slapstick—a combination of melodrama and comedy.[50] A mostly sari-clad Madhurika challenges, negotiates with and supports a range of ineffectually 'modern' Indians: her father, Diler, Miss Radha, Sevakram and Prince Ranjiit—all in varying degrees sympathetic to radical reform but unable to make this happen without Bombaiwali Madhurika. The success of the film's ideological project depends, to some extent, on how skilfully this thread is integrated into the body of the film and resolved within the moral order.

Two of the film's four songs openly advocate nationalist, reformist messages about education and exercise, and are barely contained within the diegesis. At a literacy campaign concert, the lovely schoolteacher, Miss Radha, performs a classical Indian dance to a song exhorting the townspeople to 'forge ahead a path of reading and writing ... for ... the pen is mightier than the sword', while her father, a socially enlightened community leader, lectures his audience, 'education is the first step to freedom ... vital to solve the country's problems ... knowledge is power'. Later, in Miss Radha's school playground, quasi-militaristic rows of children stretch, bend and march to patriotic music, a final Busby Berkeley–style top-shot revealing a swastika formation.[51] The song's words proclaim,

> Thank the Lord for exercise, all hail God Hanuman—to exercise is to live in bliss, always be courageous, banish weakness, be brave and strong ... let strength be your weapon—the pride of the nation is the power of its people.

Other encounters play through comedy, notably scenes where modern femininity is a point of issue, particularly sequences of Madhurika with her father and, more ambivalently, modern friends. Her father, incensed by her clothes and insistence on love marriage and an independent life beyond his authority, becomes a running joke, a rather ridiculous, reactionary old goat, mocked by the townsfolk, cheeked by Madhurika, unable to see the error of his ways or accept his 'free and fearless' daughter. Good Prince Ranjiit, disguised as a 'foreign-returned' buffoon in stripy blazer, brolly and absurd black specs, suffers Madhurika's playful, slapstick put-downs, as she deftly throws him over her sari-clad shoulder or trips him up, until he finally redeems himself—through humility, generosity, support of Madhurika and love of Radha—and turns into a benign and enlightened ruler, deserving of his kingdom.[52] There is also a comedy subplot that provides a surreal shadow of—and comment on—the main action through half a dozen comic characters who, in nonsensical vein, discourse on colonialism and women's rights.

Two romantic subplots also contribute to this thread. In her one love scene with Diler, a glamorous Madhurika in dramatic black sari and bindi, her tight, dark-looking curls profiled against a spectacular waterfall, shows the modern Indian woman in control as she leans to kiss Diler—before the camera quickly pans away across the rocky landscape to find her father, anxious for a showdown with her: 'Is this how you use your education?' On the other hand, Miss Radha and Prince Ranjiit's romance is played more conventionally, through misunderstandings and a melancholic love song, but is no less an exploration of the boundaries of modern relationships between the sexes.

Ultimately, the two threads work together to contain the radical ideas within a traditional moral order—but only just holding these ideas together. Madhurika's apparent transgressions of traditional values are justified by a greater moral and political vision than her father's. Despite her rebelliousness, she ultimately saves the community and gets married, although the farcically schematic nature of this coupling—Madhurika seated in white sari and bindi beside a miraculously transformed bandit Diler, who now wears a Western suit and tie, with Miss Radha and Prince Ranjiit in traditional Hindu wedding clothes beside them—is underlined by two comedy couples larking about on a tree behind them, a gentle parody of the main action.

However, it is the tag 'Bombaiwali' which does most to legitimise and redeem Madhurika's rebelliousness and fix a revised model of contemporary Indian feminine identity. She may be as 'foreign' as Pearl White and Douglas Fairbanks and as 'traditional' as India's warrior women, but she is ultimately Bombaiwali, the epitome of Indian cosmopolitan sophistication and modernity, and a fiery nationalist to boot. The excessive potency—and ambivalence—of her image warrants further exploration.

MIMICRY

Parama Roy, drawing on the work of Homi Bhabha and others on colonial mimicry, argues that, if we are to understand the formation of Indian national identities, we need to examine not just Anglicisation but the variety of forms of impersonation and mimicry that exist alongside this. She aims to 'open up the field of identity formation and nation formation to a more heterogeneous model than that of Anglicization' and suggests that:

> [impersonation] is … central to the ways in which nationalism imagines itself: hence the production of the nation is almost invariably mediated … through such practices as Gandhi's impersonation of femininity, an Irishwoman's assumption of Hindu feminine celibacy, or a Muslim actress's emulation of a Hindu/Indian mother goddess.[53]

The Wadias were, at one level, brilliant, Anglicising mimic men. Hollywood was their acknowledged role model and JBH, on at least one occasion, produced orientalist fare for European approval.[54] However, their films were also rich vehicles for far wider forms of mimicry and impersonation. Fearless Nadia directly reverses (and broadly challenges) the mimicry of Anglicisation: white woman mimics Indian woman. But her persona is also a conflation of other impersonations: white woman mimics white man (Douglas Fairbanks), white woman (Pearl White), Indian woman (Jhansi ki Rani—the virangana) and Indian man (masked heroine disguised as a man).

In hiring Nadia, JBH had demonstrated an astute, if unstated, understanding of the potential fluidity offered by Nadia's whiteness.

White memsahibs had been a popular exotic feature of Urdu-Parsi theatre since the early years of the century and, in the context of the nationalist movement of the day, his decision was not inherently risky. Many nationalist men had white European wives or followers—both of M.N. Roy's wives were white Westerners while Vivekananda's most loyal disciple, Nivedita, was an Irish woman. Parama Roy, in tracing the relationship between Vivekananda and Nivedita, describes how he recruited her in London in 1897, as 'a real lioness, to work for the Indians, women especially', firmly believing no man or Indian woman could do the job: a Western woman had to 'become' a Hindu woman in order to educate Hindu women.[55] She argues,

Of all the figures in the Colonial scene—western man, Indian man, western woman and Indian woman—it seems that it is only the western woman whose identity is available—for the Indian man—as relatively open, mobile, malleable. She is distinct from the Indian woman, whose identity has to be, in the nationalist context, fixed quite as much as the Indian male's is. What we have here is the familiar process of (colonial) mimicry performed in reverse, and for the Indian nationalist male; (Hindu) nationalism demands at this point its mimic woman.[56]

The parallels with the Nadia persona are interesting: Nadia was a white woman impersonating an Indian (invariably coded as Hindu) woman, whose mission was to educate and 'save' Indian women (and oppressed men). She was white but not white—and white but not (Pearl) White. But also, as Roy says of Nivedita, she was not quite/not white (or even not quite not quite/not white). While, Roy contends, Nivedita partially substitutes for Indian woman, her racial difference is crucial, for this 'guarantees ... the Indian male's ... Indianness and masculinity': a white woman impersonating an Indian (Hindu) heroine allows the Indian male to constitute himself at the centre of the project of nationalism.[57] Did the Wadias want their mimic woman in order to construct themselves as Indian nationalists?

Nadia's persona is complex as, although she was white, she was known to have grown up in India. There was considerable fluidity around 'Indianness' at that time and visual markers were (and still are) often ambiguous. Nadia described struggles over her own identity when growing up:

> [At school] I was always considered to be English. However Mummy was Greek and spoke English with a heavy Greek accent. Many of my friends would tease me about this and I felt very embarrassed.... I guess you could say that I was never too sure as to where I belonged, though I never thought of myself as un-Indian. Many people used to call me Anglo-Indian, even though I was not born in India.[58]

When she first arrived at Wadia Movietone, workers expressed anxiety about how to address her. 'You see she was a white mem and we at the studio were not sure how to react', although they soon relaxed when her unpretentious ways made her one of the gang. It was only later, especially after 1945, 'without the machinery of the studio to protect her' that we get reports that she was singled out for malicious gossip on account of her skin colour—equated with loose morals—and her status as an unmarried mother.[59] Wadia Movietone had been a particularly comfortable environment for Nadia. Owned by Westernised Parsis, the workers included a generous representation of Parsi, Muslim and other non-Hindu communities. JBH, discussing his films' feminist themes, admitted that, at least in his early days:

> I was ... out of tune ... with the overall Indian way of life.... As an insular [Westernised] Parsee I had not taken any interest in the pattern of family conventions of Hindus or Muslims.... for the world of me I could not understand ... why or how women subscribed to the male chauvinist ideology which infested the so-called social film.[60]

While the reality of India was—and still is—a hybrid society, a key imperative of the nationalist project was to negotiate the boundaries of the imagined community that was to become the homogeneous 'nation'. As Zutshi puts it:

> The key element in this process (of nationalism) is the separation of 'ourselves' from the Other, 'the outsider', since what nationalism is

crucially about is the matter of boundary/border setting.... Before political/geographical borders can be drawn on a map, psychological, social and cultural borders have to be erected.... The question 'Who are we?' is constantly being reformulated in terms of the alternative 'How are we different from them?'[61]

Films and their stars provide a terrain for such negotiation—within the broader arena of 'public culture'. Pinney, developing Appadurai and Breckenridge's seminal argument, usefully characterised public culture as 'a nexus of overlapping discourses and interests that exist in a state of interruptive tension'.[62] The melodramatic 'realist' social offers one model of negotiating national identity, tending to resolve and disavow ambivalence, hiding the exclusions necessary to define an essentialised tradition. With a more inclusive and hybrid model of Indian modernity the focus changes. The Nadia persona—in all its complexity—is a figure at play within a liminal zone of fluid racial, ethnic, gender and religious categories, where multiplicity and heterogeneity are celebrated. In the Wadias' stunt films, the key players explore new identities through mimicry and impersonation, 'fixed' only temporarily to help disguise the inherent instabilities of the border and the anxieties about what, within mainstream nationalism, is being repressed.

There were undoubtedly many reasons for the Wadias' failure to find 'respectability' through their films, not least sheer snobbery: their primary audiences were proletarian and the films were unabashed commercial entertainment. However, the Wadia films and their characters would have represented sources of profound anxiety for the nationalist project and some of their popular appeal may have derived from precisely the frisson that this engendered. Where Bombay Talkies was headed by Hindu aristocrats who could place themselves firmly at the centre of the nationalist project, the Wadias represented all that was peripheral: Parsis, Muslims, Christians and 'white trash'.[63] As JBH's attempts to fix his films within the nationalist mainstream grew ever more hysterical ('right on' themes, high-minded lectures, films without songs and films with classical music and dance), he lost his audience. One can only speculate how far it was because Homi pulled the films back from social melodrama—to playful mimicry that explored and revelled in the gamut of modern Indian identities—that the films once again succeeded with their subaltern audiences, especially the proletarian and Muslim masses.

Within the Wadia oeuvre the Nadia films represented a small but significant stream, at their best the most satisfactory resolution of the brothers' competing visions of cinema and nationalist identity. While JBH would have hated being immortalised by his 1986 obituary headline, 'King of the Stunt Film Dead', the importance of Nadia's stunt films is now undeniable. In comparison with Devika Rani, the liberal, modern, cosmopolitan beauty, Nadia was—for better or for worse—a thoroughly postmodern hybrid woman/man. While Devika ended up under the train, dead on the tracks, Nadia remains on its roof, an ebullient virangana in a modern world. While Devika is now more or less lost to time, Fearless Nadia—whip held aloft, thigh-high boots dug into her trusty steed Punjab ka Beta's flanks—looks set to ride the global media once again, this time as a Hollywood biopic star,[64] returning to Hollywood a version of its earlier self that is not quite Pearl White, ready to do new work within the cultural flows of a postcolonial late capitalist world.

NOTES

1. Trans.: 'From today I am [to be known as] the woman with the whip.'

2. See, for example, Vijay Mishra, *Bollywood Cinema: Temples of Desire*, New York: Routledge, 2002, pp. 17–18.

3. Barnouw and Krishnaswamy, for many years the key authoritative work on Indian cinema, made no reference to Nadia at all, despite a brief mention of *Hunterwali*. See Barnouw and Krishnaswamy, *Indian Film*, p. 110. Mishra et al. also fail to mention Nadia in their list of Indian imitators of Hollywood stunt stars and then proceed to claim, somewhat contentiously, that the imitations of Hollywood 'never really produced a star as text'. See Vijay Mishra, Peter Jeffery and Brian Shoesmith, 'The Actor as Parallel Text in Bombay Cinema', *Quarterly Review of Film and Video*, vol. 11, no. 3, 1989, p. 52.

4. The *Report of the Indian Cinematograph Committee, 1927–28*, together with its four volumes of evidence, gives a rich flavour of this era. For summaries of this material see Barnouw and Krishnaswamy, *Indian Film*, pp. 39–58; Prem Chowdhry, *Colonial India and the Making of Empire Cinema: Image, Ideology and Identity*, Manchester: Manchester University Press, 2000, pp. 13–21.

5. Hollywood technicians were in Bombay years before sound arrived, as we can see from the diaries of Harold Sintzenich, one of D.W. Griffith's cameramen,

posted in Bombay between 1928 and 1930 by Eastman Kodak to advise local talent on modern film and processing techniques. See Barnouw and Krishnaswamy, *Indian Film*, p. 102.

6. Ashish Rajadhyaksha, 'Neo-traditionalism: Film as Popular Art in India', *Framework*, vol. 32/33, 1980, pp. 20–67.

7. Information on Devika Rani draws primarily on a January 1989 interview with the author. This quotation also appears in Barnouw and Krishnaswamy, *Indian Film*, p. 102.

8. Previous articles, including my own, have invariably put her birth date as 1910—a fiction Nadia herself promoted. Information on Nadia's life story is drawn primarily from Nadia herself through conversations and an interview with Rosie Thomas and Behroze Gandhy in February 1986. Additional material is drawn from Girish Karnad and Riyad Wadia as indicated.

9. Girish Karnad, 'This One Is for Nadia', in *Cinema Vision India*, vol. 1, no. 2, 1980, p. 86.

10. Riyad Vinci Wadia, 'Unmasked: The Life and Times of Fearless Nadia', unpublished research notes, courtesy of Wadia Movietone Private Ltd (handed to me in 1994), p. 29.

11. Buddhi: old person.

12. Devi: goddess.

13. See chapter two for more details of Nadia's role in *Noor-e-Yaman*.

14. In 1984, J.B.H. Wadia openly admitted that 'a revolt against a tyrannical king or a minister for Azadi (freedom) was nothing if not against the British Raj, although indirectly'; quoted in Chowdhry, *Colonial India*, p. 97.

15. Behroze Gandhy and Rosie Thomas, 'Three Indian Film Stars', in *Stardom: Industry of Desire*, ed. Christine Gledhill, London: Routledge, 1991, pp. 107–16.

16. Harijan: (lit.) child of god—Gandhi's name for 'untouchables', that is, those outside the caste system.

17. M.N. Roy was a charismatic activist and political intellectual who travelled widely throughout Europe, the Soviet Union and the Americas. At one time a leading figure in the international communist movement and a confidante of Lenin, he became disillusioned equally by Communist and Congress Party politics and attempted to forge a new democratic humanism.

18. J.B.H. Wadia wrote: 'When I became a filmmaker I tried to equate [*sic*] my conscience by weaving the screenplays of some of my early talkies around the problem of emancipation of Indian womanhood', referring to the Nadia films as 'the genre which was much maligned and least understood by many "all-knowing" film critics and producers of social films'. J.B.H. Wadia, 'Those Were the Days', in *Cinema Vision India*, vol. 1, no. 1, 1980, pp. 91–9.

19. Baburao Patel in *Film India* review, August 1940.

20. Following M.N. Roy's lead, JBH argued that this should be seen as a workers' war to defeat world fascism and India should cooperate with the British, opposing the Congress policy of boycotting the war effort until India was free.

21. Riyad Wadia gave me this information (personal communication).

22. She returned to the screen in 1968 for a one-off role in Homi's film, *Khilari*, as discussed in the next chapter.

23. *Bombay Chronicle*, 30 September 1933.

24. Ashish Rajadhyaksha, 'Indian Cinema: Origins to Independence', in *Oxford History of World Cinema*, ed. Geoffrey Nowell-Smith, Oxford: Oxford University Press, 1996, pp. 408–9. Rajadhyaksha earlier wrote: 'Melodrama in the cinema, from the early 1930s, has consistently written into its various proliferations ... the transition of a "national" culture into the creation of a State: the loss of an ideal, the paradigms for belonging.' Rajadhyaksha, 'India's Silent Cinema', p. 26.

25. Sumita Chakravarty, *National Identity in Indian Popular Cinema, 1947–1987*, Austin: University of Texas Press, 1993, p. 81.

26. J.B.H. Wadia, *Looking Back on My Romance with Films*, Bombay: Jayant Art Printer, 1955, pp. 4–12.

27. This continued a well-established tradition of many studios of the silent and early sound era; see J.B.H. Wadia, 'Those Were the Days', *Cinema Vision India*, p. 94.

28. Mishra, *Bollywood Cinema*, p. 36.

29. British censorship in the 1920s was keen to protect the image of white women. This had been one of the key reasons for setting up the ICC in 1927. 'Much harm has been done in India by the widespread exhibition of Western films.... The majority of the films ... degrade the white woman in the eyes of the Indians.' *ICC Report 1927–28*, quoted in Barnouw and Krishnaswamy, *Indian Film*, p. 43.

30. Karnad, 'This One Is for Nadia', p. 86.

31. For further details of the virangana in early Indian cinema, see Thomas, 'Miss Frontier Mail'.

32. Kathryn Hansen, *Grounds for Play: The Nautanki Theatre of North India*, Berkeley: University of California Press, 1992, pp. 188–98.

33. Ibid., p. 194.

34. For lists of these films see Hansen, *Grounds for Play*, p. 195; see also Chowdhry, *Colonial India*, pp. 120–1. For description of the 1931 silent film *Diler Jigar* (Gallant Hearts, S.S. Agrawal) see Rajadhyaksha, 'India's Silent Cinema', pp. 25–40.

35. Hansen, *Grounds for Play*, p. 189.

36. Ibid., p. 189.

37. In all cases this was largely studio marketing: stunt doubles were regularly used: Arthur Wise and D. Ware, *Stunting in the Cinema*, London: Constable and Company, 1973, pp. 215–19. However, anecdotal accounts confirm that Nadia, as a former vaudeville artiste, did do most of her own stunts, especially in her early years.

38. Hansen, *Grounds for Play*, p. 192.

39. Ibid., p. 189.

40. Ibid., p. 192.

41. However, this was frequently the Maharashtrian sari—9 metres long and with much greater freedom of movement—which also refers to the virangana tradition of Maharashtrian horsewomen.

42. Gandhy and Thomas, 'Three Indian Film Stars', pp. 110–16.

43. Partha Chatterjee, 'Colonialism, Nationalism and the Colonialized Women: The Contest in India', *American Ethnologist*, vol. 16, no. 4, 1989, pp. 622–33. See also Partha Chatterjee, *The Nation and Its Fragments: Colonial and Postcolonial Histories*, Princeton: Princeton University Press, 1993.

44. Qurratulain Hyder, 'Memories of an Indian Childhood', trans. from the Urdu by Hyder, in *The Picador Book of Modern Indian Literature*, ed. Amit Chaudhuri, London: Picador, 2001 [1965], p. 213.

45. Dialogue translations from Channel Four UK's 2002 transmission of *Diamond Queen*.

46. Implicit here are references to other films in which Nadia is seen working out in her gym—which apparently stimulated a keep-fit craze at the time.

47. Richard Dyer describes how backlighting developed in Hollywood largely to ensure blonde hair looked blonde on orthochromatic stock, as a welcome consequence producing the blonde white woman's 'heavenly', 'effulgent dazzle'. In Richard Dyer, *White*, London: Routledge, 1997, p. 124.

48. The subsequent fire in which both parents die is played out in quasi-melodramatic mode, which suggests an immediate punishment.

49. Trans: 'I'm a man, a [real] man.'

50. This is a tendency rather than an absolute distinction as the opposition between narrative momentum and spectacular excess is not as strong in Hindi film as in Hollywood, the former being more of a 'cinema of attractions'.

51. The swastika here refers to the Indian peace symbol, not Nazi Germany, although in the 1940s context there might have been a curious ambivalence as some Indian National Congress supporters (not J.B.H. Wadia) supported Hitler on the basis that Britain was their common enemy.

52. There are also textual references to the playful god Krishna, especially as the name he adopts for his disguise is Krishna Kumar (Prince Krishna).

53. Parama Roy, *Indian Traffic: Identities in Question in Colonial and Postcolonial India*, Berkeley: University of California Press, 1998, p. 4.

54. The best example of this is *Raj Natarki* (Court Dancer, Madhu Bose, 1941).

55. Roy, *Indian Traffic*, p. 121.

56. Ibid., p. 123.

57. Ibid., p. 122.

58. Riyad Vinci Wadia, *Unmasked*, pp. 12–13.

59. Ibid., p. 62.

60. J.B.H. Wadia, 'Those Were the Days', *Cinema Vision India*, p. 93.

61. Somnath Zutshi, 'Women, Nation and the Outsider in Contemporary Hindi Cinema', in *Interrogating Modernity: Culture and Colonialism in India*, eds Tejaswini Niranjana, P. Sudhir and Vivek Dhareshwar, Calcutta: Seagull Books, 1993, p. 83.

62. Christopher Pinney, 'Introduction: Public, Popular and Other Cultures', in *Pleasure and the Nation: The History, Politics and Consumption of Public Culture in India*, eds Rachel Dwyer and Christopher Pinney, New Delhi: Oxford University Press, 2001, p. 14.

63. Ravi Vasudevan, describing the complexities of emergent Hindu hegemony in the 1930s Bombay industry, points out that 'the religious identity of producers, directors and actors was being related to the on-screen narrative and in fact was seen to constitute a critical social and political level to the narrative'. In 'The Politics of Cultural Address', p. 156.

64. In the mid-2000s, at least two biopics were in development, including a Cate Blanchett Hollywood project with Shekhar Kapoor.

$\mathcal{Z}$imbo and Son Meet the Girl with a Gun

INTRODUCTION

When the Beatles famously went to India in the 1960s, posters of
Zimbo Finds a Son (John Cawas, 1966) and *Khilari* (The Player, Homi
Wadia, 1968) would have been on the hoardings—and their films in
the cinemas—in all the poorer areas of India's cities and larger towns.
From everything we know, this is an India that George and the boys
never really even noticed.

While *Zimbo Finds a Son* promised its audiences alluring fantasies
of a pristine, lush, green jungle where, just like Tarzan, a handsome
couple swings from trees and tastes forbidden fruits of sexual
plenitude, *Khilari* gave tantalising glimpses of a different kind of
paradise. Here audiences could dream of the planes, helicopters,
skyscrapers and guns of an exciting modern world where, just like
James Bond, secret agents run dangerous global missions. Two exotic
utopias, two complementary fictions of modernity. Evil lurks in both:
the jungle is a space of wild and primitive nature, the city one of
villainous corruption. Our heroes and heroines posture triumphantly
across these seductive scenes, promising their audiences full-colour
thrills of gutsy innuendo and larger-than-life playful violence, all
within a recognisably Indian format.

Both films were produced by Homi Wadia at Basant Pictures,
neither was a critical success nor major hit, both were in black and
white and both were aimed at the 'C-grade circuit', the term by
which the film industry and cosmopolitan elite dismissed the barely
literate urban and rural poor who make up the largest share of
India's vast movie audiences. While Jamshed and Homi Wadia had

been known as kings of the stunt film since the 1930s, and Basant was unquestionably the leader in its field, by the mid-1960s audience tastes were changing, especially with the massive influx of the rural dispossessed into the cities in the 1960s. Many rivals had sprung up and Basant's films had begun to look tired and old-fashioned, now working their magic primarily with the poorest of these audiences. The secret of Basant's success had always been to keep their films alive to global popular culture, notably Hollywood; to push whatever technical or cultural boundaries they could; and to integrate and fuse all this with Indian entertainment conventions, traditional storytelling and populist fantasies. Theirs was a unique brand.

While the Beatles returned to Europe in the late 1960s to feed Western fantasies with a vision of a pure, timeless, spiritual India—and launch a million gap years—Basant Pictures quietly fed the Indian popular imagination over a period of almost forty years with a series of visions of East and West, jungle and city, tradition and modernity. It drew on Hollywood and popular entertainment forms, plundered with abandon and 'Indianised'. The Beatles drew on Indian classical and traditional cultures, plundered with abandon and 'Westernised'. While the Beatles fed an eccentric version of India back to Western popular culture, Basant fed an eccentric version of a *different* Western popular culture back to a *different* India. The Beatles Westernised their India, Basant Indianised its West.

But what did the two posters mean to Indian audiences in the 1960s? What might the Beatles have learnt from chatting with the drivers of those shiny Cadillacs? What might the north Indian villagers have told the most famous English lads in the world about their favourite movies, the film stars that excited them, and their passion for cinema? This chapter explores the associations of these two posters for Indian audiences and the contexts within which they would have been read at the time—not only the resonances of the global Tarzan and James Bond brands but also the local fame of Basant's daredevil star couple, Fearless Nadia and John Cawas. While the last chapter described the Fearless Nadia persona, the current chapter focuses on John Cawas, who rose to stunt stardom as Tarzan in the 193/ super hit *Toofani Tarzan* (Tempestuous Tarzan, Homi Wadia), *Zimbo*'s precursor. I illustrate how the Wadias' skilful blending of global

1966   London swings under Wilson's Labour, Christine Keeler's only just
faded out of view and the Beatles claim they are more famous than
Jesus. Indira Gandhi becomes India's third prime minister, the rupee is devalued,
and Homi Wadia releases *Zimbo Finds a Son*.

The Beatles make their first visit to India, get mobbed by fans in Delhi, visit
outlying villages in 1950s Cadillacs and George buys a sitar. Did they see those
Zimbo posters?

Figure 5.1: Poster of *Zimbo Finds a Son* (1966). *Source*: © Basant Pictures. Courtesy
Roy Wadia/Wadia Movietone and Open Editions collection.

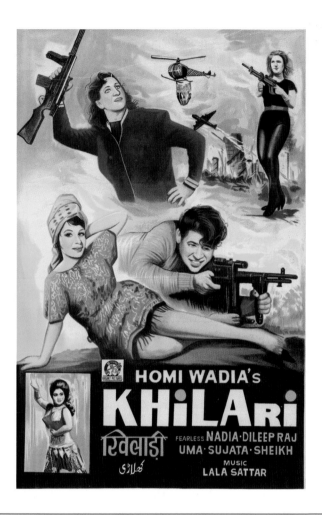

1968 Student protest sweeps Europe and America, workers man the barricades in Paris, and Mrs Gandhi prints a postage stamp to launch the Wheat Revolution. Whip-cracking Emma Peel bows out of the Avengers as actress Diana Rigg becomes a Bond girl, and Bombay movie legend, Fearless Nadia, makes her feisty come back in the James Bond spoof, *Khilari*, at the age of sixty.

The Beatles and their wives return to India, meditate in Rishikesh, find peace and love, and discover that the Maharishi is a sham. George and Patti extend their stay and study ragas with Ravi Shankar in Bombay. George does yoga and practices his sitar every day. We have heard a lot about that six-week trip but none of them has ever mentioned those *Khilari* posters.

Figure 5.2: Poster of *Khilari* (1968). *Source*: © Basant Pictures. Courtesy Roy Wadia/ Wadia Movietone and Open Editions collection.

Hollywood with Indian subject matter and cultural tradition played out within that film, and was ready to be drawn on again in the 1960s, by which time Basant was recycling its own history as well as foraging within global popular culture. Finally, through a closer reading of the two posters of *Khilari* and *Zimbo*, I compare how the legends of Fearless Nadia and John Cawas were mobilised to offer their 'C-grade' audiences an entry into the glamorous 'other' worlds of the global 1960s—the exotic primitive and the exotic West—as a vernacular, cosmopolitan form within which non-elite modes of modern Indian identities, notably gender identities, could be negotiated.

REMAKES AND HOLLYWOOD

It would be hard for Indian audiences in the 1960s to see either *Zimbo* or *Khilari* posters without thinking back to earlier movies. Both films explicitly revisited the 1930s heyday of Homi Wadia and his brother Jamshed.[1] *Zimbo* was unambiguously Tarzan and, with *Toofani Tarzan* in 1937, Wadia Movietone had brought India its own *desi* Tarzan. Proudly advertised as 'India's first jungle adventure film', this was such an extraordinary success that its box-office takings over the next five years made it, by 1942, the studio's all-time highest grosser.[2] The film continued to rake in profits for more than twenty years and by 1966 John Cawas, *Zimbo Finds a Son*'s director, had become a household name, not least through having played the original Indian Tarzan. Originally known for his astonishing world records, which had included carrying a Chevrolet containing four passengers on his bare back, he had been lovingly admired for his brawny frame, superhuman strength and simple charm. The *Zimbo* series of three films, which began in 1958, were openly advertised as *Toofani Tarzan* remakes.[3]

Khilari, on the other hand, built its appeal around an even bigger household name—and former co-star of John Cawas—Fearless Nadia, the white-skinned, blue-eyed blonde who had tossed burly villains over her golden curls and whose success had been key to Wadia Movietone's reputation and considerable fortune. *Khilari*'s promise to its audiences was another chance to enjoy Nadia, now aged sixty, nine years older than her last screen role but just as feisty.

While both films make much mileage out of their Indian pedigree, they also bathe in Hollywood's reflection. Just as Nadia had been popularly marketed as the 'Indian Pearl White'—referring to the star of *Perils of Pauline* (Louis J. Gasnier, 1914), who had been a favourite of Indian audiences in the silent era, so also had John Cawas been introduced from the first as the 'Indian Eddie Polo'. As discussed in the last chapter, while this suggests a form of mimicry familiar in colonial discourse, it was also clever marketing: J.B.H. Wadia and others clearly recognised the commercial value of the brand name.[4] Moreover, by the 1960s, the star pairing of John Cawas and Fearless Nadia was Basant's own biggest brand: parents of naughty children of the 1940s and 1950s would threaten to 'set John Cawas and Nadia onto them' if they misbehaved.

Khilari and *Zimbo* also cite Hollywood more openly, directly milking two of the biggest global phenomena of the 1960s: James Bond and Tarzan. Although both were imperialist adventure stories, these were as popular in the former colonies as in the West. *Khilari* promoted itself as a James Bond spoof. By 1968, the Bond series, based on English author Ian Fleming's racy novels, had become a worldwide success, with a string of five spectacular hits between *Dr No* (Terence Young, 1962) and *You Only Live Twice* (Lewis Gilbert, 1967). In fact, in India, with swingeing censorship cuts and import controls that limited distribution, the films were rarely seen in full and only infrequently outside the larger cities. Despite this, James Bond made his mark on the Indian market and spawned a host of local imitators. The name signalled global sophistication: Bond was a cool superhero and to know about Bond was to be up-to-date, Westernised, modern, with the additional frisson that the films were known to be more sexually explicit than anything the Indian censors allowed.

Zimbo Finds a Son and its 1937 predecessor *Toofani Tarzan* were, on the other hand, Indian versions of the Hollywood Tarzan movies: *Zimbo Finds a Son*'s English title was itself a brazen rip-off of a famous MGM title. Of course all the movies were versions of Edgar Rice Burroughs's popular American novels. While the novels' first craze was from 1912 until the 1930s, there was a global Tarzan revival in the 1960s. By 1963, one in every thirty paperbacks sold worldwide was a

Tarzan novel and Hollywood's *Tarzan Goes to India* (John Guillermin, 1962)—with music by Ravi Shankar—became the most profitable yet of the world's most lucrative film series, making more than 50 per cent of its profits outside America.[5]

However it was the 1930s MGM films starring Johnny Weissmuller that directly inspired the Wadia brothers and remain—worldwide—the classics of popular memory, notably *Tarzan, the Ape Man* (W.S. Van Dyke, 1932). While Elmo Lincoln's 1918 silent version had first popularised Tarzan throughout India, J.B.H. Wadia tells us: 'Johnny Weissmuller, with this fantastic jungle cry and swimming abilities, made Tarzan a household name even in remote small towns in India.' As JBH himself puts it (somewhat quirkily writing of himself in the third person): 'Borrowing heavily from the original, JBH placed his screenplay in an Indian setting.'[6]

Toofani Tarzan is far from being a simple copy of *Tarzan, the Ape Man*, just as the Nadia films were crucially different from anything Hollywood produced. *Khilari*'s similarities with a Bond movie lie primarily in its exuberant pace, fantasy modernity, irreverent humour and knowing jokey references. The accusation that Bombay film-makers simply copy Hollywood has often been made but does not stand scrutiny. As I have argued elsewhere, no close copy of a foreign film was ever successful in the pre-1990s era and, while borrowing elements from wherever they needed, Indian film-makers knew that the key to success lay in knowing how to adapt and 'Indianise' their material, although association with a successful foreign brand did no commercial harm. JBH was always the first to acknowledge his sources and ultimately part of the Wadia brothers' credibility with audiences lay in their being seen as 'modern' and glamorously 'Westernised' while still proudly local, in many ways the most cosmopolitan of film-makers, in others the most desi.

BASANT STUDIOS

As we have seen, the Wadia brothers had been a phenomenal force in the early sound era and the tension between JBH's aspirations to produce 'quality' cinema and Homi's populist box-office flair was productively harnessed throughout the 1930s to produce some of the era's most radical—and popular—films, notably the Nadia series. But there were an equal number of stunt films without Nadia, including *Toofani Tarzan*, and all demonstrated a pioneering technical approach. Unlike some other studios which relied on foreign technicians, Wadia Movietone encouraged enterprising, gifted local young men to find their own solutions to special effects and camera technique: they built their own camera crane and dolly, set up the best back projection and matte effects systems in Bombay and regularly shot with multi-camera set-ups. JBH and Homi scoured Hollywood technical journals and kept in touch with all new developments.

At the point that Basant Pictures was launched in 1942, the relationship between Homi and Jamshed was at breaking point. When their first social, *Mauj*, flopped in 1943, Homi, with his back against the wall, decided that instead of moving on to make fashionable realist socials, the key to Basant's survival lay in its stunt stars—the original whip-cracking Nadia and her muscle-man partner John Cawas. Although Nadia was already taking lessons in hairdressing to prepare for a new career, Homi persuaded her to give him one last chance. On borrowed time and hired studio floors he produced a shameless sequel to her original 1935 hit. *Hunterwali ki Beti* (Daughter of the Woman with the Whip, Batuk/Nanabhai Bhatt, 1943) revived the old magic and was an immediate success. Nadia was once again queen of the box office and Basant's fortunes rose. Homi's hunch had paid off and Basant's distinctive brand was launched for a new era.

Homi was soon able to build his own studio facilities at Chembur on the outskirts of Bombay. Between 1942 and 1981, Homi's well-run production company continued to produce a stream of unpretentious but quietly successful films aimed at the mass audience. Much of the success of the early years lay in being always just slightly ahead of the game. Continuing Wadia Movietone's tradition, Basant's innovative special effects department found low-cost, creative and desi solutions to the technical problems crucial to its key specialisms: stunts, mythologicals and fantasy films. A talented team grew, many of whom stayed for years, notably director Babubhai Mistry who began his career as a brilliant young SFX technician at Wadia Movietone and was still directing Basant's final film on the studio floors in 1980.[7] While stunt and fantasy films were considered C-grade fodder, the success of *Shri Ram Bhakta Hanuman* (Homi Wadia, 1948), on which Jamshed collaborated as scriptwriter, initiated a string of quality mythologicals that raised Basant's status considerably, as A-grade audiences also appreciated these. In the 1980s film industry, some older workers still jokingly referred to mythologicals as the 'Brahmins' of Indian film genres, while the stunt films were the 'shudras'. Despite the huge difference in status between Basant's two core genres, the same technicians and directors worked on both and workers used to quip: 'Mythologicals are just stunt films that happen to be about gods.'[8]

Basant's legacy is remarkable not least for the stream of stars and directors whose early careers it moulded. Meena Kumari began her adult career playing—somewhat controversially given her Muslim identity—Hindu goddesses for Basant, while the 1970s macho hero Feroz Khan started out as a hero in Basant thrillers such as *Reporter Raju* (Dwarka Khosla, 1962). Nor should we forget that other talents influenced by Basant include the masala superstar director of the 1970s/1980s, Manmohan Desai, whose brother trained as an assistant production manager at Basant and introduced him to his 'guru', Babubhai Mistry,[9] and Mahesh Bhatt, whose father, Nanabhai (aka Batuk) Bhatt, was one of Basant's leading directors, credited on many of their stunt and fantasy hits, including *Hunterwali ki Beti* and the second of the Zimbo trilogy, *Zimbo Comes to Town* (Nanabhai Bhatt, 1960). Basant's reputation amongst the businessmen of the industry for its commercial success and professionalism was such that even independent producers using Basant as no more than a hired studio facility cashed in on the kudos of its name to promote their films. And while Basant films were scorned by the upper- and middle-class nationalist elites, the name spelled magic both for many of their children (as for example Girish Karnad's testimony in the previous chapter indicates) and for India's vast subaltern audiences, for whom Basant films were an extension of the Wadias' 1930s heyday. In order to understand this heritage of appropriation and Indianisation, on which the two 1960s Basant posters drew, I will first examine the film that launched John Cawas as India's Tarzan in 1937.

TOOFANI TARZAN: INDIA'S 1937 SUPER HIT

Unlike the Weissmuller movies but in the tradition of the first Rice Burroughs's books and all good Hindi films, the storyline of *Toofani Tarzan* begins in Tarzan's childhood. Tarzan's father, Ramu, is a scientist boffin who lives with his wife and young son in a comfortable but ramshackle jungle bungalow. While Uma cooks in her kitchen, he does chemistry experiments in his makeshift laboratory next door. One day he discovers a potion that will confer immortality. He decides the family will visit his millionaire father in the city, with whom relations seem strained on account of Ramu's love marriage with the humble Uma. On the eve of the visit, where Ramu will announce his scientific discovery to the world, tragedy strikes. Ramu is killed by a pride of lions and Uma becomes separated from her son. With the help of Dada, an ape-man family retainer, and accompanied by Moti, the family's pet terrier, the young son escapes in a hot air balloon, survives a dramatic thunderstorm, and lands by a lake. Round the boy's neck is an amulet containing Ramu's miraculous scientific formula.

Fifteen years later, Ramu's father leads an expedition to the jungle to search for his long-lost grandson who, according to local rumours, survived and, now known as Tarzan, lives happily in communion with nature. With the party, in white pith helmets and hunting gear, are an adopted daughter, Leela, who obsessively makes up her face; a lecherous villain, Biharilal; a *qawwali*-singing philosopher guide, together with a buffoonish servant and an army of muscular porters and bodyguards. When local cannibals attack with poisoned arrows, Tarzan, accompanied by pals Dada and Moti, comes to the rescue, fights off the tribals and dispatches them with an elephant stampede. Out of the foliage appears a ranting mad woman wearing a necklace of stones and armbands of skulls. She rails at the party as 'liars and sinners', decries the wicked ways of city folk and urges Tarzan to follow her back into the jungle and ignore Leela's approaches. Despite this Tarzan and Leela meet again when, having rescued her from Biharilal's lecherous advances, Tarzan abducts Leela himself. Gradually, he proves his innocent and gentle nature and they fall in love. Leela joins Tarzan in his tree-top home, exchanges her blouse and slacks for a leopard skin mini-dress and spends her days riding elephants, swinging through trees and swimming in crocodile infested lakes.

After a series of adventures in which all members of the grandfather's expedition, including Leela, are kidnapped by cannibals, Leela is lowered into a pit to be fed to the cannibals' giant gorilla chief. Moti, the brave little dog, escapes and raises the alarm and Tarzan swings to the rescue, overpowers the gorilla by brute strength and finally frees the whole party. He leads them to safety by making his own taut body into a bridge over a ravine. Now fuelled by his greed for the secret in Tarzan's precious amulet, the ruthless Biharilal attacks Tarzan and, in the ensuing tussle, shoots and mortally wounds the mad harridan. Uma's memory returns and the party discovers that she is Tarzan's long-lost mother, who went insane when she believed both husband and son had perished. She dies reunited with her beloved son, Tarzan. Nudged on by the dog Moti, Biharilal falls to his death from a precipice. Leela refuses to return to the city with her adopted father and insists on living with lover Tarzan in their jungle paradise. Only when the qawwali poet reminds the old man that 'whatever God does is good', does the father finally agree to bless the union between his grandson and adopted daughter. As the sun sets, the qawwal sings: 'What you could not find in the city, you have found in the jungle, Celebrate the happiness found by love, May God fill your life with happiness, Stay Happy'.[10]

'Indianisation'

Although JBH writes of 'borrowing heavily from the original' and there are undoubtedly many echoes of, and quotes from, the Johnny Weissmuller movies, particularly in the characterisation of Tarzan and in the love scenes, the process of 'placing the screenplay in an Indian setting' has provoked substantial and significant changes.

Formally, the film follows Indian structural conventions. The first reel, set in the hero's childhood, sets up the first narrative disruption. The rest of the film traces its consequences fifteen years later. A comedy subplot with its own burlesque characters weaves through the main action and romance plot and poetic songs interrupt the narrative flow and comment on what unfolds. Heroes and villains are sharply differentiated and Biharilal, the unremittingly lecherous, callous and greedy city scoundrel, has to be killed before the narrative can be resolved. The backbone of the narrative is the drive to reunite the hero's dispersed family, which is finally resolved when the grandfather finds his lost heir and effectively provides him with a mate.

JBH also made thematic changes. Some of these key in to Indian cultural concerns, for example, the introduction of Tarzan's mad mother. Others result from a more subtle shift in the film's underlying dynamic. The explorers are not white colonialists but Westernised Indians from the city. The jungle is peopled not by black Africans but by Indian tribal peoples. The film's underlying opposition is thus between Westernised, educated, wealthy, city-dwelling 'modern' India and non-Westernised, uneducated, impoverished, rural or 'primitive' India. Evil lies in both: the former is the domain of 'false ways', immorality and greed for material gain; the latter is tainted with cruelty and savagery.[11] In the course of the film, Tarzan, Leela and other characters take a variety of positions in the space between these poles, including Tarzan's pals Moti, this curiously domesticated pet terrier, who is neither wild jungle beast nor pampered city pooch, and the mute, arm-swinging ape-man Dada, an overt cross-breed.[12] Only Leela can move freely between the two domains.

By substituting the 'nectar of immortality' for the material wealth—elephant tusks, lost jewels and suchlike—that motivates most American versions of the tale, Wadia significantly changes its thrust. Tarzan's father is a 'modern' Indian who attempts a rapprochement between city and jungle and fails. He is simultaneously a rational scientist—the epitome of the acceptable face of Westernised modernity according to the nationalist intellectuals—and a traditional ur-Indian sage, finding a magical elixir of life akin to the alleged discoveries of an ancient Indian wisdom that operated centuries before Western science. Ramu is from a wealthy city background but chooses to live in poverty in the jungle, pursuing his altruistic quest. Significantly, at the very moment when he has apparently conquered nature, his idyll is disrupted. The forces of nature—wild lions and fierce thunderstorms—punish his arrogance. Later, when the villainous Biharilal covets the wealth to be made from Ramu's discovery, he is also killed. Only when Tarzan and Leela submit to

God's will and live in harmony with the forces of nature, within the plenitude of true love—discovering that it is quality not length of life that matters—can the narrative be resolved, thereby situating the film's moral universe firmly within the emotional and metaphoric sensibilities of 'tradition', here the Indian art form of Urdu qawwali poetry and the wisdom of Sufi philosophy.

Probably Wadia's boldest innovation was Uma, the mad mother. For Indian audiences, she would be coded as a Kali figure, the goddess of creation and destruction, who conventionally represents the terrifying force within femininity. At each of her appearances Uma's insane cackle dominates the soundtrack as she harangues and challenges the city-dwellers. Ultimately, the raw, dysfunctional feminine energy thought to belong to a woman without a man— unleashed in Uma's case by the death of her husband and son and her retreat from civilisation—has to be controlled. Biharilal's bullet wound 'brings her to her senses' so that she can die as a loving, nurturing mother in her son Tarzan's arms.

Tarzan's mother scarcely figures in any American versions of the story, although Rice Burroughs's early books made something of his aristocratic father. But in Hindi cinema, mother-and-son is invariably a key dynamic. As Ashis Nandy put it, 'the mother-son relationship is the basic nexus and the ultimate paradigm of human social relationships in India'.[13] While the MGM film hints evasively at an incestuous bond between Jane and her father,[14] and her father has to die before Tarzan and Jane can live happily ever after, in *Toofani Tarzan* it is Tarzan's *mother* that has to be dispatched, releasing the Indian Tarzan from his (in all practical senses invisible) Oedipal bond.

Tarzan and Leela

If Tarzan's father and mother offer models of modernity—ways of bridging the opposition between city and jungle—which are both ultimately flawed and fail, Tarzan and Leela themselves offer more hope. Both figures provide spaces within which 'modern' identities are fluid and open to exploration and negotiation.

Leela is an intriguing mix of modern independence, coquettish helplessness and unconstrained sexuality. She encompasses two facets of decadent city femininity: the vanity and 'falseness' signalled by her obsessional attachment to her make-up bag, and the assertive toughness of a woman in slacks who stands up to men, wields a gun and defies her father in order to choose her own sexual partner. The movie transforms her into a free spirit in a mini-skirt, whose hedonistic sexuality becomes, through a series of moves and denials, acceptably identified with the innocence of the jungle. Thus, for example, an erotic bathing scene—in which she (purportedly) bathes nude while singing a sensual song about 'a burning rising in my body'—is followed by a comedy gag in which Moti the dog steals her clothes, after which she is immediately kidnapped by the cannibals. While on one level clearly presenting her as both sexually desiring and desirable, the film simultaneously disavows this. Not only does she, in a 'conversation' with Moti, coyly deny sexual relations—'You think I let Tarzan have his way? You think I'm wild (junglee) like Tarzan?'—but the overt sexual energy of the scene is also sharply displaced onto the lust of villainous cannibals and their voracious gorilla chief.[15] It is not insignificant that the figure of Fearless Nadia would inevitably have coloured any audience viewing of Leela in 1937: even the camera angles of the bathing scene echo Nadia's famous scene in *Hunterwali*.[16]

As Barbara Creed has argued of their American alter egos, Tarzan and Leela's relationship is fundamentally—and quite radically—one of mutual interdependence.[17] Both Leela and Tarzan move between being active figures that push the narrative forward and erotic spectacle for the camera. While Tarzan demonstrates brute strength and the ability to protect Leela from danger, Leela not only feminises him, by, for example, powdering his face and treating him as a naughty but charming child, but she also controls and teaches language. Their love scenes include many direct quotes from the Weissmuller movie, including the famous naming scene. But interestingly, what in the American film is simply 'Jane, Tarzan, Jane, Tarzan',[18] here becomes 'Main Leela, Tum Tarzan' (Me Leela, You Tarzan), emphatically placing control with Leela's voice.

Ultimately, however, it is Tarzan who is central to the film's power and success with its audiences. Wadia found the casting of Tarzan his greatest challenge—no suitable actors could be found in Bombay.

John Cawas, the 1930 Body Beautiful Champion of India, had to be lured away from a quiet life in Poona, where he lived with his mother and taught physical culture and weight-lifting classes at the Hercules Gymnasium.[19] Before winning the Tarzan role he first had to prove his screen charisma as second hero in *Hunterwali*. Much of *Toofani Tarzan*'s pleasure centres around admiring shots of the strength and beauty of Cawas's body and awe at his acrobatic feats and fighting skills. These include dangerous animal stunts learned through an arduous early morning training schedule with the animal tamers at Professor Deval's circus, which JBH insisted he attend before clocking in at the studio each day. As with other stars of the era who came out of popular vaudeville and showmanship traditions, the fact that he did all his own stunts was an integral part of the marketing appeal. Cawas's Tarzan is modelled closely on Weissmuller, with a similar mix of animal beauty, gruff brute strength, childish helplessness and a strong moral sensibility, although interestingly, given JBH's explicit acknowledgement of his inspiration while writing and casting the film, Cawas was billed as the 'Indian Eddie Polo' and *not* as the 'Indian Johnny Weissmuller'.[20]

TARZAN'S APPEAL IN INDIA

What seems, at first sight, most surprising about the worldwide Tarzan crazes of the early decades of the twentieth century—and again in the 1960s—is the popularity of such overtly colonialist books and films with vast audiences in former colonies. Fanon describes how audiences in the Antilles would identify with the screen Tarzan when he savaged black antagonists in the jungle.[21] In fact, the films of the 1930s made more than 75 per cent of their profits abroad: even Haile Selassie, Emperor of Ethiopia, used to demand his own African premieres of the Weissmuller films.[22]

Why did Tarzan resonate so widely? Why did Indian audiences enjoy the Hollywood Tarzans so much and what was the appeal of the Indian versions? On the one hand, the films' visceral pleasures are obvious: beautiful bodies, both male and female, thrilling shots of jungle animals, exciting stunts and fight scenes, and in the Indian version, songs and poetry. But perhaps another key lies in the points of identification the Tarzan figure itself offers.

Contrary to common misrepresentations of Tarzan, the character as originally conceived was not one-dimensionally chest-pounding and macho. As Torgovnick points out, Burroughs's early Tarzan story 'begins with scenes which dramatise confusion and contradictions about black-white relations, about maleness, and about man's treatment of women'—themes gradually suppressed as the books went on.[23] Perhaps more than most other heroes—Indian or Hollywood—the movie Tarzan is a fluid character. He is neither of the city nor properly of the jungle; neither civilised nor primitive; neither Western nor traditional; ultimately neither conventionally masculine nor feminine. As such he allows for points of fluctuating identification within the liminal zone between such oppositions, an arena within which contemporary power and gender relations can be explored. Although not in any simple sense a role model for 'modern' Indian masculinity,[24] the Tarzan figure allows space for negotiation of where modern, Indian masculine identity might lie. Three points follow in relation to India.

Firstly, in the context of India's nationalist movement, the fluidity of Tarzan's masculinity would have been particularly radical, for it moves beyond the limited oppositions that nationalist ideologies had proposed. Cawas's Tarzan offers neither the hard, callous, emotionally impoverished masculinity of the coloniser nor the more effeminate masculinity of Gandhian ideology. Instead, it keys into traditions of subaltern popular culture, from the wrestling and bodybuilding sub-cultures associated with the monkey god Hanuman, to the martial male cultures of Sikh and Muslim men, as well as to role models from popular Indian performance traditions and Hollywood. In this it harks back to the male stars of India's silent era, several of whom were wrestlers. By the 1960s, there was also another level at play as masculinity was being redefined worldwide. John Cawas as Tarzan had opened an Indian screen space which, by the 1960s, produced not just Azad, the star of the three Zimbo films and more than a dozen other Tarzan-style movies, but a number of rival 1960s Indian Tarzans, notably the bodybuilder Dara Singh, a major cult figure of the era who took the display of rippling brawn to increasingly hysterical levels.

Secondly, there is the question of mimicry. While on the one hand John Cawas was known to be a Parsi actor playing an implicitly

Hindu character (Wadia's Tarzan), he was also an Indian man playing an American actor (Weissmuller), who plays a lost English aristocrat (Burroughs's Tarzan). The Wadias' appropriation of Hollywood to their own ends was not simply good commercial sense. By incorporating and reworking MGM's and Weissmuller's Tarzan within Indian conventions, the scope for playful identification and appropriation was considerably extended. Cawas's muscular frame bears a load even more formidable than the famed Chevrolet: it simultaneously stands in for and displaces Weissmuller, accruing to itself all the power of his global marketing appeal. It becomes the white superhero of the coloniser, at one level a fictional British aristocrat, at another the global success story of American media imperialism. But at the same time it converts an overtly colonialist film to its own needs. Tarzan could be owned and played with and—interestingly—the Wadias felt no compulsion to clear copyright, at least the first time round.[25]

Thirdly, in claiming Tarzan for Indian audiences, the Wadias were also reclaiming the whole concept of 'jungle' from several centuries of colonialist appropriation. The word itself is of Sanskrit origin and is found in thirteenth-century literature meaning uncultivated ground. By 1804, we find *junglo* used in the vernacular to mean a wild or uncivilised person—here a group of Gujarati women's scathing reference to a white colonial man who did not understand their language.[26] Like thousands of other words it came into the English (and French) language—and global culture—through Anglo-Indian parlance.

Much is made of the word 'junglee' in *Toofani Tarzan*. Leela constantly but fondly berates her lover, 'Tarzan tum bilkul junglee ho.'[27] As they banter the term around between themselves, it is clearly ambivalently valued, being mostly used to mean not only uncivilised but—in the loosest sense—uncontrolled sexuality. By the mid-1960s, the word 'junglee' had acquired a new and more specific meaning following the sensational success of the film *Junglee* (Wild Thing, Subodh Mukherjee, 1961). In this film, Shammi Kapoor kick-started the 1960s for Indian youth and achieved instant stardom as an Indian rock'n'roller, a 'wild thing' with his hair slicked back in an Elvis quiff. As the persona developed, this romantic hero frolicked in the snows of fashionable mountain resorts and raced sports cars around glamorous European capitals with a new breed of 'mod' heroine, superficially Westernised but indubitably virtuous and traditional at heart. Although in his debut film the term 'junglee' in fact refers to (a caricature of) unfeeling, cold, Westernised masculinity, 'junglee' gradually became associated with Shammi himself and became an ambiguously desirable quality, with suggestions of a different sort of uncivilisedness—an excitingly dangerous sexual energy and ultra-modernity. It thus signified both the exotically primitive and the exotically Westernised, and inadvertently became one of several terms at play in the negotiation of modernity. As such it is a concept that, unconsciously and perhaps unexpectedly, underpins the *Khilari* poster as much as the *Zimbo* poster. It is time to return to the 1960s posters.

GIRLS, GUNS AND THE BASANT BRAND

The Wadias did not need Jean Luc Godard to tell them that 'all you need for a film is a gun and a girl'. *Khilari*'s poster takes no chances: three guns, four 'girls'. Its promise is clear: spectacle, action, 'thrills', sexual titillation and exciting—if jokey—violence within a glamorous modern world. Images of *Khilari*'s stars have been cut out from photographic stills of the film, overpainted in vivid colours and mounted over swirling brushstrokes, which roughly sketch in backgrounds and loosely unify the picture. While Hollywood posters often organise their imagery around an unresolved narrative dilemma, this poster offers a montage of figures in a range of settings and moods, condensing through its spatial relationships the key themes of the film.

The poster for *Zimbo Finds a Son* uses the same production technique but is, at first glance, thematically less complex. Spatial relationships set up a basic opposition around which the image is structured. Virile masculinity dominates the left-hand side of the poster, accentuated by an hysterical excess of phallic attributes: a lethal knife, rippling muscles of a bare torso, and an erect elephant trunk that dutifully echoes the bulge in the flame-red loincloth of our priapic hero. His sexy mate in tiny golden bra-top and mini-skirt averts her gaze and submits her body full-on to the camera. Bridging this exaggerated opposition between active masculinity and passive femininity (and literally placed to join the two figures) is the son, echoing his father's stance but dressed in his mother's golden loincloth. Confidently disregarding the conventions of Western perspective, his placement within the frame visually mediates the key opposition, suggesting both the nurturing qualities of his father (under—and in front of—whose arm he appears) and the potency of his mother (above whom he stands erect).

Indian audiences of the 1960s would have brought well-developed knowledge about Tarzan movies—Indian and Hollywood—to this poster: the amulets that Zimbo and his son wear around their necks, as well as the heroine's dress code and the wispy jungle background, would have provided condensed references to *Toofani Tarzan*'s storyline and city/jungle theme. Moreover, the spectre of John Cawas (and by association also Fearless Nadia, with whom he was inexorably linked in the popular imagination) would have been inescapable to viewers of this poster. Not only was Cawas India's original Tarzan, the 'authentic' Indian mimic Tarzan, now doubly mimicked with the young Dileep Raj in the title role, but his name appears in bold lettering on the poster itself, offering audiences the reassurance that John Cawas, as this film's director, is still in control, lending the glamour of the Cawas brand to this pallid remake.

Although the posters of *Zimbo* and *Khilari* might appear to the casual observer dramatically different in content, there are remarkable continuities, not least in their repackaging of elements from Basant's own history. Similar oppositions underlie and structure both, broadly a development of themes already revealed in *Toofani Tarzan*: urban vs rural, civilised vs primitive, Westernised vs traditional, masculine vs feminine, and both posters, in their different ways, make considerable play with the fluidity of gender roles.

The poster for *Khilari* offers more of a puzzle than *Zimbo*'s, coding its themes within a more complex layout, as well as assuming a broader range of cultural knowledges and references that audiences would draw on. The top right-hand corner is a dystopic urban nightmare: vivid red and yellow brushstrokes suggest the turmoil of a fiery hell. It is a site of frenzied action: an aeroplane shoots out at a dramatic angle, a helicopter hovers over toppling tower blocks, a posse of survivors hangs precariously from a net beneath. This is equally the Indian metropolitan dream turned sour, a just punishment for a wicked Western world and, for many rural audiences, a vision of Kaliyug itself.[28] Standing guard against this inferno is an exotic, gun-toting, sexy siren from the 'Westernised' world, in black catsuit and high heels, a flaming mane of auburn hair and large red belt emphasising her curvaceous body and her fiery, dangerous but powerful, sexuality. Directly opposite, in the bottom left, against the wet dream idyll of a steamy waterfall, another dangerously enticing sexuality beckons. This is nature's rural temptress, the exotic, 'primitive' tribal belle whose sexuality is 'untamed', a vamp whose skimpy ethnic clothes reveal her sensuous and alluring body as she dances seductively for the camera.

Mediating between these two extremes are three figures. The hero and his sexy 1960s babe lie across the poster's central ground, offering a promise that order will ultimately be restored and hinting that, within a glamorously Westernised world, the paradise of traditional rural life is still nearby. Hovering over this couple, like an avenging guardian angel, is the reassuringly triumphant and heroic Nadia.

Four female figures dominate the poster: two, with guns, take active control; two present themselves as erotic display. Despite this, the hero comfortably controls the centre ground, his hands firmly clasped around the biggest gun of all, his eyes masterfully focused on a distant target. As he snakes along a grassy bank, hints of the trees of the jungle behind him implicitly identify him with the virile muscular action and ur-Indian romance of Tarzan's world. But Dileep Raj's boyish, smiling features and exaggerated rock'n'roll quiff (complete with dramatic blue highlight) simultaneously evoke that other junglee, Shammi Kapoor, whose 1961 film had unleashed on India—to the scandalised tirades of traditionalists—its own energetic youth pop culture, and Dileep is excitingly 'Westernised' by these associations. Where the junglee of both Tarzan and Zimbo swings from trees in a forest, *Khilari*'s modern 'junglee' will swing from cranes and helicopters over a city skyline, leading a fast life as a debonair, handsome young man-about-town.

Dileep's sex kitten partner displays herself in classic pin-up pose, engaging our gaze and teasingly presenting herself, through contradictory signals, as both demure and sexually available. This figure combines and unifies visual motifs from the rest of the image. The towel around her head suggests that she has just bathed, evoking the sexiness of the waterfall but simultaneously modestly covering her hair. The sizzling orange flame-like pattern of her mini-dress echoes the inferno of the cityscape and the fiery sexuality and hot passion of the cat-suited femme fatale. The white brushstrokes behind her head, and arms opened to display her breasts and voluptuous but vulnerable body, echo—and subvert—the masterful figure of Nadia, commanding the skies of the top left. To fire, water and air is added earth: her snake-like, plump, bare legs, tantalisingly displayed but modestly half-crossed, lie alongside the hero, firmly grounded on the brown earth. However excitingly modern she may seem, she is still safely traditional, still a daughter of mother earth and Mother India.

Khilari's major selling point was Fearless Nadia and the two gun-toting female figures were undoubtedly key to the poster's appeal. Commanding the top left-hand corner of the frame, and echoing the placement of the Tarzan figure and his knife in the *Zimbo* poster, is Nadia's victorious and heroic spy-mistress, Madam XI. Left hand firmly on her hip in a gesture of control and authority, a masculine jacket zippered almost to the top, she brandishes her powerful gun high above her head, the only feminising touch her blood red fingernails and lips. Eyes raised heavenwards, she is the picture of the 'courage, strength, idealism' of her early years. Her cat-suited double, the fetishistic sexualised side of Nadia's feisty persona, stands guard behind. She is simultaneously a protective cover for alter ego, Madam XI, and also our protection against the terrifying cityscape.

The reappearance of Fearless Nadia after almost a decade is not only the audiences' guarantee of exciting Basant thrills, but also provides them with the reassurance they desire as they enter thrilling modern worlds. Throughout her career, Nadia's persona had been identified with the accoutrements of modern technology where she was emphatically in control: she ran, fighting, along the tops of moving trains, she drove fast cars, and she hung from aeroplanes. Throughout the 1940s and 1950s she continued to signify much that was considered dangerously exciting. Now, even at sixty, she continued to punch her weight for Basant: larger than life, sexy and irreverent, her persona was still subverting stereotypes as she confidently redefined the boundaries of what older women could do. Perhaps only Fearless Nadia could provide a viably familiar counterweight to the visceral potency of the James Bond figure and thereby temper it for Indian audiences to laugh at and enjoy.

If the Wadias' Cawas, as Tarzan, had in the pre-independence era opened a fluid space for exploration of a modern Indian masculinity that drew on subaltern male bodybuilding cultures, their Nadia persona opened a similar—and arguably even more important—space for femininity. Where Cawas had offered a 'counter-hero' to the soft romantic male leads of the mainstream social melodramas from the late 1930s onwards, Nadia offered a 'counter-heroine'. Where Tarzan's masculinity could be simultaneously virile, potent, muscular, compassionate, childish and feminised, Nadia's femininity was charming, compassionate, moral, independent, tough, aggressive and sexy. In this, the Fearless Nadia–John Cawas partnership offered—right through the 1950s and 1960s—not only a brand that audiences would trust and identify with but also a joyous imaginative space of potential resistance to the increasing hegemony of India's upper-class, upper-caste elite. While, by the late 1960s, Basant's overwhelmingly commercial sensibility had reduced their films to an astute process of assemblage—a recombination of elements that drew on brands local and global—what they still offered audiences was a visceral cosmopolitanism channelled through a subaltern vernacular, with its own distinctive take on the global 1960s.

While Mrs Gandhi was launching her Wheat Revolution, and the Beatles unleashed peace and love on the world, what did Indian audiences make of the *Zimbo* and *Khilari* posters? All but the poorest ignored them completely; these were not 'A-grade' films, the world had moved on and Nadia was well past her prime. But for subaltern audiences who still responded to the Wadia magic, here was an entry into exotic other worlds, packaged with comic-book violence, sex and a self-parodic, wacky humour, incorporated within conventions and stories they knew. Most importantly, the films were fun, playfully opening up myriad new ways of being both modern and Indian, male and female, while gently spoofing the popular culture of a transnational world.

Too bad the Beatles never made it out to Basant studios. 'Zimbo and Son Meet the Girl with a Gun'... it could almost have been on the White Album.

SIXTIES TRIVIA   In 1965, a Christine Keeler was credited with a bit part in *Tarzan and the Circus*, a cheap Bombay film aimed at the Nigerian market.[29] Azad, who'd made his name as Zimbo, starred as Tarzan.

Emma Peel's Diana Rigg spent her childhood in India (1938–46) where she learnt Hindi, went to the movies and ... well ... just *might* have seen those whip-cracking Fearless Nadia films.

In May 1968, just weeks after returning from India (and while Paris burned), the Beatles recorded the first version of 'Happiness is a Warm Gun' at George's house in Surrey. Had they, perhaps, caught a glimpse of that *Khilari* poster after all ...?

NOTES

1. As in earlier chapters, material on the Wadias draws on meetings the author had with Homi and JBH in 1980 and 1981; on her interviews with Homi and Mary (Nadia) Wadia in 1986; the documentary *Fearless: The Hunterwali Story* (Riyad Wadia, 1993); the published writings of J.B.H. Wadia, together with JBH's unpublished essays, kindly made available by the Wadia Movietone archive.

2. The combined profits of the Hindi and Tamil versions of Wadias' 1937 *Toofani Tarzan* were Rs 258,241, even more than their mega-hit, *Hunterwali* (Rs 256,148). By 1942, the Hindi version had made Rs 198,241 and the Tamil version Rs 60,000. The extraordinary success of the film in the Madras territory (both Hindi and Tamil versions showed there and together account for more than a third of the film's all-India profits) would merit further research.

3. *Zimbo* (Homi Wadia, 1958); *Zimbo Comes to Town* (Nanabhai Bhatt, 1960); *Zimbo Finds a Son* (John Cawas, 1966). See chapter six for a discussion of lobby cards for *Zimbo* in the Priya Paul archive.

4. J.B.H. Wadia, 'Those Were the Days', *Cinema Vision India*, p. 94.

5. Marianna Torgovnick, *Gone Primitive: Savage Intellects, Modern Lives*, Chicago: University of Chicago Press, 1991, p. 42; Gabe Essoe, *Tarzan of the Movies*, New York: Citadel Press, 1968, p. 187.

6. J.B.H. Wadia, 'The Making of *Toofani Tarzan*', unpublished essay quoted courtesy of Wadia Movietone archive.

7. *Mahabali Hanuman* (Babubhai Mistry, 1981).

8. Discussion with technicians and actors at Basant studios, 11 April 1980. Mythologicals were also known as *pauranik* and *dharmik* films in the 1930s and 1940s.

9. Connie Haham, *Enchantment of the Mind: Manmohan Desai's Films*, New Delhi: Roli Books, 2006, p. 9.

10. Dialogue and lyrics translations from Channel Four UK transmission of *Toofani Tarzan*.

11. Interestingly, the epitome of both evils is ultimately 'Westernised', as the evil cannibals are dressed in the generic face paint and feather headdress of the wild west 'Indians' of American movie mythology.

12. Wadia explains that he was forced to create this strange, and by today's standards offensively racist, character as Professor Deval's Circus had no trained apes. He is played by Boman Shroff, who himself had a reputation as one of the Wadias' stunt heroes, and who had played the jinni's man-servant, a very similar role, in *Lal-e-Yaman*.

13. Ashis Nandy, *At the Edge of Psychology*, New Delhi: Oxford University Press, 1980, p. 37.

14. Barbara Creed has pointed this out in 'Me Tarzan: You Jane!—A Case of Mistaken Identity in Paradise', *Continuum: Journal of Media and Cultural Studies*, vol. 1, no. 1, 1988, pp. 159–74.

15. Creed describes a similar series of moves in *Tarzan, the Ape Man* (ibid., pp. 163–5).

16. Leela, however, is neither a fighter nor a stunt woman.

17. Creed, 'Me Tarzan', p. 166.

18. It is not, as invariably misquoted in accounts of the MGM movie, 'Me Tarzan You Jane'. Creed suggests the line is so conveniently misremembered because 'Me Tarzan, You Jane' returns control to the male voice (ibid., pp. 166–7).

19. He was not quite the unwilling innocent that JBH's memoirs claim. A letter advertising that he was 'planning to join the film industry and looking for producers', with a full list of the stunts that he was in training for and would be able to perform, appeared in *Varieties Weekly*, 16 December 1933.

20. Perhaps this would have been seen as too much like copying, placing Cawas as second-rate—the MGM films were in distribution there at the time. More intriguingly, it suggests the magic of the silent era stars was still unsurpassed: the capital accrued from the brand name Eddie Polo—who never himself played Tarzan—places *Toofani Tarzan* beyond a simple copying of the US Tarzan films and into the realm of great cinema nostalgia.

21. Franz Fanon, *Black Skins, White Masks*, London: Pluto Press, 2008 [1952; 1968 in English], p. 118.

22. Essoe, *Tarzan of the Movies*, p. 87.

23. Torgovnick, *Gone Primitive*, p. 42.

24. Except, one might argue, in fantasy.

25. JBH seems genuinely astonished that a legal representative from the Burroughs estate had the temerity to visit him a couple of months after *Toofani Tarzan*'s release demanding that all references to the copyright name be wiped out. He congratulates himself on charming the agent into dropping the legal case but, with the remakes from 1958 onwards, the Wadias played safe and changed the name to Zimbo. Other 1960s Indian Tarzan producers had no such scruples and, when challenged about ten films using the Tarzan name between 1963 and 1965,

Sargaam Chitra Ltd claimed the films were 'only' for the Nigerian market. Essoe, *Tarzan of the Movies*, pp. 204–7.

26. Sir Henry Yule, A.C. Burnell and William Crooke (eds), *Hobson-Jobson: A Glossary of Colloquial Anglo-Indian Words and Phrases*, London: Routledge, 1985, pp. 470–1.

27. 'Tarzan, you're such a wild thing/uncultivated person.'

28. For more on this concept (lit. the era of Kali) expressing the degradation of the modern world, see Christopher Pinney's analysis of a calendar poster in 'Moral Topophilia: The Significations of Landscape in Indian Oleographs', in *The Anthropology of Landscape*, eds Eric Hirsch and Michael O'Hanlon, Oxford: Clarendon Press, 1985, p. 84.

29. According to Essoe, 'Released in 1965, *Tarzan and the Circus* featured Christine Keeler as the proprietess of the travelling show and carnival' (*Tarzan of the Movies*, p. 208). One presumes this was a pseudonym—and another example of the Indian film industry playfully exploiting a globally known Western brand, such as the name 'Christine Keeler' had become.

six

Still Magic
An Aladdin's Cave of 1950s B-Movie Fantasy

MAGICAL WORLDS

Fantasies permit you to stretch your imagination, to think out tricks which will thrill the audience, it's a bit like magic this fantasy film making.
Homi Wadia, film director and producer, 1991[1]

One of the greatest pleasures of trawling the Priya Paul archive is the haphazard nature of its material and the unexpectedness of what has been saved and collected. Several hundred cinema-related artefacts are here: mostly film stills, lobby cards and publicity brochures. But excitingly, the story they tell is quite unlike the conventional histories of Indian cinema. The great auteurs of Indian cinema of the 1950s and 1960s are, for the most part, barely represented: the archive boasts only a handful of stills from Raj Kapoor's key films and just one, poignantly damaged, image of a *Pyaasa* dreamscape to stand in for Guru Dutt's whole directorial oeuvre. Meanwhile, we are treated to a full set of pristine, blood-curdling collages from the 'jungle mighty thriller' *Adam Khor* (Cannibal, Akkoo, 1955) and almost two dozen charmingly theatrical photographs of *Alif Laila* (The Thousand and One Nights, K. Amarnath, 1953) (Figure 6.1).[2] Alongside these lie dozens of stills and ephemera from other B-movies of the 1950s and 1960s Bombay industry—long-forgotten films that were blithely ignored by the elite of their day, never made it into any history book, and which are now, for the most part, impossible to see. The traces of 'trash' in this archive may be one of the only keys to their fantastical worlds.

Figure 6.1 *Alif Laila* (1953) lobby card for the movie theatres. Aladdin (Vijay Kumar) and Rashid (Gope) enter the magician's (Pran's) cave.

Source: Courtesy Tasveer Ghar.

The current chapter explores this archive's visions of the overtly extraordinary: of magical worlds in which the impossible happens, of superhuman bodies pushed to their extremes. As we have already seen, two film genres dominated India's B-movie circuit in the 1950s and 1960s: stunt and fantasy films—otherwise known as 'fighting' and 'magic' (or jadoo) films. While the former referred to all manner of action films, which invariably drew openly on the Hollywood 'lower' genres popular in India since the silent era, India's fantasy films were spun around magical and wondrous happenings in a quasi-Arabian Islamic setting, most drawing loosely on oral and literary traditions of the *Arabian Nights*.[3] As chapter one demonstrated, throughout the 1950s, cheaply made fantasy films, which included plenty of action, made good money on the mofussil[4] and rural circuits, as well as the working-class areas of larger cities. Bombay production companies like Homi Wadia's Basant Pictures, the kings of these genres, flourished. What the process of immersing oneself in the Priya Paul archive makes clear is not only how ubiquitous such imagery must have been, but also just how closely linked the stunt and fantasy films were and how much they both drew on—and overlapped with—other forms of visual culture in everyday circulation, both within India and around the globe.

Magical worlds and superhuman feats have a long history within India's mythological traditions, both its Hindu religious epics and the stories and legends of the Muslim world, including qissa-dastan. Such imagery also permeated the mythology of a 'mystic East' that fired the Victorian imagination across Europe. Travellers' tales of the extraordinary happenings and sensual wonders to be found in India were accompanied by such images of snake charmers, fakirs and dancing girls as we find in many of the Priya Paul archive's postcards and prints. In turn, British designers of turn-of-the-century textile labels drew on such imagery to feed into India's own perceived appetite for the extraordinary. In fact, India had an ambivalent relationship to its own exoticism: the myth of the 'mystic East' was enthusiastically exploited by many of India's own magicians, jugglers, conjurors, fakirs and mystics.[5] Such imagery did indeed reflect some realities of subaltern performance culture: Indian 'jugglers' (magicians) were an integral part of the street culture of the bazaars, alongside acrobats, snake charmers and performing animals, even as late as the 1930s, according to Pran Nevile's accounts of his Lahore childhood.[6]

Since the mid-eighteenth century, the circus had been gradually introduced alongside this culture; by the start of the twentieth century, Indian circuses, incorporating Indian traditional martial arts, acrobatics, magic and lion-taming acts, were travelling across India's entertainment circuits alongside circuses from Europe, Russia, Japan and elsewhere, inviting audiences to wonder at apparently impossible feats that confounded the rules of the ordinary world. All such shows celebrated bodies pushed to their extremes and wild beasts subdued by men's—and women's—remarkable powers. An underclass of artistes from European, middle-Eastern, Indian and Anglo-Indian backgrounds provided the bodies that peopled these extravaganzas, which were, in many senses, transcultural shows, seen as ambiguously both modern and traditional. European and Asian traditions merged to present hybrid fantasies of exotic otherness. Anecdotal accounts suggest circus images were almost as popular as Hindu gods and goddesses in the turn-of-the-century magic lantern shows that toured

India.[7] It is perhaps not surprising that circus scenes found their way onto textile labels designed to encourage Indian consumers to buy British wares.

One textile label from the archive captures this transculturalism particularly strikingly (Figure 6.2). Speaking globalisation at every level, it is an advert for Ralli Brothers, a famous family firm of nineteenth-century global trading entrepreneurs. Originally from Greece, this formidable merchant family strategically dispatched its sons to open offices in London, Constantinople, Bombay and Calcutta, as well as Russia, Eastern Europe and the Middle East (and latterly USA and China) and exploited early international trading markets in textiles, grain, silk and much else with extraordinary vigour and success.[8]

Ralli Brothers' chosen image is of a female acrobat floating through clouds, her striped parachute held aloft. Ostensibly of a

Figure 6.2   Textile label for Ralli Brothers

Source: Courtesy Tasveer Ghar.

circus artiste, this dream-like image simultaneously invokes both the tradition of Indian acrobats and jugglers/magicians—tricks such as 'the man seated in the air' were legendary parts of their repertoires—and the ethereal qualities of the winged pari or fairy of Persian legend. In keeping with circus artistes, the woman is scantily dressed for an Indian context and of ambiguous ethnicity. The distressed condition of this textile label—torn, stained, scratched and ineptly stuck together to produce a startlingly dismembered arm and jagged storm clouds beneath her—adds to a dramatic sense of danger and other-worldliness. It is a transcultural image of thrills—erotic and visceral—which keys into one of the most pervasive of human magical fantasies, the dream of flying. It also fortuitously provides a bridge between the performance cultures of subaltern audiences and the B-movies, as we shall see.

ARABIAN NIGHTS

Nothing is predictable in a fantasy. Besides the surprising twists and turns in the plot, one could indulge in spectacular mounting—grand sets, gorgeous costumes.

Homi Wadia on fantasy films, 1991

If Ralli Brothers' aerialist was chosen to sell textiles back to India after Indian cotton's profitable journey around the world, another dreamscape of magical flying (Figure 6.3) was designed to sell Indian audiences a film based on the *Arabian Nights*—stories originally from India that were returning, embellished and transformed, after circulating global cultures over several centuries. It is perhaps fitting that this Aladdin's cave of an archive includes half-a-dozen cinema lobby display stills from Homi Wadia's (1952) *Aladdin and the Wonderful Lamp*. 'Aladdin', as probably every reader knows, is the story of a good-hearted, if feckless, young man who comes into untold, unearned wealth and magical powers through command of a supernatural being: a jinni arrives to do his will whenever he rubs a dirty old lamp he inadvertently acquired in an enchanted cave through a wicked magician's trickery. What exists in the Priya Paul archive is undoubtedly not a complete publicity set—and most of

Figure 6.3 *Aladdin and the Wonderful Lamp* (1952) lobby card for the movie theatres. Flying jinni played by Vasantrao Pahalwan.

Source: © Basant Pictures. Courtesy Roy Wadia/Wadia Movietone and Tasveer Ghar.

these photographs are damaged and fragile—but, in the spirit of the serendipity of the archive, I propose to use a selection of these fragments as pegs from which to hang my chapter, allowing each section to unfold somewhat organically around a different still from *Aladdin*.

Figure 6.3 is a composite photograph, loosely based on the film's final scene. The all-powerful jinni, the genie of the magic lamp, flies through dramatic storm clouds with Aladdin's luxurious palace balanced precariously in his arms, while the crowd in the streets of Baghdad below celebrates Aladdin's triumphant return to his mother's side, his beautiful princess bride and entourage in tow. The image has curious resonances of the Ralli Brothers' acrobat: both are dreamscapes in which apparently magical flying promises to transport consumers out of the mundane world and into an enchanted domain. In both cases, for viewers today, the burnished bronze rust stains and degraded image lend the sepia, silvery brown and cream images a heightened quality of unreality and a magical golden glow. For its contemporary audience, the gigantic flying jinni in the silver-lined clouds would have made this instantly recognisable as a fantasy film. However, this publicity image did not have too much work to do: the story of Aladdin was as well known in 1950s India as it was in Europe.

The *Arabian Nights* was a significant presence within European and Indian arts, theatre and literary cultures of the Victorian era, as detailed in chapter two. By the time cinema arrived in India, a vernacular tradition of eclectic integration of the *Arabian Nights* within other local and foreign forms was well established. The *Nights*—and their Indo-Persian variants from the qissa-dastan tradition—were enthusiastically taken up by Indian film-makers in the silent and early sound eras. The *Arabian Nights* fantasy film fell out of fashion in the 1940s, but the success of Homi Wadia's *Aladdin* in 1952 kick-started a new vogue for fantasy films on the B- and C-circuits. By the mid-1950s these and costume films together accounted for around a third of all productions.[9]

The Priya Paul archive's twenty-three stills from K. Amarnath's *Alif Laila*[10] (1953) give us a rare overview of the narrative and visual motifs of these fantastical worlds. *Alif Laila's* story is an 'Aladdin' hybrid.[11] Set in Baghdad, it tells of Aladdin's love for a beautiful princess, of a magic lamp found in a cave, and of a wicked magician who tries to thwart him (Figure 6.1). To this it adds other stock *Arabian Nights* and qissa-dastan or Persian fairy-tale elements: the pari of the magic lamp, humans transformed into animals by the wicked magician, magic rings and flying carpets.

As the glimpses of *Alif Laila* indicate, the mise-en-scène of fantasy films recycled a series of cultural clichés and architectural tropes. Onion domes, minarets, crescent moons, giant urns, terraced gardens, filigree, colonnades and scalloped Islamic arches conveyed an orientalist imaginary drawn as much from Parsi theatre as from Hollywood's *Thief of Bagdad*. Parsi theatre and early Bombay cinema both also drew on European image-makers: we may remember that Jamshed Wadia's memoirs mentioned the 'profusely illustrated

Figure 6.4 *Jahan Ara* (1964) lobby card for the movie theatres. An historical starring Mala Sinha, Prithviraj Kapoor and Bharat Bhushan.

Source: Courtesy Tasveer Ghar.

books on art, architecture, costumes and furniture designs', including 'beautifully bound German volumes', that he and Homi, together with their art director from the Parsi theatre, used for their Islamicate sets.[12] Such mise-en-scène also defined the 'legend' and 'historical' films based in a Mughal or Islamic world, in which grandeur was de rigueur. Cinema lobby cards from *Jahan Ara* (Vinod Kumar, 1964) encapsulate the dream-like beauty of this quasi-Mughal imaginary (Figure 6.4).

So why were the *Arabian Nights* such a compelling vehicle for Indian film-makers? Homi Wadia gives us some important clues: the *Nights'* licensed grandeur and unpredictable storylines—what he referred to as 'surprising twists and turns in the plot', 'grand sets' and 'spectacular mounting'. Moreover, as I argued in earlier chapters, Islamicate worlds were a ploy to appeal to India's large Muslim audiences of the day, although their appeal was by no means restricted to these communities: the tales offered recognisable motifs that would resonate with the wider Indian audiences' cultural knowledge and shared fantasies. However, I also suggest, the 'Arabian Nights fantasy film' worked with Indian audiences because it was ambiguously coded: it was simultaneously both a refusal of all things Western, and also modern and Western, in tune with global cosmopolitan modernity. Reading across the body of images within the current archive, however, we see that the Orient it peddled was a hybrid of East and West that is more complex than it first appears.

A FABULOUS ORIENT

> *The dances has [sic] to look elaborate with plenty of chorus girls and dreamy backdrops with clouds coming out from the heavens, created by smoke machines. A 'novelty' dance was a must.*
>
> Homi Wadia on fantasy films, 1991

Along with unpredictable plot twists and spectacular sets, gorgeous costumes were an integral part of this Islamicate dreamworld (Figure 6.5).

Two of the archive's six *Aladdin* stills are utopic poses of the film's leading romantic couples in extravagant 'oriental' outfits, boasting details such as a crescent moon and star hairclip or turbans dripping with pearls, which drew as much on a confused Hollywood orientalist imagination—and Parsi theatre—as on any recognisable Arabic tradition or reality. Star spectacle was arguably less crucial: while today there is a potent charge to seeing the beautiful, teenaged Meena Kumari here as the main heroine, in 1952 she was still a minor star of the B-movie world, as was her male lead, Mahipal. Basant Pictures developed its own stable of ensemble players, recognisable to its C-circuit audiences but rarely making the transition into A-grade stars that Meena Kumari—and a few others—did.[13]

Aladdin's lead actresses' costumes are reassuringly demure, promising the allure of love and romance within an exotic 'other' world, but one that is, importantly, not the decadent modern West. Presumably, the stills were designed to entice a family audience—a key aspiration of the fantasy films. But this coyness is not quite what emerges in the film itself. As Homi Wadia's quote (introducing this

Figure 6.5 *Aladdin and the Wonderful Lamp* (1952) lobby card for the movie theatres. Stars Meena Kumari as Princess Budur and Mahipal as Aladdin.

Source: © Basant Pictures. Courtesy Roy Wadia/ Wadia Movietone and Tasveer Ghar.

section) indicates, spectacular dance sequences were a sine qua non of the fantasy film. While none of the archive's six *Aladdin* stills even hints at such excess, the film did indeed flaunt 'plenty of chorus girls and dreamy backdrops'. *Aladdin* climaxes with a dramatic dream sequence song in which, above frantically belching smoke machines and choirs of nubile chorus girls, Meena Kumari is strung up in a giant spider's web as the rapacious villain makes pincer movements towards her.[14] Homi Wadia's *Hatimtai* (1956), his own favourite film, which became a cult classic on the B-circuit, is even more extravagant: its chorus lines burst with pink clouds of nymph-like fairies/paris, their richly feathered wings aflutter, as an advert in the archive for *Hatimtai*'s re-release reminds its fans.

In addition to—and quite distinct from—these displays was what Wadia calls the 'novelty dance'. In *Aladdin*, the promised scene arrives an hour into the film. Bearers bring an enormous carpet into the Sultan's court. As it gradually unrolls, a professional acrobatic dancer emerges, sensuously lithe and skimpily clad. She twirls, jumps, gyrates, is thrown through the air and balances precariously on her partner's shoulders. Often framed as 'gypsy', Arabic or Turkish dance, sometimes including belly dancing and invariably credited quite simply as 'Oriental Dances', these sequences reflected a transnational orientalist imagination: the women were always implicitly 'non-Indian', whether European, Eastern European or Middle Eastern. Moreover, their acts invoked circus and cabaret—from which many of these performers came—in a tradition reminiscent of the Ralli Brothers' aerialist (Figure 6.2).

While, on the archive's evidence, no hint of *Aladdin*'s dance spectacle—'novelty' or otherwise—appeared in its publicity, *Alif Laila*'s lobby stills were a little more forthcoming. One of these shows grand celebrations in the Baghdad royal palace for the princess's engagement. But this apparently conventional film dance image has unexpected—and for the archive adventurer exciting—historical significance: beneath the scalloped Islamicate arches and in front of a chorus of sensuously swaying dancers is the fourteen-year-old Helen Richardson, performing her first screen solo. Helen, who later made her name as the wickedly seductive, Westernised 'vamp' of countless seedy cabarets of 1960s and 1970s Bombay cinema, began her career in the B-movies as an exotic oriental attraction, dancing her way through chorus lines and solos in dozens of fantasy films, including Homi Wadia's *Alibaba* (1954) and *Hatimtai* (1956).

The fluid transition that Helen effected between oriental and Westernised versions of the exotic is not insignificant: it was indeed part of her unique appeal. Of both European and Burmese ancestry, Helen could perform 'otherness' in a number of (overlapping) dimensions.

A calendar poster of Helen from the late 1950s (Figure 6.6) epitomises this fluidity. It celebrates Helen's famous role in *Howrah Bridge* (Shakti Samanta, 1958), with her now iconic song 'Mera Naam Chin Chin Chu'.[15] Curiously, this poster takes us back once again to

235

Figure 6.6 Poster of Anglo-Burmese star,
Helen, as cabaret dancer 'Chin Chin Chu',
from the film *Howrah Bridge* (1958)

Source: Courtesy Tasveer Ghar.

the *Arabian Nights*. The song was a reference to *Chu Chin Chow*, the spectacular orientalist musical of the 'Ali Baba' story that had been the biggest hit of the London theatre world from 1916 until the late 1940s. The show successfully toured the United States and Australia and spawned a Gainsborough film (*Chu Chin Chow*, Oscar Ashe, 1934) that was undoubtedly seen in India.[16] The musical *Chu Chin Chow* permeated British popular culture and fashion of its day and its racist and orientalist tropes were exported around the world, as Helen's Chin Chin Chu persona reflects. But the song itself, set to jaunty Western jazz-style swing in a nightclub of jiving sailors, fuses several exotic worlds. With the saucy refrain 'Mera Naam Chin Chin Chu, Hello Mister, How-Do-You-Do?' Helen is simultaneously a modern city girl and an oriental sexpot, with the *Arabian Nights* implicitly providing the bridge between the two.

Helen followed in a tradition of 'unrespectable' women in cinema. From Indian cinema's earliest days, women working in film had been stigmatised—a hangover from the early-twentieth-century association of women performing song and dance in public with either Muslim courtesan culture or European variety entertainment and cabaret, from where many silent film actresses came. Women whose bodies were on public display were most comfortably seen as 'other' to the Hindu mainstream: either of Anglo-European or Eurasian origin, or of Muslim *tawaif* (courtesan) background. In some cases, such as the recording artist and courtesan Gauhar Jaan, celebrated on a matchbox cover in the archive, with pale skin and rosy cheeks, they were both. By the talkie era, more Muslim women were entering the film industry, especially from nautch (dance) and theatre, but not without problems: Meena Kumari, whose parents were a dancer and an Urdu-Parsi theatre actor, was encouraged to change her name from Mahajabeen to disguise her Muslim background. Only when she hit the A-list with the success of a 'respectable' historical, *Baiju Bawra* (Vijay Bhatt, 1952), shortly after *Aladdin* was released, was she feted amongst the pantheon of A-list stars available to grace business calendars, as we find in this 1953 calendar poster catalogue held by the archive.

If the subaltern bodies of the erotic arts—cabaret and nautch—provided many (but by no means all) of the female stars of India's silent cinema, those of the martial arts—bodybuilders and wrestlers—provided a stream of male bodies, as Kaushik Bhaumik has argued.[17] The B-movies of the 1950s inherited and perpetuated this tradition, thereby further undermining the status of fantasy and stunt films amongst the elite. However, for the C-circuit audiences this was to prove an irresistible bonus.

BRUTE STRENGTH

> *Gimmicks wasn't a dirty word then, one had to think very hard and be absolutely inventive while presenting flying carpet rides and action scenes. Chase sequences, fencing, horseback riding, daredevilry, were part of the fun.*
>
> Homi Wadia on fantasy films, 1991

Displays of fighting and pumped-up male bodies were as important to fantasy films as the special effects that created their

Figure 6.7 *Aladdin and the Wonderful Lamp*
(1952) lobby card for the movie theatres. Aladdin
(Mahipal) in a sword duel with the wicked
courtier, with the jinni (Vasantrao Pahalwan).

Source: © Basant Pictures. Courtesy Roy Wadia/Wadia
Movietone and Tasveer Ghar.

fantastical worlds, as this composite image from *Aladdin* indicates.
In Figure 6.7, Aladdin has challenged a villainous courtier to a sword
fight to save the princess he loves from the clutches of her father's
wicked usurper. Further duels to win her hand—and save her life—
take place within the enchanted palace that we see in miniature in
the top of the frame, balanced on the edge of a waterfall by the giant
jinni.[18] In another still, Aladdin arm-wrestles the villain's henchman
in front of a crowd of onlookers. As we have seen in earlier chapters,
action and 'thrills' had been a key component of all popular genres—
mythologicals, costume, stunt and fantasy films—since the silent
era, when Hollywood action serials flooded the Indian market. In

the 1920s, Douglas Fairbanks was as big a star in India as across the rest of the world: both *Mark of Zorro* and *Thief of Bagdad* made their mark on Indian audiences, with Homi and Jamshed Wadia foremost amongst their admirers. In *Aladdin*, Mahipal plays a swashbuckling hero directly in the Fairbanks mould, displaying much of the balletic agility of Fairbanks's Baghdad thief.[19] He fights, he fences, he wrestles, he jumps, he dances and he romances.

But if *Aladdin*'s swashbuckling heroics were inspired by the 1924 Hollywood *Thief of Bagdad*, the jinni borrows directly from a later, British version of the tale: *Thief of Bagdad* (Alexander Korda, 1940), which established the visual and performance style of many subsequent Indian jinns.[20] However, this is not simply a rip-off of a successful Western film: Indian audiences would have immediately recognised the figure as an archetypal wrestler's (or pahalwan's) body—indeed, the role was played by Vasantrao Pahalwan, who, like several of the stars of early action cinema and the B-movies, came from Bombay's wrestling community. Moreover, Indian wrestling developed within its own long and distinctive martial arts traditions quite independently of Western wrestling, with Hindu and Muslim variants celebrating, respectively, Hanuman and Ali. Most cities had *akharas* (gymnasia), communities in which boys and young men could learn wrestling and its strict disciplines: rigorous training regimes, high-fat diets, religious ritual and celibacy.[21] Wrestling was central to subaltern male performance cultures of early-twentieth-century India: its champions such as Gama, Imam Bakhsh and Hamida became folk heroes, celebrated with nationalist zeal, as a series of posters in the Priya Paul archive from Kanpur, which probably circulated in the 1930s, suggests.

Gama, 'Lion of Punjab', was a legend even amongst wrestling heroes. Undefeated throughout his life, his daily diet included 10 litres of milk, half a litre of *ghee*, a litre and a half of butter, and 2 kilograms of fruit.[22] In 1910, in London, Gama and his brother, Imam Bakhsh, routed a succession of Europeans who, to that date, had considered themselves 'champions'. In 1928, Gama definitively defeated the European Zbyszko, the previous world champion, in forty-two seconds in front of 40,000 triumphant spectators in Patiala. After that no one agreed to fight him again. Another hero, Hamida, who fought as one of Gama's proxies, was also part of this extraordinary Punjabi Muslim extended family, which provided nationalist role models to lower-class men.[23]

At the same time, international fantasies of superhuman masculinity and machismo circulated in India through the iconic figure of Tarzan, the half-wild man of 'civilised' origins. As discussed in the last chapter, J.B.H. Wadia's memoirs tell of the popularity in India of Hollywood's 1918 Tarzan and, especially, the films of Johnny Weissmuller in the 1930s.[24] Thus it is no surprise to find a desi Tarzan adorning Indian matchboxes in this collection. Seamlessly transposed to a fantastical south Indian setting, amidst rice fields and sugarcane groves, Tarzan plunges his dagger into a lion's jaws, his obedient ape companion at his side.

As we know, the Wadia brothers were quick to capitalise on the Tarzan brand: Homi Wadia directed *Toofani Tarzan*[25] in 1937, remaking it as the *Zimbo* series from 1958, and 'Indianising' the original story, as described in some detail in the last chapter. While much could be written about this archive's half-dozen glorious, hand-coloured cinema lobby collages from *Zimbo*, this is beyond the scope of the present chapter. Here I refer to them primarily to make some simple comparisons and to contextualise the fantasy films.

Despite their different settings, there were substantial overlaps between the stunt and fantasy films, produced side by side at studios such as Basant. Visual traces in this archive show that both deployed similar 'thrills' and used the same core actors. Both showcased lower-class performance forms such as wrestling and oriental dance. In Figure 6.8 we see a triumphant bodybuilder, as well as a perilous rope-bridge-over-ravine 'thrill', but in another *Zimbo* lobby card washed up in this archive, we catch the tantalising glimpse of an oriental dancer, her deadly knife held aloft. Both stunt and fantasy films showcased the special effects for which Basant was renowned, although in fantasies (and mythologicals) these were a more central attraction, reflecting their slightly different target audiences. Where stunt films were aimed primarily at men, fantasies were seen as family films. But their audiences in fact crossed over, not unlike circus, a form close to both. The Wadias used animals and performers from Professor Deval's Circus for many years (note *Zimbo*'s bicycling chimp

Figure 6.8 *Zimbo* (1958) hand-coloured collage used as lobby card for the movie theatres. The film stars Chitra and Azad; Azad (Zimbo/Tarzan) lifts a 'tribal'.

Source: © Basant Pictures. Courtesy Roy Wadia/Wadia Movietone and Tasveer Ghar.

in Figure 6.8) and *Aladdin*'s parallels with circus were implicit in its quasi-oriental acrobatic novelty dances, strongmen, magic and visual illusion—all attractions that celebrate human control over nature and a pushing of the boundaries of the quotidian.

Paradoxically, both *Aladdin* and *Zimbo/Tarzan* embody—and speak—modernity. Although neither is set in any (recognisable) modern world, both reflect—and draw sustenance from—the global circulation of 'trashy' images and stories of their contemporary world. Crucially, both were based on stories that had huge global appeal in the early twentieth century: the *Arabian Nights* and Edgar Rice Burroughs's *Tarzan* novels.[26] Both films 'Indianised' their sources, albeit in different ways. As discussed in the last chapter, the 'others' of *Zimbo/Tarzan*'s imaginary world were 'tribal' cannibals in an uncivilised jungle and seductively decadent 'Westernised' babes. *Aladdin*'s exotic world was a never-never land in which Muslim culture was simultaneously celebrated and casually 'othered' as decadently sensual, illusory and ultimately irrelevant. It is not insignificant to note that Muslims, tribals and the West were groups marginalised—or vilified—by the Indian nationalist project. However, these films largely reflected a different—and more cosmopolitan—form of nationalist modernity from that of the elite. As I argued in chapter four, the Wadias, unlike others of the nationalist elite, showed an astute understanding of popular passions and lower-brow vernacular cultures. They recognised the potency of transcultural popular images and the hybrid fluidity of identities within the porous borders of a modern India in a transnational context. They 'got' the visceral pleasures of Tarzan and Aladdin in a way that their elite critics did not, leaving them culturally and politically marginalised but ensuring them long-lasting enthusiasm from their loyal subaltern audiences.

AN ENCHANTED GAZE

Fantasies, simple yet imaginative, used to go down very well with the audience.... Of course the aim was to appeal to everyone from 6 to 60.... Entertainment had to cut through age barriers, the idea was to provide a jolly good time for a family which was going to the movies on a Sunday matinee.

Homi Wadia, 1991

How much can we deduce from the half-dozen *Aladdin* stills in this collection? *Zimbo* came only six years after *Aladdin* but the difference in lobby card promotion is striking. Where *Zimbo* touted for audiences with arresting, hand-coloured collages that vividly suggested stories, spectacle and stunts in a chaotic, comedic, trashy world, *Aladdin's* stills are decidedly low-key. Given the film's subject matter, the chosen images—flying jinni apart—are curiously banal. Indeed, two of these six images are happy couples and three others depict gazing crowds. One image is especially intriguing, depicting a dozen or so faces looking intently outwards but not a hint of what has amused, amazed or confused this family group. One assumes that such scenes of cosy domesticity were chosen to provide a reassuring space into which potential cinemagoers could project their fantasy selves as audience, just as in another of these stills the sight of a crowd of onlookers transforms arm-wrestling from stunt fodder into family-friendly viewing. Given that this was the era in which magic and fighting films were apparently being stigmatised by a po-faced, post-independence government,[27] promotion of a new fantasy film like *Aladdin* had to tread carefully in order to 'appeal to everyone from 6 to 60'.

But such speculation is misguided. Undoubtedly the series is not complete and we can never know whether we have here the stills *most* valued (that the cinema wanted to keep) or those *least* valued (the dregs no fans wanted to take for themselves). Instead, the archive is best approached as poetic fragments, allowing certain stories to be spun but 'proving' nothing. Indeed, by a delicious irony, any casual visitor to the archive might well assume, on the basis of its one still, that *Pyaasa*, with its smoke machine dream sequence and pari-like heroine, was the fantasy film and *Aladdin* a family social.[28] On the other hand, a new sensibility about Indian cinema history emerges from engaging with the abundance of B-movies washed up here, the patterns they conjure up and the distressed condition of many of these artefacts.

The archivist tells us these *Aladdin* stills were so brittle they almost fell apart in his hands, and two images are cropped accordingly. But such knowledge lends these a potent poetic charge: someone at some stage—whether cinema owner, distributor, fan, collector or *raddiwala*[29]—saw these stills as objects too precious to junk. Just as the torn Ralli Brothers' acrobat (Figure 6.2) is a disintegrating trace of the circuits of nineteenth-century global trade, so these B-movie stills are vivid, if random, vestiges of the global entrepreneurship of mid-twentieth century global film circulation and the forms this left on India's C-circuits. We catch fleeting glimpses of long-gone pleasures and a palpable sense of history fading.

But can we learn anything at all about the history of these images? Much of the pleasure of the archive lies in happy accidents and, with these *Aladdin* stills, there is an unexpected treat. On the back of one, in optimistic—if spidery—red ink, is written 'Novelty Cinema, Kalimpong' (Figure 6.9).

What could be more appropriate to this *Arabian Nights* treasure trove than to uncover traces of its former life in a small town high in the foothills of the eastern Himalayas? Bordering Sikkim and not far from Bhutan, this is quintessential 'C-grade' territory—up-country and, in film distribution terms, remote. In the popular imagination the

Figure 6.9 *Aladdin and the Wonderful Lamp* (1952) reverse of lobby card for the movie theatres

Source: Courtesy Tasveer Ghar.

name Kalimpong itself has an exotic ring, a place where enchanted mountains—and even Aladdin's cave itself—might lie. Magicians did indeed live here in the 1910s and 1920s, if we can believe Alexandra David-Neel, the explorer whose orientalist travellers' tales fuelled a feverish Western imagination longing for marvels (in the spirit of many of the archive's European images).[30] Moreover, Kalimpong had long been a place where Indian, Chinese, Tibetan, Nepali and European cultures crossed. Situated just off the old Silk Road to China, this trading centre was an early transcultural—even liminal—space. And we may remember that many versions of 'Aladdin', including Galland's original story, were set in China, not Baghdad—an exotic Orient deferred ever eastwards.

What might 1950s audiences holed up in the dark spaces of the Novelty Cinema, Kalimpong, with its miniscule Islamic presence, have made of *Aladdin* and its various 'novelties', including its 'novelty dance'?[31] What sense could these audiences have made of this multiply exotic tale—filmed in Bombay, set in 'Baghdad', and referencing global popular culture—taking its inspiration from some of the world's oldest stories via the detour of, inter alia, Indian theatre, Persian folktale, Arabic poetry, French literary salons, Hollywood films and English children's books?

The *Arabian Nights*, Tarzan, circus and magic shows offered images of a transcultural imagination, drawing on populist tropes of an early-twentieth-century global vernacular performance culture. These shows circulated erotica and thrills in the wake of the trading in goods and commodities and largely beneath the radar of the Indian nationalist elite. They flew the globe as easily as *Aladdin*'s giant jinni. Despite what we may like to fantasise, the Wadias' jinni did not hail from Kalimpong caves: like the Ralli Brothers' acrobat he was a transcultural hybrid, bringing his own version of modernity and 'novelty' to the Novelty Theatre, Kalimpong, ready to make all its audiences' dreams come true. In this, he was not so different from his master, Homi Wadia, that conjuror of cheap thrills, sleight of hand and visual illusion, who understood better than any film-maker of his day that 'it's a little like magic this fantasy film-making'.

NOTES

1. The quotations that introduce each of the five sections of this essay (originally the five web pages of the online visual essay) are drawn from an interview with Homi Wadia by Rajesh Rathore, 'Down Fantasy Lane', *Cinema in India*, Bombay: NFDC, April 1991, p. 40.

2. A much fuller selection of images from the archive illustrates the online version of this essay, which readers are encouraged to access at http://tasveerghar.net/cmsdesk/essay/103/.

3. As discussed in earlier chapters, generic boundaries were, as always, fluid: 'costume' films ranged from Arabian Nights fantasy to quasi-Rajput and Ruritanian settings. 'Historical' and 'legend' films could be based on Hindu legends or those of the Islamic world, including qissa-dastan. Moreover, all these genres included stunts and action. See the more detailed discussion in chapter two.

4. Meaning 'provincial'—that is, outside the metropolitan centres—notably smaller towns and rural areas.

5. See, for example, Peter Lamont and Crispin Bates, 'Conjuring Images of India in Nineteenth-Century Britain', *Social History*, vol. 32, no. 3, August 2007, pp. 308–24.

6. Pran Nevile, *Lahore: A Sentimental Journey*, New Delhi: Harper Collins, 1997.

7. Personal communication, P.K. Nair, March 2005.

8. Ralli Brothers set up their offices in Bombay and Calcutta in 1851.

9. See chapters one and two for more details.

10. Alif Laila means 'one thousand nights' in Arabic.

11. I am grateful to Radha Dayal for her help with accessing this film and her excellent notes on it.

12. J.B.H. Wadia, 'How Bagh-e-Misr Came to Be Produced'.

13. Homi Wadia gave Meena Kumari her first adult roles in a series of mythologicals at Basant in which, to the consternation of the Hindu fundamentalist lobby, she played Hindu goddesses, notably Lakshmi in *Laxmi Narayan* (Nanabhai Bhatt, 1951).

14. This sequence, in fact, drew on a scene in Alexander Korda's 1940 British version of *Thief of Bagdad*.

15. 'My Name Is Chin Chin Chu'.

16. As evidenced in the traces of *Chu Chin Chow* in the Wadias' own *Alibaba and the Forty Thieves* (Homi Wadia, 1954), notably the chain gang of slaves that is revealed to be the mechanism that opens the magic cave.

17. See Bhaumik, 'Querying the "Traditional" Roots of Silent Cinema in Asia'.

18. For more on Basant's innovative special effects department, see chapter five.

19. In this he is somewhat different from the hero of Wadia's 1933 *Lal-e-Yaman*, as discussed in chapter two.

20. Including *Alif Laila*'s jinni although, interestingly, this jinni does not appear in any of the archive's twenty-three *Alif Laila* stills, nor do we see much evidence of the film's SFX. These images are much more theatrical—and overtly fantastic—than *Aladdin*'s stills.

21. See Joseph S. Alter, *The Wrestler's Body: Identity and Ideology in North India*, Berkeley: University of California Press, 1992.

22. Ibid., p. 74.

23. S. Mazumdar, *Strong Men over the Years: A Chronicle of Athletes*, Lucknow: Oudh Printing Works, 1942.

24. J.B.H. Wadia, 'The Making of *Toofani Tarzan*', unpublished essay in Wadia Movietone archives, kindly provided by Vinci Wadia.

25. 'Tempestuous Tarzan'.

26. By the 1960s this would also include James Bond, as discussed in chapter five.

27. See article by anonymous in *India Talkie: 1931–56, Silver Jubilee Souvenir*, Bombay: Film Federation of India, 1956 (quoted in chapter one).

28. *Pyaasa*'s song 'Aapke Aankhon Main' was an 'item number' which, to Guru Dutt's dismay, the film's distributors insisted on including.

29. Raddiwala: garbage / rag-picker.

30. Alexandra David-Neel, *With Mystics and Magicians in Tibet*, London: John Lane, Bodley Head, 1931. Later English editions (of the original French *Mystiques et Magiciens du Tibet*) were titled *Magic and Mystery in Tibet*.

31. Novelty in all senses: (*a*) something new and fresh: the engine of genre cinema—and capitalist consumer culture's—appeal; (*b*) a marvel to be wondered at; and (*c*) something cheap and trashy.

part two

$\mathcal{I}$ntroduction

The second half of the book takes its starting point from the body of ethnographic fieldwork I conducted in the Bombay film industry in the early 1980s. This was the era in which the 'multi-starrer' masala film ruled the roost and in which, as described in chapter one, the 'attractions' of the B- and C-circuit movies had migrated into the mainstream and now reached an enormous mass audience, one that crossed region and class. While the films built firmly on a set of conventions that had been in place since at least the 1950s, the era was also perceived at the time as one of immense change. The Amitabh Bachchan 'angry young man' persona dominated the cinema landscape, sweeping into the sidelines the model of romantic, even tragic, heroism of the earlier socials, while roles for female stars—from Hema Malini to Zeenat Aman and Parveen Babi—challenged contemporary taboos around acceptable models of Indian femininity.

A key concern of my research at that time was how to describe the breadth and dynamism of the contemporary Bombay cinema. I wanted to know how the film-makers conceptualised what they were doing, how conditions of production impacted on their film-making, and how the films emerged from—and were read within—an intertextual field. I framed my object of study in three main ways. The first was through an ethnography of the working conditions of the industry; the second was through an exploration of film-makers' own terms of reference about the genre conventions of the films that they were making; the third was through elaboration of a number of other texts—from other films to gossip stories—through which any one film might make meaning.

Through paying attention to film-makers' discussions of their own practice, together with visual and textual analysis, I aimed to understand Bombay cinema as one element within the 'zone of cultural debate' of public culture—as an arena of contestation and debate, where meanings were in the process of constant negotiation.[1] I was looking for a set of ground rules, internalised by both film-makers and audience, with and against which any individual film played.

Theories of genre and melodrama proposed some answers, notably the concept of the 'ideal moral universe', which, it soon became clear, was a central dynamic of Bombay cinema of the day. This defines paradigms of 'good' and 'bad' (or expected and unacceptable) forms of behaviour and requires that the forces of good triumph over evil.[2] I argued that the ideal moral universe of Bombay cinema revolved around the archetypal figures of Mother and Villain, a good–evil opposition in which good was subtly conflated with the 'traditional', or that which is Indian; bad with the 'non-traditional' and the 'non-Indian'. Through this moral universe the films constructed an Other—a cold, calculating, rapacious, but exotic West/outsider—which had implications for the construction of notions of modern Indianness.[3] The narrative function of the hero/heroine was not to embody good but to mediate between these two poles. Through such mediation certain elements of the non-traditional could become gradually legitimated and incorporated within the 'traditional' modern—that is, connotations, for example, of love marriage or women driving motorbikes could be shifted over time through careful negotiation of the contexts within which they appeared.[4] Thus, films—together with texts such as film star gossip—could be seen as an important locus for the ongoing negotiation and transformation of a modern Indian identity. At the time, I saw kinship, sexuality and modernity as the key discourses. Today, with hindsight, I would contextualise these as interlinked discourses of the nationalist movement. But my key point still stands: we needed a dynamic model that incorporated in-built systems for change.

An essay I wrote in the 1980s used the examples of *Kartavya* (Duty, Mohan Segal, 1979) and *Deewar* (The Wall, Yash Chopra, 1975) to describe how skilful negotiation of this universe by successful film-makers allowed transgressions to be pleasurably enjoyed and,

Figure II.1   Mother (Nirupa Roy) and her villainous son
(Vinod Mehra). A still from *Kartavya* (Mohan Segal, 1979).

Source: © Kamat Foto Flash. Courtesy Neha Kamat at Kamat Foto Flash.

through pushing at its boundaries, the genre's ground rules to be gradually transformed.[5] Amitabh Bachchan's now classic films with star script-writing duo Salim–Javed provide masterful examples of this kind of operation and were of undoubted influence in breaking new ground in the 1970s and setting the terms for the era that followed.[6] In particular, they explored and developed a new model of male heroism that was powerful, aggressive, defiant, self-respecting, sophisticated, successful, and at home with the accoutrements of a Westernised lifestyle, yet still respectful of 'traditional' values.[7]

What particularly fascinated me was how film-makers talked about and evaluated their own practice. A central preoccupation among directors, writers and producers that I knew was whether or not their audience would 'accept' a certain representation or narrative outcome—that is, they worked with an explicit concept of their audience as imposing constraints on their film-making. Thus, the moral universe within which the films operated was a form of self-censorship based not, like the Hays Code of Hollywood in the 1930s and 1940s, on any ideology of social responsibility or concern about the public image of the film industry, but on a firm belief that the audience would simply boycott a film that was 'immoral' or clumsily transgressed the moral code.

It was believed that the Hindi film audience expected a drama that put a universe of firmly understood—and difficult-to-question—rules into crisis and then resolved that crisis within the moral order. This meant that transgressions had either to be punished or, more excitingly, be made 'acceptable', that is, be rigorously justified by, for example, an appeal to humane justice, a mythological precedent, or a perceptible contradiction within the terms of the moral code itself. If the film-maker stepped outside the moral universe to construct the resolution, the film was said to have cheated, to be inept, to be unconvincing, and to be a failure. Particular pleasure—both for audiences and for film-makers in script sessions—seemed to derive from a film-maker finding new ways of bending the comparatively inflexible system, which meant that values and meanings were continually being negotiated on the fringes. Thus the total system was undergoing gradual change, to the extent that certain taboos of ten or fifteen years earlier had become more acceptable by the early 1980s.

Films were developed in script sessions that would involve one or two screenplay writers, usually a separate dialogue writer, together with the director or producer (or both) as well. These might often be sumptuous affairs, held in five-star hotels or glamorous holiday resorts. Considerable time and energy was spent in discussing what was or was not acceptable and in devising screenplay ideas that would 'please' their audience. It was common to hear in script development sessions phrases such as 'they'll burn the cinemas down if we show ...' and 'it will never run beyond Thane ...'.[8] There was much discussion of other films—Hollywood, Indian classics and recent Indian releases—and post-mortems on recent successes and failures were a topic of keen interest. Discussions of films that flopped invariably adduced evidence that the box-office failure was related to unskilled transgression of the moral universe. Thus, for example, one of the most tenacious rules of Hindi cinema, according to these film-makers, was that it was 'impossible' to make a film in which a protagonist's real mother was villainous or even semi-villainous: the industry was aghast at the temerity of one film-maker who, in 1981, produced *Kaaran* (Reason, B.R. Ishara), in which a hero killed his mother, who was a prostitute. The film proved their point by folding after three days, for apparently no audience would watch a film that violated the rules of Hindi cinema so boldly and ineptly. How far this was true was probably not ascertainable and is anyway irrelevant here: the point is that discussion of the possible reasons for the film's failure went no further. Similarly, film-makers ascribed the failure of *Jaanbaaz* (Gambling with Life, Feroz Khan, 1986) almost completely to the fact that the central hero and his father were depicted smoking, drinking and discussing women together—behaviours that were, it was claimed, 'unbelievable' and 'unrealistic' in a hero figure.[9] In fact, very few film-makers bothered to watch films with the mass audiences and there was none of the formalised audience research that has been routine in Hollywood for many decades.

Although the film-makers often explained that their perceived constraints were based on the fact that their audience was conservative and would not accept being shocked, many factors—not least the widespread and enthusiastic consumption of gossip about film stars—suggest that audiences could derive great pleasure from being shocked in certain situations.[10] It is important to stress that the ideal moral universe was not necessarily believed by anyone: it was a construct of the film-makers, with the collusion of their audiences, and was as much a product of the history of Indian cinema and the genre conventions it had evolved as of other discourses in Indian society.

There is of course a limit to how far one can spell out the forces at play within any intertextual arena: in the final analysis there is an infinite regress of context. But it is important to recognise that film-makers operated within an apparatus that had its own momentum and logic: they were crucially constrained not only by their internalised systems of rules and their own perceptions of audience expectations but also by many other factors in the field, not least the economic context of the film industry within which they worked. Even the average-budget Hindi film had to make money in most, if not all, of the distribution territories if it were to make a profit, and therefore beliefs about what 'pleased' audiences invariably became the ultimate reference point. This led to a—mostly knowing—exploitation of crude populist sentiment and a model of a heterogeneous audience to which films had to cater by putting in elements 'for everybody'. Thus, for example, the apparent 'national integration' that the films were said to promote could be seen as a direct effect of the economic pressures of the industry, as chapter seven describes.

Two of the four chapters in this section were first published many years ago but, as they express my central conclusions on that era more lucidly than anything I might write afresh, I was encouraged to reproduce them here more or less unchanged. Moreover, I am assured that they may still be useful for students new to the field. I frame these two essays with two new chapters, which complement and extend my earlier insights. These both build on my own original fieldwork archive, which it seems appropriate to put into the public domain now that Indian cinema studies is a burgeoning discipline. Chapters seven and eight are primarily ethnographic. Chapters nine and ten explore intertextuality and are best seen as bookends of the era in question: while the 1957 film, *Mother India*, was invariably quoted as an ur-text by the film-makers of the 1970s and early 1980s, the ongoing saga of Sanjay Dutt provides us with an intriguing—and far from final—coda.

Chapter seven is an overview of how Bombay film production was organised in the early 1980s, drawing on accounts from insiders that include 'secrets' of how financing, production and distribution operated at that time; the role of the laboratories in regulating an apparently anarchic system; and how personal power was negotiated within the industry. The chapter demonstrates that the way films were produced depended crucially on who the producer was. Moreover, I argue that, despite the apparent chaos, the system worked quite well for some of the more powerful players within it, however much it constrained the form of the films it produced.

Chapter eight outlines the conventions and pleasures of popular Bombay cinema of the 1970s and early 1980s as uncovered through film-makers' own terms of reference and their internalised beliefs about their audiences. I set these in the context of the patronising assumptions of their European and Indian critics. My focus is on the Bombay film industry's own discussion of key films of the era, including Manmohan Desai's *Naseeb* (Destiny, 1981). I build on the film theory concept of 'genre' to analyse the material in terms of conventions of narrative, mode of address and verisimilitude.

Chapter nine offers an analysis of the quintessential Bombay film, *Mother India*, highlighting the complexity of reading and writing about films, both within and across cultures. Reading the film across an intertextual field that includes colonialist propaganda, film industry publicity and gossip rumours about the star Nargis and her family, the chapter argues that *Mother India* is most usefully seen as an arena within which a number of discourses around female chastity, modern nationalism and, more broadly, morality intersect and feed on each other with significant political effects.

The final chapter updates the saga of Nargis and the Dutt family to the mid-1990s, the point at which India and the film industry began to change in significant ways. It provides a sequel to the *Mother India* essay and sketches in the remarkable crossovers between real life and screen fiction—notably with *Sadak* (The Street, Mahesh Bhatt, 1991) and *Khalnayak* (The Villain, Subhash Ghai, 1993)—that allowed public debates about nationalist identities to continue. It argues that by the early 1990s these were being played out over a traumatised male, rather than female, body. In a brief coda I update this material to the present day, examining the star persona of Sanjay Dutt in 2012, from which I trace a line back through the action, fantasy and masala films that have been the focus of this book.

NOTES

1. Arjun Appadurai and Carol A. Breckenridge, 'Why Public Culture?' *Public Culture*, vol. 1, no. 1, Fall 1988, p. 6.

2. See Peter Brooks, *The Melodramatic Imagination: Balzac, Henry James, Melodrama and the Mode of Excess*, New York: Yale University Press, 1976. As Douglas Sirk, master of Hollywood melodrama, put it, melodrama as a form required the 'deux ex machine of the happy end'. This does not, however, preclude its strength lying in 'the amount of dust the story raises along the road, a cloud of overdetermined irreconcilables which put up a resistance to being neatly settled in the last five minutes'. Laura Mulvey, 'Douglas Sirk and Melodrama', *Australian Journal of Screen Theory*, vol. 3, 1977, pp. 26–30.

3. I was not suggesting that the Occidental Other was a simple reversal of the Oriental Other. Said himself argued that there was no such thing as Occidentalism.

See Said, *Orientalism*. Gayatri Spivak, among others, made the important point that the play of power relations already in the field meant that it was a different experience for the West to see itself marginalised within Indian representations than for India to see itself constantly so positioned within colonial (and neocolonial) discourse. See Gayatri C. Spivak, 'The Rani of Sirmur', in *Europe and Its Others*, vol. 1, ed. F. Barker, P. Hulme, M. Iversen and D. Loxley, Colchester: University of Essex, 1984, p. 128. The concept does seem useful, however, in pointing out some of the unspoken assumptions within Indian popular culture of that era about Indianness (and non-Indianness).

4. Riding a motorised two-wheeler appeared to brand a woman as 'fast', and even in Indian cities (apart from Pune, for mainly historical reasons) few women would risk their reputations in this way. Women on scooters were also a recurrent image in saucy popular calendar art in the 1960s and 1970s. Gradually, through the early 1980s, film-makers played with placing heroines on motorbikes; a notable breakthrough was Hema Malini, the 'dream girl' of the industry, in *Naseeb* (Destiny, Manmohan Desai, 1981).

5. Rosie Thomas, 'Melodrama and the Negotiation of Morality in Mainstream Hindi Film' in *Consuming Modernity: Public Culture in a South Asian World*, ed. Carol Breckenridge, Minneapolis: University of Minnesota Press, 1995, pp. 157–82.

6. Salim Khan and Javed Akhtar were a film-writing duo that emerged in the early 1970s with *Zanjeer* (Shackles, Prakash Mehra, 1973). *Zanjeer* established Amitabh's reputation as an 'angry young man' and as the superstar of Hindi cinema in the 1970s and early 1980s. Salim–Javed went on to write a string of films starring Amitabh that were almost all very successful. They themselves became celebrities and were instrumental in raising the status—and fees—of Bombay screenplay writers.

7. While tough masculinity had been seen in mainstream Hindi cinema before Amitabh, it was rarely in a central hero figure. Thus, for example, in *Mother India*, it was the mother, Radha, who was the focus of audience sympathy, not her son Birjoo. On the other hand, as discussed in part one, the space for tough, aggressive masculinity had been primarily in the B- and C-grade movies, with heroes such as John Cawas and Dara Singh.

8. Thane is a railway terminus and suburb on the north-eastern edge of Mumbai and was, at that time, seen as an outer boundary of Bombay, both culturally and geographically.

9. Such behaviour was the mark of a villain and his family. Although discussed within the industry as a flop, *Jaanbaaz* did subsequently do fairly well at the box office, allegedly on account of a steamy sex scene.

10. Hundreds of film gossip magazines peddling interviews with, and scandalous innuendo about, stars were already being published—and making money—in the 1970s and 1980s. They were printed in most languages, although those published in English (*Stardust*, *Super*, *Star and Style*, *Cine Blitz*) were the glossiest and most salacious.

$\mathcal{W}$here the Money Flows, the Camera Rolls

INTRODUCTION

When I was doing fieldwork in the early 1980s, the Bombay film industry was popularly pictured—within India and elsewhere—as a locus of seedy glamour and glittering corruption. It was seen as a place awash with untold wealth that was squandered in wild parties and extravagant hedonism, a jungle where the unwary could be relieved of their life savings and where the simply 'lucky' could suddenly find themselves possessors of undreamed of fortunes. This picture was firmly linked with ideas of a Bombay underworld: the film industry was said to be a 'dirty' place, the people unscrupulous and immoral, driven by greed, base materialism and lust for worldly power. I even heard both industry and films referred to by orthodox Brahmins as 'impure' and 'heating'. Much of this image centred on the fact, generally well known at least among the urban literate, that a lot of the money that circulated in the industry was 'black'[1] money, and that film financing was a way of money laundering for corrupt industrialists, builders, politicians, 'smugglers' and other racketeers. The picture was given substance—and arguably its specious glamour—in part by the Hindi films themselves, which regularly depicted an underworld in which whisky-sodden, whore-crazed smugglers exchanged suitcases bulging with thousand-rupee notes at rendezvous in luxury hotels. On the other hand, the press made frequent mileage out of stories on the film industry, from sensationalised accounts of tax raids on film stars' homes in which lakhs in black money were reportedly found stashed inside Lakshmi[2] statues or hidden under gold-tiled bathroom floors, to politicians' self-righteous denouncements of this den of depravity as a shame upon society.

Whatever role this mythology may have served in the popular imagination, another part of the fascination with the 'dirty' film industry was fuelled by the fact that its economic basis was supposedly shrouded in secrecy. In fact, the dirty secret was a very open secret. Anyone could read published, sober accounts of the extent of the involvement in the black economy: a government report of 1980 clearly stated *that*—although not precisely *how*—money was laundered by financiers who charged illegal interest rates.[3] Moreover, Barnouw and Krishnaswamy's authoritative *Indian Film* had clearly spelled this out within a more academic arena.[4] Nevertheless, almost everyone I talked to in the industry delighted in telling me the same facts and invariably expressed surprise that I already knew. On one occasion, a dapper film broker and former bank clerk exclaimed conspiratorially, after a cursory twenty-minute summary of well-known facts, 'There, now you know everything about the economics of the Hindi film industry. But don't tell anyone I told you: these are things a producer will not even tell his wife.'

Uncovering an accurate picture of the economics of the Hindi film industry was both easier and more difficult than I expected. I had embarrassingly good access: in the early 1980s a young, female, foreign anthropologist was a novelty and, once I had established a few judicious contacts, I could meet anyone I wanted; nor was I taken seriously enough for anyone to take much care to hide things from me. However, it was clear from the beginning that verifiable figures would be hard to find. Two factors distorted these. On the one hand, embroilment in the black economy meant that amounts tended to be routinely misrepresented as lower than they were. On the other hand, status in this industry was importantly measured by the price any individual player could command. All producers, financiers, distributors and stars were involved in delicate negotiations in which their bargaining strength depended on a degree of secrecy about true prices. This led to a tendency for figures to be exaggerated. To some extent, perhaps, these two tendencies cancelled each other out, but the second probably distorted information more. Thus, 1981 press reports regularly published the 'fact' that the leading star of the day,

Amitabh Bachchan, commanded a 'price' of Rs 25 lakh[5]—a figure that included payments in black and probably did represent the price his secretary quoted to new producers asking for his services. Not so easy to ascertain was the amount any individual producer actually paid him for their film, for such fees were always subject to negotiation, fluctuating according to who the producer was and how much the star wanted—or needed—to do that film.

Ultimately, figures seemed of less consequence than understanding how the system as a whole worked and the implications of this for the films. At a distance of thirty years, this is even truer. My key concern at the time was to understand how the economic conditions of production influenced the films that got made. I aimed to understand who had what kinds of power in the system and what that power allowed—or compelled—them to do. I was also curious about how such an apparently dysfunctional system worked and whose interests it served. Over the course of my eighteen-month fieldwork in Bombay, I spent many hours in producers', distributors' and exhibitors' offices, hanging out on film sets and at parties: interviewing, chatting and just listening. The exceedingly complicated jigsaw, that I was picking up piecemeal, only fell into place months later, in particular after long conversations with the late Uday Row Kavi, associate editor of *Trade Guide*, who was born into the film industry and for whom production and distribution were in his DNA. The snapshot that follows owes much to Uday for patiently answering my questions, letting me in on the 'secrets' and checking many, many facts for me. Given that no reliable documents exist, this was an extraordinary resource.

A key problem was that, as with all ethnographic research, the system in practice was considerably more complex than the ideal model that circulated so freely. Firstly, as indicated above, the way in which film production was financed and organised depended very much on *who* the producer was and, crucially, his or her standing— or negotiating power—within the industry. Secondly, all models were complicated by a whole range of rule-bending, trickery and slippery negotiations that went on, about which most people were understandably reticent. In some cases, people genuinely appeared not to have noticed contradictions between model and practice; in others their negotiating power depended on secrecy about the tricks

of the trade; yet others were concerned about their 'reputations'—
both individually and as an industry. I encountered considerable
concern generally that I should not give the industry 'a bad name'.
While almost everyone I spoke to in the industry—at all levels—
decried its disorganisation and inefficiency, they invariably exonerated
themselves by focusing complaints upon the government, crucially
the fact that it refused to recognise the film industry as an industry,
thereby precluding their raising institutional finance or insurance or
implementing labour laws. Moreover, everyone vociferously decried
the enormous percentage of 'our' profits that the government took
in taxes. But that was clearly only half the story.

I begin with an account of how films were funded and the ground
rules within which players operated: the system ran almost entirely
on face-to-face verbal agreements and the film-processing laboratories
played a central policing role. I move on to explore the implications of
this system for how production was managed, notably the importance
of having and accruing status and 'clout'. Finally, I speculate on
different kinds of power within the system and the impact all this
had on the films.

FINANCING FILM PRODUCTION

'Where the money flows, the camera rolls', went an industry saying,
and one of the central headaches for almost every producer was
actually keeping finance flowing. Three potential sources of finance
were available: loans from financiers, advances from distributors
and credit from laboratories, studios, equipment hire and workers.
Almost every Bombay producer used a combination of these three,
the relative proportions depending primarily on how well established
the producer was. Those with a string of successful films behind
them could obtain many of their costs on credit and would make
good distribution deals with reliable distributors at an early stage
in the production. They therefore had little need for costly loans
from financiers, although as the distributors' full payments only
came in on final delivery of the print, almost all needed some
under-production bridging loans. By contrast, small, new producers,
especially those whose team and product were at all 'risky', might

have to borrow substantial amounts over long periods at exorbitant interest rates.

These three core sources might sometimes be supplemented in a small way by investment of personal capital and, *very* occasionally, by bank loans. However, since a post-independence ruling by the Reserve Bank of India, the film industry was declared ineligible for bank finance, and the few producers who had raised bank loans had done so against substantial personal collateral.[6] In fact, very few producers would risk using their own money (or loans against collateral) for anything beyond a small injection of starting capital because, as even the largest Bombay producers were still comparatively small companies and never dealt with more than a couple of films at a time, the risk would be very high. On the other hand, financiers and distributors could spread their risks over a number of films—and in the case of financiers, a number of businesses.

Apart from naïve newcomers, the only producers who did invest in their own films were people who *began* as financiers or distributors and branched out into production as a subsidiary part of their business. Gulshan Rai was the most significant—and successful—example of this: his company, Trimurti Films, had been lucky with a succession of big-budget projects throughout the 1970s, which he financed and distributed himself, including *Deewar* (The Wall, Yash Chopra, 1975) and *Johny Mera Naam* (My Name Is Johny, Vijay Anand, 1970). By contrast, Rajshri Productions, a family company that also invested in its own films, made small-budget movies with minor stars and owed its success to a degree of vertical integration unique in the industry at that time. The company comprised three arms—production, distribution and exhibition—each conveniently run by one of founder/owner Tarachand Barjatya's three sons. Rajshri operated by spreading risks: the production department worked on several films at a time and ensured their distribution through the company's block booking of chains of cinemas throughout the country. Rajshri's film financing was equally unique at that time in Bombay: it combined reinvesting in its own productions with a system whereby a number of investors bought shares in a film, the company having the status of a private limited company. What no Indian production company at that time could do was offer stock market shares, as, unlike

Hollywood, film companies could not be public limited companies. The only other option for raising film production finance was through the government's National Film Development Corporation (NFDC) loans. These loans were given to very small-budget productions (less than Rs 10 lakh) that the government considered to be 'serious', or of artistic or cultural merit, and which were unlikely to find commercial backing.[7] For mainstream, commercial Hindi films, government funding was unobtainable.

Credit

Depending on the producer's standing and assets, a large proportion of the costs could be acquired on credit. Given the competition between the ten laboratories in Bombay, they, in particular, liked to encourage business by offering substantial credit facilities—under-production processing and, for established producers, often all their

Figure 7.1   Flow of Finance in Bombay Film Production

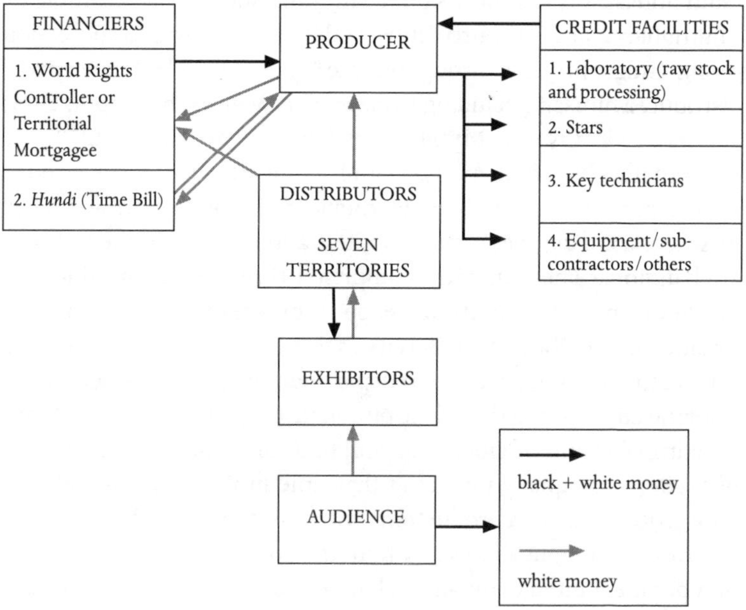

raw stock, a facility that alone could be worth Rs 5 or 6 lakh. Given their crucial role in policing the system (see Figure 7.1), laboratories had considerable security and could insist their debts had first priority. Many of the key workers on the film also effectively gave credit by accepting payment in instalments: in the case of the stars, the white money was often not paid until the film's release—or later, if ever. The system was open to much abuse, particularly at the lower levels of contractual workers, as I will discuss ahead.

Financiers

Financiers were mostly men who wished to 'launder' black money and who were prepared to take some risks with their money in exchange for very high interest rates and the glamour of being involved with the film business—the opportunities to mix with film stars and, sometimes, even be directly supplied with 'girls' (aspiring starlets) by the producers. Many financiers were Gujaratis, notably Marwaris and Sindhis, with large sums of black profits from businesses such as commodities and hotels and as diamond merchants. There were also a number of outright criminals and smugglers—often allegedly involved in dealings with Gulf countries—with totally unaccounted money to launder. Producers would be asked to sign blank chits (cheques or promissory notes), so that account books could be 'adjusted': the chits would eventually show *smaller* amounts of money being borrowed, which could either be turned into 'white' profits or 'lost' in the producers' books via inflated prices on some items—notably publicity, premieres and junior artistes. Money was usually borrowed in equal proportions of black and white, although the producer had absolute choice in the matter. Black money borrowed would be used to make black payments direct to stars and key personnel who demanded that. This money was borrowed under one of two main schemes, world rights control and territorial mortgage, as well as occasionally the 'time bill'.

World Rights Control

Under the world rights scheme, one person (or financing company), known as the world rights controller, undertook to finance the whole film, ostensibly in return for a 2 per cent commission on all sales, plus 25 per cent of the producer's share of the 'overflow' (profit on box-office returns). However, the 2 per cent commission on sales was a legal fabrication and what was actually charged was monthly interest on the loan at anything from 2.5 per cent to 3.25 per cent per month (up to 40 per cent per annum—and in actuality sometimes more). This clearly contravened the legal limit on interest rates, which in the early 1980s was 18 per cent per annum (and from 1985, 21 per cent). The illegal rates were generally accepted in the film industry as inevitable, although some 'reliable' producers were able to negotiate better rates because, in these cases, the 25 per cent of the 'overflow' could be expected to be substantial.

Accounting was done in such a way that the terms of the contract appeared to have been fulfilled. Once the distribution territories were sold, the original loan, plus 2 per cent of sales price, was paid to the financier by cheque, usually in instalments as the distribution monies came in—and in many cases paid directly by the distributors. Meanwhile, the total interest actually due was calculated and the difference outstanding then paid in cash, as 'unaccounted'—hence 'black'—money. Clearly, financiers could have no easy recourse to legal action if the black money was not paid and so, as security, they held joint ownership of the film's negative with the producer, meaning that they had control of world rights. Only when the producer had repaid the full amount—in black and white—would the financier relinquish rights on the negative and allow prints to be made and released.

In fact, in practice, the system allowed considerable scope for negotiation and double-dealing, as both producer and financier might attempt to outwit each other to gain control of the negative. The producer might wish to renegotiate the interest due, especially if the film had taken much longer than expected and the interest risen excessively. The producers' bargaining strength was that only they could sign the censorship certificate and without this the negative was worthless, so that they might simply prevaricate and refuse to sign until the financier had agreed to a compromise.[8] However, once the censorship certificate was complete the financier was able to foreclose on the negative if the producer could not afford the interest, the financier's strength being the blank chits signed on receipt of every loan, which could simply be filled in to present the interest as an additional—legal—loan.[9]

As the legal machinery in India moves so slowly and cumbersomely that it is used only as a last resort—a case might take years to actually come to court—the laboratories, as keepers of the negative, effectively moderated in these disputes. Anyone who extended credit to the producer—from financiers to actors or equipment suppliers—was given a lien letter, signed by the laboratory owner, who affirmed that the lab would not part with prints until this particular lien was cleared. The lien might be against first release of the film anywhere in the world or, alternatively, against its release within a particular territory. In the case of a dispute, the laboratories brought the various parties together to negotiate a settlement. In some cases, films were never released, because no agreement could be reached.

Producers who could not pay their debts at the time of a film's release, either because of excessive interest or because not all distribution territories were sold, usually had the option of negotiating instalment payments. The debts to the laboratory took first priority (raw stock and under-production processing charges), those to the financier second priority, while debts to the cast and other creditors had third priority on any subsequent incoming money. To secure this arrangement, the producer had to mortgage something—an established producer would usually mortgage the negatives of previous films—to the laboratory. In any case the laboratory would refuse to release prints of the film until it had received letters from financiers, stars and all other creditors stating that they had received full payment or would accept instalment conditions. Where necessary, labs would also ask the producer for written confirmation of monies owed, the order of priority of creditors and their intention to repay. In fact, quite often stars—and some technicians—agreed to accept the profits of one distribution territory as their repayment, so that, if the film did not do well, they never received their full wage. However, it was said that they would always get their black money. Naturally, unscrupulous distributors could manipulate accounts to ensure that their creditors never got paid.

The crucial role played by the laboratories is quite unusual in world cinema production. Referred to as 'the nerve centre' of the film industry, they were a regular source of information for trade press and other journalists seeking gossip on current disputes, on people's credit ratings and on their business reputations, as well as on the state of readiness of any film under production. More importantly, insofar as the laboratories offered a neutral forum in which disputes could be played out, backed up by real powers to uphold decisions— by releasing or refusing to release prints—they were the effective linchpins in a system so full of verbal contracts, loopholes and outright illegalities that it could never be policed by the law. In fact, the only true safeguards were carefully negotiated balances of bargaining power—a minefield for the unwary novice.

Territorial Mortgage

While the world rights control system was the ideal (both ideal model and preferable for all concerned), in practice only 10 to 15 per cent of productions were financed in this way. The rest had to raise money piecemeal from a number of different financiers and, although the terms were similar, in these cases financiers got no share of the 'overflow'. The interest payable would still be 40 per cent but the contract dispensed with the '2 per cent of the sales price' fiction and, instead, formally set down the interest at the legal limit (18 per cent), with full understanding by all concerned that this was hogwash. Under the 'territorial mortgage' system, the financier's security was that a distribution territory—or sub-division of a territory, depending on the amount loaned—would be mortgaged to them and the laboratory would not release prints for that territory until the financier concerned had given written permission.

Once again the system was open to abuse and sharp negotiation, with the financiers, in this case, in a rather weaker position, for although they would have collected blank chits from the producer, their security was less reliable: prints might be released for one territory, which had been cleared, and subsequently moved illegally to another. Thus, in the 1970s and early 1980s, Miraj railway station in southern Maharashtra had an infamous reputation for 'losing' prints in transit. It was said that prints of any film could be obtained from there at a price.

Bombay before Bollywood

Despite the comparatively stronger position for the producer under this scheme, there were a number of disadvantages, not least the time and energy involved in chasing up unreliable payments from a number of different sources. The financiers themselves generally kept a low profile and unscrupulous ones used tricks of the trade to short-change producers. A common sight on film sets of the early 1980s was the arrival of the financier's representative, in white polyester safari suit, with a brown leather suitcase of cash. 'He's the shark, the financiers are the barracudas', quipped one producer, as a rep who had, the day before, short-changed him arrived on set. When I later asked the rep for his side of the story, he kept stressing the lure of 'Vitamin Moola' and explained, 'Deepak thinks I cheated him. But there was a hole in my case and some "vitamins" fell out.... I had to reimburse him from my own money. It was my responsibility.' He went on to assure me, stony-faced, that there was no black money in the film industry: 'Stars get less than the technicians—they're very poorly paid.'

In many ways, financiers who knew the rules and pitfalls of negotiation in the film industry were comparatively secure, for recovery of their investment did not depend on the box-office success of the film—a variable that was notoriously unpredictable. Financiers only faced real risks when dealing with new producers who had no assets such as studios or negatives of previous films.[10] In these cases, if the film was not completed, or if some distribution territories remained unsold, the investment would be unrecoverable, even with a court case. However, as so much of industry business depended on reputation, such a producer would be unlikely to be able to borrow again for any subsequent venture and such people were either driven out of the industry or had to find a new front person.

Hundi *or 'Time Bill'*

Money flow could be uncertain from any of these sources and most producers at times needed to resort to quick, short-term loans to help cash flow crises, for example, if the producer unexpectedly got a few days of the stars' time and could fit in an extra shooting schedule, or if the distributors were late in paying their monthly instalment.

Short-term loans were borrowed from small-time moneylenders—mostly either Marwaris or Sindhi Shikarpuris—by taking out a *hundi*, known as a 'time bill'. This referred to a loan of up to Rs 10,000 for a period of ninety days at the legal interest rate. The interest would be deducted when the loan was handed over (that is, for a Rs 10,000 loan, the producer received Rs 8,200). No black money would be involved and a producer who failed to repay (or renegotiate) after ninety days could be taken to a small claims court.

Distributors

Most producers aimed to sell off rights to distribution territories as soon as possible because, once distributors' payments started to come in, repayments to financiers could begin, thereby minimising interest charges. Distributors paid 40 per cent of their purchase price while the film was under production, the remaining 60 per cent on delivery of prints. The under-production money was usually paid in monthly instalments over a negotiated period—on average 18 months—calculated according to the requirements of shooting schedules and subject to ongoing evidence that shooting was indeed proceeding. It might be paid to the producer or, in some cases, directly to the financiers: many producers relied on 'strong' financiers to extract resources from recalcitrant distributors.

As, in fact, most films took at least two years to complete—and many considerably longer—there was continual negotiation around these instalments. Producers would complain of the distributors' tardiness in paying up, thereby holding up the progress of the film; the distributors would complain that there was not enough evidence of how their money had been spent, or that they did not like what had been shot. Often the distributors did face genuine hardship and occasionally had to borrow from financiers on interest themselves. How much control the distributors could exert depended on the prestige and 'reliability' of the producer. Some 'big' producers were able to insist that the distributors buy blind and see nothing of the film until delivery of prints: Ramesh Sippy, golden boy of the 1970s following the success of *Sholay* (Flames, Ramesh Sippy, 1975), was able to do this with *Shaan* (Pride, 1980). By contrast, a 'high-risk' producer might regularly have to show what had been shot and could be forced—by threat of halting the payments—to change or modify the film. Most producers negotiated a middle way between these extremes. Much depended on personal relationships being built up between producers and their regular distributors, although for the most part, by the 1980s, such alliances were said to be comparatively short-lived. Distribution contracts would be drawn up for a stipulated period—usually seven or eleven years, but sometimes more or less than this—after which rights would revert to the producers, unless the laboratories or financiers still had claims on the film. There were three types of distribution deal.

Minimum Guarantee

The producers' preferred deal, used in around 90 per cent of cases, was known as 'minimum guarantee' or 'MG'. In this, the distributor took all the risk: he paid an agreed price and sought to recover it from box-office returns, together with the print and publicity costs he had borne, plus 20 per cent commission. Any profit the film made on top of this was shared between producer and distributor, usually equally. If the film failed to recoup the original investment, the loss was entirely the distributor's and the producer owed nothing. Before the 1980s, the MG included agreements about the sharing of print costs and publicity: usually radio and railway publicity would be paid for by the producer, while costs of local publicity were the distributor's responsibility, thereby adding significantly to the distributor's overheads.[11] By the time I was researching this, these costs were no longer included in MG.

Advance

For producers who were either very confident of their own film, or whose films were known to be so bad that no distributors would take the risk, there was another option, known as the 'advance' or 'commission' deal. In this kind of agreement, used in 7–8 per cent of cases, the producer took most of the risk. The distributor paid the producer an agreed price as advance against recovery and then proceeded to recover this investment, together with print and publicity costs and a 15 per cent commission, from the first box-office returns. Once the distributor had recouped this investment, all profits, minus 15 per cent commission, belonged to the producer. If the box-office returns fell short of the original price paid, the producer had to reimburse the distributor with the shortfall after a stipulated period, usually eighteen months. As this usually meant that the producer had also not made any profit on the film and therefore could not easily repay immediately, a compromise was often negotiated on the rights of the producer's next venture.

Outright

In the third option, known as the 'outright' sale, the distributor bore the brunt of the risk, but stood to make much greater profits if the film was successful. Once the agreed price had been paid, the producer had no further rights on the film for the duration of the contract and any profits the film made belonged to the distributor. Only 2–3 per cent of producers would accept such a deal—those who were either very unsure of their film or in a very weak bargaining position—although it was often used for the overseas territory, where the producer had limited ways of assessing the true box-office takings. However, an MG deal might sometimes be converted to an outright deal after the film's release if the film was a success and the producer did not trust the distributor to repay him honestly. If both parties agreed to convert the deal to 'outright', the distributor would pay an additional sum, on top of the MG already advanced, and all subsequent profits belonged to him. This kind of deal would also suit a producer who wanted to raise money for his next production without borrowing on interest.

Territories

The total market was divided into seven[12] territories, which more or less corresponded to those established before independence—and reflected British India's geographical divisions, rather than the linguistic/cultural/state divisions of the post-independence era—although modifications were necessitated by Partition and the consequent loss of almost one-third of the total market: that is, half of Punjab, Sind and East Bengal, together with a separation off of Aden, the Persian Gulf, Burma and Ceylon (as they were then known).[13] These seven territories were subdivided into twenty-one main sub-territories, and beyond that into A-, B- and C-circuits, which reflected both the quality of their cinemas and the class backgrounds of their audiences.

Table 7.1   Cinema distribution territories in 1981

Territory	Market Potential
1. Bombay: comprising Gujarat, Maharashtra (excluding Marathwada, Khandesh and Vidarbha), four districts of Karnataka (Belgaum, Hubli, Bijapur and Dharwar), Goa, Daman and Diu.	17%
2. Delhi/Uttar Pradesh: comprising the union territory of Delhi and the state of Uttar Pradesh.	17%
3. East Punjab: comprising Punjab, Haryana, Himachal Pradesh, Jammu and Kashmir and the union territory of Chandigarh.	6%
4. Bengal: comprising West Bengal, Bihar, Orissa, Assam, Nagaland, Arunachal Pradesh, Meghalaya, Tripura, Manipur and Sikkim. It also includes Nepal and Bhutan.	15%
5. Central Provinces and Central India (CPCI): comprising Madhya Pradesh and Rajasthan, plus Khandesh and Vidarbha regions of Maharashtra.	14%
6. South: comprising Karnataka (excluding Belgaum, Hubli, Bijapur and Dharwar), Tamil Nadu, Kerala and Andhra Pradesh, plus Marathwada area of Maharashtra.	5%
7. Overseas: comprising all countries except India, Bhutan and Nepal. This also excluded Eastern European countries.[14]	26%

Note: Percentages represent 1980/81 figures. By 1984, the strength of the overseas territory had plummeted due to video and television distribution.
Source: Information courtesy of *Trade Guide*.

Prices were negotiated according to the assumed market potential— or 'strength'—of each territory. The Bombay territory was considered to have the potential to bring in about 17 per cent of the total all-India returns, thus Bombay distributors paid 17 per cent of the total 'price' of the film. The south was said to be a less lucrative territory—because of its own large regional language film industries—and so these distributors paid only 5 per cent of the total. The money-making potential of each sub-division of the major territories was again proportionately assessed to guide prices for sub-distributors.[15] In fact, all these percentages were only guidelines for negotiation and had evolved as understandings between distributors and producers rather than being the result of rigorous calculation or research. Precise percentages of returns in each circuit would fluctuate from film to film, some subject matters suiting some circuits better than others.

Although the real prices paid might be kept secret, the 'major territory' asking prices—Delhi and Bombay—did soon become common knowledge and were supposed to represent about one-sixth of the cost of producing the film (including a 5–7½ per cent producer's margin). These figures would be used as shorthand to talk of the cost of the film. Thus the average price of films in 1980–81 was said to be Rs 65 lakh (see Appendix 7.1 for details over the years). Somewhat confusingly, this referred to the price of the major territories, not of the film in total (which would, accordingly, be Rs 390 lakhs).[16] However, these prices were never a very reliable guide to the *actual* cost of production for, apart from anything else, producers would inflate costs as far as they could get away with, in order to increase their profit. I was told of several big-name producers who routinely expected to make a significant percentage on the production cost by competent 'fooling' of the distributors who, on their part, eagerly looked out for evidence of spending (or 'production values') in pre-sale and under-production trials of the film in order to haggle over the price.

However, agreeing to a distribution price and deal was no guarantee of the final price or terms—contracts were unofficially always renegotiable and tentative.[17] In the case of the successful, top producers, who were in a position to ask whatever they thought they could get away with, the final price was never agreed until the film was complete. Their distributors accepted this because, with the promise of a top producer's film on their hands, they could pull in advance payments from theatre owners eager to screen a potential blockbuster: theatre owners not only wanted to secure full houses but also healthy profits from extra canteen sales and parking slots.

On all productions, distributors might back out at any point—particularly in the early stages before they had invested too much money—using their dissatisfaction with the film's progress as a pretext. Once a film was complete, it was common practice—although not wholly approved of—for the price to be renegotiated on either side. Depending on how well the film was expected to do and how desirable hanging onto distribution rights was, the producer was often able to increase the price at the time of release by arguing that costs had escalated since the original agreement and exerting pressure by delaying signing for release of the prints, thereby tying up the distributors' investment. On the other hand, distributors might hold to ransom a producer of a film carrying less favourable reports—especially one that had been released and flopped in one territory—by holding back money and delaying release, putting the producer into an increasingly desperate situation as interest to the financier escalated.

In fact, distributors did take considerable risks—albeit spread risks: a very large percentage of films failed to make any money for distributors, at least in the crucial first months. Somewhat confusingly, films were spoken of as 'hits' or 'flops' on the basis of how much profit, if any, distributors made on the prices they had paid for the territories (not on whether or not the film made money for producers, nor on total box-office takings).[18] On this measure, even in the heyday of the 1970s, only around 20 per cent made profits, and by the early 1980s the figure had dropped considerably. Thus, according to *Trade Guide*, in 1980, out of 114 films released, 54 (47.7 per cent) lost money, 36 (31.56 per cent) broke even and only 24 (21.05 per cent) made profit (and only two of these were blockbusters over the crucial first eighteen months). In 1982, out of 135 films, the figures were 69 (51.12 per cent) loss-makers, 46 (34.07 per cent) 'coverage' and 20 (14.81 per cent) money-makers (with, again, two 'blockbusters').[19]

Exhibitors

The distributors' money came, of course, from ticket collection revenue via the exhibitors. It was unofficially calculated that only 24 per cent of the money paid at the box office reached the distributors—and thus only a portion of this, the producers—as not only did the exhibitor often massage the figures and have significant overheads, but the state government extracted a massive 58 per cent entertainment tax. This, as mentioned above, was a source of much discontent among all in the film industry, particularly, as was repeatedly grumbled: 'The government does nothing to help us.' The fact that most *state* governments did, to some extent, subsidise *regional* language film-making was little consolation for Bombay film-makers. Moreover, the central government's heavy capital input in the early 1980s into cinema's direct rival, television, wildly infuriated the film industry.

Although entertainment tax would never be included when box-office collection figures were quoted,[20] a very approximate guide to where an individual's ticket money went (averaged across the country) shows the following breakdown.[21]

58%	Entertainment tax
6%	Theatre running costs
5%	Wages
4%	Local (municipal) show tax
24%	Distributor and producer
3%	Exhibitor
100%	

There were several types of relationship between exhibitor and distributor. The main 'A-class' cinemas in the big cities (Bombay and Delhi) were in a position to demand more than 50 per cent of the cinema's 'capacity' (that is, potential collections from a full house, minus taxes) from the distributor, usually 5 per cent of this in cash (black), payable in advance.[22] If the film did not run to full houses, the distributor would suffer the loss. 'Strong' (lucrative or prestigious) cinemas in city suburbs or towns could charge more than 50 per cent of the capacity. Smaller cinemas elsewhere in the country, on the B- and C-grade circuits, were generally leased out by the cinema owners to weekly contractors, who acted as middlemen between exhibitor and distributor, and who organised the cinemas in chains. In these cases, the exhibitor would usually keep either 50 per cent of actual collections or 'theatre protection' (40/45 per cent of the capacity), whichever was the greater. As cheating was rife, not only would a 'representative' always accompany a cinema print on outstation bookings, but the bigger distributors would, from time to time, send their agents unannounced to the more remote cinemas to do spot checks on audience numbers. However, given how low their wages were, such reps were frequently either paid off by theatre owners or threatened with muscle power: cinema owners might well be local strongmen.

There was a comparative shortage of cinema houses in India at that time. A government report estimated that in January 1980 the total number of cinemas stood at 10,392 (of which 6,368 were permanent and 4,024 were temporary—that is, touring cinemas, either in tents or the open air).[23] Assuming a population of 646,800,000, this worked out at 7 seats per 1,000 people—one of the lowest ratios in the world.[24] As there was always a queue of films waiting to be released, the exhibitors were more or less in a position to dictate their terms to distributors. To the distributors' concern, something of an exhibition monopoly began to build up in certain territories in the early 1980s. Even the block-booking strategies of distributor/exhibitors such as Gulshan Rai and Rajshri were powerless to control this, largely because the distribution sector was fragmented into a large number of rather small companies in competition with each other. [25]

ORGANISATION OF FILM PRODUCTION

Terms of Employment

Black money was fundamental in establishing how production was organised in Bombay in the early 1980s. Barnouw and Krishnaswamy describe how the studios of the 1930s broke down when entrepreneurs, with black money from illicit arms deals and wartime profiteering following World War II, set themselves up as independent producers and lured the stars away from the studios where they had formerly worked under exclusive contract.[26] By the early 1980s, studios were no more than locations and facilities that could be hired by any producer.[27] Films were produced by a large number of small independent production companies, most working on no more than one film at a time—even the larger companies on only two or three. These had no effective central organisation, despite three notional producers' associations, the Indian Motion Picture

Producers' Association (IMPPA) and two smaller ones.[28] Distribution similarly operated through a large number of comparatively small, decentralised companies.

Most film industry employees worked on a freelance basis and were hired by the producer—or a sub-contractor appointed by the producer—either by the day or by contract for the duration of the production. The contract in theory specified a number of days per month over a certain period that must be worked, but in practice these contracts were infinitely flexible and negotiable, not least because most films were at least two years in production and many ran on much longer. Most of the more highly regarded people involved in film-making worked on such contracts: the director and assistants, the sub-directors (for example, music, dance and stunt directors) and other major technicians together with their assistants, stars and actors, writers and major sub-contractors. Those paid on a daily basis[29] were primarily the lower-ranking personnel in jobs where individuals were interchangeable: junior artistes/extras, dancers, electricians, set builders/painters, hairdressers, make-up artists, and—largely on account of their strong unions—musicians, singers and stuntmen. The only workers in permanent salaried employment were laboratory staff, production office employees and some studio and facility/equipment hire workers, for example, gatekeepers, equipment supervisors and small numbers of office staff.

The daily wage workers and salaried employees were, on the whole, fairly effectively unionised. Although rates of pay were very low compared with the amounts that circulated in the film industry,[30] the rates generally compared favourably with those that could be earned by the same people doing similar kinds of work outside the film industry. Of course, the wages of those lower in the hierarchy such as manual labourers on sets were meagre—in many cases below subsistence level—but this was a reflection of the gross exploitation that existed in the wider society and was a scandal not specific to the film industry. However, the higher-paid of the daily wage workers— stuntmen, some extras and musicians among others—did consider themselves quite well off, provided they got a regular supply of work. Thus one stuntman assured me: 'If there is a paradise on this earth it is the Hindi film industry.' In fact, the stunt union was so unusually well organised that the union itself collected wages from the various producers, so that union members could simply turn up at the union office each evening for their wages. Moreover, if a producer failed to keep his obligations, these unions effectively blacklisted him and no worker attended his shoots.[31] Nevertheless, all kinds of compromises might be necessary for a daily wage worker to *get* work regularly from the sub-contractors: many had to accept less cash than they actually signed for, female workers might have to provide sexual favours, and several groups took enormous risks with their lives, notably light 'boys' and stuntmen. Among these latter there had been a number of fatal accidents, with no form of insurance or statutory compensation, for another consequence of the film industry having no government recognition as an industry was that even the minimum protection afforded by Indian labour laws did not apply to these employees.

Infinitely more disorganised was the apparently more prestigious contractual work sector. The position of these workers was very insecure: not only did their contracts have no effective legal validity, but they were frequently obliged to work, at least in part, on credit with no form of redress if the producer could not, or would not, pay up. The producers regularly exploited the fact that there was a constant supply of eager, ambitious people who would suffer considerable hardship for the chance to 'make it', knowing that, for those at the top in each of these fields, there were rewards of unparalleled fame and fortune. Thus, although there were unions for every category of worker, and theoretically membership was compulsory and minimum wages fixed, it was well known that most unions had no power even to enforce membership, let alone minimum wages. Even many union members resigned themselves to working for less than the minimum wage, for if they alienated the producers—or whoever they assisted—they were out of work for good. This was often justified (on both sides) by claiming that the worker had an 'obligation' to a certain producer, either because of kinship and 'friendship' bonds or because the producer was giving, or had given, the person their 'break' in the industry.

Condoning this exploitation in a similar way was an ideology of 'struggling', which implied that every successful person had to serve their apprenticeship and suffer hardship in their early days to earn their later rich rewards. The long-suffering aspirants to stardom (in any field, but particularly acting) were literally referred to as 'strugglers'. Those who became successful smugly outdid each other with extravagant descriptions of the toughness of their days of 'struggle'—from how rough they slept, to how sadistic their employers. The unsuccessful strugglers that I met were mostly resigned but rather angry at what they unequivocally perceived as the unfairness of the system, which forced them to humiliate themselves again and again at the expense of callous producers or exploitative star directors and technicians, while privileging those with the right connections, particularly the sons of successful film-makers and stars. Everyone knew that very many jobs in the industry did depend on kinship connections, and that well-established fathers saw it as their 'duty' to launch their sons into their own profession, whether as stars, directors, producers or light 'boys'.[32] In fact, many of the daily wage workers, notably junior artistes and stuntmen, stated explicitly that they preferred to accept their comparatively lowly status and 'an easy life' rather than let themselves in for the anxieties, insecurities and humiliations of contractual work and 'struggling'.

The Producer

As in film-making around the world, the producer was the central pivot of a project. The producer put the package together, persuading stars, music director and director to work on the project, finding a story and writers, and with these raising finance. Once the film was under way, the producer's job was ostensibly an organisational one—setting up shooting schedules, coordinating employees, getting the film sold and organising post-production. But in fact this involved a continual round of wheeling, dealing, pleading and placating in order to keep stars and key technicians turning up on sets, the laboratory providing raw stock and, most crucially, money coming in from financiers and distributors. Smaller producers might do much of this work themselves; larger companies employed a production executive and/or production managers to do such legwork.

As most negotiations were formalised by little more than verbal contracts and as, because of the prevalence of black money, little was enforceable by law, the successful producer had to be exceptionally skilled in negotiating personal relations, as well as street-wise. A cynical writer who had been in the industry a long time quipped, 'An experienced producer is someone who has got their fingers burnt and been cheated and is now learning how to cheat others without getting caught.' A saying among film people, 'Ghore ki laat, Bombay ki barsaat, Producer ki baat, In pe kabhi bharosa nahi karna', likened the word of a producer to two other dramatically unreliable and potentially dangerous phenomena: the kick (leg) of a horse and the Bombay monsoons.[33]

Most crucially, a producer needed to have, or to negotiate, clout or bargaining power. A track record of hit films was the best asset, but 'respect' might also accrue through kinship, 'friendship' or other connections with power inside and outside the industry. Clever image management, built upon personal charisma, charm and hospitality or a reputation—however unwarranted—for 'decent' behaviour was also crucial. Personal financial resources were, of course, an important added bonus, but money alone was not enough to buy viable power as a producer: I was told, 'Without contacts, a top industrialist couldn't even get to talk to Rishi Kapoor.'[34] Production was the point at which people without personal finance—or even knowledge about film—could come into the industry if they had the requisite connections or persistence to build these, although such producers were often, somewhat disparagingly, referred to as 'proposal makers', that is, people with nothing behind them but a skill in wheeling and dealing (at worst little more than conmen). Production was generally regarded as one of the most stressful and thankless jobs: 'You have to become something of a shock-absorber, to accept any kind of jolt or setback …' or, 'I returned to distribution because I couldn't put up with all the insults you have to bear as a producer …'. Several times I heard film production referred to as 'a pimp's game', although production was one area in which one did find (a very few) women working, mostly mothers and sisters of female film stars.

Even for established producers with considerable clout, the film industry was so anarchic that little ever went according to even the best-laid plans, meaning that they had to become masters of flexibility and the contingency plan. For those with less power, the pressures and delays could be nightmarish and many simply gave up: in the early 1980s well over half the films started were never completed.

Setting up a Production

Assuming some connections—and hence working capital—in the industry, a newcomer who wanted to set up a film production needed only to take three simple steps. S/he needed to join the producers' association, IMPPA or WIFPA; to have—or to borrow from financiers on interest—a minimum starting capital (at the time said to be around a lakh of rupees); and to obtain a raw stock permit from the JCCI, a government body designed to weed out the uncreditworthy but allegedly not averse to accepting bribes—Rs 4,000–5,000 was said to be enough to oil those wheels. With these basic prerequisites, aspiring producers could begin to put a 'proposal' ('deal') together. Where they started depended on where their most prestigious contacts were. The relative or friend of a star would begin with the star and on this basis interest director and storywriters. Otherwise, a director was usually approached first and would be asked to indicate which male star they would prefer to work with.[35] A story and/or writers would be chosen next and a hotel suite might have to be hired for some preliminary 'story sittings' to produce a story outline with which to persuade stars to join the project.[36]

The degree of detail required of a story outline at this stage depended almost entirely on the status of the producer: it was said that Amitabh agreed to a Manmohan Desai story 'narrated to him in three sentences across a corridor'.[37] With a little-known producer, a star would insist on much greater detail—even a complete story outline—although the usual practice was for the writers to visit the star and narrate the story face-to-face, and it was said that one of the prerequisites of a successful writer was the ability to *narrate* a script entertainingly and, crucially, to flatter the star in the process. Writers were often flown great distances to narrate stories to stars on location, as this was thought to flatter the star and thus predispose him/her to the project. Narration sessions often continued even after shooting had begun, as the story evolved. The star would usually want to know whether the role would enhance their image—'is it "negative" or "positive"?'—how large the part was and who the co-star would be. The male stars had a crucial say in which female star would be engaged and the female stars' status depended almost entirely upon which men would co-star with them. In the late 1970s/early 1980s, any woman whom Amitabh refused to act opposite could not become an 'A-grade' heroine.[38] This naturally put enormous pressures on the women to 'cooperate' with the male stars—who routinely exploited their power. From the producer's point of view, it was usually preferable to engage real-life lovers as screen partners, as they were more likely to cooperate in giving shooting dates together, particularly if the film could also offer a spell of location shooting in some pleasant spot outside Bombay—preferably abroad. However, there was always a risk that if the liaison finished before the film was complete, it might be impossible to get them to attend the same shooting sessions again.

The stars', music directors', writers' and chief technicians' agreement to the project would be confirmed by their accepting a 'signing amount'. Tentative 'dates' would be negotiated, which the person supposedly set aside for this project. On the basis of the signatures of this team of names (that is, the 'proposal'), the producer could begin to interest distributors and, if these had not already been agreed, financiers. Producers without contacts could hire brokers to arrange money; such brokers charged between 0.25 and 2 per cent of the sum raised.[39] Given that the deals involved illegal interest rates and large amounts of black money, financiers were best organised through trusted channels and by word of mouth. Moreover, as the distribution sector was as fragmented as production, intermediaries were an asset to both sides.

At this stage the producer would probably start putting advertisements in the trade press to announce the new venture and, as soon as feasible, would hold a *muhurat* (lit. auspicious moment to begin something). The muhurat was a ceremony to mark the switching on of the camera for the first shot of a new film. Its precise timing would invariably have been chosen in consultation with an astrologer and would be accompanied by a puja or ritual offered to the producer's family's preferred deities, invariably including Ganesh (the elephant-headed god—overcomer of difficulties), Saraswati (goddess of learning, music, the arts) and—crucially—Lakshmi (goddess of wealth). Almost every Hindi film would have a muhurat, including Muslim teams, who would usually bless the occasion with prayers.

The size and grandeur of the muhurat ranged from a small family ceremony to an opulent party. Any producer who wanted publicity would ensure that as many prestigious guests as could be mustered were invited—along with brokers, distributors and financiers. While the womenfolk of the producer's family tended to join the *purohit* (priest) and take an active part in blessing the briefcase of account books, together with the film's 'script' and clapperboard, most of the other guests more or less ignored the puja, which was usually set up in some quiet corner of the studio. Once they had greeted the producer, these guests concerned themselves with business pleasantries and with checking out who else had deigned to grace the occasion— shorthand for the producer's current standing in the industry. The producer himself[40] would divide his time between welcoming the guests (and receiving armfuls of stiff cellophane-wrapped bouquets), preliminary business negotiations and occasional visits to the puja fire whenever his presence was deemed ritually necessary. When the stars arrived they were surrounded at once by crowds of well-wishers and taken to receive blessings by the purohit. In fact, there was a long tradition of stars arriving late for muhurats,[41] but as near as possible to the appointed time the crew would set up the shot. The producer would break a coconut, some prestigious guest would sound the clapperboard, and the camera, garlanded with marigolds, was set rolling—usually by some other important guest. As soon as the shot was complete—at most a matter of a few seconds—there would be applause, *peda*[42] (auspicious sweets) would be distributed, and the main guests and stars would pose for an extended photo session, the results of which served as trade press publicity for the film. In some cases a gala party in an expensive hotel would follow. It was said that some producers might spend Rs 40,000–50,000 or more on the muhurat in order to demonstrate publicly that the money would flow (and the camera would roll) on this production—usually a convenient way of using up black money.

The scale of the muhurat depended largely on the main purpose it had to serve. Film people suggested three functions, none of which had much to do with capturing the first image of the film, for the shot taken was rarely intended for use in the final film. Firstly, the muhurat was said to be importantly concerned with attracting the distributors: not only would a number be invited, with whom business negotiations might commence on the spot,[43] but the trade press photographs would advertise more widely that the 'proposal' was at least viable enough to get stars to attend the ceremony. If the guest list was impressive, the photos would also indicate that the producer had adequate standing in the industry to have a good chance of getting cooperation to complete the project. Secondly, cynical poses and public disclaimers notwithstanding, the blessing of the project with a traditional puja was clearly genuinely important to very many producers—from 'sentimental reasons' to nervous pragmatism in the face of the great uncertainty and risk that surrounds film production. Thirdly, the muhurat provided a forum where alliances or 'camps' and hierarchies in the industry could be checked out, re-established and adjusted if necessary—a function that all the numerous 'star-studded' film industry parties also served. Even the forms of greeting used would code, at a glance, the power hierarchies: whether someone received a back-slapping bear hug or deferential touching of feet (or kneecaps)—and their response to this form of 'respect' would also be noted. Moreover, forms of obligation could be negotiated at such a function: thus any guest who did make the effort to attend and 'wish' the producer would, by this, impose some obligation—comparatively mild in this case—on the producer to return a favour at a later date. Questioning a number of guests at one muhurat, I was given reasons for attending that ranged from the ruthlessly honest friend who took me, who went because the producer was a fellow Bengali and a very rich man (ex-financier), whom he wanted to ask to invest in his own film, to the reply of a prestigious senior film-maker and his director/producer son: 'It's a nice gesture, we want to wish him well.' Some minutes later this became, 'Well, Hema is in our film as well, so it's like a big family ... and besides the success of our film is linked to the success of this'—meaning that if this film should do well, Hema's box-office rating would go up, and their film would sell more easily. They also suggested that the muhurat's producer would become somewhat obligated to give way—or at least be cooperative—on any potential shooting date clashes over the stars they shared.

Further work on the film might not take place for several months. The first dates were usually for song recordings and song picturisations, which were also routinely photographed for publication in the trade press. Both provided a good selling point to attract distributors.[44] Once shooting was under way, all but the very top producers would have to give regular under-production 'trial' shows, both to attract new buyers and to convince those already committed that their advance payments were being well used and that further instalments were required. Both sides engaged in various forms of subterfuge: producers exaggerated numbers of shooting days, never edited rushes too sharply ('so that it looks like we've shot more'), flattered the distributors (for example, by introducing them, with extravagant praise, to foreign anthropologists), and paid particular attention to their wives—with whom, it was commonly asserted, 'the more they cry, the better the film'. On their part, distributors sent cheques they had 'forgotten' to sign, arrived hours—and sometimes days—late for the trial screenings, and would routinely denounce the script as 'unworkable'.

As well as keeping money flowing in, producers also had to keep the raw stock coming. As stock control was very tight in those days—being limited by import regulations, film stock had a high black-market value—laboratories had to sign consumption certificates after every batch they processed: only with these would the government allocate further permits. However, the bulk of the producer's energy was spent in keeping everyone involved in the project motivated, or obligated, enough to turn up to shoots—in particular the elusive stars and, in some cases, the (star) directors. Although dates were supposedly negotiated months, even years, ahead, they had to be reconfirmed a week or so beforehand and were susceptible to impromptu change of heart on the day itself: excuses might range from another film to shoot, to a headache or a solar eclipse. In fact, almost every star that could would multiple-book themselves. Beyond the broad division of the working day into two eight-hour shifts, stars might spread their time between any number of productions in different parts of the city, sometimes spending as little as an hour on each set. Somewhat confusingly, each such appearance was also referred to as a shift—thus stars would talk of doing eight or nine 'shifts' a day.

Producers could spend the day driving around Bombay, chasing stars up, attempting to extract them from 'the clutches' of another producer or cajoling them out of bed, for their verbal contract with the star had no legal status and producers depended wholly on whatever kind of bargaining power they had or could negotiate.

Many producers had no option but to smile grimly and rush to flatter a star who nonchalantly arrived on set several days late, at a cost of thousands of rupees in sets, a waiting unit and other idle and angry actors. They would subsequently rationalise this, 'What could I say? S/he is my friend ... if s/he walks out of my picture I am finished.' At other times I heard, 'This industry runs on friendship', and even, 'This industry runs on love'. A fiction of friendship was often the producer's only tool to obligate the star to cooperate. Some producers negotiated this with great dedication. It was well known that one producer would visit his two stars, Hema and Dharmendra, with 'morning greetings' every day—either calling in at their houses before breakfast or landing up at their first shoot of the day. He would bring them presents and on occasions touch their feet—despite which Dharmendra was noticeably unreliable. On one occasion, when the second hero, Jeetendra, after waiting several hours made-up and in a sailor-suit to shoot a song picturisation in a park outside Bombay, eventually got tired and took off, I watched the producer chase him half a mile to his Mercedes, pleading tearfully, gesturing to touch his feet and regaling him with heart-rending tales of the plight of his family should the film fail. All to no avail, although this particular producer's dogged persistence was legendary in the industry. A story circulated of his having once been so preoccupied in negotiating his stars' dates that when he pulled off the remarkable coup of persuading three top stars to converge on the same studio one Saturday morning, they all arrived to discover he had quite forgotten to build the set.

At every stage, the future of all but the most established producers' films was uncertain and very many simply folded—or got 'stuck up'. A large number of the others were continually modifying their project: I commonly heard of films being restarted two or three times with different stars because the producer had given up trying to negotiate with an uncooperative star. Reshooting a film that had reached even eleven or twelve reels (three-quarters of its final length) might be necessary, either because the distributors had abandoned it or, in some cases, because the director had lost interest. In any case, story sittings and constant refinement of the screenplay would take place throughout the entire shooting period of the vast majority of films, changes being introduced either to please distributors or stars, to keep up flagging interest over a number of years, or often to adapt to the exigencies of last-minute shooting schedules, which had to exploit whatever resources were at hand. One very busy director told me of dropping into bed at midnight, after working on three different films that day, to be woken an hour later by a producer on his doorstep with the news that he had a certain star's dates for the next morning and they had to begin immediately to work out the screenplay for whatever could be shot with the resources available.[45] In fact, on the whole, very long hours were worked in the industry by anyone who was successful, including a seven-day working week, the only statutory holiday being the second Sunday of each month.

Given that cancellations, delays and last-minute changes of plan were so prevalent, one has to ask how it was that films did get made—in such impressive numbers—and how people lived this uncertainty. In fact, almost everyone double- or multiple-booked themselves if they could, knowing that there was a high chance that one or several schedules would fall through for other reasons. All plans were, at best, tentative approximations, hedged around with contingency plans. From the producer's perspective: 'You learn always to expect the worst that could happen.' From the point of view of the stars (including star directors and top technicians), the system had considerably more advantages than was sometimes suggested and the stars' *nakhras* (airs and graces) could be far from simply whimsical. What the laxity offered was flexibility to keep reassessing, in a highly risk-laden and speculative field, where their best next move lay. As a star's status ultimately depended on their making a string of box-office hits and ensuring that their rivals made fewer, they benefitted from signing with a large number of producers. They thereby blocked their competition (in the form of other star aspirants), while remaining able to allocate shooting dates primarily to the films they assessed would do their own career most good. Should they find themselves disenchanted with a film or producer, they had only to become 'difficult' and the film would get stuck.

To some extent all this backfired on these star players and they suffered almost as much inconvenience as everyone else. They put in many hours of wasted labour on films that were never finished, they had to cooperate with necessarily disorganised producers who could not get money, and the furiously negotiated 'friendships' and obligations did effectively coerce them into unwieldy work schedules, for few could afford to be totally callous. The ones who were, notably Rajesh Khanna, were seen to have met their downfall. However, the stars' behaviour was a not irrational response to the system that had evolved and it impacted ultimately on the films themselves.

CONSEQUENCES OF THE BOMBAY SYSTEM OF PRODUCTION

The snapshot I have drawn of the ground rules of economic transactions within the film industry and the implications of these for the day-to-day organisation of Bombay film-making highlights one recurring theme: the delicacy—and lack of legal backup—of all transactions. Players relied centrally on personal contacts and public reputation, on forms of obligation and negotiated power. Most people were consequently preoccupied with building any kind of clout that they could. The crucial power struggles were between stars and producers; between distributors, financiers and producers; and among competitors within each category, notably between stars. As discussed above, the government was repeatedly blamed by film-makers for what they unanimously described as the disorganisation of the film industry.

Two questions emerge. Who had most power in the system overall? What were the implications of this system of checks and balances on the films themselves? Neither can be answered through generalisations. Firstly, one must distinguish between three different types of 'power' in the industry. The first stemmed primarily from the security of the person's position, so that, in general, financiers, stars, exhibitors, the government—and one might add, audiences—risked least and therefore, having various kinds of strangleholds, could dictate terms to others. A second form of power was a function of the degree of risk the person was prepared to take, so that distributors—and some producers—who took risks that no one else would take, had the power to dictate terms. The third form of power accrued through status in the industry at an individual level. This was the 'respect' an individual commanded for reasons largely to do with how well established they—or their family—were and, crucially, how likely they were to make a hit film. This included people in all categories, but applied particularly to producers, stars and top directors, leading technicians and key writers. People in this bracket could dictate terms to those who took risks. Thus, the question of who had most 'power' must always consider the overall power—accumulated in all of the three domains—in any specific situation. Moreover, these forms of power play took place within the context of two key structural constraints: the black economy and the shortage of cinemas, both of which broadly impacted the types of films produced.

Consequences of the Black Economy

'Only financiers, stars and the government are the winners in this industry', was a common gripe throughout the other sectors. The lack of legitimate finance, thereby compelling producers to turn to private financiers, was cited as the root of most problems: the financiers' power to charge illegal and crippling interest rates produced an escalation of prices. Moreover, the impossibility of regulating the industry through the law, and hence at all, led to a 'star system' whereby stars were said to run a rule of terror, in the face of which producers and others were helpless. Undoubtedly, private finance was a crucial determinant of the system that evolved and clearly benefitted financiers, stars and the government.[46] However, despite much public rhetoric and the considerable inconvenience caused to all, the system was workable for *all* the most successful people in it, including top producers. Once government or institutional finance were made available, these people would lose some of their advantage. Large numbers of people at the bottom of the hierarchy would also lose out.

Firstly, black money benefitted all who received large parts of their remuneration tax-free, which included many top producers, writers and directors. Secondly, with a constant supply of ready 'black' money, producers did not have to reinvest any of their own profits in the risky film business. More crucially, while the black money undermined the power (type 1) of producers in general vis-à-vis the stars, it enhanced the power (type 3) of the currently well-established producers vis-à-vis other producers. Any form of 'fair' regulation of the industry—whereby stars would have to keep to contracts and limit shooting shifts per day—would erode the top producers' current advantage, for they got preferential treatment and had comparatively much less problem with stars. Regulation would increase the opportunities of—and hence competition from—talented people at that time disadvantaged in terms of access to the resources of the industry, especially to stars, by lack of clout.[47]

A revealing incident had occurred in 1970, when the IMPPA agreed to limit any star's shooting commitments to no more than four films at a time. Producer, director and veteran star, Dev Anand, was the first to defy it: he openly took the overbooked starlet, Mumtaz, to Kathmandu for his production *Hare Rama Hare Krishna*, justifying his action in terms of 'freedom of artistic expression'. Few were fooled and feelings ran so high that an armed guard had to accompany their cars to the airport, but the IMPPA ban collapsed soon after. Significantly, Dev Anand was one of the most highly 'respected' men in the whole industry, with such an unassailable accumulation of power (type 3)[48] that he could survive this—and even keep intact his reputation for 'decency' and public-spiritedness. Throughout his long career—and despite a succession of flop films—he would only ever be criticised in whispers.

The people who had most to gain from legalising finance were those with less clout (type 3 power). However, given the large number of speculators in the field, for many of those at the bottom of the hierarchy the introduction of bank finance would be of equally little advantage, as they would probably have greatest difficulty in accessing this. They might still have to borrow privately—competing against even greater odds—or be driven out of business. To this category, one might add the producers and financiers/producers who were *in* the business in order to launder money, who naturally had no interest in change. Thus, the only sector to benefit unambiguously from legal finance would be the more sincere and talented of the new or middle-status producers, together with all contractual employees who were not in the 'black' bracket.

Distribution/Exhibition Strangleholds

The shortage of cinema houses undeniably placed power (type 1) in the exhibition and distribution sectors. Repercussions of the black economy accentuated this: escalating prices—from high interest rates and stars' fees—meant that films had to be part-financed by distributors, which gave them power (type 2) and some control over production. The production sector—and the numerous 'concerned' critics of Indian cinema—perennially grumbled that the distributors continually inflicted their ideas about form and content on the films and constrained the 'creativity' and innovation of the film-makers. Again, the complete picture was somewhat more complicated.

It was true that the need to sell a film in an over-producing market meant that buyers could dictate terms. As distributors were also the people who took the most risk, they naturally demanded a product that reduced risk as far as possible. Thus, they insisted on what they considered to be saleable ingredients: stars, good music/songs, action, eroticism, and certain sorts of storylines. Well-established producers and directors—those with clout—were again advantaged by the distributors' need to minimise risk.

However, the Indian distributors' power was of a different order from that of their Hollywood counterparts at that time. There, when the studio system broke down, the legacy of the Paramount decision of 1948 left intact the stranglehold of the six 'majors' over distribution, which had by the 1980s evolved into a system in which seven mega-corporations (business empires in which film was a minor subsidiary) dominated the field and controlled the market by vertical integration—linking production, distribution and exhibition. In Bombay, while the studios of the 1930s were never so hegemonic as in Hollywood, their breakdown fragmented the fields of both production and distribution. In the early 1980s, there were estimated to be around 3,000 major distributors in India and up to 10,000 sub-territory distributors.[49] Only the Rajshri business operated across the whole of India and this dealt predominantly with its own films. The result was great competition, with comparatively little mutual cooperation between distributors to exploit their potential stranglehold. Moreover, they took so great a degree of risk with each individual film that they were very truthfully constrained to caution.

Thus the apparent power of the distributor was substantially modified: they were vulnerable on two counts. Firstly, they were squeezed by escalating prices of films—caused in part by their own validation of the 'value' of stars but also by the loopholes through which 'good' producers could negotiate higher prices. Secondly, they were unable to organise themselves against the increasing demands of the exhibitors, where monopolies had begun to be set up. An attempt to form a cartel by some top Bombay distributors—nick-named the Super Eight—in 1981 ended in disaster, for whenever strategies for action were agreed, scarcely masked self-interest emerged and split them. The overall effect was that, again, power effectively depended on a combination of structural power in the system and individual personal clout. The only group that, as a whole, came off comparatively well within the system as it stood were exhibitors with theatres in prime locations.

Consequences for Film Form and Content

The producers' need to keep the money flowing at any cost had obvious consequences for the films that the industry produced. On a practical level, uncertain finance and inevitable delays, together with the high interest that mounted daily, meant films might lack continuity and be shoddily finished due to the pressure for a quick release once shooting was over. The fragmented distribution system also influenced more broadly the form and content of the films. As a film needed sales in all territories to be financially viable, the fact that there were no pan-Indian distributors (Rajshri apart) meant that each distributor would insist on ingredients that would sell the film in their area. There was consequently little room for films with a regional focus or even for regional/cultural specificity.

The emphatic demand was that the films had 'Indian' rather than regional identities, resulting in the ongoing construction and elaboration of a bland, pan-Indian, never-never land. This also led to a preoccupation with themes drawn from Hindu mythology and other pan-Indian stories, including dastan, as well as with songs and stunts. As the evidence of the ICC had suggested as early as 1928, mythologicals, stunt and fantasy films were deemed most likely to transcend regional boundaries. The commercial imperative to incorporate such elements into mainstream socials continued to be a pressure in the early 1980s, as seen in the ubiquitous 'masala' films that drew on the safety net of ingredients that had, in earlier decades, been the fare of B- and C-circuits. Moreover, the high risk involved in distribution emphasised the need for films to have the widest possible appeal even within regional territories, undoubtedly one of several factors in the development of the 'all-India film' that included 'something for everyone'. But by the early 1980s, even Homi Wadia's strategy of using in-house facilities to make genre films cheaply for the B- and C-circuits was no longer commercially viable: Basant closed down in 1981.

Without any form of market research—or even trips to watch films with their audiences—directors, producers and distributors sustained a system built around an imagined audience crudely demarcated in regional, religious, class and gender terms. This pressure was openly acknowledged even at the scripting stage: I attended script sessions with Manmohan Desai's team at which a children's blackboard was set up in the corner of the glamorous five-star hotel suite, on which wild scribbles in coloured chalks marked up a fiendishly complicated kinship diagram of the script's key cast, with red chalk for the Hindu characters, green for the Muslims and yellow for the Christians. A picture of who their audience was and what they wanted was being continually built up and refined by all—as discussed in the next chapter.

From the perspective of 2012, the system I have just described was byzantine and bizarre. Since 1998, the government has recognised the Indian film industry as such, with the result that it can now raise bank finance and a streamlined and well-capitalised industry is emerging. But, however much its players may have decried its shortcomings and whilst few, if any, would want to turn back the clock, the industry of the early 1980s had its own logic and its own checks and balances, including the unique role played by the laboratories and the sophisticated system of negotiated relationships and mutual obligation. It worked well enough for all the most successful people within it. Without contracts or institutional finance, this (non-)industry made more films than anywhere else in the world, with an overall success and failure rate no worse than Hollywood's. The money flowed and the camera rolled.

Appendix 7.1 Major territory average prices, 1935–83

Year	Major Territory (Rs)	
1935	10,000	
1940	25,000	
1945	45,000	
1950	60,000	
1951	75,000	
1952	100,000	
1954	125,000	
1955	150,000	
1956	200,000	
1957	300,000	
1958	400,000	
1960	400,000	colour era starts
1965	600,000	
1968	700,000	
1970	900,000	
1972	1,100,000	
1974	1,200,000	
1975	1,800,000	
1976	2,500,000	
1977	3,500,000	
1978	5,000,000	
1979	6,000,000	
1981	6,500,000	
1983	7,500,000	

Source: Information courtesy of *Trade Guide*, Bombay.

NOTES

1. Money from illegal profits or those undeclared for tax purposes. In the early 1980s, a huge amount (estimated at Rs 200,000 crores) circulated as a 'parallel economy' in India and almost every big transaction—including house/flat purchase in Bombay—required a percentage of the price in black.

2. Goddess of wealth.

3. K.S. Karanth (ed.), *Report of the Working Group on National Film Policy*, New Delhi: Ministry of Information and Broadcasting, May 1980.

4. Barnouw and Krishnaswamy, *Indian Film*, pp. 127–30.

5. At that time equivalent to around £160,000.

6. Before independence, British-owned banks did, to some extent, finance film-making. The argument against institutional finance was that in the current system producers had no assets except negatives, which had no intrinsic value.

7. However, as the NFDC had failed to establish any viable independent distribution circuit, most such films, once made, never got screened in India, as commercial distributors were unwilling to take risks on them—particularly as there was already a surfeit of commercial films in which they had invested, waiting for release. On the other hand, films in regional languages (that is, other than Hindi) did frequently get *state* government financial backing and find efficient local distribution.

8. It would be unskilful business practice to do this openly. Clever producers manipulated the situation so that stories simply circulated that the film was having 'problems' in censorship.

9. Although the blank chits would appear extraordinarily dangerous for the producer, it was said that financiers 'do not' (are very unlikely to) abuse the system without reasonable grounds, as their future business depended largely on reputation. There did appear to be a general consensus on where the line between astute business practice and cheating lay, and I was told on several occasions that in certain matters—especially those that concern black money (that is, 'cheating' an 'iniquitous' government that demands 'excessive' taxes)—there was an 'honour among thieves'.

10. Houses and other personal capital were standardly kept in the names of wives and other family members for this reason.

11. Excise duty on processed prints and customs duty on the import of raw stock were high throughout the 1970s.

12. This list of territories broadly corresponds to those published in Karanth, *Report of the Working Group on National Film Policy*, p. 23. By the mid-1990s, according to Tejaswini Ganti (*Bollywood*, New York: Routledge, 2004, pp. 57–8), this was talked about as six territories, with the East Punjab territory amalgamated with the Delhi territory. Presumably by the 1990s this territory (which in pre-independence days had included the large Lahore area and been much more significant) was finally recognised to be too small to stand alone.

13. In the days of the studio system (1920s/30s) most films were distributed by the studios themselves, which established links with the exhibitors direct or, in the case of producers such as Madan, actually owned chains of cinemas. There were very few distributors at this time and these served mostly the smaller studios and the comparatively few independent producers. With the rise of the independent producer in the 1940s, the distributors came into their own, but worked for a straight commission. The system of a large number of independent distributors and their financing of under-production films evolved slowly through the 1950s and 1960s. See Barnouw and Krishnaswamy, *Indian Film*, pp. 145–7.

14. Despite the fact that Bombay films were very popular in most Eastern European countries, industry sources suggest that no formal distribution deals were signed. The films may have arrived illegally there via other countries, notably Russia, where a fixed number of prints were bartered every year. This needs more research.

15. In fact, any distributor would aim to sell the sub-divisions for as much as possible—sometimes as much as was originally paid for the whole territory.

16. Information courtesy of Uday Row Kavi and *Trade Guide*, Bombay.

17. Compared with Western business practice, an extraordinary amount was done by word of mouth, without written or clearly formalised contracts. The system was held together through the importance of 'reputation' and connections in ensuring survival in the industry.

18. Tejaswini Ganti elaborates on this important point in reference to a slightly later period, the 1990s, when she did her own fieldwork. See Ganti, *Producing Bollywood*, pp. 190–1.

19. These ratios are said to be not dissimilar to those of Hollywood films in those years.

20. Entertainment tax was collected on the government's behalf. Moreover, different states had different tax structures.

21. Figures given to me by Uday Row Kavi, associate editor of *Trade Guide* in 1985.

22. By way of example, the Maratha Mandir, Bombay's most prestigious luxury cinema, cost Rs 47,000 per week in 1980—a price that even the powerful Tarachand Barjatya found excessive.

23. Karanth, *Report of the Working Group on National Film Policy*, 1980, p. 24.

24. Ibid., p. 24. These figures include cinemas showing *all* types of film, not just Hindi films. Britain's seat to population ratio at the time was 15 seats per 1,000 population. Even other Asian countries had better ratios: Singapore had 27 seats per 1,000; Malaysia, 21 per 1,000; and Sri Lanka, 13 per 1,000.

25. In fact, despite their power, something of a stigma attached to exhibitors—and film exhibition as a sector. It was sometimes explained as being because the original cinemas were situated in the red-light areas of cities. However, when I pressed people on this, these explanations changed. Those in the film industry's other sectors suggested that it was because the exhibitors were the ones to deal with the 'dirty' public, and were contaminated by this contact and by being the ones to take money from this public. This was interesting in view of the popularly circulating image of the film industry itself as the 'dirty' place, from which perspective the exhibitor presumably represented the public face/point of contact with this 'dirty' industry and was thus contaminated from both sides.

26. Barnouw and Krishnaswamy, *Indian Film*, pp. 127–8.

27. The owner of a studio might also be a producer—for example, Raj Kapoor or V. Shantaram—but these would be run as two separate business concerns.

28. The IMPPA, the largest of these, primarily settled disputes between members and had been notoriously unsuccessful in organising any cooperative action. The Film Producers' Guild was a small 'invite-only' group of elite film-makers. Western India Film Producers' Association (WIFPA) had only regional or small-time film-makers as its members.

29. Per shift, either 9 a.m. to 6 p.m., or 7 p.m. to 2 a.m., although a common stint was 10 a.m. to 10 p.m., representing one-and-a-half shifts.

30. While Hema Malini's earnings (in 1981) were estimated at between Rs 15,000 and Rs 30,000 (£1,000–2,000) per day (and Amitabh's over twice this), a woman carrying bricks on set construction earned Rs 10 per day.

31. These unions also had a strong apex body, the Federation of Western India Cine Employees (FWICE), which from time to time renegotiated payment rates and working conditions with producers' associations.

32. In the 1980s, daughters were generally 'protected from', rather than launched into, the industry.

33. The implication being that all three can provoke sudden and transient changes of state, are not to be trusted and can potentially do a lot of damage, that is, watch out!

34. There was something of a vicious circle as stars were justifiably wary of producers without the right connections, knowing that only those with connections would be able to persuade others to cooperate at every stage, and therefore finish the film. Moneyed outsiders usually began in the comparative safety of financing, rather than producing, films.

35. The male star was considered to be the key to the film's saleability.

36. With established teams, sittings were usually sober occasions often at the director's or producer's house. In other cases, drinks, prostitutes and general debauchery were on hand 'to relieve tensions'.

37. He would have known that Desai's films were almost certain to enhance his star status even further by being hits. He might also have claimed that he had an obligation to Desai, who had done so much for his present status. It could be considered disrespectful for a star—particularly minor stars—to demand to know the story when a high-status producer did them the 'honour' of approaching them.

38. This was particularly exacerbated by the predominance then of male-centred, 'buddy' storylines.

39. The precise percentage depended on who the producer was and his negotiating power.

40. I never attended the muhurat of a female producer.

41. Hence vindicating the astrologers' claims that their calculations were always reliable: it was just human error in carrying them out which meant that fewer than 20 per cent of films made money.

42. Peda may, or may not, be the same as *prasad* (blessed food) from the puja.

43. Interested distributors would indicate their intention to buy by bringing along a cheque for a token amount, thereby giving them first option on the film, subject to terms and conditions being negotiated later.

44. If the songs were good and their picturisation spectacular, the film was considered to have a good chance of doing well. But music directors saved their best songs for prestigious producers who would make hit films of them. This was a vicious circle: good songs were an indication not only of a producer's judgement in selecting songs but also of his standing in the industry.

45. Another reason for rarely finalising script details until shortly before shooting was that, given the many uncertainties about what or who might be available and whether the film would even get that far, it would be a waste of time.

Bombay before Bollywood

46. The government had very little incentive to change the regulations, as they received a huge tax levy from an industry (or a non-industry) in which no government or institutional money was involved in any form of risk. The real problem was the much wider one of the parallel economy itself, and until that was stemmed it might appear convenient that black money was what was risked—and mostly lost—in films. In the tradition of Gandhi's disapproval of films, a quasi-ascetic, rhetorical stance—which could decry the dirty industry by refusing to recognise it—was also advantageous to the government.

47. This was not to argue that those at the top were not talented: the crucial importance of continuing box-office success ensures that, in film industry terms, they were most highly talented. However, there were undoubtedly many others who, given equal access to resources, could offer real competition.

48. Dev Anand's very considerable personal clout derived from having been one of India's mega-stars since 1949, from considerable charm and a reputation for 'decency' and 'honesty' and, as a long-standing producer, from giving 'breaks' to many established industry players. He was also the figure-head of the Anand 'camp', based around himself, Chetan and Vijay, his two very talented producer/director brothers, together with a second generation of sons and nephews. Quite extraordinarily, such immense power accrued to Dev Anand through all this that it overrode the (seldom emphasised) fact that few of the films he produced and directed ever made money.

49. Information courtesy of *Trade Guide*, Bombay.

$\mathcal{I}$ndian Cinema
Pleasures and Popularity

The pseudo-intellectuals here try to copy Westerners. We think we're better than Westerners—they can't make films for the Indian audience.

Bombay film-maker[1]

A discussion of Indian popular cinema as 'other' cinema is immediately problematic. There is no disputing that, within the context of First World[2] culture and society, this cinema has always been marginalised, if not ignored completely, especially in the era before 1984, when this chapter was originally written. It was defined primarily through its 'otherness' or 'difference' from First World cinema, and consumption of it in the West, whether by Asians or non-Asians, was something of an assertion: one had chosen to view an 'alternative' type of cinema. However, this was a cinema which, in the Indian context, was an overridingly dominant, mainstream form, and was, in the 1970s and early 1980s, itself opposed by an 'Other': the 'new', 'parallel', 'art' (or often simply 'other') cinema which ranged from the work of Satyajit Ray, Shyam Benegal and various regional film-makers, to Mani Kaul's 'avant-garde' or Anand Patwardhan's 'agitational' political practice. In these terms, Indian popular cinema was neither alternative nor a minority form. Moreover, in a global context, by virtue of its sheer volume of output, the Indian entertainment cinema still dominated world film production, and its films were distributed throughout large areas of the Third World (including non-Hindustani-speaking areas and even parts of the Soviet Union), where they were frequently consumed more avidly than both Hollywood and indigenous 'alternative' or political cinemas. Such preference suggests that these films were seen to be offering something positively different from Hollywood and, in fact, largely because it always had its own vast distribution markets, Indian cinema, throughout its long history, evolved as a form that had resisted the cultural imperialism of Hollywood. This is not, of course, to say that it has been uninfluenced by Hollywood: the form has undergone continual change and there have been both inspiration and assimilation from Hollywood and elsewhere, but thematically and structurally, Indian cinema has remained remarkably distinctive.

Corresponding to this diversity of contexts, each of which constructs Indian popular cinema as a different object, there has been considerable confusion of critical and evaluative perspective. This chapter examines the ways in which this cinema was discussed by critics in India and abroad prior to 1980 and suggests that, as a first step, the terms of reference of the Indian popular cinema itself should be brought into the picture. It attempts to do this, using material from discussions with Bombay film-makers[3] about what, for them, constituted 'good' and 'bad' Hindi cinema in the 1970s and 1980s.[4] Points will be illustrated through the example of one very popular, and at the time of release generally lauded film, *Naseeb* (Destiny, 1981),[5] whose producer/director, Manmohan Desai, was Bombay's most consistently commercially successful film-maker of his day. I will suggest that, while First World critical evaluation outside these terms of reference is, at best, irrelevant and also often racist, to impose a theoretical framework developed in the West—particularly one concerned with examining textual operations and the mechanisms of pleasure—does allow useful questions to be asked, as well as opening up the ethnocentrism of these debates.

The most striking aspect of First World discourse on Indian popular cinema must be its arrogant silence. Until home video killed the market in the 1980s, the films had been in regular distribution in Britain for more than thirty years, yet ghettoised in immigrant areas, unseen and unspoken of by most non-Asians. Even in 1980, when the first Bombay film (*Amar Akbar Anthony*, Manmohan Desai, 1977) was shown on British television, it passed more or less unnoticed: the BBC not only programmed it early one Sunday morning, without even troubling to list it with other films on the *Radio Times* film preview page, but pruned it of all its songs and much narrative, including most of the first two reels, which are, not surprisingly, crucial to making any sense of the film. Although the situation began to change in the early 1980s, largely through the initiative of Channel Four's first two seasons of Indian entertainment cinema, the traditional attitude remained one of complacent ignorance. Clichés abounded: the films were regularly said to be nightmarishly long, second-rate copies of Hollywood trash, to be dismissed with patronising amusement or facetious quips. British television documentaries had a long tradition in perpetuating these attitudes, for the baroque surface of the Hindi film, particularly if taken out of context, made for automatic comedy. *Time Out*'s television listings section in 1984 announced *Gunga Jumna* (Nitin Bose, 1961)—a classic of Indian cinema, but obviously unpreviewed—with the smug throwaway: 'Sounds turgid, but who knows?'[6]

Where popular Indian films were taken at all seriously, it was either to subject them to impertinent criticism according to the canons of dominant Western film-making—'*Mother India* is a rambling tale of personal woe, narrated episodically in unsuitably pretty Technicolour'[7]—or to congratulate them patronisingly—'All told, a disarmingly enthusiastic piece of Eastern spectacle, exaggerated in presentation and acting, exotic, and yet charmingly naïve.'[8] They were generally looked at as 'a stupendous curiosity'—even in the 1950s, as an ethnographic lesson, a way to 'get to close grips with a handful of [India's] inhabitants. That Indians make the same faces as we do when they fall in love astounds me beyond measure.'[9]

But the most general theme since the 1960s was the unfavourable comparison with Indian art cinema 'It all goes to prove once again that Satyajit Ray is the exception who proves the rule of Indian film-making.'[10]

As Indian art cinema was comparatively well known and enthusiastically received in the West in the 1970s and 1980s, and much conformed to conventions made familiar within European art cinema, the Western audience's assumptions about film form could remain unchallenged. In fact, the art films served mostly to confirm the 'inadequacy' of popular cinema to match what were presumed to be universal standards of 'good' cinema—and even of 'art'. Western critics were perhaps not completely to blame, for they took their cues from the Indian upper-middle-class intelligentsia and government cultural bodies, who had a long tradition of conniving in this denunciation and, somewhat ironically, themselves insisted on evaluating the popular films according to the canons of European and Hollywood film-making. One would commonly hear complaints about the films' 'lack of realism', about the preposterous 'singing and dancing and running round trees', and that the films were 'all the same' and simply 'copy Hollywood'. To dislike such films was, of course, their privilege. What is disturbing is the tone of defensive apology to the West and the shamefaced disavowal of what was undoubtedly a central feature of modern Indian culture. Thus, for example, Satish Bahadur, comparing popular cinema unfavourably with Satyajit Ray's *Pather Panchali* (Song of the Road, 1955) which 'was a work of art … an organic form', referred to the former's 'immaturity' and asserted: 'The heavily painted men and women with exaggerated theatrical gestures and speech, the artificial-looking houses and huts and the painted trees and skies in the films of this tradition are less truthful statements of the reality of India.'[11] Even Firoze Rangoonwalla, who devoted considerable energy to compiling much of the published material available on popular Indian cinema, dismissed the work of the 1970s as 'a very dark period, with a silly absurd kind of escapism rearing its head'. He was tolerant of popular cinema only if it attempted 'sensible themes'.[12]

One of the central platforms for this kind of criticism was the English-language 'quality' press. Week after week, the Indian *Sunday Times* and *Sunday Express* produced jokey review columns which scored easy points off the apparent inanities of Hindi cinema. Typical is a *Sunday Times* feature entitled 'Not Only Vulgar But Imitative', which skims through all the critical clichés: absurd stories, poor imitations of Hollywood, lack of originality, and finally the myth of a 'golden age'—of the 1960s—when commercial films were 'gentle, warm-hearted, innocent'. Most significant is the fact that the article appeared—by no coincidence—in precisely the week that Bombay was full of Western delegates to the annual film festival. It makes no bones about its intended audience, to whom it defers: 'Not surprisingly the West cares little for these films. All that they stand for is exotica, vulgarity and absurdity.'[13] *Naseeb* was, of course, received within this tradition. The *Sunday Express* review was captioned 'Mindless Boring Melange' and, for example, described a central scene—in fact one that was spectacularly self-parodic, in which many top stars and film-makers make 'guest appearances' at a party—as follows:

> [A] 'homage' to ... all those who have, in the past thirty years, brought the Hindi film down to its present state of total garish mediocrity. In fact, the film encapsulates the entire history of our sub-standard 'entertainment'—elephantine capers ... the manufactured emotion, the brutalism in talk and acting, the utterly 'gauche' dances.[14]

The tone was echoed throughout the popular English-language (hence middle-class) press. Even among regular (middle-class) filmgoers there appeared to be huge resistance to admitting to finding pleasure in the form. Thus letters to film gossip magazines ran the following:

> Want to make *Naseeb*? Don't bother about a story or screenplay. You can do without both. Instead rope in almost the entire industry.... Throw in the entire works: revolving restaurant, London locales, and outfits which even a five year old would be embarrassed to wear to a fancy dress competition. Now, sit back, relax, and watch the cash pour in.[15]
>
> Manmohan Desai's concept of entertainment still revolves around the lost and found theme, with a lot of improbabilities and inanities thrown in.... But how long can such films continue to click at the box-office? Soon audiences are bound to come to their senses.[16]

There were also, of course, more serious and considered critical positions within India, notably of the politically conscious who argued, quite cogently, that Hindi cinema was capitalist, sexist, exploitative, 'escapist' mystification, politically and aesthetically reactionary, and moreover that its control of distribution networks blocked opportunities for more radical practitioners. It should, of course, be remembered that what may be pertinent criticism within India may be irrelevant—or racist—in the West, and apparently similar criticisms may have different meanings, uses and effects in different contexts. However, two central objections to all the criticisms do stand out. One is the insistence on evaluating Hindi cinema in terms of film-making practices which it had itself rejected, a blanket refusal to allow its own terms of reference to be heard. The second is the reluctance to acknowledge and deal with the fact that Hindi cinema clearly gave enormous pleasure to vast pan-Indian (and Third World) audiences. In view of this, such supercilious criticism does no more than wish the films away. Dismissing them as 'escapism' neither explains them in any useful way, nor offers any basis for political strategy, for it allows no space for questions about the specifics of the audiences' relationship to their so-called escapist fare. What seems to be needed is an analysis which takes seriously both the films and the pleasures they offer, and which attempts to unravel their mode of operation.

Clearly, a body of film theory developed in the West may mislead if it is used to squash Hindi cinema into Western film-making categories, particularly if it brutalises or denies the meanings and understandings of participants. Thus, for example, Hollywood genre classification was, especially in that era, quite inappropriate to Hindi cinema. Although almost every Hindi film contained elements of the 'musical', 'comedy' and 'melodrama', to refer to the films in any of these ways imposes a significant distortion. Certainly no Indian film-maker would normally have used such classifications. Important distinctions were marked instead by terms such as 'social', 'family social', 'devotional', 'stunt' or even 'multi-starrer' (terms hard to gloss quickly for a Western readership). However, the *concept* of genre, in its broadest sense—as structuring principles of expectation and convention, around which individual films mark repetitions and differences[17]—does appear to be potentially useful in opening up questions about Hindi cinema's distinctive form. In the first place, it moves immediately beyond the tired rantings about Hindi cinema's 'repetitiveness' and 'lack of originality'—although, on this point, some of the Bombay film-makers were in fact many steps ahead of their so-called 'intellectual' critics:

People seem to like the same thing again and again, so I repeat it ... but you always have to give them something different too.... There can be no such thing as a formula film—if there were, everybody would be making nothing but hits.[18]

Secondly, it points to questions about narrative structure, modes of address and conventions of verisimilitude that, at the least, help to organise description which can take Indian cinema's own terms of reference into account. From this, further questions about spectatorship and pleasure become possible. The rest of this chapter attempts to illustrate such an approach.

Contrary to common 'intellectual' assumptions within India, the Indian mass audience was ruthlessly discriminating: over 85 per cent of films released between 1983 and 1985 did not make profits, and these included films with the biggest budgets and most publicity hype.[19] There was a clear sense among audiences of 'good' and 'bad' films, and the film-makers, committed as they were to 'pleasing' audiences, made it their business to understand, and internalise, these assessments. While the yardstick of commercial success was of course central—for film-makers a 'good' film was ultimately one that made money—they did also have a working model of (what they believed to be) the essential ingredients of a 'good' film and the 'right' way to put these together. This model evolved largely through the informal, but obsessive, post-mortems that followed films whose box-office careers confounded expectations, and it underwent continual, if gradual, redefinition and refinement.

Bombay film-makers frequently stressed that they aimed to make films that differed in both format and content from Western films, that there was a definite skill to making films for the Indian audience, that this audience had specific needs and expectations, and that to compare Hindi films to those of the West—or those of the Indian 'art' cinema—was irrelevant. Their statements implied both a sense of the tyranny of their audience and a recognition of the importance of a class link between film-maker and audience. The example of the barely educated Mehboob Khan, whose cult classic *Mother India* (1957) still drew full houses in the 1980s, was often cited proudly—buttressed by assertions that his film was 'of our soil', 'full of real

Indian emotions'—and by that token inaccessible to the emotionally retarded, if not totally cold-blooded, West.[20]

Whatever the critics' clichés may suggest, no successful Bombay film-maker ever simply 'copied' Western films. Of course, most borrowed openly both story ideas and sometimes complete sequences from foreign cinemas, but borrowings had always to be integrated with Indian film-making conventions if the film was to work with the Indian audience: no close copy of Hollywood had ever been a hit up to then.[21] Film-makers said that the essence of 'Indianisation' lay in the way the storyline was developed; the crucial necessity of 'emotion' (Western films were often referred to as 'cold'); and the skilful blending and integration of songs, dances, fights and other 'entertainment values' within the body of the film. There was also the more obvious 'Indianisation' of values and other content, including reference to aspects of Indian life with which audiences would identify, particularly religion and patriotism. It was, for example, generally believed that science fiction would be outside the cultural reference of the Indian audience, and censorship restrictions meant that films about war, or overtly about national and international politics, risked being banned.

The film-makers' terms of reference often emerged most clearly when discussing a film which was judged a failure. A trade press review of *Desh Premee* (Patriot, 1982), one of Manmohan Desai's few unsuccessful films, is particularly revealing.[22]

> *Desh Premee* has all the ingredients that make a film a hit, yet every aspect is markedly defective. Firstly, the story has a plot and incidents but the narration is so unskilled that it does not sustain interest. There is no grip to the story. The situations are neither melodramatic, nor do they occur spontaneously, but look forced and contrived. Secondly, the music side is not as strong as the film demands. All songs are good average, but not one song can be declared a superhit. Thirdly, emotional appeal is lacking. Although there are a few scenes which try to arouse feelings, they fail to hit their objective. Fourthly, production values are average, considering the producer. The traditional grandeur of Manmohan Desai is missing, as are technical values.

Desh Premee has no sex appeal. The romantic part is too short. Comedy scenes and melodramatic scenes are missing.... [*Author's précis*: the stars' roles are not properly justified ... several appear for too short a time ... action, thrills and background music are only average]

Several of the scenes look like repetitions from many old hits and there is no dose of originality in the film.... Although every formula film is basically unrealistic and far from the truths of life, everything can still be presented with acceptable realism and logic. But in this film there are several 'unbelievables' even with normal cinematic license granted. This is not expected from any seasoned film-maker.[23]

Particularly interesting is the order in which defects are listed: the screenplay is recognised to be crucial, the music (that is, the songs) of almost equal importance, 'emotional appeal' a significant third, and fourth are production values, or expensive spectacle. A 'dose of originality' and 'acceptable realism and logic' are additional points of general importance. Big stars are a decided advantage (viz., 'the ingredients that make a film a hit'), but cannot in themselves save a film—particularly if not exploited adequately. By contrast, *Naseeb* on its release had been particularly praised for 'assembling the biggest star-cast ever [and] ... justifying each and all of them'.[24]

Two themes emerge from this review: firstly, that of the expected narrative movement and mode of address, and secondly, the question of verisimilitude.

NARRATIVE

Indian film-makers often insisted that screenplay and direction were crucial and the storyline only the crudest vehicle from which to wring 'emotion' and onto which to append spectacle.

It's much more difficult to write a screenplay for *Naseeb* than for a western or 'art' film, where you have a straight storyline. A commercial Hindi film has to have sub-plots and gags, and keep its audience involved with no story or logic.[25]

The assertion that Hindi films have 'no story' is sometimes confusing to those unfamiliar with the genre. 'Who cares who gets the story credits? Everyone knows our films have no stories', and, in fact, the story credits were often farmed out to accommodating friends or relatives for 'tax adjustment' purposes. However, Hindi cinema has by no means broken the hallowed bounds of narrative convention. The most immediately striking thing about *Naseeb* is the fiendishly complex convolutions of this multi-stranded and very long succession of events, which nevertheless culminate in an exemplarily neat resolution. What was meant by 'no story' was, first, that the storyline would be almost totally predictable to the Indian audience, being a repetition—or rather an unmistakable transformation—of many other Hindi films, and second, that it would be recognised by them as a 'ridiculous' pretext for spectacle and emotion. Films that really had 'no story' (that is, non-narrative), or were 'just a slice of life', or had the comparatively single-stranded narratives of many contemporary Western films, were considered unlikely to be successful. 'The difference between Hindi and western films is like that between an epic and a short story.'[26]

Not only was a film expected to be two-and-a-half to three hours long, but it was usual for the plot to span at least two generations, beginning with the main protagonists' births or childhoods and jumping twenty or so years (often in a single shot) to the action of the present. There is of course good evidence that Hindi films evolved from village traditions of epic narration, and the dramas and the characters, as well as the structure, of the mythological epics were regularly and openly drawn upon. Film-makers often insisted that 'Every film can be traced back to these stories', and even that 'There are only two stories in the world, the Ramayana and Mahabharat'.[27] In fact, it is the form and movement of the narrative that tends to distinguish the Hindi film, the crux of this being that the balance between narrative development and spectacular or emotional excess is rather different.

As the *Trade Guide* review implies, audiences expected to be addressed in an ordered succession of modes. *Desh Premee* had failed allegedly because, among other reasons, there was no comedy, no melodrama, too little 'romance' and no 'emotion', while *Naseeb* had earlier been commended because 'everything' was there:

'balancing beautifully the story, the plot, the screenplay, the dialogue and dramatic situations ... [and] providing properly the thrills, the action, boxing, chasing and other modes'.[28] Film-makers talked about 'blending the *masalas*[29] in proper proportions' as one might discuss cookery, and (defensive stances for the benefit of Westerners or 'intellectuals' notwithstanding) they had a clear perception that these elements, including the inexcusably maligned songs and dances, were an important part of the work of the film, which was to achieve an overall balance of 'flavours'. Clearly, something of a commercial motivation was at work here (one put in 'something for everybody'), but it was also considered very important that one did not 'just shove these things in', for, it was said, 'the audience always knows if you do'.

Naseeb's narrative movement is by way of swift juxtaposition of cameo scenes of spectacular—or humorous—impact, rather than steady development of drama. Clearly, as in all mainstream cinema, Hindi films work to offer the viewer a position of coherence and mastery, both through narrative closure and by providing a focus for identification within the film (in *Naseeb* this is a male hero with, as will be argued below, a particularly reassuring mastery of potent phantasy). However, spectacular and emotional excess were invariably privileged over linear narrative development. The spectator was expected to be involved not primarily through anticipation of *what* would happen next, but through *how* it would happen and affective involvement in the happening: excitement, thrill, fear, envy, wonder, not to mention the eroticism which lies behind the desire for spectacle itself. While many Hindi films depend essentially on emotional drama (although with spectacle always of importance), *Naseeb* is primarily about spectacle—with song and dance, locations, costumes, fights and 'thrills' (or stunts), most of Bombay's top stars, and sets which range from a luxury glass mansion to a baroque revolving restaurant and a fanciful 'London' casino. 'If the story is weak, you have to be a showman and show the public everything', said Desai.[30] But unregulated, uncontained spectacle, however novel, interesting and pleasurable, always risks losing its audience's involvement (for example: 'The narration is so unskilled that it does not sustain interest'[31]). *Naseeb* depends on two strategies to avoid this. One is its skill at swift transition between well balanced 'modes' of spectacle, the

Figure 8.1 *Naseeb* (1981): Amitabh Bachchan, Rishi Kapoor and Shatrughan Sinha sing and dance in the revolving restaurant.

Source: © MKD Films. Courtesy Ketan M. Desai.

other the strength and reassuring familiarity of the narrative, which is, in fact, structured by discourses that are deeply rooted in Indian social life and in the unconscious (and in this its relationship with Indian mythological and folk narrative becomes particularly apparent).

Briefly, the story of *Naseeb* concerns the friendships, love affairs, family reunions and fights between the (adult) children of four men who won a lottery ticket together and fell out over the division of the spoils. Any attempt at succinct summary of the intricacies of this extraordinarily convoluted plot and its characters' relationships is doomed to failure—nor is it strictly relevant. It is probably enough to point out that the story is built around three chestnuts of Hindi cinema which were particularly popular in the late 1970s/1980s, the themes being: (*a*) 'lost and found' (parents and children are separated and reunited years later following revelation of mistaken identities); (*b*) '*dostana*' (two male friends fall in love with the same woman and the one who discovers this sacrifices his love—and often life—for the male friendship or dostana); and (*c*) revenge (villains get their just deserts at the hands of the heroes they wronged). Analysis of the narrative

Figure 8.2 *Naseeb*: sword fight in the revolving restaurant

Source: © MKD Films. Courtesy Ketan M. Desai.

suggests that the discourses that structure it are those of kinship (the blood relationship and bonds expressed in its idiom); 'duty' and social obligation; solidarity and trust; and also a metaphysical discourse of 'fate' or 'destiny' and human impotence in the face of this. Order, or equilibrium, is presented as a state in which humans live in harmony with fate, respecting social obligations and ties of friendship or family. Disruption of this order is the result of selfish greed, fate (or human meddling in fate) and (hetero-) sexual desire.

The narrative is built upon a simple opposition between good/ morality and evil/decadence. Connotations of 'traditional' and 'Indian' are appended to morality, which is an ideal of social relations which includes respect for kinship and friendship obligations, destiny, patriotism and religion (and religious tolerance) as well as controlled sexuality. Evil or decadence is broadly categorised as 'non-traditional' and 'Western', although the West is not so much a place, or even a culture, as an emblem of exotic, decadent otherness, signified by whisky, bikinis, an uncontrolled sexuality and what is seen as lack of 'respect' for elders and betters, and (from men) towards womanhood.

Film-makers were quite aware of building their narratives around the terms of an opposition so basic that audiences could not easily avoid immersion:

> Kinship emotion in India is very strong—so this element always works—that's what 'lost and found' is about. It doesn't work so well with educated audiences who go several days without seeing their families, but it works with B and C grade audiences who get worried if they don't see a family member by 6.30 p.m., whose family members are an important part of themselves and their experience of the world.[32]

However, the films also appear to deal with these basic family relationships at a much deeper level, and what appears to be highly charged imagery, which is not organised into conscious narrative coherence, regularly erupts in these films. Thus, for example, *Naseeb* boasts a scene whose parallels with the Oedipal scenario are hard to ignore, in which the father and 'good' son/hero, unaware of their blood relationship, are locked in mortal combat—the father wielding a knife above his prostrate son. Just as one is about to kill the other, the hero's foster mother, who had fallen and lost consciousness, revives, appears at the top of the stairs with a bleeding wound on her head prominently bandaged, and shrieks. The action freezes, mistaken identities are explained, and the son agrees to follow his father into combat with the villains. For this encounter the father hands over to him a special ring, bearing the mark of Hindu religion (the sacred symbol OM), which protects him in a succession of fights and later becomes the mechanism by which he escapes, on a rope, from a burning tower in which the villains (that which is not socialised) meet gory deaths. In fact, somewhat bizarrely, the film can be read as a narrative of masculine psychic development (the emergence of the sexed subject within the social order), with the early scenes of anarchic sexuality followed by an Oedipal crisis and a subsequent drama of sons following the Father into the Symbolic Order.

To point to the kind of reading that a very literal psychoanalysis produces is not to advocate reducing *Naseeb*—or psychoanalysis—to this. However, it does raise interesting questions about the relevance of psychoanalysis in the Indian context and, in fact, the greatest problem is not how to *apply* such concepts, but whether one can *ignore* patternings which obtrude in so implausibly striking a manner. Although few films order their imagery in so fortuitously neat a diachrony, its potency and overtness is not unusual, and what a letter writer could dismiss as nothing but 'the lost and found theme with a lot of improbabilities and inanities thrown in' can be very far from inane in the context of the spectator's own phantasy.

VERISIMILITUDE

Beyond the basic suspension of disbelief on which cinema depends, any genre evolves and institutionalises its own conventions, which allow credibility to become unproblematic within certain parameters.[33] Compared with the conventions of most Western cinema, Hindi films appear to have patently preposterous narratives, overblown dialogue (frequently evaluated by film-makers on whether or not it is 'clap-worthy'), exaggeratedly stylised acting, and to show disregard for psychological characterisation, history, geography and even, sometimes, camera placement rules.[34]

Tolerance of overt phantasy has always been high in Hindi cinema, with little need to anchor the material in what Western conventions might recognise as a discourse of realism. Moreover, slippage between registers does not have to be marked or rationalised. The most obvious example is the song sequences, which are much less commonly 'justified' within the story (for example, introduced as stage performances by the fictional characters) than in Hollywood musicals. Hindi film songs are usually tightly integrated, through words and mood, within the *flow* of the film—'In my films, if you miss a song, you have missed an important link between one part of the narration and the next'[35]—and misguided attempts to doctor Hindi films for Western audiences by cutting out the songs are always fatal. However, the song sequences (often also dream sequences) do permit excesses of phantasy which would be more problematic elsewhere in the film, for they specifically allow continuities of time and place to be disregarded, heroines to change saris between shots and the scenery to skip continents between verses, whenever the interests of spectacle or mood require it.

Although Hindi film phantasy needs comparatively slight authenticating strategies, *Naseeb* does negotiate the terrain with care, and this is undoubtedly one of its strengths. In fact, the viewer is immersed gradually, as the film moves through three phases: an initial mode bordering on 'social realism', a second period of self-reflexivity and parody, and a final phase in which dream imagery and dream logic are unproblematic. Particularly interesting are the middle scenes, which make self-conscious and sophisticated play with the ambiguity between registers. Thus, for example, in the party song mentioned above, 'real' Bombay film stars appear, as themselves, at a film party located firmly within *Naseeb*'s fiction, and, throughout, the central hero's romance is presented largely as a parody of Hindi cinema clichés, with him commenting, after a dazzling display of kung-fu skills to rescue his pop singer girlfriend from rapacious thugs: 'It's just like a Hindi film.' Later, when he finds her modelling for a throat

Figure 8.3 *Naseeb* party scene. Amitabh Bachchan as the waiter John Jani Janardan.

Source: © MKD Films. Courtesy Ketan M. Desai.

pastille advertising film on the riverside, he 'mistakes' the film scenario for 'reality' and, as the director yells, 'Start camera' and a crew member runs into frame with a microphone, the hero (speaking to camera in both the film and the film within the film) begins a flowery proposal of marriage in the style of Hindi film dialogue.

Naseeb was undoubtedly unusual in taking the self-reflexive and self-parodic elements inherent in most Hindi cinema so far, but the fact that it *was* acceptable is significant. Despite what middle-class critics implied, it was clear, if one experienced an Indian audience irreverently clapping, booing and laughing with the films, that they knew perfectly well that the films were 'ridiculous', 'unreal' and offered impossible solutions, and that pleasure arose in spite of—and probably because of—this knowledge.

However, this is not to say that 'anything goes': as the *Trade Guide* review implied, there was a firm sense of 'acceptable realism and logic', beyond which the material was rejected as 'unbelievable'. In fact, the criteria of verisimilitude in Hindi cinema appeared to refer primarily to a film's skill in manipulating the rules of the film's moral universe. Thus one was more likely to hear accusations of 'unbelievability' if the codes of, for example, ideal kinship behaviour were ineptly transgressed (that is, a son kills his mother, or a father knowingly and callously causes his son to suffer), than if the hero was a superman who single-handedly knocked out a dozen burly henchmen and then burst into song.

Any rigorous discussion of the conventions of verisimilitude and the apparent tolerance of 'non-realism' in Hindi cinema would have to consider much wider issues, including concepts and conventions of realism in Indian culture generally. However, even an examination of the cinematic heritage on which *Naseeb* drew is suggestive and, significantly, Manmohan Desai and two of his writers learned their craft as apprentices to directors from the Wadias' Basant studios, producers of the most popular genres in Indian film-making history, 'mythologicals', fantasy and stunt films. As discussed in earlier chapters, although mythologicals were generally considered to be of higher status ('the Brahmin of film genres'), film-makers recognised their overlap ('mythologicals were just special effect and stunt films which happened to be about gods rather than men'), for both were primarily moral stories with displays of magical happenings, supermen and gods. On the other hand, the influence of Hollywood cannot be ignored, from James Bond, whose idiom inflected many 1970s/1980s films, to the phenomenal impact of Douglas Fairbanks in the 1920s (when *Thief of Bagdad* was the decade's most popular film),[36] or of Charlie Chaplin, who was as big a star in India as elsewhere. Echoes can be found of all these traditions in *Naseeb*.

THE SPECTATOR

It would appear that the spectator-subject of Hindi cinema was positioned rather differently from that of most Western cinema. In fact, even at the most overt level, Indian cinema audience behaviour was, and mostly still is, distinctive: involvement in the films was intense and audiences clapped, sang, recited familiar dialogue with the actors, threw coins at the screen (in appreciation of spectacle), would 'tut tut' at emotionally moving scenes, cry openly and laugh and jeer knowingly. Moreover, it was expected that audiences would see a film they liked several times. So-called 'repeat value' was deliberately built into a production by the film-makers, who believed that the keys to this were primarily the stars, music, spectacle, emotion and dialogue— this last having a greater significance than in Western cinema.[37]

What seemed to emerge in mainstream Hindi cinema was an emphasis on emotion and spectacle rather than tight narrative, on *how* things would happen rather than *what* would happen next, on a succession of modes rather than linear denouement, on familiarity and repeated viewings rather than 'originality' and novelty, on a moral disordering to be (temporarily) resolved rather than an enigma to be solved. The spectator was addressed and moved through these films primarily via affect, although this was structured and contained by narratives whose power and insistence derived from their very familiarity, coupled with the fact that they were deeply rooted (in the psyche and in traditional mythology).

Whether, and how, one can relate the 'spectator-subject' of the films to the Indian 'social audience'[38] is not immediately clear, although certain comparisons with other discourses within India through which subjectivity might be lived are suggestive. For example, it has been suggested that Hindu caste, kinship and religious ideologies, in particular beliefs in destiny and karma, position a decentred, less individuated social subject.[39] One can also point to specific cultural traditions of performance and entertainment which must be of direct relevance, notably the forms on which early cinema drew, from the performances of the professional storytellers and village dramatisations of the mythological epics, to the excesses of spectacle ('vulgar' and 'garish' according to contemporary critics) of the late-nineteenth- and early-twentieth-century Urdu-Parsi theatre with its indulgent adaptations of Shakespeare and Victorian melodrama. Beyond this, one must remember that Sanskrit philosophy boasts a coherent theory of aesthetics which bears no relation to Aristotelian aesthetics. Rejecting the unities of time and place and the dramatic development of narrative, the theory of *rasa* (flavours/moods) is concerned with moving the spectator through the text in an ordered succession of modes of affect (rasa), by means of highly stylised devices. All Indian classical drama, dance and music draw on this aesthetic.

Of course, most film-makers I spoke with made no conscious reference to this heritage; and the privileging of spectacle and music can be accounted for in many other ways, not least the pragmatic one, that to make money the films needed to appeal across wide linguistic and cultural divides within India itself. 'Tradition' cannot be used to provide too neat an 'explanation' of the present form—apart from anything else, Indian cultural 'tradition' is a heterogeneous assimilation of Sanskritic, Islamic, Judaeo-Christian and many other influences, and could be selectively drawn upon to 'explain' almost any present form. Moreover, invoking tradition also holds dangers of uncritically romanticising the present form as exotically other and ignoring its diverse influences and constant evolution. Tradition should rather be seen as a framework of terms of reference within which certain developments have been stifled, others allowed to evolve unproblematically, and which can be used to throw light on the different possibilities of forms of address which might be expected or tolerated by an Indian audience.

This chapter has attempted to examine Indian popular cinema's terms of reference by placing this cinema within a number of contexts:

primarily that of the film-makers' own descriptions of their films and generic expectations, but also briefly that of audiences, and of earlier and coexisting cultural forms and traditions. There is, of course, the problem of the infinite regress of context: no description of conditions and discourses could ever be adequate to contextualising Indian cinema. But any criticism that ignores the specificity of the textual operations and pleasures of Indian popular cinema will remain caught up in the confusion and condescension which marked British responses to the London release of *Aan* in 1952: 'But having proved themselves masters of every cliché in the western cinema, its remarkable producers should have a look around home and make an Indian film.'[40]

NOTES

1. Quotes from film-makers were all collected during a period of fieldwork in Bombay in 1979–81, in many cases in the course of informal interviews and discussion. Following the conventions of this kind of ethnography, informal quotes are anonymised wherever specific permission to quote was not obtained at the time.

2. At the time this essay was written, the terms 'First World' and 'Third World' were common currency in critical discourse. I would not use these terms today.

3. This refers here primarily to those employed in the film industry as producers, directors, writers and distributors.

4. Films produced in the Hindustani language (and primarily in Bombay) accounted, in 1981, for less than 20 per cent of pan-Indian film production. However, they alone were distributed throughout the country and, having the biggest budgets, stars and hence prestige, influenced most regional language film-making.

5. *Naseeb*'s box-office returns rank with those of three other films as the highest of 1981. It was one of the most expensive 'multi-starrers' ever produced in India to that date (distribution rights sold for a little over £2 million in total: see chapter seven for an explanation of what this means).

6. Geoff Andrew in *Time Out*, 2–8 August 1984.

7. James Green in the *Observer*, 26 March 1961, referring to *Mother India*.

8. 'ER' in the *Monthly Film Bulletin*, September 1952, vol. 19, no. 224, referring to *Aan*.

9. Virginia Graham in the *Spectator*, 18 July 1952, referring to *Aan*.

10. *Monthly Film Bulletin*, August 1963, vol. 30, no. 355, referring to *Gunga Jumna*.

11. Aruna Vasudev and Philippe Lenglet (eds), *Indian Superbazaar*, New Delhi: Vikas Publishing House, 1983, p. 112.

12. Rangoonwalla, *Indian Cinema: Past and Present*.

13. Khalid Mohamed in the *Times of India*, 'Sunday Review', 8 January 1984.

14. *Sunday Express*, 3 May 1981.

15. *Star and Style*, 13 November 1981.

16. Iqbal Masud in *Cine Blitz*, July 1981.

17. Stephen Neale, *Genre*, London: British Film Institute, 1980.

18. Manmohan Desai in interview with the author, May 1981.

19. *Trade Guide*, 5 January 1985. Video piracy had a particularly harsh effect on the Bombay film industry. However, even in the late 1970s it is alleged that only 10 per cent of releases made 'sizeable' profits. (Karanth, *Report of the Working Group on National Film Policy*, p. 17).

20. The film has, in fact, been generally well received in the West and until 1988 was the only Indian film ever to have won an Oscar nomination (Best Foreign Film, 1958).

21. Where European and Hollywood cinemas have drawn upon literary traditions for their story ideas, Hindi cinema has primarily looked to other films for basic stories to adapt. Inspiration from Hollywood was often integrated with storylines from the Indian mythological epics, for example, a recent proposal 'for a cross between *The Omen* and the Mahabharat'. The only (more or less) frame-to-frame remakes of Hollywood films: *Khoon Khoon* (Mohammed Hussain, 1973) of *Dirty Harry* (Don Siegel, 1971) and *Manoranjan* (Shammi Kapoor, 1974) of *Irma La Douce* (Billy Wilder, 1963) flopped disastrously. So did *Man Pasand* (Basu Chatterjee, 1980), based closely on *My Fair Lady*, a failure which the BBC ignored in its dismissive documentary on the film in 1982.

22. In the early 1980s, there were two weekly Bombay trade papers, *Trade Guide* and *Film Information*. Their reviews were generally respected in the film industry (unlike all other press reviews, especially the Sunday critics') and they did in fact have a good record in predicting subsequence box-office performance.

23. *Trade Guide*, Special Edition, 2 April 1982 (with slight stylistic adaptations by author).

24. *Trade Guide*, 3 May 1981.

25. K.K. Shukla, screenplay writer of *Naseeb*, in interview with the author, April 1981.

26. Javed Akhtar, screenplay writer, in an interview with the author, February 1981.

27. The two key mythological epics of India.

28. *Trade Guide*, 3 May 1981.

29. Literally, spices.

30. Manmohan Desai, quoted in *Bombay* magazine, 22 April 1981.

31. *Trade Guide*.

32. K.K. Shukla, screenplay writer, in interview with the author, May 1981.

33. Neale, *Genre*, pp. 36–41.

34. Camera placement rules can be disregarded, particularly in action (fight) scenes, which seem to be allowed something of the non-continuity conventions of song sequences.

35. Raj Kapoor, film-maker, in interview on *Visions*, Channel Four, February 1983.

36. Barnouw and Krishnaswamy, *Indian Film*, p. 47.

37. Audiences often talked about dialogue (or 'dialogues' in local parlance) as a central draw, and books and records of film dialogue sometimes sold better than collections of film music.

38. Annette Kuhn, 'Women's Genres', *Screen*, vol. 25, no. 1, 1984, p. 23.

39. Louis Dumont, *Homo Hierarchicus*, trans. from the French by Mark Sainsbury, London: Weidenfeld and Nicolson, 1970 [1963].

40. Unreferenced in BFI microfiche collection of *Aan* reviews in UK newspapers, 1952.

nine

Sanctity and Scandal
The Mythologisation of Mother India

A rumour widely quoted in Bombay film circles in the 1980s was that when *Mother India* (Mehboob Khan, 1957) was screened in Europe in 1958, it was beyond the comprehension of the hard-boiled, amoral Western audience. 'Why didn't the heroine simply sleep with the moneylender? Then she could have fed her family without all that suffering', a bewildered Englishman is supposed to have asked of a horrified Mehboob Khan. Whether or not the story is apocryphal, its wide currency and endurance suggest something deeper.

Mother India, in fact, has received considerable acclaim from Western audiences over the years—probably more than any other mainstream Indian film. It received an Oscar nomination in 1958, patronising but generally favourable reviews at its London release in 1961, and a flood of enthusiastic letters following its first transmission on British television in 1983. The wide circulation of the rumour almost certainly says less about actual Western audiences than about the terms of discourse of Indian cinema itself. Since it first emerged in the context of colonial India's fight for independence, Indian cinema has, for a number of reasons, been concerned with constructing a notion of Indian cultural and national identity. This has involved drawing on concepts such as 'tradition'. But a chaste and pristine India has also been constructed by opposing it to a decadent and exotic Other, the licentious and immoral 'West', with the films' villains invariably sporting a clutter of signifiers of Westernisation: whisky bottles, bikini-clad escorts or foreign limousines. In this case, however, there appears to be a telling displacement. The decadent Other is

Figure 9.1 Poster for *Mother India* (1957)

Source: © Shaukat Khan. Courtesy Mehboob Productions Private Ltd, Mumbai, India.

transposed from the narrative of the film itself—where colonial rape is nevertheless an implicit subtext—to the wider narrative of the film's conditions of circulation; from an element within the narrative that must be punished by the forces of virtue to the gaze of a Western audience whose control must be wrested or arrested.

It can be no coincidence that such a story circulated around this particular film. *Mother India*'s status in Indian cinema mythology and popular consciousness is legendary: it was the all-time box-office hit and still guaranteed full houses well into the 1990s, allegedly playing in some part of India every day of every year.[1] Imbued as it was with the apparently untroubled optimism of the post-independence decade, and referred to as 'of our soil' or 'full of Indian emotions', *Mother India* is in many ways the quintessential Indian film. Clearly, the rumour articulated a not unreasonable mistrust of Western appropriation of Indian cinema: the West's desire to see and know cannot be divorced from the ethos of colonialist adventuring, which controls its subjects both through voyeuristic fantasy and through attaining knowledge by means of which it can define and judge the rest of the word and thus consolidate its power.[2]

Beyond this general warning lies a disturbing specific history, for *Mother India* is also the title of a notorious book published in 1927 by Katherine Mayo, an American.[3] This book purported to reveal research on the abuse suffered by Indian women at the hands of their menfolk but was an overtly sensationalised and very dubious diatribe that linked hysterical accounts of horrific sexual abuse—maimed and lacerated child brides, rampant venereal disease and grossly unsanitary childbirth—with a spurious genetic argument that India was unfit for independence. A best-seller in the West, it provoked a storm of controversy and has now come to exemplify the crudest of colonialist propaganda, particularly since recent research has revealed that rather than being a naïve, misguided evangelist for women's causes, Mayo was almost certainly knowingly involved in a cynical British propaganda exercise.[4] The film's reference to this controversy was not incidental,[5] and the fact that both film and rumour so neatly invert the terms of the book in their construction and use of female sexuality is a feature of central significance, with wider ramifications, to which we will return.

What both the rumour concerning the film and the controversy around the book more broadly highlight are the complex issues involved in the reading of texts across cultures. Assuming that the text is not an object that contains meaning in itself, but that meanings arise in the process of reading and that texts open continuously onto other texts,[6] I am concerned broadly with the implications—and difficulties—of this notion of intertextuality for how we talk about any individual film, particularly across cultures. At its most basic level, this chapter is an uncovering (necessarily partial) of some of the other stories and imagery that open onto, and through which a mainstream Indian audience might read, the film *Mother India*. It is not intended, of course, to fix the film—or simply to explain it to a Western film buff eager to consume such knowledge—but to illustrate the complexities involved in the processes of meaning production. On the one hand, I argue that the film offers a number of fissured, partial and contradictory representations that address, construct and produce meaning and illusory coherence for the spectator through the process of narrative—and the resolutions narrative appears to effect. On the other hand, I show that underlying the film are a number of other discourses that range from the imagery and rhetoric of nationalism to ideas current in Indian society about female chastity, including those derived from other films and books and gossip about film stars.[7]

The central argument of this chapter is that *Mother India* is most usefully seen as an arena within which a number of discourses around female chastity, modern nationalism and, more broadly, morality intersect and feed on each other, with significant political effects. The first part of the chapter describes the film and discusses some of the play it makes with notions of femininity and tradition, ordering its material, somewhat precariously, within the narrative. The second part focuses on two written texts which bear on the film and describes how these fix and use two very different constructions of female sexuality and tradition. While some understanding of the Indian concept of *izzat/laaj* (honour or chastity)[8] is important to making sense of the film, and knowledge of mythological and other culturally specific references further enriches it, vital and invariably undervalued is knowledge of the expectations Indian audiences have of Hindi film as a genre and the usually extensive fund of information they have about film stars. Thus, *Mother India* is known to be a remake of Mehboob Khan's earlier film *Aurat* (Woman, 1940), to work within (and against) the conventions of mainstream Indian cinema, and to be mythologised now as *the* all-time classic, its songs, imagery and dialogue firmly ensconced in the popular preconscious.

However, Nargis, who plays the heroine, was equally a legend in the 1980s, particularly since her tragic early death in 1981, and her star persona provided a further, crucial inflection to the film. The third part of this chapter focuses on the gossip stories through which Nargis's star persona was constructed and argues that these also constitute a discourse on chastity, nationalism and morality. While their comparatively open-ended form constrains this material in a manner different from film narrative, these stories work in crucial counterpoint to the film. Thus, for example, as the top star of her era, Nargis was popularly seen not only as glamorous and enviable but also as scandalously sullied because of a very open romance she enjoyed over a number of years with her married co-star, Raj Kapoor. It may not be altogether frivolous to suggest that the most significant differences between the European and Indian audience's understanding of *Mother India* may have had less to do with the Europeans' ignorance of Indian ideas about female chastity (as the 1958 rumour implied) than with their ignorance of India's prurient interest in the star's purported lack of chastity.

THE FILM

Mother India is the story of a poor peasant woman, Radha, who, left alone with her children, defends her self-respect and an ideal of virtuous womanhood against tremendous odds: famine, flood, and a corrupt and lecherous moneylender, Sukhilal. Although his attempts to seduce her fail, he does keep her *kangan* (wedding bangles) in pawn and pauperises the family by extracting usurious interest on a small loan for over twenty years. Her son, Ramu, grows up to be gentle, obedient and supportive, but her favourite, Birjoo, turns outlaw in a single-handed fight against Sukhilal and the oppression he represents. Having failed to persuade the conservative, law-abiding villagers to join him, Birjoo then antagonises them further by joking with, and disrespectfully touching, the young unmarried women of the village. His excesses are seen as a threat to the community's izzat, and the angry villagers start a fire in which both Birjoo and his mother nearly die. When Birjoo finally unequivocally oversteps the bounds of community morality by kidnapping Sukhilal's daughter on her wedding day, Radha takes the decision to kill her own son.

The film is, of course, constructed within the formal conventions of Hindi cinema: the narrative is not tightly linear but builds in more or less circular fashion through a number of climaxes that are counterposed with scenes of humour, spectacle or pure emotional import, notably, a series of visually powerful and musically splendid songs.[9] The film as a whole falls under the rubric of melodrama. A number of irresolvables, primarily in the arena of kinship and sexuality, are set in motion, resolutions are proposed which are only tenuously satisfactory and the excess (the emotional overspill; that which cannot be convincingly resolved) is siphoned off in music and spectacle.

> The undischarged emotion which cannot be accommodated within the action, subordinated as it is to the demands of family/lineage/inheritance, is traditionally expressed in the music and ... in certain elements of the mise-en-scene. That is to say, music and mise-en-scene do not just heighten the emotionality of an element in the action, to some extent they substitute for it.[10]

Nowell-Smith's description of Hollywood melodrama is highly relevant, for Indian mainstream cinema as a genre tends to address and move its spectator through a film importantly by way of affect, although this is structured and contained by deeply rooted and familiar narrative. The emphasis is on *how* things will happen, not *what* happens next; on a moral disordering to be (temporarily) resolved rather than an enigma to be solved, as stated earlier. This positioning depends for its full effect on certain kinds of cultural competence, most notably, a knowledge of the parameters of the ideal moral universe of the Hindi film—that is, the paradigms of 'good' and 'bad' (or expected and unacceptable) behaviours through play with, or defiance of, which the film derives its dramatic tensions and within which the ensuing crises must be safely resolved.

The most common ploy of Indian cinema is to throw the domain of kinship morality into crisis. In this, *Mother India* is exemplary. Drama is wrought, firstly, by exposing contradictory injunctions within the domain itself and, secondly, by opposing ties of kinship to the demands of the law and religious and moral duty to the community. The crises are dramatised through a series of dilemmas that face the heroine. Radha's first apparent choice is between being an ideal wife (honouring her *suhaag*[11] and refusing Sukhilal's advances) and being an ideal mother (feeding her starving children). Later, she must choose between being an ideal mother (unconditionally loving and protecting her son) and being an ideal woman of the village community (protecting its izzat, which has been tainted by Birjoo's abduction of one of its daughters), itself considered a kinship group. While the narrative momentum, and identifications offered, must position most spectators adequately to make sense of these dilemmas, they gain in power with cultural knowledge of the conventions of Hindi cinema's ideal moral universe, which lays particular stress on both the sanctity of the blood relationship—above all, the mother–son bond—and the sanctity of marriage (and suhaag), together with the controlled sexuality of wife and mother figures. Careful negotiation of values accruing to each character is crucial to the working of the film, so that, for example, much is made of the ambiguity of Birjoo's villainy. Although he endangers the village girls' izzat, he is also a passionately devoted and, in many ways, exemplary son whose breaking of the law is fired primarily by a desire to avenge the affronts to his mother's chastity: he dies pulling from his chest the blood-soaked kangan he has recovered for her—a restitution of her symbolically violated honour.

Although the spectator appears to be positioned primarily through the figure of Radha, this identification is, of course, partial and fragmented, and one is simultaneously offered the infinitely more dangerous position of Birjoo. From here, a familiar underlying structure, the Oedipal drama, unfolds: the son's fantasy of displacing the father and taking his place with the mother is a violation of the law against incest and must be punished by castration or death. This is not overt, of course, but its resonances underlie the poignancy and emotional power of, for example, Birjoo's offerings of the blood-soaked bangles. While the film can be seen to play out, on one level, this most recurrent preoccupation of human mythology—the conflict, from a male perspective, between desire and the law—around this it also weaves other material which is more specific to Indian culture and film conventions.

All such ordering works to give apparent mastery of (and to cover over) ambivalence and contradiction, none more fraught than in the construction of woman.[12] In *Mother India* we, in fact, find Radha constructed though a number of partial and, at times, conflicting representations that refer to a spectrum of archetypes of ideal femininity in Indian culture, and the figure appears to operate as a terrain on which a notion of the ideal Indian woman is negotiated.

The types of images that erupt in the course of the film vary from shots of Radha heroically enjoining the villagers not to desert their motherland to images of her being trampled underfoot by them; from being carried out of a blazing haystack in her son's arms to stuffing *chapatis* (flatbreads) into her sons' mouths as they pull a plough through their fields; from shots that look down on her blushing coyly behind a wedding veil or as *sindoor* (vermillion) is placed in her hair to shots that look up at her proudly striding forward harnessed to her plough; from shots of her crying on her son's shoulder and pleading with him as a lover might to the images of her wielding a heavy stick, axe and, finally, gun. The most powerfully horrifying image is of Radha's levelling a shotgun at her son. But, in fact, all the central male figures are destroyed or implicitly castrated by association with her: she kills her favourite son; her husband loses both arms (and implicitly his manliness) following her insistence that they plough some barren land; the villainous Sukhilal ends up covered in cotton fluff, cowering like a naughty infant as she beats him with a big stick, and pleading abjectly with her to save his daughter's izzat; and her elder son Ramu becomes ineffectual in her shadow. Thus, she is both venerator of men and venerated by them as devi (goddess) and *maa*

Figure 9.2   Mother India (Nargis) and her two sons. Still from
Mother India.

Source: © Shaukat Khan. Courtesy Mehboob Productions Private Ltd, Mumbai, India.

(mother), and she is, in turn, in need of men's protection and also a protector and destroyer of men.

The cultural competence of most Indian audiences means they would, on some level, recognise within this Radha allusions to a variety of figures of Hindu mythology: Sita (archetypal dutiful, loyal wife and embodiment of purity, whose trial by fire and abandonment with two young sons are implicitly invoked);[13] Savitri (exemplarily devoted wife); Radha herself (the cowherd who was Krishna's lover); Lakshmi (goddess of wealth and good fortune, to whom brides are customarily likened and to whom Sukhilal explicitly, and somewhat ironically, given the context of his attempted seduction, likens Radha); and the more fearsome mother goddesses, Durga and Kali, powerful symbols of female sacred authority and embodiments of Shakti (female power), who punish and destroy if they are displeased. There are also more covert references, for example, to Surabhi, the holy cow, and to Mother Earth, the fertility principle.

This diversity of allusions and a degree of incoherence are undoubtedly crucial to the experience and dramatic power of the film. But while the Oedipal subtext may operate as one form of ordering of this diversity, it is elaborated within another important, and more culturally specific, patterning. As Wadley has pointed out, in the Hindu tradition not only does femaleness embody a fundamental duality—woman as bestower and as destroyer—but female sexual energy is always potentially dangerous, but can become beneficent (to men) if controlled through marriage or otherwise subjugated to male authority.[14] Thus, the goddesses who have no regular consort (primarily those known as mother goddesses) are considered the most aggressive and fiery—often demanding blood sacrifice—due to the 'fierce power of chastity',[15] a power that accumulates through sexual abstinence but, if carefully handled, can also be tapped to male advantage.

In fact, the film relates each manifestation of Radha's apparently threatening power or strength to her exemplary chastity, and this then serves (male) traditional values and the izzat of the community. Radha's defiant refusal of Sukhilal's advances is thus constructed less as a stand against male sexual oppression of women than as evidence of faith in Lakshmi and as a refusal to dishonour her husband and hence her suhaag. It is by virtue of this noble chastity and faith that Radha derives strength to uphold the morale of the village and save it from a string of natural disasters. Similarly, her subsequent killing of her son is less a display of solidarity with the women of the village than a defence of the community's izzat (ensuring the chastity of young women given to other villages in marriage). The pattern has overtones of a blood sacrifice, Radha's own 'fierce power of chastity' being tested and consolidated before the act, first by the fire ordeal and then by a purification in water (as she and Birjoo swim to escape). The film's resolution produces Radha—and her upholding of female chastity— as the saviour of the village and implicit cause of its prosperity and liberation from oppression: it is *her* hands, still bloody from the sacrifice of her son years before, that are respectfully entreated to inaugurate the village dam, signifier of technological plenitude.

In describing the film as a play of tensions between a number of apparent irreconcilables—primarily within the domain of kinship morality and notions of femininity—and the (tenuous) mastery and coherence the narrative seems to offer, it is important to remember that these irreconcilables draw on, and slip between, a number of discourses. Mulvey has described melodrama's fundamental appeal and power as lying in 'the amount of dust the story raises along the road, a cloud of overdetermined irreconcilables which put up a resistance to being neatly settled in the last five minutes.'[16] *Mother India*'s central celebration of a notion of female chastity does, in fact, work some particularly complex elisions and denials, most notably through its slippage between discourses of sexual and national identity.

For any Indian audience, the title *Mother India* immediately situates the film within the discourse of the freedom movement, and the film is seen to be as much about nationhood as womanhood. Although the British are not overtly represented, there are a number of oblique but highly charged allusions, notably, the metaphor of colonial rape that underlies the whole film: the predatory oppressor appropriates a defenceless woman's wedding bangles through force backed by a corrupt law. However, the villainous Sukhilal is simultaneously the tyrannical feudal lord, and the film can be read as a description of the triumphant emergence of a new India from both feudal and colonial oppression. The long introductory credit sequence together with the film's final moments—between which the body of the film unfolds as flashback—is most revealing. Following a long montage of dams, pylons, power stations, cranes, bulldozers and bridges, Radha, who appears as a venerated but dumb and mud-stained old woman, is asked to inaugurate and bless an irrigation project by the men of the village who, as paragons of patriotic deference, signified by the white cotton *kurta* (shirt) and Gandhi-*topi*,[17] humbly address this champion of female chastity as maa. It is a vision of a new utopia that integrates features of both alternative deposed societies. The traditional society, it is implied, was fundamentally morally sound, its evils concentrated in a villain who could be vanquished. Here Sukhilal evokes the mythological villain, Raavana, the rapacious king of Lanka who abducted Sita. However, this society was vulnerable to the vagaries of nature. Western society, the locus of male violence and notoriously uncontrolled female sexuality, is fundamentally morally unsound, but it does have technological mastery. Thus, controlled female sexuality and uncontrolled nature are opposed to controlled nature and uncontrolled female sexuality. Power in the new society is generated by control of both: oppression is ousted and the hazards of nature overcome with modern technology, but the purity of traditional values—symbolised by female chastity—must still bless, and ultimately legitimise, technological advance. Mother India must open the dam.

In celebrating Radha's power and her defence of chastity in this way, the film implicitly, but crucially, denies the essential role played by Birjoo's act of violence in killing Sukhilal and the conscious sacrifice Birjoo made of his own life. As Birjoo explained: 'Ma, our troubles will never end as long as Sukhilala lives.... My death will assure ... the farmers will have grain in their homes and fuel to burn.... The fate of the village will change forever.'[18] To which Radha, who was throughout a conservative force remonstrating with him against the use of excessively radical or violent action, replied: 'No, Birjoo. You won't change anything with a gun.... Don't lose heart, my son.... We'll work hard, we'll toil. God will change our lives and He will change the fate of the village.'

Within the framework of the Oedipal subtext, the denial of the desire and subsequent violence of the son and its displacement onto woman are not so mysterious. But this denial can also be related to the context of early post-independence India and the wide currency of Gandhi's ideas, which drew on notions of bhakti (redemption through selfless devotion) and a concept of potent, active femininity to oppose two models of (male) behaviour. The Gandhian ideal used a non-violent, 'feminine' and supremely potent force; the other, the violence, machismo and uncontrolled aggression seen to mark Western as well as various Indian warrior traditions.[19] The film appears to echo this by denying and destroying Birjoo's potency, while celebrating and saving Radha and the gentler son, Ramu.[20]

One of the most traumatic aspects of independence was, of course, the amount of violence that was involved and that erupted so horrifically during Partition. The film's seeming denial of the effectiveness of revolutionary violence is rather more fraught than at first appears. Throughout the film one finds examples of highly charged imagery and covert reiteration of the denial: for example, one central and powerfully emotional song begins with images of streams of refugees leaving their homeland (which could not but evoke Partition, particularly in 1957 India) but ends with them returned to peace and prosperity, dancing by sheaves of wheat on a map of *pre-Partition* India. Although a coherent explanation of the song is feasible, for an Indian audience much of the power of such sequences undoubtedly lies in the emotional impact of this dream-logic reworking and censoring of Indian history.

The slippages effected by the notion of female chastity itself permit the most complex disavowal, however, for within India, the notion conflates a number of not wholly compatible ideas and discourses. First, female chastity represents female sexual energy not dissipated by sexual activity and, as such, it is a potent force in nature that can either be tapped to male advantage or become positively dangerous to men. Second, it implies a passive sexuality, woman constrained as a pawn of male power networks and locus of displaced male anxieties. Third, it is used as a metaphor for purity and, hence, for the 'purity' of traditional values, for an ideal society uncontaminated by colonial oppressors, and for India itself. This slippage between woman and nation means, for example, that the film can construct woman as an ultimate authority and power, disavow this by relegating woman to metaphor for India or ideal morality, and simultaneously preserve a construction of woman as pawn of male desire.

BACKGROUND READING

The rumour that *Mother India* puzzled Western audiences because they could not understand the Indian stress on female chastity is not, in fact, so misconceived. Although female chastity is familiar in the West as a symbol of purity, this draws primarily on a Christian equation of sexuality with sin, an association scarcely present in the Indian formulation. The range of ideas the concept encompasses in a Hindu or Muslim context would certainly be lost on most Westerners. It was ostensibly to contextualise *Mother India* for international audiences that the film-makers produced a special brochure.[21] This was a twenty-two-page, full-colour booklet containing reproductions of oil paintings illustrating both themes and scenes from the film together with a number of short essays (in English) purporting to explain Indian traditional beliefs about womanhood, nature and destiny and to give a flavour of peasant life in village India. The whole is resonant of a sentimental, and somewhat hysterically moralistic, Victorian religious picture book, each image capped with an overblown title and a florid prose description.

The booklet begins and ends with the assertion that the film is about Indian women's chastity and its sanctity. It refers to:

> this epic drama of an Indian mother, the nucleus around which revolves the tradition and culture of ages in this ancient land ... [where] ... chastity, the sacred heirloom of an ancient race, demands the supreme sacrifice, even of her children, from the mother.[22]

It brazenly asserts that woman exists only in terms of man.

> In India, woman is part of man ... her single prayer is to die in the presence of her husband.... To this eternal Indian woman, the home is her temple, her husband her god, the children his blessings and the land her great mother.[23]

This is finally neutralised in a historical perspective.

> The woman is an altar in India. She is loved and respected, worshipped and protected.... Indians measure the virtue of their race by the chastity of their women. To them a woman's person is sacred, her chastity a virtue to be nursed and her character a prize to be envied.... Indian women have thrown themselves into the sacrificial fire to escape even the defiling shadow of a foreign invader.... This India of the olden days still lives in the 700,000 villages of India.[24]

Throughout the booklet, Radha/Mother India is described as ideally pure and an exemplary mother and wife and repeatedly compared to the goddesses Sita and Savitri. However, in stressing analogies with these paragons of purity and selfless devotion to husbands and sons, there is a significant omission: the booklet ignores all reference to the more powerful and terrifying facets of ideal Indian femininity, as embodied in the punitive and destructive mother goddesses such as Kali and Durga, although these are in fact implicit in the film. The effect of this construction of a comparatively uncontradictory model of femininity is to close off whole areas of themes and tensions apparent in the film, presenting instead an ideal moral universe free from disorder or ambiguity, with woman safely controlled and idealised.

A similar disavowal operates in the booklet's description of traditional India, which is shown as an unequivocal utopia where 'an ancient peace-loving people ... lead a harmonious community life', with colourful festivals and mothers telling 'stories of virtue and valour' from mythology to build the character of their sons. The theme of rural oppression and Sukhilal's corruption is scarcely mentioned: hardships are ascribed to the 'inscrutable smiles and frowns of nature', designed by God and destiny to make 'heroes out of men and mothers out of women'. Furthermore, 'the Indian farmer likes his sweat to mix with the perspiration of his bullock', so that even those who know of tractors often prefer not to use them. In this context, Birjoo becomes a virtual villain for having 'hatred in his heart' and for losing faith in divine justice. Again, this shift of emphasis closes off much of the narrative play of the film: if traditional society is a utopia, questions about the ethics of revolutionary violence become less compelling; if Birjoo is a villain, Radha's dilemma is less acute; if peasants prefer bullocks to tractors, Western technology need not be incorporated.

It would be easy to dismiss this as simply a sexist and reactionary rant. However, as with the film (whose complex workings and contradictions particularly defy simplistic categorisation), such blanket dismissal is dangerously reductionist. As an aside we might note that, intriguingly, Mehboob Khan himself was not coy about contradiction: his studio emblem blithely combined a hammer and sickle with an Urdu couplet meaning 'Man proposes, God disposes'.[25] While the use of the figure of woman to signify a vestibule of traditional purity and power undoubtedly works to oppress women on many levels, in the context of the nationalist struggle it can be simultaneously a tool to counter imperialist oppression. We cannot ignore a history in which an American book, brazenly appropriating the nationalist catch-phrase 'Mother India' to its own title, had sensationalised a picture of degradation purporting to be of Indian womanhood and had claimed not only that 'Indian women of child-bearing age cannot safely venture, without special protection, within reach of Indian men',[26] but even that 'a very small percentage of Indian women seem ... well and strong.... This state I believe to be accounted for by a morbid and unawakened mentality, by venereal infection, and by sexual exhaustion. They commonly experience marital use two and three times a day.'[27]

While an Indian rumour constructs a West so licentious and amoral that it cannot remotely comprehend Mother India's bid for chastity and must have the concept spelled out in a proselytising picture pamphlet, a Western book—far more sinisterly—constructs and projects onto India a sexuality so depraved that chastity is inconceivable, where women are routinely abused to the point that Indian genetic stock is depleted and Indians' 'hands are too weak, too fluttering, to seize or hold onto the reins of government'.[28] In this context, the insistences of the film booklet, the rumour and the film itself seem less excessive, for they are implicitly involved in reclaiming Mother India for India, in exorcising the defamation and pollution of the term by Mayo—and, similarly, that of India by the West and of Indian women by colonialist men.[29]

THE STAR

These are not the only discourses within which the film is read. Other texts at play within the broader arena of *Mother India* already undermine too seamless a construction of an ideal India. Although Bombay film-makers assert that certain transgressions of an ideal morality are impossible in Hindi films because the Indian audience is conservative and easily shocked, this same audience appears very eager to be shocked in certain contexts, if one is to believe the evidence of the network of gossip that surrounds the scandals in the lives and loves of film stars in India. These stories are consumed almost as avidly as the films themselves and, over the years, many publications have been regularly produced devoted exclusively to such narratives, which become tacitly—and at times, even quite overtly—interwoven in the Indian audience's readings of the films. Compared to the films, the form of the gossip narrative is somewhat open-ended and most usefully likened to soap opera. There is a long-standing core of central characters, whose careers and romances have been the focus of obsessive public scrutiny over the years and are standard cultural knowledge throughout the Hindi film-going centres of India. There are a number of ongoing and intertwined storylines, within which short, self-contained dramas are played out. Crises erupt and are temporarily resolved but, as in soap opera, the elements of the drama remain to be re-used, re-explained and resolved again in a new drama, thus allowing a continual reworking of the obsessions of the discourse, which turn primarily around sexuality and kinship but also deal with modern Indian identity.

Nargis became a star in the late 1940s and, although she retired from films in 1957, she remained very much in the public eye until her death. She is undoubtedly a central legendary figure of Indian cinema, and most Indian audiences were, until recent years, familiar with—and still discussed—the details of her story. It is not possible to reconstruct precisely how the stories would have been inflected in

1957, as film publications then were more discreet and much was told by word of mouth as rumour. What was available in the 1980s were primarily modern retellings of her story: rumours circulating among the general public, stories told by people who claimed to have known or have met her, features in gossip magazines of those years, some archival features, and a small number of published interviews.[30] The questions and issues that structure the legend have been inevitably and importantly reworked over the years, according to the preoccupations of each generation, and it is crucial to stress that my concern here is with the persona of Nargis as publicly constructed rumour, not with an accurate biography.[31]

The story of Nargis is that of an unfortunate girl, born in 1929 to a famous Muslim courtesan-singer and a young Hindu doctor later ostracised from his 'respectable' family for this association. The story goes that even as a child, Nargis had dreamed of redeeming herself by becoming a doctor. Her mother had sent her to a good Bombay school and disciplined her strictly, largely keeping her away from the film industry throughout her childhood. Once she reached adolescence, however, Nargis's mother not only tricked her into (most unwillingly) starring in a film for her friend Mehboob Khan but also allegedly put her daughter's *nath* (virginity) on the market and allowed a wealthy Muslim prince to pay handsomely for her. (This episode is sometimes denied, or recounted as her first affair. Its purpose seems to be to construct her as already tarnished before meeting Raj Kapoor.)

By the late 1940s, Nargis had become a top star, but it was her professional and personal partnership with Kapoor, handsome young star, producer and director, that brought superstardom and notoriety. The couple's bold and very open love affair captured the prurient imagination of the nation. On the one hand, it was enviously celebrated: they were young, glamorous, beautiful, rich, and said to be passionately in love. They epitomised a modern freedom and lack of inhibition. They flew around the world, were seen photographed with Truman at the White House in 1952, were popular as pin-ups in bazaars throughout the Arab world, and were household names in Russia following the unprecedented success there of *Awaara* (The Vagabond, Raj Kapoor, 1951).[32] Many versions of the gossip justify the affair not only because of their (anomalous) status as film stars, but also because their love is said to have been pure, blind, an all-consuming passion, and even divine. Moreover, Nargis is applauded for having had the courage to live her life openly and show total devotion to 'her' man, for example, wearing only white saris in deference to his whims, slaving with exemplary dedication at his studios for minimal pay, and even wearing sindoor in her hair despite the fact that he continually refused to marry her. On the other hand, the affair was a source of voyeuristic titillation and completely scandalous. As Kapoor was a married man with children, Nargis was denounced as a whore and a home-breaker, and the affair as squalid. It is also stressed that Kapoor exploited her, although it is simultaneously suggested that, of course, as a good Hindu, he could not have left his arranged marriage to marry a tarnished woman. After seven years, Nargis eventually 'saw the light' and, 'heartbroken', left him. She scrupulously kept a vow to avoid his presence for more than twenty years.

The next episode is recounted particularly often and with overt fascination. Some time after the breakup, Nargis was shooting the fire scene for *Mother India* in Mehboob Studios when the blaze got out of hand, and she was trapped behind a wall of burning haystacks. In a dramatic gesture, Sunil Dutt, the young and comparatively unknown actor who played her son, Birjoo, dived heroically into the flames and carried her to safety in his arms. After he saved her life, they fell in love and later married quietly. When news of the marriage broke, there was a sensation, fuelled by a distinct frisson of scandal that a younger man (and screen son of Mother India) was marrying the notorious First Lady of the Indian screen.

Riding high on the phenomenal success of *Mother India*—and national and international accolades for her performance—Nargis retired from the dirty world of the film industry and gave birth to a son, Sanjay. Gossip invariably stresses how crucial leaving films was in saving her reputation. For the next twenty years, she continued to devote her energies to caring for her husband and three children, for whom she was said to be a 'tower of strength'. Much is made of her performance as an ideal wife and mother, keeping traditional Hindu fasts for her husband's well-being—Sunil's prospering career was taken as evidence of her devotion—and idolising her son. As Sanjay grew up, the gossip press made much of this exemplary mother–son relationship: 'for a minute we looked in admiration at this wonderful, dignified, first lady of the Indian screen. I turned to Sanjay. His eyes held sheer idolatry and respect as he gazed fondly at his mother.'[33] She also gave dedicated service to community charities, especially those relating to cerebral palsy. The family suffered various hardships. At one point, Sunil's films began to fail, he had indiscreet affairs with other actresses (although Nargis remained the long-suffering, faithful wife), and they were constantly harassed by a public loath to forget the colourful Kapoor affair. Sanjay was taunted by schoolmates, and, most bizarrely, when Kapoor in 1970 chose a young unknown beauty, Dimple, to co-star in his son's debut film, a decidedly far-fetched rumour gained ground that Dimple was Raj and Nargis's secret illegitimate daughter who had been farmed out to a local businessman for adoption. Moreover, Sanjay was clearly developing into something of a rebel: while Nargis wanted him to be a doctor, he wanted to become a film star. Before long, stories started to circulate of his teenage romance with a top starlet—of whom Nargis was said to disapprove.

In accordance with a pattern that has been remarked on in the construction of other stars,[34] stories about Nargis construct her as both ordinary and extraordinary, as a housewife with her share of mundane domestic joys and trials and simultaneously as both an extraordinarily talented actress and a bold rebel who had uninhibitedly followed through a grand and divine passion and who continued to live among the rich and powerful. She began to be referred to respectfully and affectionately as *bhabhiji* (lit., elder brother's wife) by the film industry, becoming their public spokesperson and president of the IMPPA. More significantly, she is said to have built up a close friendship with Indira Gandhi over the years and in 1980 was rewarded with a seat in the Rajya Sabha (House of Lords).[35] She was by then a national symbol of dignified glamour and respectability, the other first lady of India—Indira Gandhi's glamorous alter ego. Nargis's first parliamentary intervention was stoutly patriotic and wildly controversial: she denounced Satyajit Ray's films for showing India's poverty to the West, rather than 'Modern India ... [for example], dams', and a national debate ensued.[36]

Later that year, aged 51, Nargis was discovered to have cancer and, when Indian doctors gave up hope, she was rushed to New York's foremost cancer specialist. For weeks on end her distraught husband kept constant vigil at her bedside and his prayers and superhuman endurance appeared to have been rewarded when the specialists declared a 'miracle'. Nargis was triumphantly brought home and fondly anticipated her newfound dream of seeing her beloved son make his public debut as a film star. Weeks later she suffered a relapse, and just three days before Sanjay's film premiere, she died. The nation mourned, and the family was devastated.

Stories continued to circulate about Sanjay.[37] After his mother's death, he became a self-destructive rebel, allegedly ruining his health and film career with drugs, wild nights and alcoholic binges. In Nargis's daughters' rare appearances in gossip, they were invariably constructed as 'good', and, with a touch of fortuitous symmetry, the eldest married the son of Rajendra Kumar, who had played Mother India's good son, Ramu. Sunil, Nargis's husband, became a pillar of the community. In 1985, pledging his support for the bereaved son of Nargis's friend, Indira, he was elected a member of Rajiv Gandhi's new government.

The parallels between the film and star texts are, of course, remarkable: both are preoccupied with the control of female sexuality and patterned around sacrifice and the burgeoning of female power and authority. Both involve mothers' relationships with rebellious sons and both work towards a definition of a modern Indianness, with dams recurring, somewhat bizarrely, as key signifiers in each. Direct crossovers occur, with Nargis's star persona increasingly integrated with Mother India in later years; but there are also some crucial inversions. To the extent that the star persona is always implicit in the Indian audience's reading of a film, these inversions provide a counterpoint and tensions that can, at times, explosively exacerbate the apparent coherence of the film.

Just as the film had played with a diversity of representations of 'woman', so the star persona of Nargis ties a number of facets of modern Indian womanhood loosely together: the Muslim courtesan, the Westernised free lover, the passionate Radha, the devoted Hindu wife, the adoring mother, the powerful politician, and so forth. While some coherence is provided through the overriding linear narrative (sexuality placed under social control leads to redemption and power), the facets still to some extent coexist in the gossip, which orders this material primarily through spinning stories around the questions that such conflicts throw up: Can a daring, uninhibited seductress be a dutiful wife and mother? Can the daughter of a courtesan be a respected symbol of national propriety? While the film more or less contained such irreconcilables through the process of classic narrative, and the booklet's didacticism closed off even more, the star persona exists primarily in the telling and retelling—with varying emphases, moralistic commentaries and speculations—of a heterogeneous collection of anecdotes over many years (which the present account has necessarily had to linearise, standardise and condense), and resolutions are always temporary. It can thus accommodate more internal incoherence and more overt transgressions of ideal morality. If the star persona is a discourse on how to live modern Indianness and the crises of conflicting moralities this entails, stars become more fascinating the greater the contradictions they embody and the greater their transgressions.

Similar themes structure both texts, however, and the most obvious inversion—that the persona of Nargis at the time she played Radha was very far from a paragon of maternal chastity—masks a deeper structural similarity. In the film, Radha's chastity was tested when kinship duty and economic necessity (feeding her children) crossed wider social morality (preserving izzat) and, in fact, the film ultimately allows her both. In the gossip, Nargis must choose between kinship duty (obeying her mother) and economic necessity on the one hand, and wider social morality (preserving her izzat and becoming a doctor) on the other hand. But here the former constrains her and she loses her chastity with dire social consequences.[38] Thus, underlying and interwoven in the film's blanket celebration of ideal chastity is a text that opens up a number of questions sealed over by the film: which women must be chaste? What is the place of India's various erotic traditions—from goddesses such as Radha to the Muslim courtesan? How is modern Indian woman's sexuality negotiated?

Probably the most dramatic subversion of the film's denials lies in the moment at which the two texts literally overlap: Birjoo/Sunil Dutt rescues Radha/Nargis from a wall of blazing haystacks. It is in fact a turning point in both texts. Within the film, it is the point at which Radha's devotion to her son is most acutely tested and recognition of the need to sacrifice him begins; within the gossip, the purging of the 'unchaste' woman is the point from which Nargis can achieve redemption and power by self-sacrificing devotion to husband, son and community. The film booklet adds its own significant inflection to this moment with a painting of a modestly draped woman lost in swirling (womb-like) blood-red and orange flames. The caption reads:

Fire, the crucible of virtue…. Like Sita, the fabled goddess of purity, she stepped into the ordeal of fire only to come out into the dawn of a new life. Those who sacrifice never die. They only inherit a greater existence.[39]

Somewhat strangely, this description fits the gossip story better than the overt sense of the film scene, which not only makes no explicit reference to Sita but is more obviously about testing Radha's devotion to, and unflinching protection of, her *son*—and his devotion and protectiveness towards her. The fact that the film's testing of the mother's devotion and son's power is played out in an idiom that echoes Rama's testing of the chastity of his wife, Sita, leads to an interesting elision: Birjoo the son plays out the role of Rama the husband, the fantasy of the son displacing the husband/father. These are, in fact, peculiarly intense scenes: around these moments, Radha and Birjoo appear most like lovers, the mise-en-scène becomes revealingly extravagant and patently excessive. The sequence culminates in a crescendo of orchestral strings and a wild camera pan through trees, before dropping down into a lilting, lyrical song: 'O Mere Laal Aa Jaao' (My Beloved Son, Come Back), soothingly reinstating the 'proper' mother–son relationship. That the gossip stories represent the fire scene as the precise moment at which the stars fall in love is thus a dizzy exacerbation of an already dangerous Oedipal subtext, for it provides the 'knowledge'/fantasy that the scene was really played out. Sunil married Nargis. The son 'got' the mother.

It is, of course, primarily through controlled sexuality and motherhood—rather than chastity per se—that Nargis is seen to have consolidated her power and authority. Moreover, the obsessional interest of the gossip in Nargis's very ideal relationship with her son suggests that her power, and the completeness of her redemption, must be continually asserted and tested. Radha, the doting mother whose rebel son has to be killed when she can no longer control him, becomes Nargis, whose beloved rebel son becomes wild and self-destructive when she dies and can no longer control him. The film's significant denial of the effectivity of revolutionary violence is echoed, although more tamely, in the gossip. Where Radha's struggles had been against the villain Sukhilal, Nargis struggled first against her semi-villainous mother and then against the film industry—a veritable Sukhilal with its black money, extortionate interest rates, rapacious exploitation of young women, and sex and violence in its films. Like Radha, Nargis's fight against social injustice was gentle and non-violent, eventually moving into voluntary social work and institutionalised politics. She was known for opposing both radical politics (supporting Mrs Gandhi throughout) and even radical film-making (decrying Satyajit Ray's 'Westernised' films, Mrinal Sen's Marxist films, Mani Kaul's 'avant-garde' practice), and her centrality as an icon of respected Indian female power was crucially bound to this conservatism. Mother India had blessed the new India by opening a dam at the request of devout male villagers. In her final months, Nargis sanctioned a similar vision of modern India by insisting to an assembly of male politicians that Indian film-makers should show not poverty to the West but dams. We thus find the model of controlled female sexuality invoking the image of controlled water to generate power for a new India—while still fighting the shadow of the controlling gaze of an ever-critical West: 'When I go abroad, foreigners ask me embarrassing questions … like "Do you have cars in India?" I feel so ashamed my eyes are lowered before them.'[40]

To the end, the gossip stories attempted to negotiate a harmonious marriage of Western technology and Indian traditional values. As Nargis lay in a prestigious American hospital, paying huge fees to take advantage of the latest medical technology, she and Sunil were, according to the gossip press, displaying to the admiring Western world the sublime devotion of the traditional Indian married couple and the power of Hindu faith and prayer. 'After seeing this, I think I will convert to Hinduism', one American specialist allegedly announced.

Between a curious Western gaze denied any comprehension of Indian chastity and one that must be solicited with vistas of an India by which it might be benignly awed lies a history of difficult shifts and uneasy negotiations around the construction of a modern India within a postcolonial world. *Mother India* must be regarded as a broad terrain of multilayered, interrelating and conflicting texts that not only have historical and economic dimensions but also crucial political ramifications.[41] Although the complexities of shifting and alternative readings and positionings must render blanket categorisations such as 'radical' or 'reactionary' inadequate (and suggest that texts are worked with rather than simply consumed), the conflations and

Figure 9.3   Poster on Bombay streets in 1985

Source: © Behroze Gandhy. Courtesy Behroze Gandhy.

slippages that this wider text negotiates have produced *Mother India* as a site of extraordinary emotional potency and clear political effectivity—whether in the arena of gender relations or the narrower forum of national politics. The figure of controlled female sexuality continued to be tapped to generate power for husbands and sons—in the national interest. In 1980, Indira Gandhi's election campaign had used the image of a raised hand with the caption, 'The hand that rocks the cradle rules the world'. In Rajiv Gandhi's 1985 election campaign following his mother's assassination, Sunil Dutt, Nargis's 'saviour' and devoted husband, stood as parliamentary candidate for Bombay. His poster showed a map of India within which stood the figure of Indira Gandhi, sheathed in a decorous sari. Beneath this was the raised hand, to one side Sunil's photograph and, above it all, the caption 'Mother India needs you' (Figure 9.3). He was returned with an overwhelming majority.

NOTES

1. Whilst the film is still iconic, by the mid-1990s, with the advent of cable television and a new 'Bollywood' generation, it no longer had such a guaranteed box-office draw. See discussion in Gayatri Chatterjee, *Mother India*, London: British Film Institute, 2008 [2002], p. 19, also pp. 76–7.

2. This should, of course, be read as a serious—and ever relevant—warning for European and American publications devoted to the examination of Indian cinema. See, for example, Robert Crusz, 'Black Cinemas, Film Theory and Dependent Knowledge', *Screen*, vol. 26, nos 3–4, 1985, pp. 152–6. However, in the context of a multicultural Western society, institutionalised disdain for, and ignorance and marginalisation of, mainstream Indian cinema seems equally dangerous, as this is not only a symptom of, but also feeds directly into, racism.

3. Katherine Mayo, *Mother India*, London: Jonathan Cape, 1927.

4. See Manoranjan Jha, *Katherine Mayo and India*, New Delhi: People's Publishing House, 1971. Jha's book renders naïve Mary Daly's uncritical praise of Mayo's 'exceptional' understanding in *Gyn/Ecology: The Metaethics of Radical Feminism*, Boston: Beacon Press, 1978, p. 119.

5. Although I was unaware of this when I wrote the original essay on which this chapter is based, Gayatri Chatterjee's research in the Mehboob Studio archives has now shown that, in fact, the allusion was a knowing one (Chatterjee, *Mother India*, p. 20.)

6. Roland Barthes, *Image-Music-Text*, Glasgow: Fontana/Collins, 1977, pp. 147–8.

7. While the former broadly describes the spectator in process, a subject positioned by the film (and offers a way out of the impasse of a relativism whose

ultimate logic must be to posit as many—equally valid—readings as readers), the latter indicates the kinds of cultural competence that the intended audience might be expected to bring to the film. The distinction is, of course, primarily conceptual and, as the chapter makes clear, the two are less easily separable in practice. See Charlotte Brunsdon, 'Crossroads: Notes on Soap Opera', *Screen*, vol. 22, no. 4, 1981, pp. 32–7, and Kuhn, 'Women's Genres', for discussion of these issues in relation to so-called women's genres.

8. Izzat and laaj can both refer to controlled female sexuality. The connotations of izzat are broader, conveying a general sense of prestige, honour, respect, while laaj refers more specifically to female chastity / virginity. Both embody the idea that female 'honour' reflects on the honour of the whole kin / affine network.

9. For further discussion of these conventions, see chapter eight.

10. Geoffrey Nowell-Smith, 'Minnelli and Melodrama', *Screen*, vol. 18, no. 2, 1977, p. 117.

11. Suhaag: the auspicious state of being blessed with a living husband. The concept has wide currency and is symbolised by the woman placing sindoor (vermillion) in her parting and wearing kangan (bangles). Widows may no longer do these things and become, themselves, inauspicious.

12. Drawing on psychoanalytic theories, Mulvey and others have suggested that, in cinema, the denial of male anxiety around the figure of woman (due to the threat of castration that she represents) takes the fetishistic form of disavowal through idealising woman. See Laura Mulvey, 'Visual Pleasure and Narrative Cinema', *Screen*, vol. 16, no. 3, 1975, pp. 6–18.

13. In the *Ramayana*, when Sita was rescued from the clutches of the monstrous Raavana, the wicked king of Lanka who had abducted (but not 'touched') her, her husband Rama would not be convinced of her 'purity'—and consequent worthiness to remain queen of the land—until she had undergone an ordeal by fire. Although her survival 'proved' her innocence, as the people of his kingdom remained sceptical, Rama banished her for many years, until their two sons were grown.

14. Susan S. Wadley 'Women and the Hindu Tradition', in *Women in India: Two Perspectives*, eds D. Jacobson and S. Wadley, New Delhi: Manohar, 1977, pp. 118–19.

15. Chris Fuller, 'The Divine Couple in South India', *History of Religions*, vol. 19, no. 4, 1980, p. 327.

16. Mulvey, 'Douglas Sirk and Melodrama'.

17. Gandhi-topi: white oblong cap popularised by Gandhi and adopted by many politicians since as a symbol of earnest, sober respectability. By the 1980s it already had an additional popular connotation of hypocrisy.

18. Dialogue translations by Nasreen Munni Kabir, *The Dialogue of Mother India*, New Delhi: Niyogi Books, 2010, p. 236.

19. See Ashis Nandy, *The Intimate Enemy: Loss and Recovery of Self under Colonialism*, New Delhi: Oxford University Press, 1983.

20. Genre also operates here: for years the standard hero of Hindi cinema was a passive melancholic who accepted his fate with resignation as his duty or else destroyed himself. *Mother India* marked an early breakthrough in negotiating a model

of masculinity that used violence but was not wholly villainous, and Birjoo could, therefore, be only marginally heroic.

21. The booklet, entitled *Mother India*, was apparently co-written with Baburao Patel, the feisty editor of the trade journal *Film India* (subsequently renamed *Mother India*). It was published in Bombay around the time of the film's release.

22. Anonymous (studio publicity booklet), *Mother India*, p. 1.

23. Ibid., p. 1.

24. Ibid., p. 16.

25. 'Muddai laakh bura chhahe toh kya hota hai
Vahi hota hai jo manzoor-e-khuda hota hai'
(It matters little if the plaintiff wishes you countless ills
What comes to pass is only what is acceptable to God)
(Trans. Nasreen Munni Kabir in *The Dialogue of Mother India*, 2010, p. 2.)

26. Mayo, *Mother India*, p. 186.

27. Ibid., pp. 60–1.

28. Ibid., p. 32.

29. See, for example, Kenneth Ballhatchet, *Race, Sex and Class under the Raj: Imperial Attitudes and Policies and Their Critics, 1793–1905*, London: Weidenfeld and Nicolson, 1980. The potential effectiveness of this kind of reversal of colonial discourse is, however, always constrained by other power relations already in the field. For the West to see itself as marginalised within Indian representations may be salutary, but it is a different experience from India seeing itself continually so positioned within colonialist (and neocolonialist) discourse. See Spivak, 'The Rani of Sirmur', p. 128.

30. A star persona is also built up around the accumulation of meanings from previous film roles. For reasons of space, I have not dealt with this here, although, interestingly, one finds distinct echoes of the gossip persona in these: Nargis frequently played Raj Kapoor's lover, a Westernised sophisticate, and even a coquette but always ultimately a 'good' woman who suffered for her lover.

31. This point needs stressing: over the years, this has been one of the most regularly misunderstood aspects of this essay. A number of excellent biographies of Nargis and the Dutts have been published since 1989, to which readers are referred for factual details. These include Kishwar Desai, *Darlingji: The True Love Story of Nargis and Sunil Dutt*, London: Harper Collins, 2007; Namrata and Priya Dutt, *Mr and Mrs Dutt: Memories of Our Parents*, New Delhi: Lustre Press, Roli Books, 2007; T.J.S. George, *The Life and Times of Nargis*, New Delhi: Indus, 1994; Reuben, *Mehboob, India's De Mille*.

32. Barnouw and Krishnaswamy, *Indian Film*, p. 160.

33. *Film World* (Bombay), August 1980.

34. See Andrew Britton, *Katharine Hepburn: The Thirties and After*, Newcastle upon Tyne: Tyneside Cinema, 1984; Richard Dyer, *Stars*, London: British Film Institute, 1979; John Ellis, *Visible Fictions: Cinema, Television, Video*, London: Routledge & Kegan Paul, 1982.

35. The two women were also connected by older family connections: Nargis's mother, Jaddanbai, is believed to have known the Nehru family in Allahabad in the

early 1900s. See Desai, *Darlingji*, p. 17. See also George, *Life and Times*, p. 24, who claims that Jaddanbai made a *rakhi* brother of Jawaharlal Nehru in her youth.

36. *Probe India*, October 1980, p. 14.

37. See chapter ten.

38. 'As long as I was in school my friends were all with me.... But [after acting in Mehboob's *Taqdeer* in 1943, aged fourteen] ... going to picnics or calling me to birthday parties was stopped. And that hurt a lot.... I was completely shattered.' Interview with Nargis in Vasudev and Lenglet, *Indian Superbazaar*, p. 252.

39. Anonymous (studio publicity booklet), *Mother India*.

40. *Probe India*, October 1980, p. 14.

41. More precise articulation of these is, of course, important, although outside the scope of the present chapter.

ten

*M*other India Maligned
The Saga of Sanjay Dutt

Almost a quarter of a century after Sunil Dutt won his parliamentary seat for the Congress Party in Bombay, with the implied blessings of Mother India in all her incarnations, including the public's memories of his recently deceased wife Nargis, their film star son, Sanjay Dutt, announced that he was standing in India's 2009 elections for the Samajwadi Party.[1] This was the culmination of a decade and a half of extraordinary turmoil for the Dutt family. On 19 April 1993, Sanjay, then one of the top stars of the Bombay industry, was arrested on terrorism charges and imprisoned under the Terrorist and Disruptive Activities [Prevention] Act (TADA). Over the next twenty years Sanjay spent more than eighteen months in prison and the rest out on bail, forced to attend court hearings and forced to plead his innocence of 'anti-national' activities. Only in July 2007 was Sanjay cleared of terrorism conspiracy charges in connection with the 1993 'Black Friday' bomb blasts in Mumbai, although he was still found guilty of illegal possession of firearms, for which he was sentenced to six years in jail. He accordingly withdrew his Samajwadi candidacy and parliamentary ambitions and, in 2012, he reasserted his support for the Congress Party. Sanjay had successfully rebuilt his film star career throughout the previous decade: his starring role as the monstrous drug baron villain, Kancha Cheena, contributed to *Agneepath* (Path of Fire, Karan Malhotra, 2012) becoming one of the blockbusters of 2012 and one of the Bombay cinema's all-time highest-grossing films. However, on 21 March 2013 the Supreme Court upheld the 2007 verdict, albeit reducing his sentence to five years. He surrendered

himself to the TADA court on 16 May 2013 and is, at the time of
going to press, imprisoned in Yerwada jail in Pune.

INTRODUCTION

When I originally wrote on *Mother India* in the mid-1980s, I could
never in my wildest dreams have imagined either the painful human
story that would unfold for this beleaguered family or the uncanny
way in which life and art would continue to intersect.[2] I first returned
to this complexly layered material in the mid-1990s. I was intrigued to
discover how relevant my earlier analysis still was. Not only were there
continuities between the themes structuring Mehboob Khan's 1957
film, *Mother India*, and those of Sanjay Dutt's major hits of the early
1990s, but I was also struck by the way in which the threads of a tale
that began in the 1950s with the legendary Nargis, top screen heroine
of the era of post-independence optimism, could be traced through to
the 1990s where, in a very different India that was apparently cracking
apart at the seams, her star son, Sanjay Dutt, was at the centre of an
astonishing and, in human terms, unquestionably appalling drama.

Moreover, the developments of the 1990s revealed a subtext to
the Nargis story that had been more or less obscured in the 1980s.
As Parama Roy perceptively pointed out in 1998, public interest in
Nargis was not only focused upon her scandalous sex life and perceived
redemption but also on her Muslimness, however unmarked this may
have been during her lifetime.[3] Extending my original analysis, Roy
argued that, after Nargis's death—and with the events of the 1990s—
Sanjay, and to a lesser extent Sunil, came to substitute for her in the
public imagination, crucially as embodiments of her Muslimness.[4]
Roy asked, 'How are we to read the process by which Sanjay Dutt
becomes Nargis, and becomes Muslim, in the current moment?' Many
found the most shocking revelation in the saga of Sanjay Dutt to be
his alleged response to his father's question, on arrest at the police
station, as to why, in the context of the Mumbai riots of 1993, he had
bought the guns: 'Because I have Muslim blood in my veins. I could
not bear what was happening in the city.'[5] Roy's insightful and elegant
argument has more than stood the test of time and I can add nothing
to that here. But I would like to complement it with other material,

drawn largely from my own field notes of the mid-1990s, including research for a documentary on the Dutt saga that I co-produced in 1996.[6] In particular, I want to look more carefully at an area Roy's analysis ignores, Sanjay Dutt's films of the early 1990s, and to explore how the parallel threads of fictional and factual stories inevitably inflected readings of these fictions.

In the context of the Indian film industry, the years around 1994 are significantly known as the period in which the old Bombay cinema began to break down and the new Bollywood began to emerge.[7] Of course there is no break point: as I have argued in earlier chapters, Indian cinema has always been in constant and gradual evolution. But, in many ways, *Mother India* and *Khalnayak* (The Villain, Subhash Ghai, 1993) are convenient bookends for the classic era of mainstream Hindi cinema: the former was the archetypal Bombay cinema epic of the nation-state, the latter its dangerously twisted transformation, as the nation-state consensus collapsed. Moreover, in retrospect, we can discern the seeds of a new cinematic—and political—era in *Khalnayak*.[8] That Nargis and her real-life son respectively played the leading—and very public—roles in these two films and in the very different kinds of dramatic public stories that surrounded their release, is an irresistibly intriguing twist. Sanjay Dutt is in any case central to any evaluation of 1990s Bombay cinema, as two of his films were among the biggest successes of the early 1990s. *Sadak* (The Street, Mahesh Bhatt, 1991) was one of the box-office triumphs of 1992; *Khalnayak* the mega-hit of 1993. However, the fact that Sanjay was the son of two of the biggest stars of the previous generation, Nargis and Sunil Dutt, lent another dimension both to his screen roles and to his star persona and its involvement in a horrifying real-life drama.

My chapter on *Mother India*, the 1957 legendary classic of Indian cinema, looked at both the film and the stories woven around its stars as a 'zone of cultural debate', to quote Appadurai and Breckenridge.[9] In the manner of a sequel, I choose to approach the Sanjay Dutt material in a similar way and find remarkable continuities and coincidences as well as some suggestive discontinuities between the material of the 1950s and the 1990s. While female chastity was still being exploited as a central structuring device and crude signifier of the purity of India, by the early 1990s the emphasis had shifted to

exploring and worrying notions of masculinity: tensions around a—
by that time already problematic—notion of nationalism were being
played out within the web of images and stories that constructed the
male star.

As in the *Mother India* chapter, I focus on intertextuality, in
particular on the recognition that in India the arena of popular
cinema has, since the early sound era, been considerably more than
the films themselves: the songs circulate and achieve popularity
through channels other than the cinema and the stars are sites
for a network of stories, gossip, rumour, poster portraits, photo
opportunities and the accumulated baggage of the screen roles
they have played. Taking the Sanjay Dutt persona as my core text,
the current chapter draws together threads from the network of
stories—both fact and fiction—circulating around this star in the
mid-1990s. I begin with *Sadak*, the 1992 hit that consolidated Sanjay's
place as one of Bombay's top stars—at the time second only to
Amitabh Bachchan—following a tumultuous decade in the wake
of his mother's death, during which he had battled drug addiction,
frustrated producers with his wayward lifestyle, and married and
then separated from his first wife.[10] I argue that the film deals with
the breakdown of all forms of social and moral order through a
stream of imagery and dreamwork that is particularly intriguing in
the context of the political upheavals of 1990s India. I am primarily
concerned to understand *Sadak* in relation to *Mother India*, drawing
out some of the more obvious continuities and discontinuities
between the two films and noting *Sadak*'s notable breakthroughs
in its representations of villainy and the male body. I move on to
consider the broader web of stories around Sanjay Dutt, which
both fed into any reading of *Sadak* and also played off against each
other, looking more broadly at the operation of this star persona
in the popular imagination of the early 1990s. Finally, I consider
Khalnayak, released just eighteen months after *Sadak* in 1993, reading
this in the context of the unfolding saga of the arrest and jailing of
Sanjay Dutt. I argue that, while the film is—like many films of the
1970s and 1980s—a knowing reworking of the *Mother India* theme
of two brothers on opposite sides of the law, the crucial change is
that the crisis of the nation is played out over a traumatised male

body, rather than female chastity alone. I conclude with some brief thoughts about the subsequent developments within the Sanjay Dutt star text.

SADAK

Mahesh Bhatt's *Sadak* was released in January 1992. The six distribution territories were sold for Rs 16 lakh each and the film made Rs 100 lakh in each territory, having, according to industry rumours, cost no more than Rs 40 lakh to produce.[11] The film was an instant success. The consensus of belief among my film industry trade sources was that this was because of Sanjay's star appeal, because the violence was 'well done' (although some thought it excessive), because the story flowed well and was 'logical' (although 'usual') and because the dialogue was so earthy and 'shocking'. They made much of the 'daring' *hijra* (eunuch) villain.[12] Their unquestioned assumption was that its core appeal was to young, urban, working-class men, as it mobilised a number of populist elements, including a taxi driver hero (albeit an educated one) and spectacular violence. Moreover, it was one of two films that year to launch a new female star, Mahesh Bhatt's own daughter, Pooja.

The film tells the story of a Bombay taxi driver, Ravi (Sanjay Dutt), who is troubled by the memory of his own sister who, when their parents died, had been tricked into prostitution and ended up taking her own life because her uncle then disowned her: the Brahmin family could not be sullied by her impurity. One evening Ravi meets a beautiful young woman, Pooja (Pooja Bhatt), lost in the centre of Bombay, carrying a gilded birdcage. He discovers that she too is an innocent orphan, in this case sold into prostitution by a weak and unscrupulous uncle. The film follows the hero's struggle to rescue her from the clutches of the hijra brothel owner, Maharani. Ravi borrows money and bids successfully against a rich old man for Pooja's *nath* (virginity). He takes her for the night but spends it at the temple and returns her unsullied. He then mortgages his taxi to buy her for a second night but the brothel owner refuses to let him have her: 'I can tell from the way she walks that she's still a virgin. You're either mad or in love and both are dangerous for us.' Ravi takes her away from the brothel by force and the couple must go into hiding as Maharani's network chases after them. The lovers ask an apparently trustworthy cop to help them by arresting Maharani, but the cop is, in fact, in the pay of Maharani and tricks them into a deadly rendezvous with Maharani's men in an underground car park. Ravi and Pooja survive but must go on the run again.

The lovers escape to Ooty where Pooja's uncle is the caretaker of a remote grand house. Meanwhile, Maharani's men, in a bid to get information on Ravi's whereabouts, torture and kill his friend and father figure, the poor, honest restaurant owner, Salim. When Ravi hears about this he vows revenge. Pooja insists on returning to Bombay with him but first they marry at the local temple and romance briefly in the hill station. There follows an intricate dreamscape of Ravi and Pooja on the run back to Bombay. Chased by cops and criminals, dripping with blood, they drag themselves through rivers and across beaches. Eventually a bloody Ravi is nailed to a cross—the mast of a boat—on Versova beach, while Pooja is carried back to the brothel. All looks hopeless, as the red-light area is decorated for Pooja's return and, what promises to be her first real sale. Suddenly Ravi, miraculously escaped from his crucifixion on Versova beach (Figure 10.1), appears on the scene, challenges Maharani's men to a fight and single-handedly destroys them all. He rescues Pooja from the blazing brothel—set on fire by Maharani himself—and serves his statutory three years in jail

Figure 10.1   Ravi (Sanjay Dutt) tied up on Versova beach in *Sadak* (1991)

Source: © Vishesh Films Pvt. Ltd. Courtesy Mahesh Bhatt.

for taking the law into his own hands, before walking out into the sunset with his astonishingly still unsullied wife Pooja.

While the story is superficially very different from *Mother India*, there are some interesting underlying continuities. I had argued that kinship and female sexuality (notably ideas about female chastity) were key structuring discourses of *Mother India*: Radha's choices were between being an ideal wife and an ideal mother, later between being an ideal mother and an ideal woman of the village community.

The most significant continuity between the two films is the central importance of female chastity as a structuring device. If, following Todorov, we posit narrative as a movement between two equilibriums that are similar but not identical,[13] we find, in *Sadak*, that the original equilibrium is an implied scenario in which female chastity is protected within the family: both Pooja and Rupa (Ravi's sister) were 'once upon a time' protected and controlled by their male kin. The narrative disruption results from the breakdown of kinship solidarity, due both to economic forces and to a crisis of masculinity that puts female chastity at risk, in Pooja's case from an uncle who uses her to settle an old debt. As the cynical Maharani tells her, 'This is all a part of the game of relations (*rishtedaar*): when things start to hurt you dispense with them', a particularly shocking transgression of the ideal moral universe of that era, according to my film industry sources at the time. Her chastity is also at risk from other deviant males: the hijra Maharani, his lecherous clients and the corrupt cops, emblems of a butch masculinity that has run out of control. The narrative re-equilibrium—the re-ordering of the narrative threads—is effected when female sexuality is protected and controlled within marriage. In the final scene, Ravi and Pooja walk out into the sunset, the forces of deviant masculinity having been vanquished and questions about the purity of the heroine purged through a trial by fire: Pooja has to jump from the flames on the roof of the burning *kotha* (brothel) into Ravi's arms—providing closure to the traumatic image of his own sister jumping to her death, that had haunted Ravi for years. The focus of identification is fairly uncomplicatedly masculine, unlike *Mother India*, which offered more complex positionings across gender. The implicit logic of this structure is that, just as in *Mother India*, female sexuality under male control leads to power for men and social salvation. There are direct echoes of *Mother India*—notably the trial by fire—that in turn echoes the Sita story of the *Ramayana*. There are also direct echoes of other iconic films, from Martin Scorsese's *Taxi Driver* (1976), to *Pakeezah* (Pure Heart, Kamal Amrohi, 1972), in which the 'pure' prostitute is saved by the asexual and pure love of a good man, including direct visual references such as the metaphor of the bird in the gilded cage.[14]

At a more superficial level, there are also interesting and significant differences between *Mother India* and *Sadak*. *Mother India* operates within a fundamentally optimistic universe: Radha and her family are concerned with vanquishing one particular villain, the exploitative and lecherous feudal landlord-cum-moneylender, Sukhilal. While they also have to fight against the vagaries of nature—flood, famine, fire—and the added complexity of Radha's son, Birjoo's incipient villainy (or more properly anti-heroism as he primarily wants to use violence and revenge to destroy a discredited older order), these threats are all overcome. The moral order, symbolised by Mother India's chastity, remains intact leading to economic plenitude through modern technology within a new India.

Sadak is by contrast a fundamentally pessimistic vision of a disintegrating universe: the hero is at sea in a dark, corrupt world and villainy and moral breakdown are all around. The police are untrustworthy and corrupt, in the pay of pimps and hijras. Old men are killed for their taxis and meagre savings. Young women are forced into prostitution for economic survival—or sold into it by their own families. It is the world of rootless, urban anomie through which our hero stumbles as half-crazed saviour and avenger. Fuelled by the power of love and the memory of his own sister, his mission is to rescue the chaste prostitute and take revenge on the forces of evil. His overt physical violence is tempered by a crudely literal reference to a saviour who suffered to save the world, as he bleeds from his crucifix on Versova beach.

Most significantly, this is a world without family: kinship, a key structuring dynamic of so much Bombay film narrative of that era, is alluded to but here takes the form of a significant absence. The hero is completely without family, apart from the haunting tragic memory of his 'fallen' sister who literally fell to her self-inflicted death. The heroine's family sells her into prostitution, and the villain, as hijra, is firmly placed outside the nexus of family and reproductive kinship systems. The only family is an ersatz one, a group of friends who face a hostile world together, comprising Ravi's friend and father figure, the Muslim restaurant owner, Salim, and his buddy Gotya, who is also in love with a prostitute who needs rescuing from the brothel. This is a crude, idealised, anti-communal family that clings together in the face of a hostile world.

As noted in the introduction to part two, in Bombay cinema's ideal moral universe the Mother and the Villain represent conceptual poles within and against which the tensions of the narrative are built and resolved.[15] The mother figure is the signifier of moral probity—and all that is valued in the moral universe—and is in a large number of instances literally present as the hero's mother, or maa. Given the role of kinship as a key ingredient of the Hindi film dynamic up to that date, *Sadak*'s lack of any literal family for the key players seems interesting. Where is the Oedipal subtext? There is a hint that the sister had been 'like a mother' to Ravi but the answer may be more interesting and I will return to this later.

As for the villain figure, *Sadak* marks both continuities and innovation within the moral universe of the Hindi film genre. In line with a trend that had been growing since the mid-1970s, notably with *Deewar* and other Salim–Javed films with Amitabh, villainy in *Sadak* is diffused into a dark underworld peopled by gangs of urban thugs. The film further reflects the breakthroughs of Bombay cinema of the 1980s, where, since *Ardh Satya* (Half-Truth, Govind Nihalani, 1983) and *Andha Kanoon* (Blind Law, T. Rama Rao, 1983), the traditional forces of moral authority—the police and politicians—could finally, after many years of censorship, be shown to be corrupt. But as one might expect from an extremely successful film, *Sadak* also pushes at the boundaries of the moral universe: the hijra/eunuch as villain was a novel ingredient. Maharani, the brothel owner, is a blackly comic but sinisterly evil character and was cited by many viewers and film industry professionals as one of the reasons for the film's success.

The hijra villain pushes to extremes the representation of a world in which both family values and patriarchal authority have broken down. His threat is the classic power of the anomalous being—one that is neither 'properly' man nor woman—and, crucially, the eunuch/ hijra represents an ultimately deviant form of emasculation to which Indian traditions have long attributed special powers. Significantly, this is a 'traditional' Indian deviance that owes nothing to the threat of Westernisation that had been a preoccupation of so many films of the previous decades. In *Sadak*, the breakdown of order is due not to Westernisation but to a fundamental crisis within patriarchy and male sexuality: the father has disappeared and the rebellious sons run wild in an amoral universe where eunuchs rule the roost.

Interestingly, the film is structured as much by tensions around male sexuality as by those around female chastity, the latter operating as a cipher around which male sexuality is explored. The film's divergence from the norms of Hindi cinema to that date is set up in the very first song of the film. Here, a chorus line of male taxi drivers and other good subalterns of the idealised footpath community dance benignly in formation behind Ravi/Sanjay, as if signalling that it is the male body and male sexuality that are at issue in this film.

THE STAR—SANJAY DUTT

If the continuities and discontinuities between *Mother India* and *Sadak*, two films thirty-five years apart, are interesting, the undertones that would have inflected any mainstream reading of *Sadak* through audiences' knowledge of gossip stories are even richer. Sanjay Dutt has, throughout his long career, been publicly known as Sunil and Nargis's rebellious son.[16] The last chapter described the extent to which the gossip mythology dwelt on the idealised relationship between Nargis and her only son: he idolised his mother, was devastated by her death in 1981, and subsequently turned to drugs and alcohol in a wild self-destructive binge, cleaning up and making a temporary comeback with his marriage—albeit short-lived—to a 'good girl' in the late 1980s.

However, for the purposes of this analysis, we need to revisit the stories around Nargis herself. In particular, much of the gossip pivoted around the fact that her mother, Jaddanbai, was a *gannewali* (*thumri* singer and hereditary courtesan) from Allahabad, via Calcutta and Lahore,[17] who, while protecting Nargis from the 'dirty' film industry during childhood, lost no time in tricking her into films at age thirteen and (allegedly) selling her nath to a wealthy Muslim prince soon after. As in the film *Mother India*, the gossip stories through which Nargis's star persona was constructed also constituted a discourse about chastity, nationalism and morality. Thus, for example, while Nargis's film role was about the defence of a poor, exploited but honourable village woman's chastity, as the top star of her era Nargis was popularly seen as not only glamorous and enviable but also scandalously sullied on account of the very open romance she enjoyed over a number of years with married co-star, Raj Kapoor. As discussed earlier, although she scandalised the nation in the 1950s, Nargis finally made good by marrying Sunil Dutt, retiring from films while her starring role in *Mother India* was fresh in the public's memory, giving birth to her son Sanjay, and becoming active in politics and charity work.

All this 'knowledge' was still in circulation in the early 1990s and if, as Parama Roy argued, Nargis was a structuring absence—'a contagion from beyond the grave, an unquiet specter'—*Sadak*, too, would have been read, to some extent, in relation to the Nargis gossip.[18] Moreover, if gossip knowledge operates both to reinforce and to undermine the coherence of film narrative, providing a set of interwoven narratives that offer tools for thinking and feeling the anxieties and tensions of living in the contemporary world, then our understanding of the film text must engage with it. Within the rich material that emerges from the *Sadak*/Sanjay nexus, two extraordinary interconnections propose themselves.

Firstly, I suggest that the absence of 'maa' within the film text is filled in through displacement and elisions between the film and gossip texts. If film star Nargis was an innocent whose only family sold her nath at puberty, *Sadak*'s Pooja character becomes a substitute for Nargis. This produces a dangerously subversive subtext within the film, which then becomes about Sanjay saving his mother, Nargis's, virtue and with that all that she stood for: India, a pure India, Mother India. Moreover, given that producer/director Mahesh Bhatt's own life story has been a source of gossip and semi-autobiographical films—he was the illegitimate son of the Hindu fantasy film producer/director, Nanabhai/Batak Bhatt and Shirin, his Muslim actress mistress—an additional subtext suggests that Sanjay is simultaneously rescuing both his own mother, Nargis, and Mahesh's mother, Shirin (two Muslim actresses who scandalously fought against convention to follow their desires) through the figure of Shirin's granddaughter, Pooja Bhatt. It is a muted challenge to an outmoded form of Indian society.

The second suggestive continuity is between Sunil Dutt, Sanjay's father who played Mother India's rebellious son, and both the film *Sadak* and the gossip stories about Sanjay. The 'bad' son, Birjoo, had wanted to save a corrupt world by sacrificing his own life and killing the villain with a gun. Mother India/Radha had warned him against revolutionary violence: 'No, you won't change anything with a gun.... Don't lose heart, my son.... God will change our lives and He will change the fate of the village.'[19] In *Sadak*, thirty-five years later, we find Sanjay, Mother India's real-life son, set to save a corrupt India with machismo and violence, tempered by an anomalous image of Christ-like sacrifice. However, one enduring image from this film— one that was published more than any other in the Indian press—is of Sanjay lovingly fondling his guns. At this point the interplay between fact and fiction—gossip, real-life drama and film fantasy—escalates at dizzying speed.

When in April 1993 Sanjay Dutt was arrested at Bombay airport charged with possession of an AK56 automatic assault rifle and illegal ammunition, directly in the wake of the communal riots and bombings, the gossip went wild. Sanjay Dutt was said to be a terrorist, in the pay of terrorists, or in cahoots with the Dubai underworld, notably with the notorious godfather, Dawood Ibrahim, his brother Anees, and Bombay-based 'Tiger' Memon, believed—or known—to be the masterminds behind the 1993 Bombay bomb blasts. Others suspected another kind of conspiracy: Sunil Dutt, Sanjay's father, had over the past years spoken out firmly against communalism and was working openly on the ground in Bombay to protect Muslims threatened by BJP/Shiv Sena violence that winter. They suggested that the arrest of Sanjay was on charges trumped up by enemies keen to get back at Sunil Dutt père. Others insisted that Sanjay was just a wild and rather foolish kid, who, as spoiled movie brat, simply enjoyed playing macho games with powerful rifles. Sanjay's own version, once he had admitted the offence, was that he had bought the rifle to protect his father and family who had been threatened in the aftermath of the communal violence.

Whatever the truth, the stories spun on dramatically after April 1993. In the early months the drama brought catastrophic upheavals: from the soap opera gossip melodrama of Sanjay's alleged girlfriend, the respectable middle-class Maharashtrian, Madhuri Dixit, publicly finishing the relationship and denouncing him while he languished in jail, to a hate campaign run by elements in the vernacular press, notably *Saamana*, the Shiv Sena–owned Marathi daily, which denounced the whole Dutt family as traitors and 'anti-nationalists', as a result of which many major bodies of the film industry distanced themselves from the family. Exhibitors in Hindu fundamentalist strongholds such as Pune refused to screen any Sanjay or Sunil Dutt films at all.

By the summer of 1993, the film industry predicted that Sanjay's career as a star was finished. His next film due to release, *Khalnayak*, was anyway rumoured to be a serious gamble as Sanjay's leading role was that of a villain—a daring challenge to the boundaries of Hindi cinema's moral universe. While carefully negotiated anti-heroes had been common throughout the history of Indian cinema, up to that point only one major male star/hero had successfully played a totally villainous character—Dilip Kumar, once. By an appalling, even uncanny, coincidence—for the film was mostly made many months before Sanjay's arrest—in *Khalnayak* Sanjay was playing a terrorist, bent on destabilising his country. Just as his real-life arrest drama took off, Bombay was flooded with posters of Sanjay Dutt's face alongside the text, 'I am Khalnayak' (I am the villain). Few believed he could possibly survive this.

Following the release of *Khalnayak* in August 1993, it soon became clear that the patchwork of stories and mythologies surrounding Sanjay Dutt and underpinning any contemporary reading of the film had most definitely touched the pulse of contemporary India. *Khalnayak*, directed and produced by Subhash Ghai, was, on release, Bombay's biggest-grossing film since *Sholay* in the 1970s, with opening box-office takings of more than Rs 12 crore—of which the Bombay and Delhi circuits alone accounted for almost half. For a number of reasons, this much-hyped film quickly became a national controversy.

KHALNAYAK

Khalnayak reworks *Mother India*'s central plot device, which is also that of *Gunga Jumna* (Nitin Bose, 1961), *Deewar* (Yash Chopra, 1975) and many other key Bombay films: two brothers—in this case childhood friends—end up on opposite sides of the law, one a 'principled' traditionalist, the other an angry rebel. The father is in each case an idealist who loses out in life and disappears (or dies), and the brothers/ friends are in competition for the mother's love and approval.

Khalnayak tells the story of a violent, gun-toting thug, Ballu (Sanjay Dutt), who works for a villainous 'foreign' boss involved in drug racketeering, who masterminds attacks on the political stability of India from 'abroad'.[20] Ballu's long-lost childhood friend, Ram (Jackie Shroff), is a police officer who is determined to capture, punish and reform Ballu from 'khalnayak' (villain) to 'nayak' (hero/good citizen). Ram's girlfriend, Ganga (Madhuri Dixit), also a police officer, goes undercover as a decoy dancing girl to help Ram in his mission. After a long series of adventures, Ram, Ganga and Ballu's long-lost mother, who rejected him when he joined the terrorists and is subsequently blamed for Ballu's villainy, help Ballu to see the light. In the process, Ganga's reputation is undermined and her chastity doubted. She ends up in court, her professional and personal integrity on trial. Ballu redeems himself by storming into the courtroom, swearing on his mother's name that Ganga is 'pure like Sita' and that 'Ram is Bharat's true son', repents of his sins and offers himself up for the jail sentence that he accepts he deserves.[21]

The film was yet another reworking, inflected for the 1990s, of the perennial threads of conflicting moralities of sexuality, kinship and modern Indian nationalism. However, the film pushed at the boundaries of the moral universe in remarkably adventurous ways, while finally resolving these transgressions firmly within its order. While villainy was ultimately located in an 'outsider' who corrupted the good sons—and grandsons—of Mahatma Gandhi's India, for most of the film the central hero, Sanjay Dutt, was unambiguously a criminal thug at loose in a violent, hypocritical and unjust modern India. He drank, he leered, he taunted good citizens and he killed without compassion. Similarly, the mother defied the rules of Hindi cinema's moral universe by apparently rejecting her son, and the heroine played vamp, but the resolution redeemed them all through the villainous hero's final public recognition of the heroine's purity and the mother's love, played out within a set of Hindu mythological references to Ram, Balaram and Ganga. Ultimately, in *Khalnayak*, as in *Mother India*, female chastity is a force of social control and a crude signifier of the purity of India (Sita/Ganga/Mother/Mother India/ Bharat). Where *Mother India* begins and ends with the elderly mother blessing dams and technological progress (carefully motivated within the story), *Khalnayak* quite transparently begins and ends with the Indian flag. Many spectacular and subversive elements erupt within this generic frame, providing the film's pleasures and ensuring its popularity: catchy music, erotic dances and exciting fights, sensation, humour and action, not to mention dazzling performances by its then megastars, Sanjay Dutt and Madhuri Dixit.

One ingredient that firmly captured the contemporary Indian imagination and mood of the day was *Khalnayak*'s daring play with female sexuality. The song, 'Choli ke Peeche Kya Hai?' (What's underneath Your Blouse?), suggestively picturised on the alluring heroine Ganga/Madhuri Dixit, in her masquerade seduction of Ballu/ Sanjay, became *the* song of 1993 and was banned on Doordarshan and All India Radio for obscenity—thereby guaranteeing the film both an audience and the ever coveted 'repeat value'.[22] The double entendre song lyrics themselves were not significantly more obscene than many traditional Indian songs: Subhash Ghai got them past the film censors by pointing out that the song was based on a Rajasthani folk song and somewhat disingenuously insisting that they referred to her heart. However, the song's ostensible meaning within the film is interestingly at odds both with its reception within the wider social domain in which it circulated so successfully and with how it was picturised—focusing pruriently on Dixit's heaving, thrusting breasts.[23] While the film resolved such apparent transgressions within a traditional and conservative moral order, within the wider public imagination the *dupatta* was in jeopardy: female sexuality as cipher of purity was up for grabs as Madhuri Dixit flaunted her torso in a defiant provocation of the restrictive codes around male and female sexuality. Indeed, as Monika Mehta argues, the controversy may have been less to do with the apparently obscene words and more about the film's depiction of overt female desire.[24] With this song and Khalnayak's plot device of the undercover cop, the Ganga character pushed the split persona of the Hindi film heroine further than almost any film before: on the one hand, Ganga was a tough, avenging policewoman in the tradition of Hema Malini and other avenging women in the films of the 1980s;[25] on the other hand, the Ganga role adumbrated a new breed of sexually assertive heroines. From this point on, distinctions between heroine and vamp began to crumble, as the item number became de rigueur for the female stars.

A second element that captured the public imagination was the complex set of representations around 'Bad Boy' Sanjay. He was both a locus of masculine strength and power—gun-toting and brutal—and, at the same time, a body marked by the blows and tortures of the zealous police officer jailor. The first scenes of the film are intriguing. Having first introduced Ballu's abandoned mother wistfully contemplating his photograph while she reads the Ramayana, the film sets up key plot points through an extended fifteen-minute credit sequence, at the end of which we see Ballu tied up in a police cell and being brutally beaten by Ram's police officers. The song 'Nayak Nahiin, Khalnayak Hoon Main' (I'm Not a Hero, I'm a Villain) intercuts images of Ballu's beaten muscular body and his tortured and bloody face with erotic shots of his girlfriend, Sonia, both alone in her bedroom and dancing seductively in high silver boots in the master villain's opulently decadent nightclub, flanked by a chorus of muscular male bodies, wearing cossack hats and black leather boots. Just as in Sadak, the male body is, from the start of the film, presented as an object of spectacle and desire, but this time the torsos are bare and the macho energy is threateningly subversive. Just a few scenes later, when Ram challenges Ballu to their first fist fight, the camera lingers, lovingly, on their respective biceps as the two superheroes, nayak and khalnayak, prepare to slug it out.

Structurally, the place Sanjay occupies in the narrative directly echoes that of his father Sunil in Mother India: he is the rebellious son who believes in guns and violence to change the world. However, Sanjay as Ballu is infinitely more villainous than Sunil as Birjoo.

Moreover, this time the 'good' son, Ram, also believes in force and violence: the traditionalist is no longer a weakling. Ram fights back.

Khalnayak, of course, sits all too neatly within the political events of 1990s India: it can be read as a metaphor for—or even a celebration of—the rise of militant Hinduism against the perceived threats from 'abroad'. However, the other forms of knowledge that we have about Sanjay, in particular that, by the time of the film's release, he was awaiting trial on charges of anti-national terrorism, make readings more complex and problematic. As no one really knew, for the next fourteen years or so, whether or not Sanjay was guilty of terrorist conspiracy, this unresolved narrative was inexorably threaded throughout the text.

Over the period of *Khalnayak*'s run and for a couple of years on from Sanjay's arrest, with applications for bail consistently refused, the stories in the gossip press began to change, constructing an almost saintly, martyr-like figure. By 1995, according to *Stardust*, where once Sanjay lived a fast life, playing with guns, drink and drugs, now he spent his long days meditating and praying.[26] Where once he wore exotic perfumes and expensive shoes, his clothes now smelled of a musty prison and he walked barefoot. While at one time crowds of sycophantic industry colleagues came to visit him, now—apart from one lone loyal producer—only his close family and a new, goddess-like girlfriend, dressed in white salwar-kameez, were there for him.[27] Many of the stories concerned Sanjay's increasing ill-health—he was at one point rumoured to be dying of emphysema—and his main sightings in central Bombay were at his regular hospital visits. His once taut muscles were now said to be flabby and photos showed a haggard face with a long *sannyasi*-like beard, or the star, like a caged animal, behind the bars of the prison van. Stills from the film were even used to illustrate stories from his real life. The headlines proclaimed: 'Is Sanjay Cracking under Pressure?' or 'Has the Industry Forgotten Sanjay Dutt?'[28]

The *Khalnayak* hero turned anti-Indian 'terrorist' because, among other things, he believed that his mother had turned against him, nicely inverting the knowledge audiences had that Sanjay was the wild, rebellious and adored son of committed nationalists.[29] By summer 1993, *Mother India*'s real-life son was in jail on charges of possessing illegal firearms, held under Indian anti-terrorist laws while he insisted that the gun was simply to protect his family: it was the archetypal Hindi film conflict between being an ideal son and a good citizen. Meanwhile, Nargis's screen son, Birjoo/Sunil Dutt (Sanjay's real-life father), who stepped into his wife's political shoes after her death and until 1995 was a Congress Member of Parliament (MP) actively working for communal harmony and the ideals of a secular Indian nationalism, was now tirelessly supporting a son accused of being a 'terrorist', despite his fervent belief that, in his words, his son was 'the type of guy who does not know anything about politics and who never indulged in politics'.[30] Dutt senior faced the conflict between being a good father and a good nationalist, and between being a good nationalist and caring for his fellow citizens.

In 1990s India, the discourse of nationalism was complexly inflected and was being increasingly appropriated by the Hindu right. What was it to be a 'good nationalist' in the 1990s? The post-independence, secular, nationalist modernity of Nargis and Sunil Dutt was in question: Sunil's old Congress seat went to the Shiv Sena in the 1995 elections and his support of oppressed Muslims in the 1993 riots and their aftermath led to accusations from some quarters of being 'anti-national', perhaps the worst insult Sunil could imagine. As he told *Sunday* magazine, in the context of his son's arrest: 'You can call me a murderer. Call me a criminal. Call me a smuggler. But don't call me anti-national. That is what really hurts after all I have done for my country.'[31]

I had suggested that, in *Mother India*, the female body was the site on which the politics of post-independence modern Indian nationalism was played out, and that the preoccupations of the film and gossip were with notions of chastity. By the early 1990s, the tensions and debates around nationalism were being played out more centrally on the male body. Hindi cinema had for long worked with a tension between two versions of masculinity, implicitly two modes of political action: the law-abiding, god-fearing, non-violent (Gandhian) man of principles and the man who uses violence and guns to take the law into his own hands. By the mid-1990s, other options were emerging: from the castrated villain of *Sadak*, to the once powerful male body flagellated, bloody, broken, diseased—the flip side of the brawny muscleman. The images of Sanjay hanging like a martyr on the cross in *Sadak*, or those of his flesh, bloody and beaten, in *Khalnayak*, were now fused with media images of his haggard face and flabby muscles, a body locked behind bars that was succumbing to a life-threatening lung disease. The physical body of Sanjay was directly bearing the burden of the contradictory imperatives of a corrupted discourse of nationalism.

CODA

At the point at which he went into jail in 2013, the body of the 'Deadly Dutt' may have been ageing but it was still working out. 'Bad Boy' Sanjay had continued to be a major and marketable force within the Indian film industry. His star persona had developed in two directions over the films of the previous decade, reflecting two dimensions of the new masculinity that came with the 1990s Bollywood era, characterised by Ranjani Mazumdar as the rebellious *tapori* (vagabond) rascal of Aamir Khan's films such as *Rangeela* (Carefree, Ram Gopal Varma, 1995) and the psychotic hoodlum of Sharukh Khan's breakthrough film, *Baazigar* (The Player, Abbas-Mastan, 1993).[32]

On the one hand, Sanjay made the comic tapori figure his own with *Munnabhai MBBS* (Rajkumar Hirani, 2003) and *Lage Raho Munnabhai* (Rajkumar Hirani, 2006), in which he played a loveable rogue, a minor gangster with a heart of gold, and rehabilitated a populist notion of *Gandhigiri* (non-violent good works) for a twenty-first-century audience. On the other hand, his persona has encompassed the wild anger of the psychotic anti-hero (with shades of his roles in *Sadak* and *Khalnayak*) and Sanjay is now increasingly associated with brawny, sadistic psychopath figures, from semi-villainous cops in films such as *Shootout at Lokhandwala* (Apoorva Lakhia, 2007) to two outright villain roles in *Aladin* (Sujoy Ghosh, 2009) and *Agneepath* (Path of Fire, Karan Malhotra, 2012). His niche by 2013 has become that of cult comic villain: he is a scary, bloated, larger-than-life character with a sinister leer and deadly black humour.

Having begun this book with Alibaba, we find ourselves nearing its end with Aladdin: the *Arabian Nights* fantasy film has followed us

Figure 10.2   Bad Genie Ringmaster (Sanjay Dutt) in *Aladin* (2009)

Source: © Eros International & Bound Script. Courtesy Sujoy Ghose.

well into the twenty-first century. In Sujoy Ghosh's *Aladin*, Sanjay Dutt plays bad genie to Amitabh Bachchan's good genie, thereby pitting the 1990s anti-hero against the superstar hero of the 1970s masala heyday. In this context, Dutt's evil carnivalesque role is especially fascinating: his bad genie, 'Ringmaster' (Figure 10.2), is a psychotic, sadistic, circus owner, a former genie of the magic lamp, who terrorises Kwaish, an Islamicate fantasy land perched high in the mountains of a nebulous somewhere-outside-India. Wearing black and scarlet top hat and tails, with a Batman-style cape, leather gloves and a sneering laugh, he fronts a female chorus of Indian and European beauties dolled up in fetishistic black leather boots, hot pants, suspenders and scarlet bikini tops, who gyrate to his *Giri Giri* tune. Meanwhile, between stunts, fights and magic trickery, he flirts with a succession of dumb geisha girls in purple bikinis, faces hidden by grotesque white masks. Here we have it all: the exotic *gori bibi*—ambiguously European or East Asian—as white-masked dancing girl; exciting hard-nosed action; spectacular CGI special effects fantasy, a cabinet of horrors and a red-and-white striped circus tent. We have come almost full circle back to the origins of Bombay cinema.

In fact, *Aladin* was a box-office flop but Dutt's next outing as pure villain was one of the top money-spinners of 2012. In *Agneepath*, a

Figure 10.3 Kancha Cheena (Sanjay Dutt) in *Agneepath* (2012)

Source: © Dharma Productions. Courtesy Dharma Productions.

retro neo-masala remake of a 1990 film of the same name, Sanjay Dutt plays Kancha Cheena (Figure 10.3), an ageless, shaven-headed, tattooed and lumbering giant, the monstrous son of the owner of Mandwa island. Having cheated the poor islanders out of their lands, he runs a cocaine business within a fiefdom that the law cannot penetrate. For this role, Sanjay allegedly worked out in the gym twice a day, shaved his head and had his eyebrows digitally removed. His sheer bulk and sly menace dominate the screen.

If, as Parama Roy argued in 1998, the 'specter of Mother India' continues to haunt Sanjay, it is perhaps inevitable that the son of Mother India should morph into the arch villain of Bombay cinema. His enormous frame now embodies within itself the very motor of Indian cinema, the two dynamic poles of the ideal moral universe: Mother and Villain. Over the years the Hindi cinema villain has been transformed from the puny body of the nasty, snivelling creep, Sukhilal, who collapsed like a naughty child under the righteous force of Mother India's big stick, to Kancha Cheena, an hysterically-male monster that grows and grows and, like a grotesque cockroach, must be repeatedly stabbed before he is finally vanquished from the world.

Sanjay Dutt's performance and the sheer bulk of his physical presence encode not only the trauma of his own life story—the wild youth who went astray, the naïve 'bad boy' imprisoned on terrorism charges—but also the longer story of the Dutt family, and thereby of the Indian nation. Within this monstrous frame lurk many dark tales: his own family's troubled history, the terrorist attacks of 1993, the dirty politics of modern India, and urban gang warfare. This is a journey from the optimistic nationalism of Nargis and Sunil Dutt in the 1950s to an India fraying at the edges in the 1990s. Finally, in the current moment, referring to *Agneepath* as 'an operatic film about gangster violence', Kaveree Bamzai wrote in *India Today*: 'The film is a metaphor for the world we live in and Mandwa, the benighted Mandwa, which sold its soul for the money it expected to come from cocaine is India today.'[33]

Dutt's arch villain is no longer straightforwardly of the West but ambiguously within and outside India. The character's name is Kancha Cheena, perjorative terms for Nepalis and Chinese, encoding evil, oriental Otherness. Although no attempt is made to orientalise Dutt's features, the shadow of the original Kancha Cheena of the 1990 *Agneepath* (Mukul Anand), the Sikkimese star villain, Danny Dengzongpa, remains a racist subtext. But Danny was a slick, Westernised, corporate villain, in sharp suits. His otherness was of the global Western world. Dutt's is a different kind of exotic otherness.

The visual references are multiple and transcultural. Dutt himself cites Marlon Brando in *Apocalypse Now* (Francis Ford Coppola, 1979) as a conscious influence, while reviews suggest allusions to other dark creatures from global popular culture, including Smeagol from *Lord of the Rings* (Peter Jackson, 2001 / 2 / 3) and Voldemort from the *Harry Potter* films.[34] But Dutt's character is also overtly Raavana from the *Ramayana*: he speaks a Sanskritised Hindi, he quotes the *Bhagavad Gita*, and he explicitly refers to his island off India as a modern Lanka. Moreover, his massive frame is one which is long familiar to Indian audiences: it is the body of the pahalwan wrestler; the body of the gods and demons of the B studios' mythologicals; and the body of the jinni of Homi Wadia's fantasy films such as *Aladdin and the Wonderful Lamp*. Dutt's 'bulking up' for the role reminds us of nothing so much as Gama's extraordinary diet of ghee and meat. It is the male body of India's 'magic and fighting' films, but also that of the visceral, transcultural, spectacular entertainment forms of the early twentieth century, including circus, wrestling and variety shows.

Finally, despite certain current orthodoxies about the 'new Bollywood', the success of *Agneepath* suggests that we must recognise the continuities as well as the differences between this era and those of the past: the break is not so radical. Despite the emergence of a plethora of new forms and small films in all genres today, there is still room for what is being dubbed 'neo-masala'—Manmohan Desai with CGI—and these films, from *Dabangg* (Audacious, Abhinav Kashyap, 2010) to *Agneepath*, still do excellent business at the box office. While *Agneepath* is overtly a remake of a 1990 film, it is *not* played as knowing, postmodern pastiche. The adaptation draws on the core storyline and characters of the 1990 film, which it transforms and makes its own. And, surprising as it may seem and against all the odds, at its heart the film is structured by—and plays deftly with—the same ideal moral universe of the classic era, which also underpins its system of verisimilitude. It draws on—and is a permutation of—*Mother India* via *Deewar* and *Khalnayak*, including such perennial tropes as female chastity under threat and the pure mother torn between duty and filial love. The challenge for new histories of Indian cinema will be to engage with the complex multitude of cross-currents that feed relentlessly into the contemporary moment.

NOTES

1. The Samajwadi Party is a Uttar Pradesh–based democratic socialist political party, and a main opposition to the Congress and BJP Parties. Its key support comes from other backward classes (OBCs), notably the Yadav caste and Muslim communities. Founder and leader, Mulayam Singh Yadav, is a former wrestler.

2. That essay, originally published in *Quarterly Review of Film and Video*, is reprinted as chapter nine in this book.

3. Parama Roy, 'Figuring Mother India: The Case of Nargis', in *Indian Traffic*, Berkeley: University of California Press, 1998, pp. 152–73.

4. Ibid., p. 156.

5. 'The Sanjay Dutt Cover-Up: How the Star Escaped TADA', *Tehelka*, 24 March 2007, http://www.tehelka.com/story_main28.asp?filename=Ne240307How_the_ CS.asp (accessed on August 2012).

6. *To Hell and Back*, documentary produced by Behroze Gandhy and Rosie Thomas. Broadcast on UK's Channel Four Television on 2 November 1996.

7. See discussion in chapter one of this book.

8. I am not arguing that any one film definitively changes things: changes are always cumulative. However, *Khalnayak*'s release preceded by several months that of the other 1993 breakthrough film, *Baazigar* (The Gambler, Abbas-Mastan, 1993), in which Shahrukh Khan played an unambiguously psychotic villainous hero, a film often cited as a game-changer. See Mazumdar, *Bombay Cinema*, pp. 32–40.

9. Appadurai and Breckenridge, 'Why Public Culture?' p. 6.

10. Richa Sharma, who died of a brain tumour in 1996.

11. Information from trade paper *Box Office*.

12. Draws on conversations with many people, including film industry journalists.

13. Tsvetan Todorov, *The Fantastic: A Structural Approach to a Literary Genre*, trans. Richard Howard, Ithaca: Cornell University Press, 1973, p. 163.

14. Arguably, this also places Pooja within the frame of India's Islamicate fantasies of earlier decades.

15. This does not mean that every film includes a literal mother and villain character. See Thomas, 'Melodrama and the Negotiation of Morality'.

16. To a young twenty-first-century generation, Sanjay's own real-life dramas have extended beyond this, and his star persona has developed its own dynamic and charisma.

17. See Desai, *Darlingji*, pp. 8–26. See also George, *The Life and Times of Nargis*, pp. 21–39.

18. Full quote: 'She features as a contagion from beyond the grave, an unquiet spectre inhabiting both the renegade Hindu husband and the violent weak-minded and affectionate son' (Roy, *Indian Traffic*, p. 171).

19. Dialogue translations by Kabir, *The Dialogue of Mother India*, p. 236.

20. The master criminal is said to work from an unspecified 'abroad' (*videsh*)—with the only reference to a concrete location being a scene set in Singapore in the final reels. Wherever it is, this videsh is clearly not the West. Parallels with Dawood Ibrahim's masterminding of drug-running and terrorist plots from his base in Dubai were not lost on audiences at the time.

21. Ballu is short for Balram—referring to Krishna's older brother, sometimes seen as an incarnation of Vishnu.

22. Newspapers of the day reported that many 'repeat viewers' went regularly to the film but left the cinema immediately after that song.

23. For an excellent and detailed analysis of both the song picturisation and the censorship controversy around this song, see Monika Mehta 'What Is Behind Film Censorship? The *Khalnayak* Debates', *Jouvert: A Journal of Postcolonial Studies*, vol. 5, no. 3, 2001, http://english.chass.ncsu.edu/jouvert/v5i3/mehta.htm (accessed 21 August 2012). A version is reprinted in Monika Mehta, *Censorship and Sexuality in Bombay Cinema*, Austin: University of Texas Press, 2012, pp. 159–84.

24. Ibid., p. 166.

25. Before we meet Ganga, her 'boyishness' is discussed by the jailor and his wife: she is referred to as a *larkha* (boy). For discussion of avenging woman in Indian

cinema, see also Lalitha Gopalan, *Cinema of Interruptions*, London: British Film Institute, 2002, pp. 34–62.

26. Omar Qureshi, 'Has the Industry Forgotten Sanjay Dutt', *Stardust*, March 1995; and Omar Qureshi, 'Stardust Meets Sanjay Dutt', *Stardust*, May 1995.

27. Rhea Pillai who became his second wife, 1995–2005.

28. *Stardust*, December 1994 and March 1995.

29. There are direct echoes within *Khalnayak* of both *Mother India* and of the 'real-life' gossip about Sanjay and Nargis: for example, the mother always covered for her son's wild transgressions when his morally upright father tried to discipline him.

30. Gandhy and Thomas, *To Hell and Back*, 1996.

31. *Sunday*, 22–28 August 1993. But he added: 'I must say that the silver lining in all this was that I came to appreciate the support of my family.'

32. Mazumdar, *Bombay Cinema*, pp. 32–78.

33. Kaveree Bamzai, *India Today*, 27 January 2012.

34. Sukanya Verma on rediff.com, 26 January 2012, http://www.rediff.com/movies/report/review-agneepath-less-of-a-remake-more-of-a-tribute/20120126.htm (accessed 25 October 2012).

References and Select Bibliography

Adarsh, B.K., *Film Industry of India, 1913–1963*, Bombay: Trade Guide, 1963.

Alter, Joseph S., *The Wrestler's Body: Identity and Ideology in North India*, Berkeley: University of California Press, 1992.

Anonymous, in *Indian Talkie, 1931–56, Silver Jubilee Souvenir*, Bombay: Film Federation of India, 1956.

Appadurai, Arjun, and Carol A. Breckenridge, 'Why Public Culture?' *Public Culture*, vol. 1, no. 1, 1988, pp. 5–10.

Apte, M.L., *Mass Culture, Language and Arts in India*, Bombay: Popular Prakashan, 1978.

Bakhle, Janaki, *Two Men and Music: Nationalism in the Making of an Indian Classical Tradition*, New York: Oxford University Press, 2005.

Ballhatchet, Kenneth, *Race, Sex and Class under the Raj: Imperial Attitudes and Policies and Their Critics, 1793–1905*, London: Weidenfeld and Nicolson, 1980.

Bandyopadhyay, Samik (ed.), *Indian Cinema: Contemporary Perceptions from the Thirties*, Jamshedpur: Celluloid Chapter, 1993.

Barnouw, Erik, 'Shards of the Silent Era', *Cinema Vision India*, vol. 1, no. 1, 1980, p. 102.

Barnouw, Erik, and S. Krishnaswamy, *Indian Film*, second edition, New York: Oxford University Press, 1980 [1963].

Barthes, Roland, *Image-Music-Text*, Glasgow: Fontana / Collins, 1977.

Bate, David, *Photography and Surrealism: Sexuality, Colonialism and Social Dissent*, London: I.B. Tauris, 2004.

Bernstein, Matthew, 'Introduction', in *Visions of the East: Orientalism in Film*, eds Matthew Bernstein and Gaylyn Studlar, London: I.B. Tauris, 1997.

Bhaskar, Ira, and Richard Allen, *Islamicate Cultures of Bombay Cinema*, New Delhi: Tulika, 2009.

Bhaumik, Kaushik, 'The Emergence of the Bombay Film Industry, 1913–36', unpublished DPhil thesis, University of Oxford, 2001.

Bhaumik, Kaushik, 'Sulochana: Clothes, Stardom and Gender in Early Indian Cinema', in *Fashioning Film Stars: Dress, Culture, Identity*, ed. Rachel Moseley, London: British Film Institute, 2005, pp. 87–97.

―――, 'Querying the "Traditional" Roots of Silent Cinema in Asia', *Journal of the Moving Image*, no. 7, 2008, http://www.jmionline.org/jmi7.htm (accessed 6 January 2011).

―――, 'Cinematograph to Cinema: Bombay 1896–1928', *BioScope*, vol. 2, no. 1, 2011, pp. 41–67.

Bilimoria, M.B., 'Foreign Market for Indian Films', in *Indian Talkie: Silver Jubilee Souvenir 1931–56*, Bombay: Film Federation of India, 1956.

Booth, Gregory D., 'Musicking the Other: Orientalism in the Hindi Cinema', in *Music and Orientalism in the British Empire 1780s–1940s: Portrayal of the East*, eds Martin Clayton and Bennett Zon, Aldershot: Ashgate, 2007, pp. 315–38.

Britton, Andrew, *Katharine Hepburn: The Thirties and After*, Newcastle upon Tyne: Tyneside Cinema, 1984.

Brooks, Peter, *The Melodramatic Imagination: Balzac, Henry James, Melodrama and the Mode of Excess*, New Haven, Conn.: Yale University Press, 1976.

Brunsdon, Charlotte, 'Crossroads: Notes on Soap Opera', *Screen*, vol. 22, no. 4, 1981, pp. 32–7.

Chabria, Suresh, and Paolo Cherchi Usai, (eds), *Light of Asia: Indian Silent Cinema, 1912–1935*, New Delhi: Wiley Eastern, 1994.

Chakravarty, Sumita, *National Identity in Indian Popular Cinema: 1947–1987*, Austin: University of Texas Press, 1993.

Chatterjee, Gayatri, *Mother India*, London: British Film Institute, 2008 [2002].

Chatterjee, Partha, 'Colonialism, Nationalism and the Colonialized Women: The Contest in India', *American Ethnologist*, vol. 16, no. 4, 1989, pp. 622–33.

―――, *The Nation and Its Fragments: Colonial and Postcolonial Histories*, Princeton: Princeton University Press, 1993.

Chatterjee, Ranita, 'Journeys In and Beyond the City: Cinema in Calcutta 1897–1939', unpublished PhD thesis, University of Westminster, 2011.

Chattopadhyay, Sajal, *Aar Rekho Na Andhare*, Calcutta: Jogomaya Prakashani, 1998.

Chion, Michel, *The Voice in Cinema*, trans. from the French by Claudia Gorbman, New York: Columbia University Press, 1999 [1982].

Choudhury, Ranabir Ray, *Early Calcutta Advertisements, 1875–1925*, Bombay: Nichiketa Publications, 1992.

Chowdhry, Prem, *Colonial India and the Making of Empire Cinema: Image, Ideology and Identity*, Manchester: Manchester University Press, 2000.

Cosquin, Emmanuel, 'Le Prologue-cadre des Mille et Une Nuits', *Revue Biblique*, vol. 6, no. 7, 1909, pp. 7–49.

Creed, Barbara, 'Me Tarzan: You Jane!—A Case of Mistaken Identity in Paradise', *Continuum: Journal of Media and Cultural Studies*, vol. 1, no. 1, 1988, pp. 159–74.

Crusz, Robert, 'Black Cinemas, Film Theory and Dependent Knowledge', *Screen*, vol. 26, nos 3–4, 1985, pp. 152–6.

Dadi, Iftikhar, 'Registering Crisis: Ethnicity in Pakistani Cinema of the 1960s and 1970s', in *Beyond Crisis: Re-evaluating Pakistan*, ed. Naveeda Khan, New Delhi: Routledge, 2010, pp. 145–76.

Daly, Mary, *Gyn/Ecology: The Metaethics of Radical Feminism*, Boston: Beacon Press, 1978.

Das, Sisir Kumar, *Sahibs and Munshis: An Account of the College of Fort William*, Calcutta: Orion Publications, 1978.

Dass, Manishita, 'The Crowd outside the Lettered City: Imagining the Mass Audience in 1920s India', *Cinema Journal*, vol. 48, no. 4, 2009, pp. 77–98.

David-Neel, Alexandra, *With Mystics and Magicians in Tibet*, London: John Lane, Bodley Head, 1931.

Desai, Kishwar, *Darlingji: The True Love Story of Nargis and Sunil Dutt*, London: Harper Collins, 2007.

Dharamsey, Virchand, 'The Script of Gul-e-Bakavali (Kohinoor, 1924)', *BioScope*, vol. 3, no. 2, 2012, pp. 175–207.

———, 'The Advent of Sound in Indian Cinema: Theatre, Orientalism, Action, Magic', *Journal of the Moving Image*, vol. 9, 2010, http://www.jmionline.org/film_journal/jmi_09/article_02.php (accessed 9 June 2013).

Dudrah, Rajinder, *Bollywood Travels: Culture, Diaspora and Border Crossings in Popular Hindi Cinema*, London: Routledge, 2012.

Dumont, Louis, *Homo Hierarchicus*, trans. from the French by Mark Sainsbury, London: Weidenfeld and Nicolson, 1970 [1963].

Dutt, Namrata, and Priya Dutt, *Mr and Mrs Dutt: Memories of Our Parents*, New Delhi: Lustre Press, Roli Books, 2007.

Dwyer, Rachel, *Filming the Gods: Religion and Indian Cinema*, London: Routledge, 2006.

Dwyer, Rachel, and Christopher Pinney (eds), *Pleasure and the Nation: The History, Politics and Consumption of Public Culture in India*, New Delhi: Oxford University Press, 2001, pp. 1–34.

Dwyer, Rachel, and Divia Patel, *Cinema India: The Visual Culture of Hindi Film*, London: Reaktion Books, 2002.

Dwyer, Rachel, and Jerry Pinto (eds), *Beyond the Boundaries of Bollywood: The Many Forms of Hindi Cinema*, New Delhi: Oxford University Press, 2011.

Dyer, Richard, *Stars*, London: British Film Institute, 1979.

———, *White*, London: Routledge, 1997.

Ellis, John, *Visible Fictions: Cinema, Television, Video*, London: Routledge and Kegan Paul, 1982.

Encyclopaedia Britannica, *Encyclopaedia of Hindi Cinema*, New Delhi: Encyclopaedia Britannica (India) Pvt. Ltd, 2003.

Erdman, Joan L., 'Dance Discourses: Rethinking the History of the "Oriental Dance"', in *Moving Words: Rewriting Dance*, ed. Gay Morris, London: Routledge, 1996.

Essoe, Gabe, *Tarzan of the Movies*, New York: Citadel Press, 1968.

Everett, William A., '*Chu Chin Chow* and Orientalist Musical Theatre in Britain during the First World War', in *Music and Orientalism in the British Empire, 1780s–1940s*, ed. Martin Clayton and Bennett Zon, Aldershot: Ashgate, 2007, pp. 277–96.

Fanon, Franz, *Black Skins, White Masks*, London: Pluto Press, 2008 [1952; 1968 in English].

Fuller, Chris, 'The Divine Couple in South India', *History of Religions*, vol. 19, no. 4, 1980, pp. 321–48.

Gandhy, Behroze, and Rosie Thomas, 'Three Indian Film Stars', in *Stardom: Industry of Desire*, ed. Christine Gledhill, London: Routledge, 1991, pp. 107–16.

Ganti, Tejaswini, *Bollywood*, New York: Routledge, 2004.

———, *Producing Bollywood: Inside the Contemporary Hindi Film Industry*, Durham: Duke University Press, 2012.

George, T.J.S., *The Life and Times of Nargis*, New Delhi: Indus, 1994.

Ginzburg, Carlo, *Clues, Myths and the Historical Method*, trans. from the Italian by John and Anne C. Tedeschi, Baltimore: John Hopkins University Press, 1989 [1986].

Gool-i Bukawulee, trans. from the Urdu by Thomas Philip Manuel, Lucknow: Naval Kishore Press, 1882.

Gopal, Sangita, *Conjugations*, Chicago: Chicago University Press, 2011.

Gopalan, Lalitha, *Cinema of Interruptions*, London: British Film Institute, 2002.

——— (ed.), *The Cinema of India*, London: Wallflower Press, 2009.

Gorbman, Claudia, *Unheard Melodies: Narrative Film Music*, London: British Film Institute; Bloomington and Indianapolis: Indiana University Press, 1987.

Gupt, Somnath, *The Parsi Theatre: Its Origins and Development*, trans. from the Hindi and edited by Kathryn Hansen, New Delhi: Seagull Books, 2005 [1981].

Haddawy, Husain (trans.), *The Arabian Nights* (based on the text edited by Muhsin Mahdi), New York: Norton, 1995/2008.

Haham, Connie, *Enchantment of the Mind: Manmohan Desai's Films*, New Delhi: Roli Books, 2006.

Hansen, Kathryn, *Grounds for Play: The Nautanki Theatre of North India*, Berkeley: University of California Press, 1992.

_____, 'The *Virangana* in North Indian History: Myth and Popular Culture', in *Ideals, Images and Real Lives: Women in Literature and History*, eds Alice Thorner and Maithreyi Krishnaraj, Mumbai: Orient Longman, 2000.

Hansen, Miriam Bratu, 'The Mass Production of the Senses: Classical Cinema as Vernacular Modernism', in *Reinventing Film Studies*, eds Christine Gledhill and Linda Williams, London: Arnold Publishers, 2000, pp. 332–50.

_____, 'Falling Women, Rising Stars, New Horizons: Shanghai Silent Film as Vernacular Modernism', *Film Quarterly*, vol. 54, no. 1, 2000, pp. 10–22.

Hodgson, Marshall G.S., *The Venture of Islam: Conscience and History in a World Civilisation*, 3 vols, Chicago: University of Chicago Press, 1974.

Hughes, Stephen Putnam, 'Is There Anyone Out There? Exhibition and the Formation of Silent Film Audiences in South India', unpublished PhD thesis, University of Chicago, 1996.

_____, 'When Film Came to Madras', *BioScope*, vol. 1, no. 2, 2010, pp. 147–68.

_____, 'The Production of the Past: Early Tamil Film History as a Living Archive', *BioScope*, vol. 4, no. 1, 2013, pp. 71–80.

Hyder, Qurratulain, 'Memories of an Indian Childhood', trans. from the Urdu by Hyder, in *The Picador Book of Modern Indian Literature*, ed. Amit Chaudhuri, London: Picador, 2001 [1965], pp. 206–19.

Indian Cinematograph Committee, *Indian Cinematograph Committee 1927–28, Evidence*, Calcutta: Government of India Central Publication Branch, 1928.

_____, *Report of the Indian Cinematograph Committee, 1927–28*, Calcutta: Government of India Central Publication Branch, 1928.

Indian Talkie, 1931–56 Silver Jubilee Souvenir, Bombay: Film Federation of India, 1956.

Irwin, Robert, *The Arabian Nights: A Companion*, London: Allen Lane, 1994.

_____, 'Introduction', in *The Arabian Nights: Tales of 1001 Nights*, trans. Malcolm Lyons with Ursula Lyons, London: Penguin, 2008.

Jain, Madhu, 'The Day of the Villain', *India Today*, 30 November 1988.

Jha, B., 'Profiles of Pioneers', *Cinema Vision India*, vol. 1, no. 1, pp. 54–5, 1980.

Jha, Manoranjan, *Katherine Mayo and India*, New Delhi: People's Publishing House, 1971.

Kabir, Nasreen Munni, *The Dialogue of Mother India*, New Delhi: Niyogi Books, 2010.

Kakar, Sudhir, 'The Ties That Bind', *Indian Popular Cinema*, ed. Pradip Krishen, *Indian International Centre Quarterly*, vol. 8, no. 1, 1981, pp. 11–21.

Kapur, Geeta, 'Revelation and Doubt: *Sant Tukaram* and *Devi*', in *Interrogating Modernity: Culture and Colonialism in India*, eds Tejaswini Niranjana, P. Sudhir and Vivek Dhareshwar, Calcutta: Seagull Books, 1993, pp. 19–46.

Karanth, K.S. (ed.), *Report of the Working Group on National Film Policy*, New Delhi: Ministry of Information and Broadcasting, May 1980.

Karnad, Girish, 'This One Is for Nadia', in *Cinema Vision India*, vol. 1, no. 2, 1980, pp. 84-90.

Kaur, Raminder and Ajay Sinha, *Bollyworld: Popular Cinema through a Transnational Lens*, New Delhi: Sage, 2005.

Kendall, Elizabeth, *Where She Danced*, New York: Kopf, 1979.

Kesavan, Mukul, 'Urdu, Awadh and the Tawaif: The Islamicate Roots of Hindi Cinema', in *Forging Identities: Gender, Communities, and the State in India*, ed. Zoya Hasan, Boulder, Colorado: Westview Press, 1994, pp. 244–57.

Kuhn, Annette, 'Women's Genres', *Screen*, vol. 25, no. 1, 1984, pp. 18–28.

Lamont, Peter, and Crispin Bates, 'Conjuring Images of India in Nineteenth-Century Britain', *Social History*, vol. 32, no. 3, August 2007, pp. 308–24.

Lyons, Malcolm C., with Ursula Lyons (trans.), *The Arabian Nights: Tales of 1001 Nights*, introduction by Robert Irwin, 3 vols, London: Penguin, 2008.

Majumdar, Neepa, *Wanted Cultured Ladies Only! Female Stardom and Cinema in India 1930s–1950s*, Urbana: University of Illinois Press, 2009.

Marzolph, Ulrich (ed.), *Arabian Nights Reader*, Detroit: Wayne State University Press, 2006.

Marzolph, Ulrich, Richard van Leeuwen and Hassan Wassouf (eds), *Arabian Nights Encyclopedia*, Santa Barbara, CA: ABC-CLIO, 2004.

Mayo, Katherine, *Mother India*, London: Jonathan Cape, 1927.

Mazumdar, Ranjani, *Bombay Cinema: An Archive of the City*, Minneapolis: University of Minnesota, 2007.

Mazumdar, S., *Strong Men over the Years: A Chronicle of Athletes*, Lucknow: Oudh Printing Works, 1942.

McLean, Andrienne L., 'The Thousand Ways There Are to Move', in *Visions of the East: Orientalism in Film*, eds Matthew Bernstein and Gaylyn Studlar, London: I.B. Tauris, 1997.

Mehta, Monika, 'What Is behind Film Censorship? The *Khalnayak* Debates', *Jouvert: A Journal of Postcolonial Studies*, vol. 5, no. 3, 2001, http://english.chass.ncsu.edu/jouvert/v5i3/mehta.htm (accessed 21 August 2012).

———, *Censorship and Sexuality in Bombay Cinema*, Austin: University of Texas Press, 2012.

Mishra, Vijay, *Bollywood Cinema: Temples of Desire*, New York: Routledge, 2002.

Mishra, Vijay, Peter Jeffery and Brian Shoesmith, 'The Actor as Parallel Text in Bombay Cinema', *Quarterly Review of Film and Video*, vol. 11, no. 3, 1989, pp. 49–67.

Mitra, Jatindra Nath, 'A Review of Indian Pictures', *Filmland*, Puja issue, 1934, [reprinted] in *Indian Cinema: Contemporary Perceptions from the Thirties*, ed. Samik Bandyopadhyay, Jamshedpur: Celluloid Chapter, 1993.

Mohan, Ram, 'The Closely Guarded Secrets of the Special Effects Men', *Cinema Vision India*, vol. 1, no. 1, 1980, pp. 89–90.

Mukherjee, Prabhat, 'Hiralal Sen', in *70 Years of Indian Cinema, 1913–1983*, ed. T.M. Ramachandran, Bombay: CINEMA India-International, 1985, pp. 49–53.

Mukherjee, Sushil Kumar, *The Story of the Calcutta Theatres: 1753–1980*, Calcutta: K.P. Bagchi, 1982.

Mulvey, Laura, 'Visual Pleasure and Narrative Cinema', *Screen*, vol. 16, no. 3, pp. 6–18, 1975.

———, 'Douglas Sirk and Melodrama', *Australian Journal of Screen Theory*, vol. 3, 1977, pp. 26–30.

Nandy, Ashis, *At the Edge of Psychology*, New Delhi: Oxford University Press, 1980.

———, 'The Popular Hindi Film, Ideology and First Principles', in *Indian Popular Cinema*, ed. Pradip Krishen, *Indian International Centre Quarterly*, vol. 8, no. 1, 1981, 89–96.

———, *The Intimate Enemy: Loss and Recovery of Self under Colonialism*, New Delhi: Oxford University Press, 1983.

Neale, Stephen, *Genre*, London: British Film Institute, 1980.

Nevile, Pran, *Lahore: A Sentimental Journey*, New Delhi: Harper Collins, 1997.

Nochlin, Linda, 'The Imaginary Orient', *Art in America*, no. 71, 1983, pp. 118–31 and 187–91.

Nowell-Smith, Geoffrey, 'Minnelli and Melodrama', *Screen*, vol. 18, no. 2, 1977, pp. 113–18.

Ojha, Rajendra, *75 Glorious Years of Indian Cinema*, Bombay: Screen World Publication, 1988.

Orsini, Francesca, *Print and Pleasure: Popular Literature and Entertaining Fictions in Colonial North India*, New Delhi: Permanent Black, 2009.

Pinney, Christopher, 'Moral Topophilia: The Significations of Landscape in Indian Oleographs', in *The Anthropology of Landscape*, eds Eric Hirsch and Michael O'Hanlon, Oxford: Clarendon Press, 1985.

_____, 'Introduction: Public, Popular and Other Cultures', in *Pleasure and the Nation: The History, Politics and Consumption of Public Culture in India*, eds Rachel Dwyer and Christopher Pinney, New Delhi: Oxford University Press, 2001.

_____, '*Photos of the Gods': The Printed Image and Political Struggle in India*, London: Reaktion Books, 2004.

Prasad, M. Madhava, *Ideology of the Hindi Film: A Historical Construction*, New Delhi: Oxford University Press, 1998.

_____, 'Surviving Bollywood' in *Global Bollywood*, eds Anandam P. Kavoori and Aswin Punathambekar, New York: New York University Press, 2008, pp. 41–51.

Pritchett, Frances, *Marvellous Encounters: Folk Romances in Urdu and Hindi*, Delhi: Manohar, 1985.

Purohit, Vinayak, *Some Aspects of Sociology of Indian Films and Profile of the Hindi Hit Movie, 1951–1989*, Bombay: Indian Institute of Social Research, 1990.

Rajadhyaksha, Ashish, 'Neo-traditionalism: Film as Popular Art in India', *Framework*, vol. 32/33, 1980, pp. 20–67.

_____, 'The Phalke Era: Conflict of Traditional Form and Modern Technology', in *Interrogating Modernity: Culture and Colonialism in India*, eds Tejaswini Niranjana, P. Sudhir and Vivek Dhareshwar, Calcutta: Seagull Books, 1993, pp. 47–82.

_____, 'India's Silent Cinema: A "Viewer's View"', in *Light of Asia: India's Silent Cinema 1912–1934*, ed. Suresh Chabria, New Delhi: Wiley Eastern, 1994, pp. 25–40.

_____, 'Indian Cinema: Origins to Independence', in *Oxford History of World Cinema*, ed. Geoffrey Nowell-Smith, Oxford: Oxford University Press, 1996, pp. 398–409.

_____, 'The "Bollywoodization" of the Indian Cinema: Cultural Nationalism in a Global Arena', in *Global Bollywood*, eds Anandam P. Kavoori and Aswin Punathambekar, New York: New York University Press, 2008, pp. 17–40.

Rajadhyaksha, Ashish, and Paul Willemen (eds), *Encyclopaedia of Indian Cinema*, new revised edition, London: British Film Institute and Oxford University Press, 1999.

Ramachandran, T.M. (ed.), *70 Years of Indian Cinema, 1913–1983*, Bombay: CINEMA India-International, 1985.

Rangoonwalla, Firoze, *Indian Filmography*, Bombay: J. Udeshi, 1970.

_____, *Indian Cinema: Past and Present*, New Delhi: Clarion Books, 1983.

Rathore, Rajesh, 'Down Fantasy Lane', *Cinema in India*, Bombay: NFDC, April 1991.

Reuben, Bunny, *Mehboob, India's De Mille*, New Delhi: Indus, 1999.

Rothfeld, Otto, *Women of India*, London: Simpkin, Marshall, Hamilton, Kent & Co. Ltd, 1920.

Roy, Parama, *Indian Traffic: Identities in Question in Colonial and Postcolonial India*, Berkeley: University of California Press, 1998.

_____, 'Figuring Mother India: The Case of Nargis', in *Indian Traffic*, Berkeley: University of California Press, 1998, pp. 152–73.

Said, Edward W., *Orientalism*, London: Routledge and Kegan Paul, 1978.

Salazkina, Masha, 'Soviet-Indian Co-productions: Alibaba as Political Allegory', *Cinema Journal*, vol. 49, no. 4, 2010, pp. 71–89.

Sarkar, Kobita, *Indian Cinema Today*, New Delhi: Sterling, 1975.

Sarkar, Nikhil, 'Printing and the Spirit of Calcutta', in *Calcutta Living City*, vol. 1, ed. Sukanta Chaudhuri, Calcutta: Oxford University Press, 1995 [1990], pp. 128–36.

Shawn, Ted, *Gods Who Dance*, New York: Dutton, 1929.

Singer, Milton B., *When a Great Tradition Modernizes: An Anthropological Approach to Indian Civilization*, London: Pall Mall, 1972.

Spivak, Gayatri C., 'The Rani of Sirmur', in *Europe and Its Others*, vol. 1, eds F. Barker, P. Hulme, M. Iversen and D. Loxley, Colchester: University of Essex, 1984, pp. 128–51.

Stark, Ulrike, *An Empire of Books: The Naval Kishore Press and the Diffusion of the Printed Word in Colonial India*, Ranikhet: Permanent Black, 2007.

Steedman, Carolyn, *Dust*, Manchester: Manchester University Press, 2001.

Studlar, Gaylyn, 'Douglas Fairbanks: Thief of the Ballets Russes', in *Bodies of the Text: Dance as Theory, Literature as Dance*, eds Ellen W. Goellner and Jacqueline Shea Murphy, New Brunswick, NJ: Rutgers University Press, 1995.

_____, 'Out-Salomeing Salome: Dance, the New Woman, and Fan Magazine Orientalism', in *Visions of the East: Orientalism in Film*, eds Matthew Bernstein and Gaylyn Studlar, London: I.B. Tauris, 1997.

Suhrawardy, Shaista Akhtar Banu, *A Critical Survey of the Development of the Urdu Novel and Short Story*, London: Longmans, Green, 1945.

Sunder, Pushpa, *Patrons and Philistines: Arts and the State in British India, 1773–1947*, New Delhi: Oxford University Press, 1995.

Thomas, Rosie, 'Indian Cinema: Pleasures and Popularity', *Screen*, vol. 26, nos 3–4, pp. 116–31, 1985.

———, 'India: Mythologies and Modern India', in *World Cinema since 1945*, ed. William Luhr, New York: Ungar, 1987, pp. 301–29.

———, 'Sanctity and Scandal: The Mythologization of Mother India', *Quarterly Review of Film and Video*, vol. 11, no. 3, pp. 11–30, 1989.

———, 'Melodrama and the Negotiation of Morality in Mainstream Hindi Film', in *Consuming Modernity: Public Culture in a South Asian World*, ed. Carol Breckenridge, Minneapolis: University of Minnesota Press, 1995, pp. 157–82.

———, 'Not Quite (Pearl) White: Fearless Nadia, Queen of the Stunts', in *Bollyworld: Indian Cinema Through a Transnational Lens*, eds Raminder Kaur and Ajay Sinha, New Delhi: Sage, 2005.

———, 'Zimbo and Son Meet the Girl with the Gun', in *Living Pictures: Indian Film Poster Art*, eds David Blamey and Robert D'Souza, London: Open Editions Press, 2005.

———, '*Miss Frontier Mail*: The Film That Mistook Its Star for a Train', in *Sarai Reader 07: Frontiers*, eds Monica Narula, Shuddhabrata Sengupta, Jeebesh Bagshi and Ravi Sundaram, Delhi: Centre for Study of Developing Societies, 2007, pp. 294–308.

———, 'Still Magic: An Aladdin's Cave of 1950s B Movie Fantasy', visual essay, http://tasveerghar.net/cmsdesk/essay/103/ (accessed 7 June 2011), n.d.

Todorov, Tsvetan, *The Fantastic: A Structural Approach to a Literary Genre*, trans. Richard Howard, Ithaca: Cornell University Press, 1973.

Torgovnick, Marianna, *Gone Primitive: Savage Intellects, Modern Lives*, Chicago: University of Chicago Press, 1991.

Varshey, D., 'Modern Hindi Literature 1850–1900', unpublished PhD thesis, Allahabad University.

Vasudev, Aruna, and Philippe Lenglet (eds), *Indian Superbazaar*, New Delhi: Vikas Publishing House, 1983.

Vasudevan, Ravi, 'Genre and the Imagination of Identity, 1935–1945', in *From Ali Baba to Jodhaa Akbar: Islamicate Cultures of Bombay Cinema*, eds Ira Bhaskar and Richard Allen, New Delhi: Tulika Press, forthcoming.

———, 'The Politics of Cultural Address in a "Transitional" Cinema: A Case Study of Indian Popular Cinema', in *Rethinking Film Theory*, eds Christine Gledhill and Linda Williams, London: Arnold, 2000, pp. 130–64.

_____, *The Melodramatic Public: Film Form and Spectatorship in Indian Cinema*, New Delhi: Permanent Black, 2010.

Vitali, Valentina, *Hindi Action Cinema*, New Delhi: Oxford University Press, 2008.

Wadia, J.B.H., 'How *Bagh-e-Misr* Came to Be Produced', unpublished memoirs, Wadia Movietone archives, Bombay, 1980.

_____, 'Joseph David—Tribute to a Forgotten Pioneer', unpublished memoirs, Wadia Movietone archives, Bombay, 1980.

_____, 'JBH in Talkieland', *Cinema Vision India*, vol. 1, no. 2, pp. 82–3, 1980.

_____, 'The Making of *Toofani Tarzan*', unpublished manuscript, Wadia Movietone archives, n.d.

_____, 'The Story behind the Making of *Lal-e-Yaman*', unpublished memoirs, Wadia Movietone archives, Bombay, 1980.

_____, 'The Wadia Movietone Partnership', unpublished memoirs, Wadia Movietone archives, Bombay, 1980.

_____, 'Those Were the Days, Part Two', unpublished memoirs, Wadia Movietone archives, Bombay, 1980.

_____, 'Those Were the Days', *Cinema Vision India*, vol. 1, no. 1, pp. 91–9, 1980.

_____, *Looking Back on My Romance with Films*, Bombay: Jayant Art Printer, 1955.

Wadia, Riyad Vinci, *Unmasked: The Life and Times of Fearless Nadia*, unpublished research notes courtesy Wadia Movietone Private Ltd, 1994.

_____ (director), *Fearless: The Hunterwali Story* (Documentary), India, 1993.

Wadley, Susan S., 'Women and the Hindu Tradition', in *Women in India: Two Perspectives*, eds D. Jacobson and S. Wadley, New Delhi: Manohar, 1977, pp. 113–39.

Wenner, Dorothee, *Zorro's Blonde Schwester*, Berlin: Ullstein Buchverlag, 1999.

Wise, Arthur, and D. Ware, *Stunting in the Cinema*, London: Constable and Company, 1973.

Wollen, Peter, *Raiding the Icebox: Reflections on Twentieth-Century Culture*, London: Verso, 1993.

Yagnik, R.K., *The Indian Theatre: Its Origins and Later Development under European Influence, with Special Reference to Western India*, London: Allen and Unwin, 1933.

Yule, Sir Henry, A.C. Burnell and William Crooke (eds), *Hobson-Jobson: A Glossary of Colloquial Anglo-Indian Words and Phrases*, London; New York: Routledge, 1985.

Zutshi, Somnath, 'Women, Nation and the Outsider in Contemporary Hindi Cinema', in *Interrogating Modernity: Culture and Colonialism in* India, eds Tejaswini Niranjana, P. Sudhir and Vivek Dhareshwar, Calcutta: Seagull Books, 1993, pp. 83–142.

NEWSPAPERS & MAGAZINES

Bombay
Bombay Chronicle
Cine Blitz
Cinema
Film India
Film Information
Film World
Madras Mail
Monthly Film Bulletin
Mouj Majah
Observer
Probe India
Screen
Spectator
Star and Style
Stardust
Sunday Express
Sunday
Super
The Tatler
Tehelka
Times of India
Time Out
Trade Guide
Varieties Weekly

Index

anomie 279
dystopia 143
India 50, 104
poor 20, 21, 127
theatre 36, 67
vs rural 127, 143
Urdu-Parsi theatre *see* theatre, Urdu-
Parsi
USA 48, 153

Vaidya, R.N. 100
Vakil, Nanubhai 40–1
Vantolio (Whirlwind) 29, 82–3, 86
Varieties Weekly 58, 74
Varma, Ram Gopal 290
Vasudevan, Ravi 6
Veer Bharat (Indian Warrior) 112
verisimilitude 15, 16, 179, 228, 230,
236, 238, 294
Victorian India 36
Vidyavinode, K.P. 8, 31, 36
Ali Baba 31
villain 19, 82–3, 100, 110, 112–15,
129, 134–5, 159, 163, 174, 179,
233, 235, 244, 254, 257–8, 266,
272, 274, 276, 279, 280, 283–5,
287, 289–93
violence 127, 142, 146, 254–5, 258,
266, 276, 279, 283–4, 287–9, 293
virangana 29, 95, 108–11, 113, 116,
118, 122
visual 2, 4, 13–14, 25–6, 29–30, 44,
56, 66–7, 76, 78–83, 86, 107, 119,
145, 152, 156, 164, 166, 170, 174,
279, 293
culture 29, 152
effects 82
ephemera 2, 4, 25, 29
illusion/magic 44, 79–83, 166, 170
references 13, 14, 56, 279, 293

style 26, 164
vs aural 29, 78, 81
Vivekananda 119
voice 18, 29, 45, 54–5, 66–7, 69–84,
86, 98, 138
acousmatic 74–7
and song 82
coach 98
divine 67, 78–9, 81, 83, 86
off-screen 86
power of the 29, 66–7, 78, 80–1
singing 69, 71, 78
voice-over 18
Voltaire 35

Wadia, Homi 11–13, 15–16, 18, 25–9,
33, 41–3, 45, 53–5, 58, 66–78, 80–2,
84–6, 92–105, 107, 109–10, 112,
114, 120–2, 127–33, 136–8, 141,
146, 150–1, 154–60, 162–5, 166–7,
170, 216, 293
on fantasy films 154, 158, 162
Wadia, J.B.H. 16, 26, 28–9, 33, 42, 45,
54, 66–9, 72–3, 75, 82, 85, 92, 95,
97–106, 118, 120–2, 130–2, 135–6,
139, 165
Wadia, Mary *see* Nadia, Fearless
Wadia Movietone 26–9, 41, 45, 54,
58, 66, 68, 71, 73, 78, 84, 93, 95,
97, 99–105, 109, 114, 120, 129, 132
Nadia and 97
Walsh, Raoul 9, 32, 80
Weissmuller, Johnny 45, 80, 131,
134–5, 138–9, 141, 165
westerns 25
WIFPA 204
Wirsching, Joseph 96
woman 9, 13, 26, 29, 43, 47, 50, 53,
68, 75–6, 92, 94–5, 99–100, 102,
104, 107–20, 122, 132, 134, 137–8,